THE LAST MAN — Ring of Truth

Y: THE LAST MAN – Ring of Truth

Brian K. Vaughan
Writer

Pia Guerra
Penciller

José Marzán, Jr.
Inker

Zylonol
Colorist

Clem Robins
Letterer

Massimo Carnevale
Original series covers

Y: THE LAST MAN created by Brian K. Vaughan and Pia Guerra

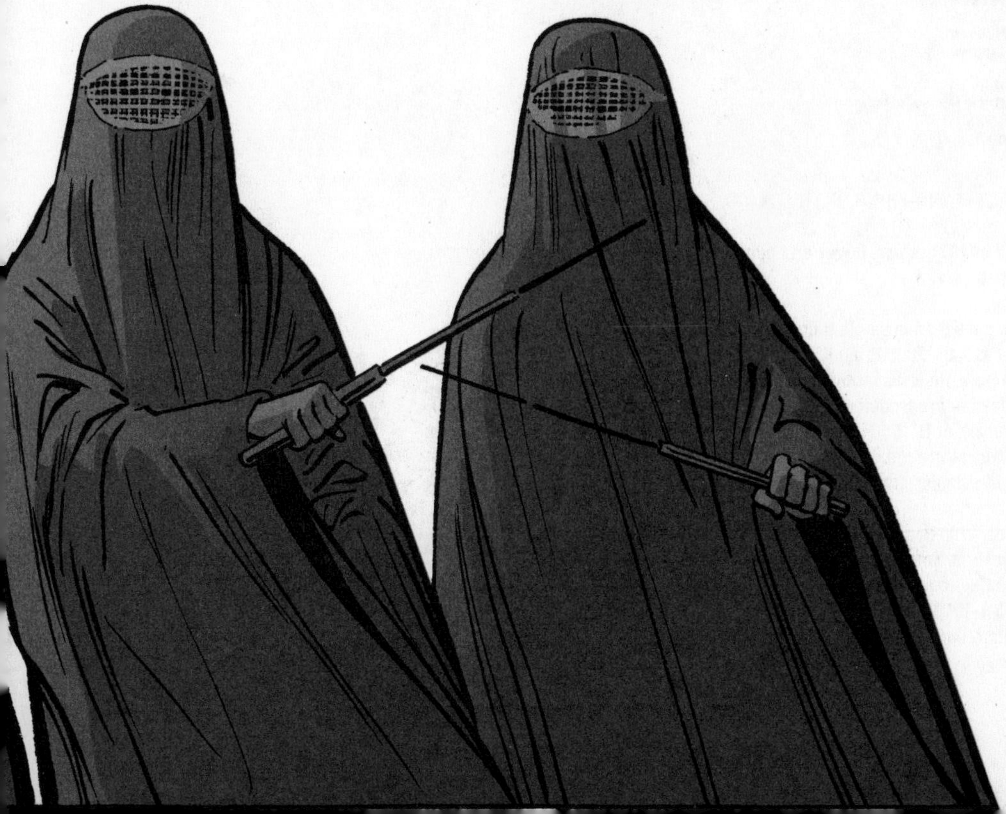

Y: THE LAST MAN — RING OF TRUTH

DC Comics, 1700 Broadway, New York, NY 10019
A Warner Bros. Entertainment Company.
Printed in Canada. Third Printing.
ISBN: 978-1-4012-0487-7
Cover illustrations by Massimo Carnevale.
Logo design by Terry Marks.

Y THE LAST MAN — Contents

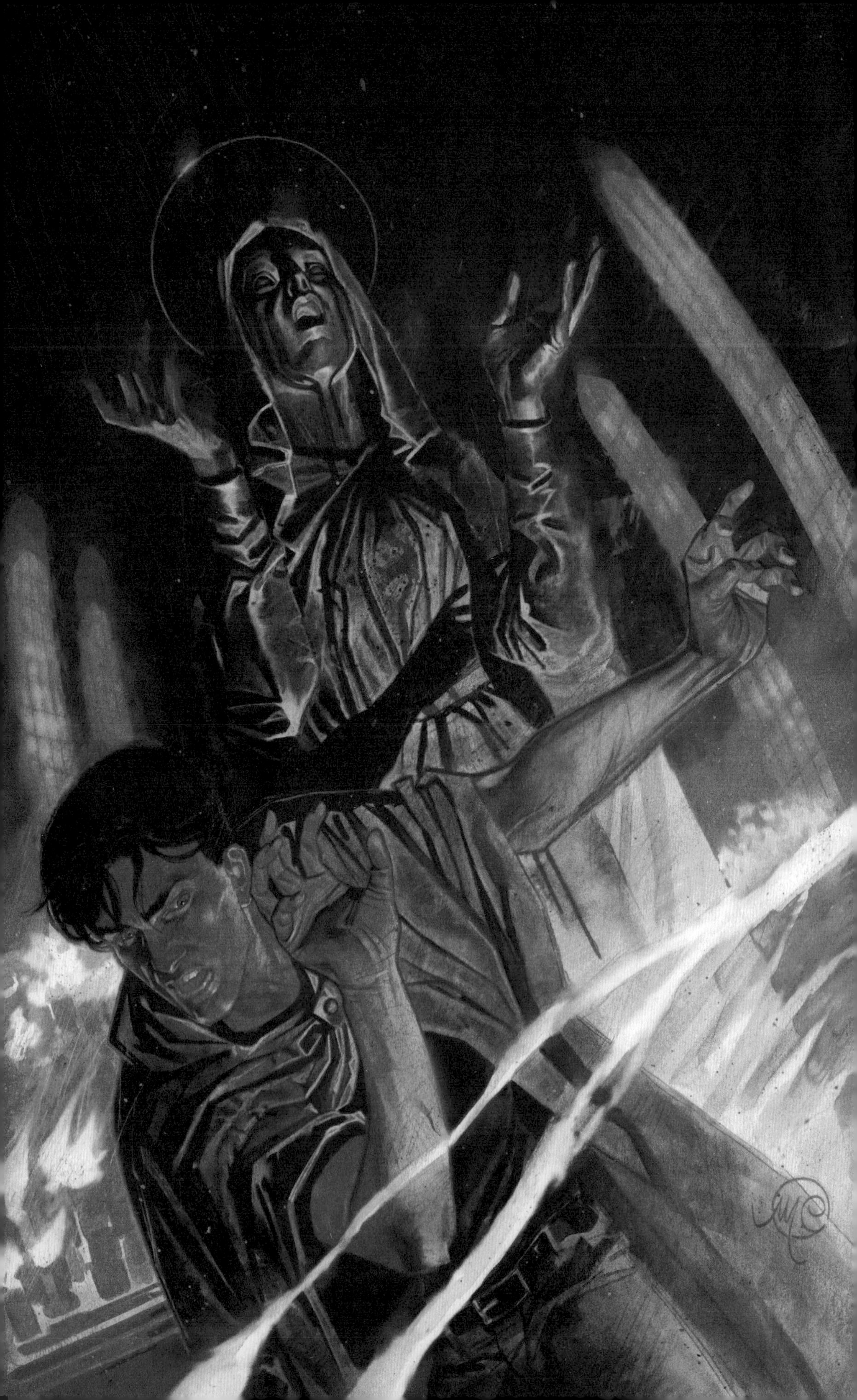

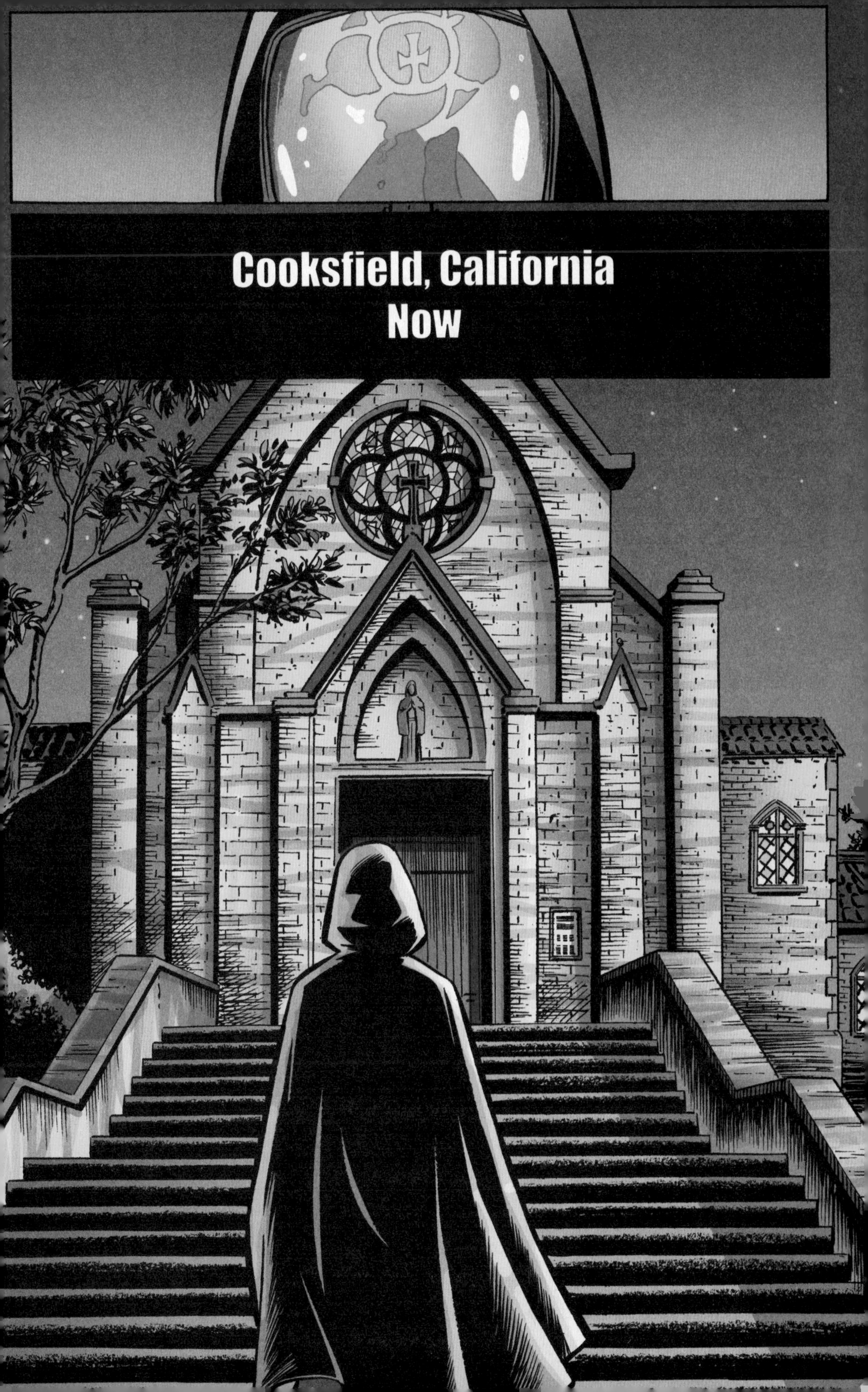
Cooksfield, California
Now

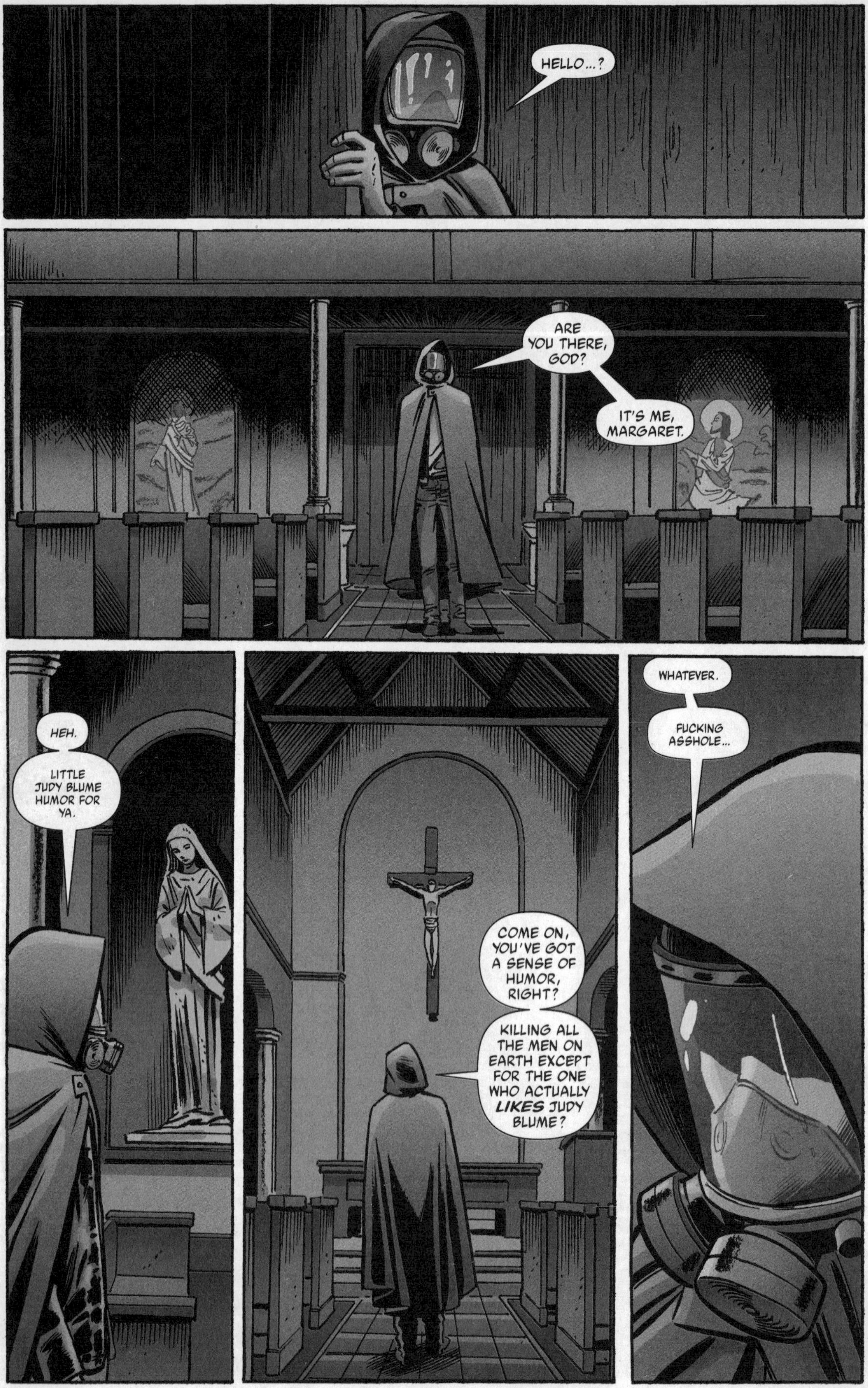
HELLO...?
ARE YOU THERE, GOD?
IT'S ME, MARGARET.
HEH.
LITTLE JUDY BLUME HUMOR FOR YA.
COME ON, YOU'VE GOT A SENSE OF HUMOR, RIGHT?
KILLING ALL THE MEN ON EARTH EXCEPT FOR THE ONE WHO ACTUALLY LIKES JUDY BLUME?
WHATEVER.
FUCKING ASSHOLE...

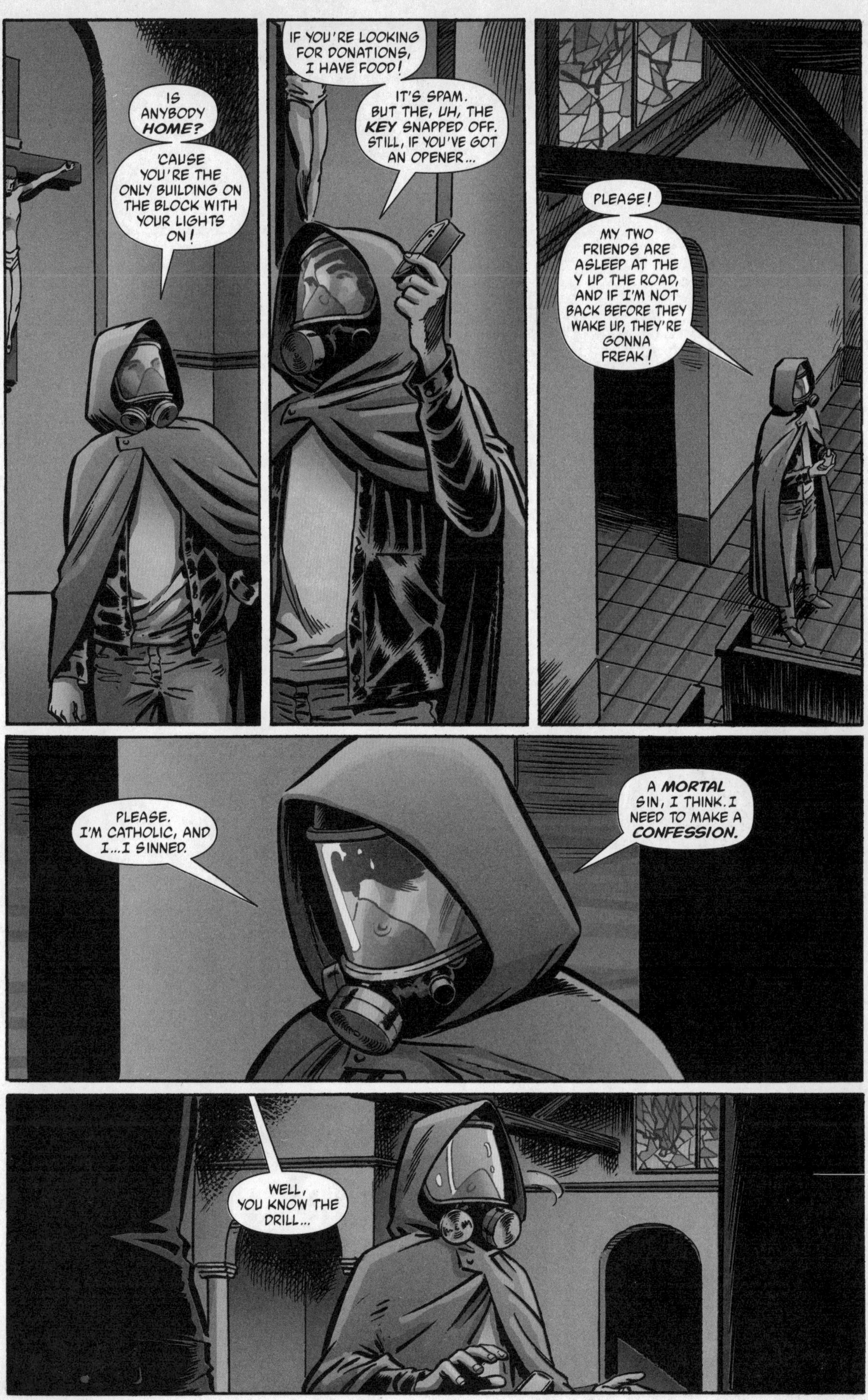
IS ANYBODY HOME?
'CAUSE YOU'RE THE ONLY BUILDING ON THE BLOCK WITH YOUR LIGHTS ON!
IF YOU'RE LOOKING FOR DONATIONS, I HAVE FOOD!
IT'S SPAM. BUT THE, UH, THE KEY SNAPPED OFF. STILL, IF YOU'VE GOT AN OPENER...
PLEASE!
MY TWO FRIENDS ARE ASLEEP AT THE Y UP THE ROAD, AND IF I'M NOT BACK BEFORE THEY WAKE UP, THEY'RE GONNA FREAK!
PLEASE. I'M CATHOLIC, AND I...I SINNED.
A MORTAL SIN, I THINK. I NEED TO MAKE A CONFESSION.
WELL, YOU KNOW THE DRILL...

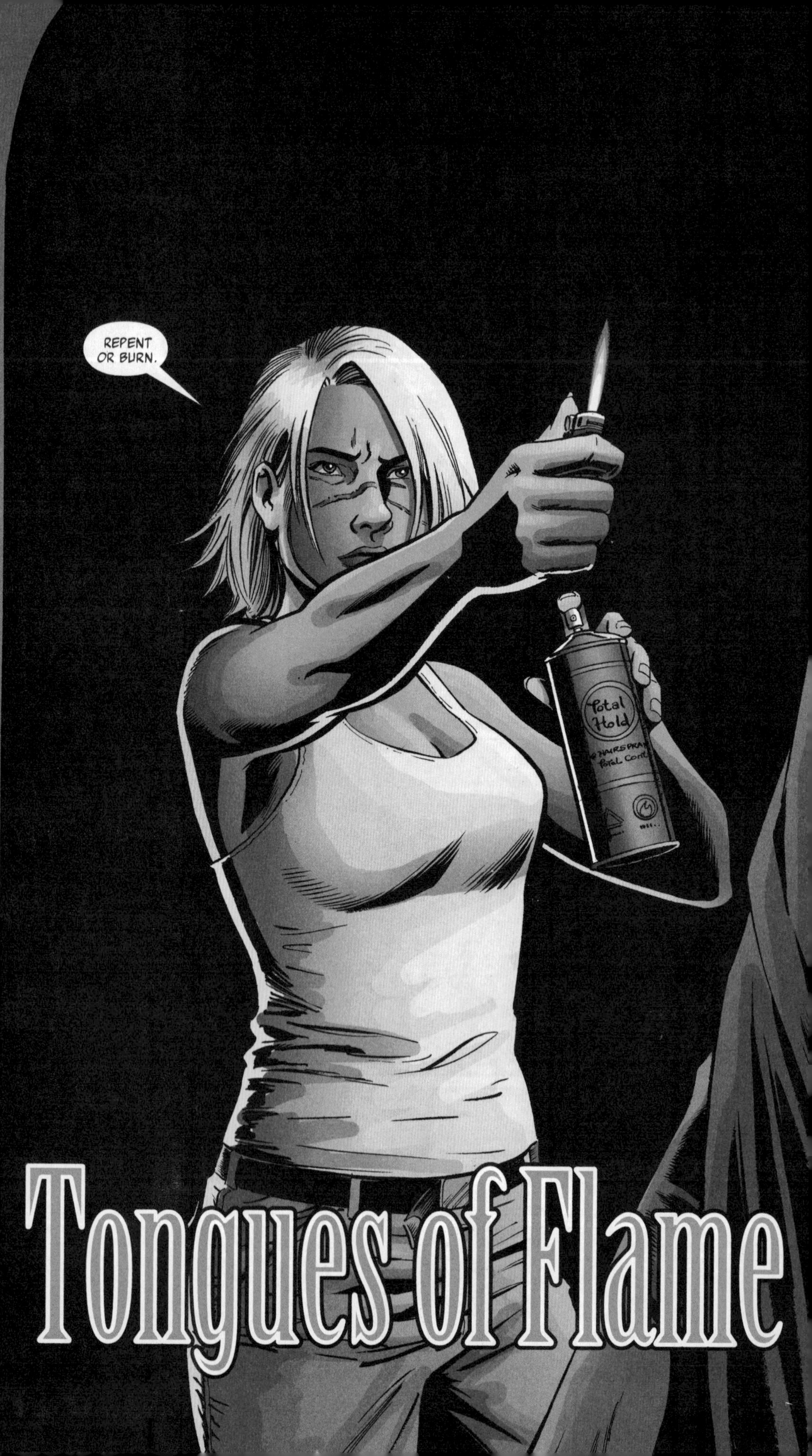
REPENT OR BURN.
Total Hold
Tongues of Flame

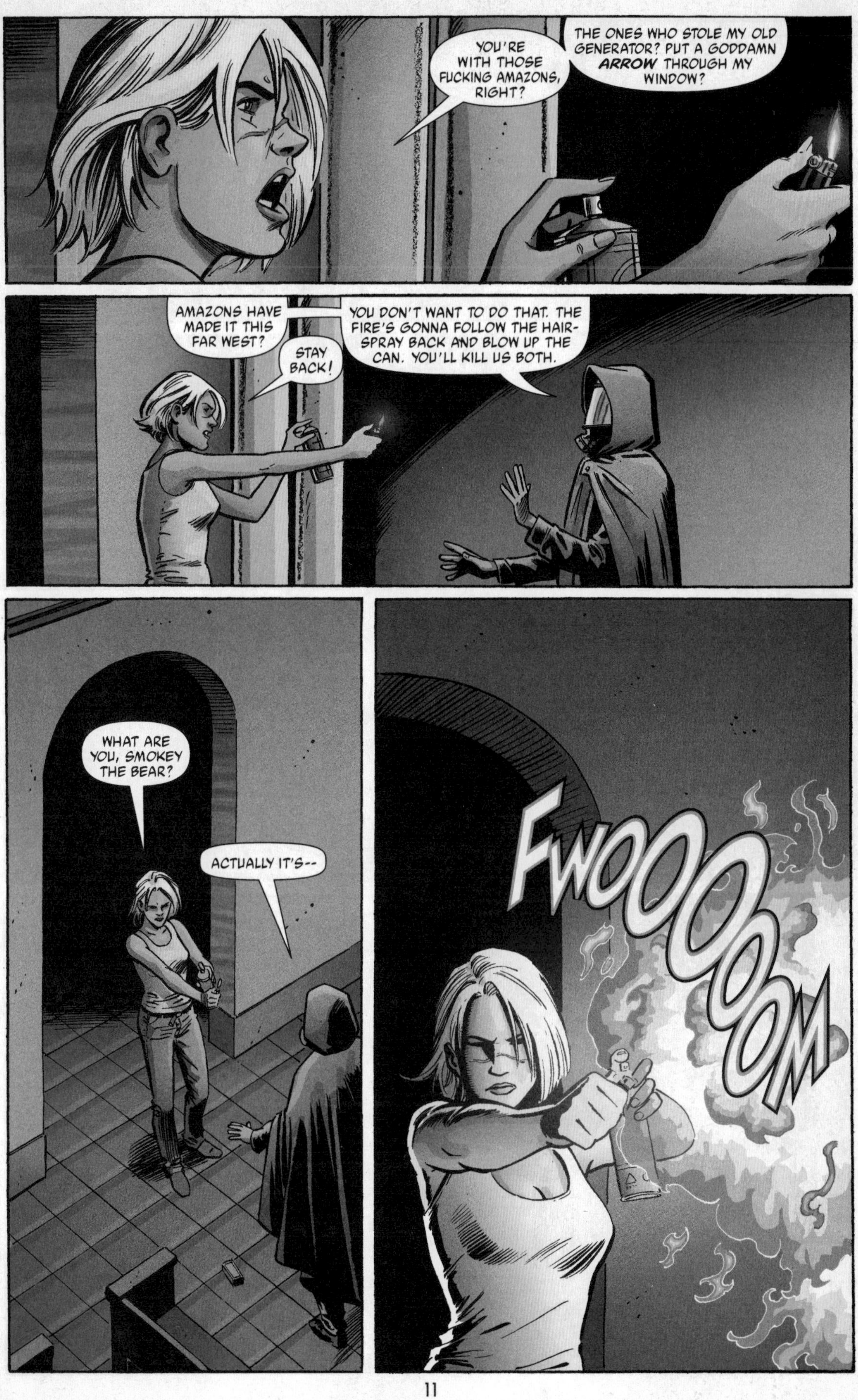
YOU'RE WITH THOSE FUCKING AMAZONS, RIGHT?
THE ONES WHO STOLE MY OLD GENERATOR? PUT A GODDAMN ARROW THROUGH MY WINDOW?
AMAZONS HAVE MADE IT THIS FAR WEST?
STAY BACK!
YOU DON'T WANT TO DO THAT. THE FIRE'S GONNA FOLLOW THE HAIR-SPRAY BACK AND BLOW UP THE CAN. YOU'LL KILL US BOTH.
WHAT ARE YOU, SMOKEY THE BEAR?
ACTUALLY IT'S--
FWOOOOOOM

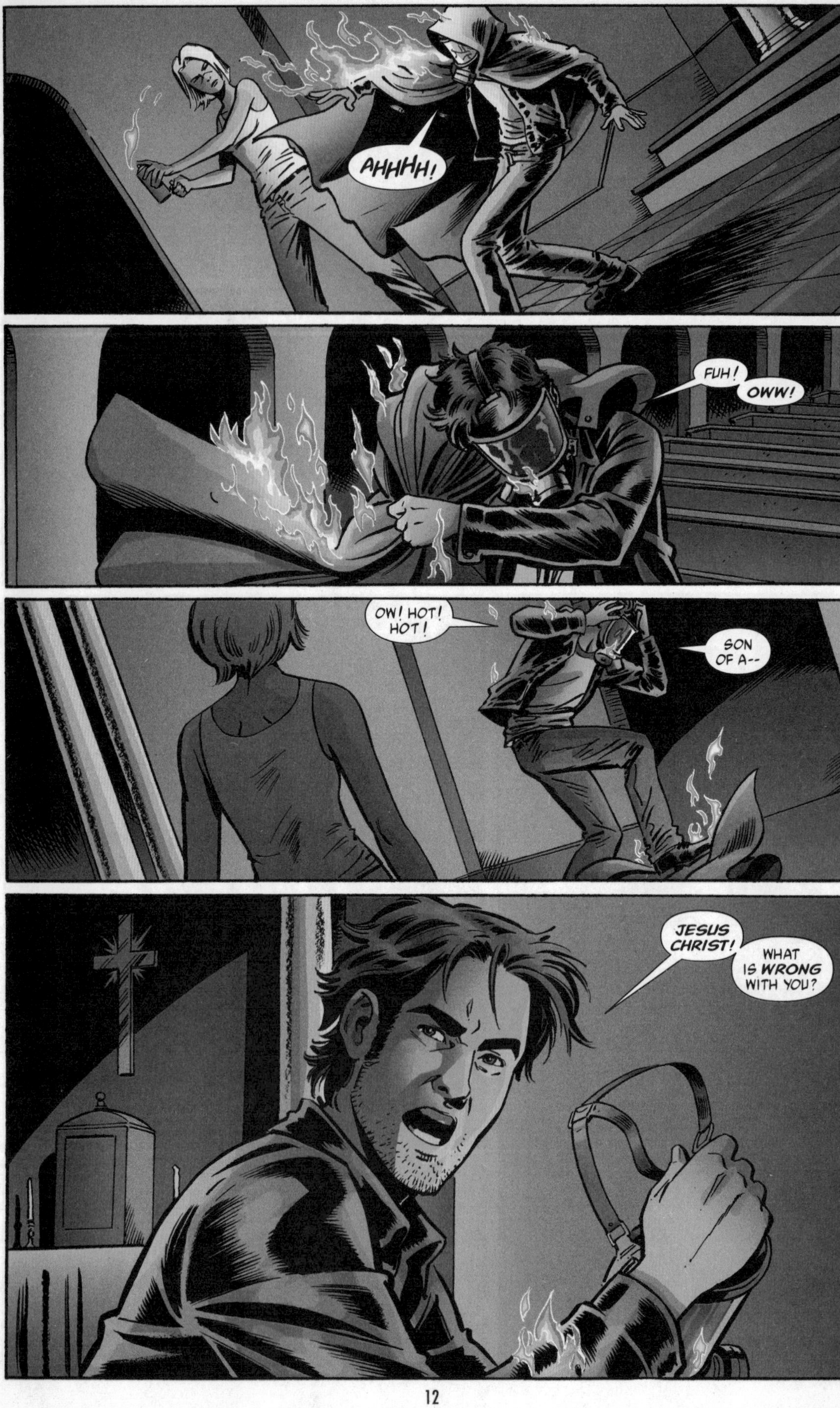
AHHHH!
FUH!
OWW!
OW! HOT! HOT!
SON OF A--
JESUS CHRIST!
WHAT IS WRONG WITH YOU?

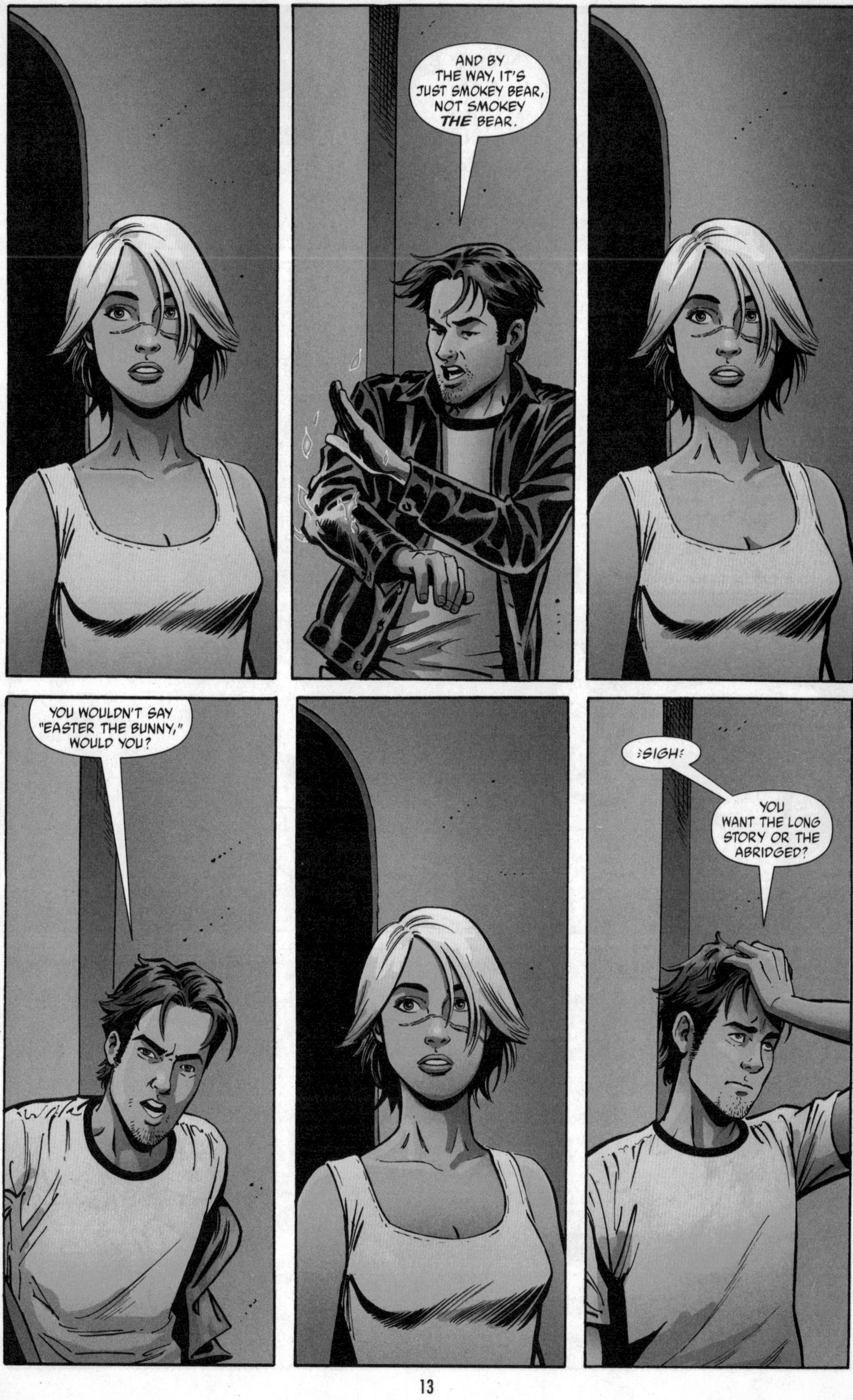
AND BY THE WAY, IT'S JUST SMOKEY BEAR, NOT SMOKEY THE BEAR.
YOU WOULDN'T SAY "EASTER THE BUNNY," WOULD YOU?
SIGH
YOU WANT THE LONG STORY OR THE ABRIDGED?

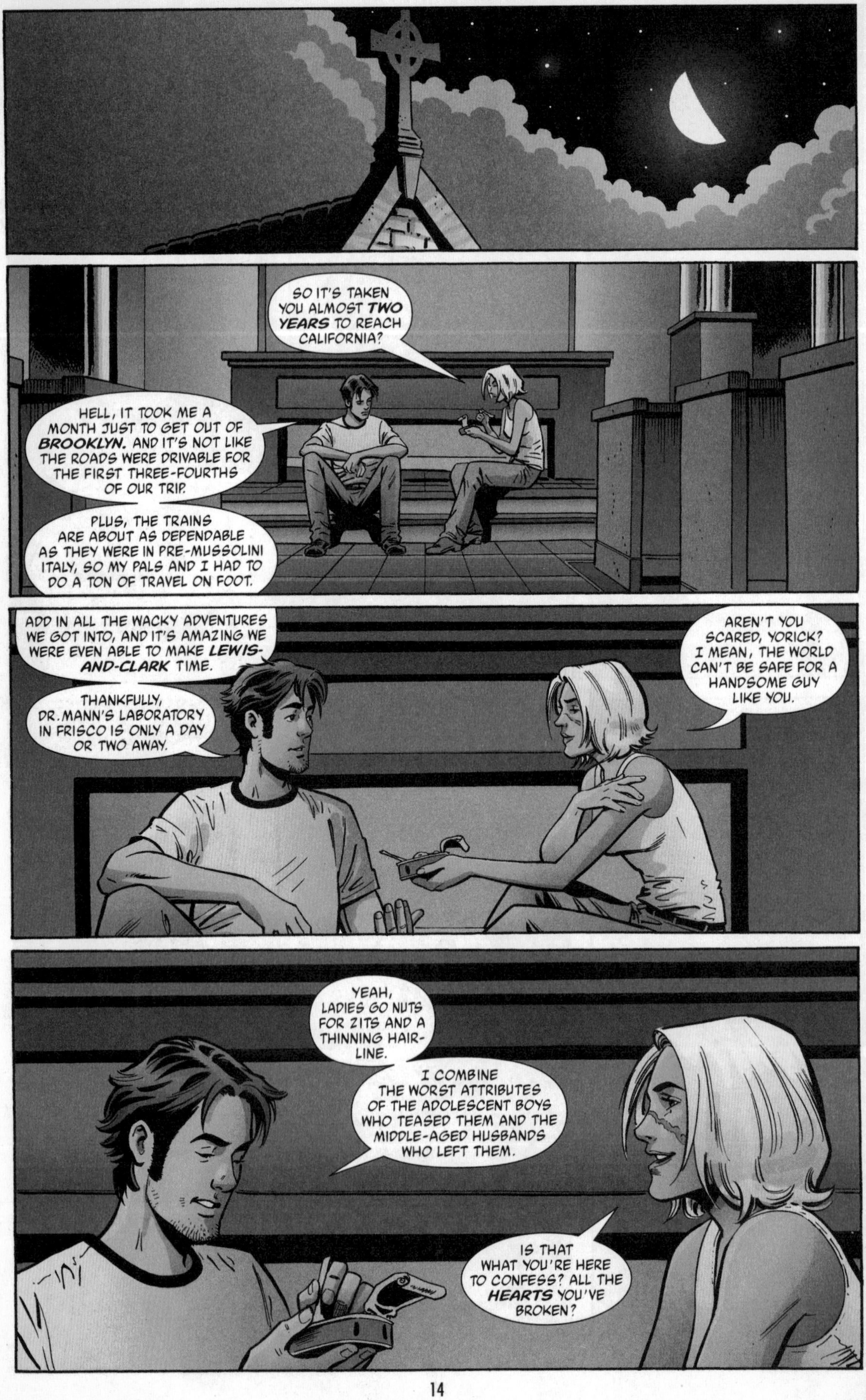
SO IT'S TAKEN YOU ALMOST TWO YEARS TO REACH CALIFORNIA?
HELL, IT TOOK ME A MONTH JUST TO GET OUT OF BROOKLYN. AND IT'S NOT LIKE THE ROADS WERE DRIVABLE FOR THE FIRST THREE-FOURTHS OF OUR TRIP.
PLUS, THE TRAINS ARE ABOUT AS DEPENDABLE AS THEY WERE IN PRE-MUSSOLINI ITALY, SO MY PALS AND I HAD TO DO A TON OF TRAVEL ON FOOT.
ADD IN ALL THE WACKY ADVENTURES WE GOT INTO, AND IT'S AMAZING WE WERE EVEN ABLE TO MAKE LEWIS-AND-CLARK TIME.
THANKFULLY, DR. MANN'S LABORATORY IN FRISCO IS ONLY A DAY OR TWO AWAY.
AREN'T YOU SCARED, YORICK? I MEAN, THE WORLD CAN'T BE SAFE FOR A HANDSOME GUY LIKE YOU.
YEAH, LADIES GO NUTS FOR ZITS AND A THINNING HAIR-LINE.
I COMBINE THE WORST ATTRIBUTES OF THE ADOLESCENT BOYS WHO TEASED THEM AND THE MIDDLE-AGED HUSBANDS WHO LEFT THEM.
IS THAT WHAT YOU'RE HERE TO CONFESS? ALL THE HEARTS YOU'VE BROKEN?

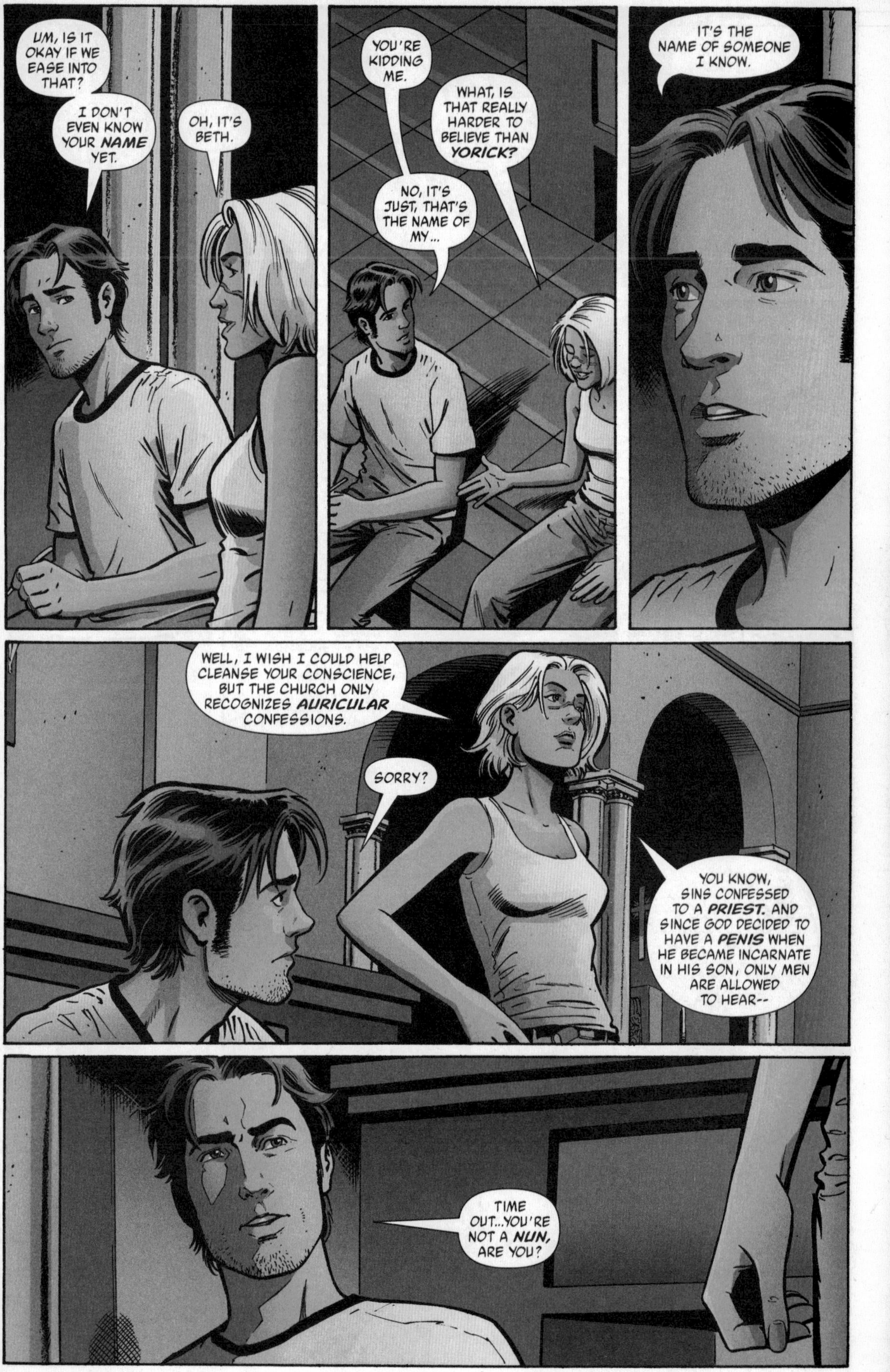
UM, IS IT OKAY IF WE EASE INTO THAT?
I DON'T EVEN KNOW YOUR NAME YET.
OH, IT'S BETH.
YOU'RE KIDDING ME.
WHAT, IS THAT REALLY HARDER TO BELIEVE THAN YORICK?
NO, IT'S JUST, THAT'S THE NAME OF MY...
IT'S THE NAME OF SOMEONE I KNOW.
WELL, I WISH I COULD HELP CLEANSE YOUR CONSCIENCE, BUT THE CHURCH ONLY RECOGNIZES AURICULAR CONFESSIONS.
SORRY?
YOU KNOW, SINS CONFESSED TO A PRIEST. AND SINCE GOD DECIDED TO HAVE A PENIS WHEN HE BECAME INCARNATE IN HIS SON, ONLY MEN ARE ALLOWED TO HEAR--
TIME OUT...YOU'RE NOT A NUN, ARE YOU?

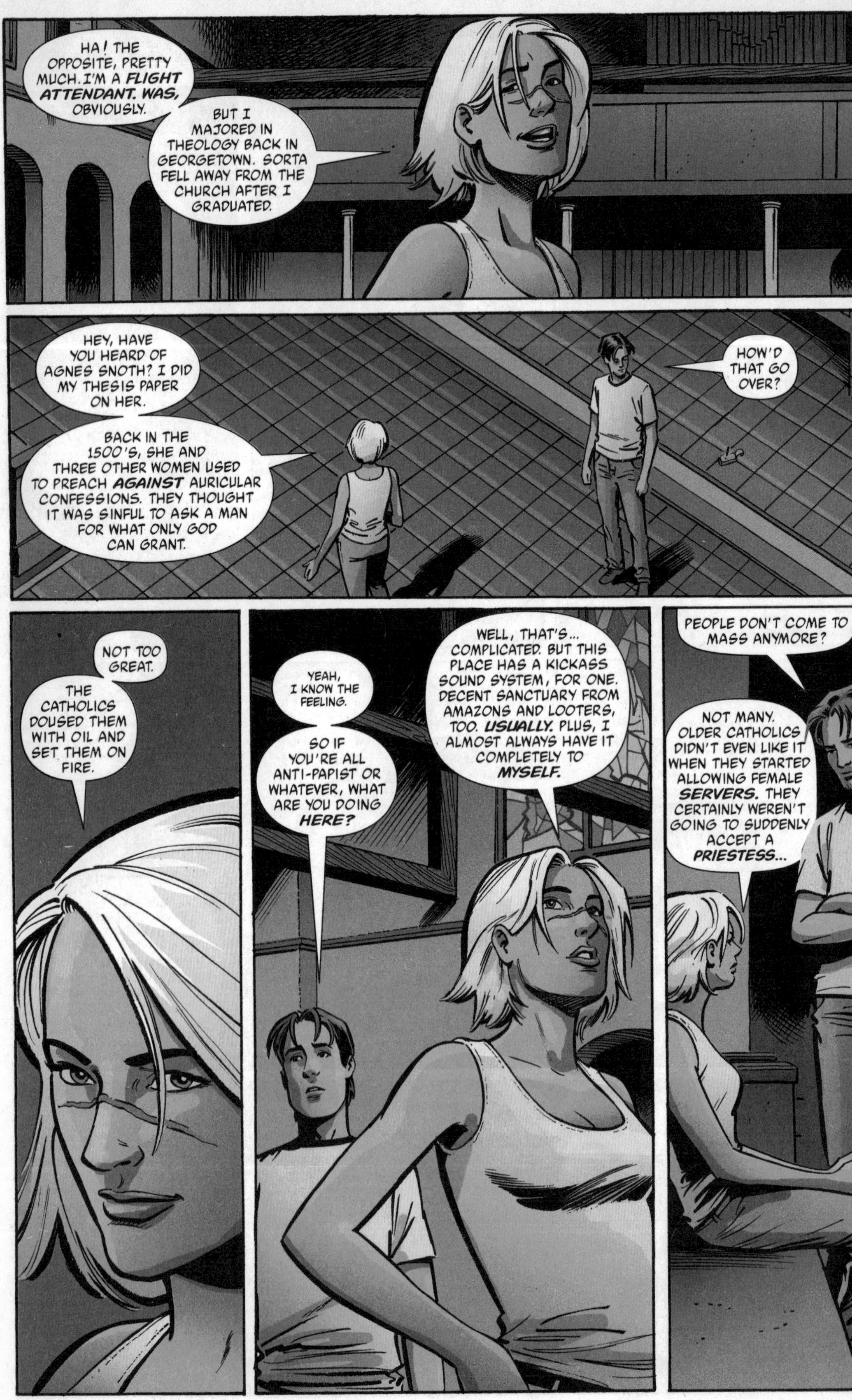
HA! THE OPPOSITE, PRETTY MUCH. I'M A **FLIGHT ATTENDANT. WAS,** OBVIOUSLY.
BUT I MAJORED IN THEOLOGY BACK IN GEORGETOWN. SORTA FELL AWAY FROM THE CHURCH AFTER I GRADUATED.
HEY, HAVE YOU HEARD OF AGNES SNOTH? I DID MY THESIS PAPER ON HER.
BACK IN THE 1500'S, SHE AND THREE OTHER WOMEN USED TO PREACH **AGAINST** AURICULAR CONFESSIONS. THEY THOUGHT IT WAS SINFUL TO ASK A MAN FOR WHAT ONLY GOD CAN GRANT.
HOW'D THAT GO OVER?
NOT TOO GREAT.
THE CATHOLICS DOUSED THEM WITH OIL AND SET THEM ON FIRE.
YEAH, I KNOW THE FEELING.
SO IF YOU'RE ALL ANTI-PAPIST OR WHATEVER, WHAT ARE YOU DOING **HERE?**
WELL, THAT'S... COMPLICATED. BUT THIS PLACE HAS A KICKASS SOUND SYSTEM, FOR ONE. DECENT SANCTUARY FROM AMAZONS AND LOOTERS, TOO. **USUALLY.** PLUS, I ALMOST ALWAYS HAVE IT COMPLETELY TO **MYSELF.**
PEOPLE DON'T COME TO MASS ANYMORE?
NOT MANY. OLDER CATHOLICS DIDN'T EVEN LIKE IT WHEN THEY STARTED ALLOWING FEMALE **SERVERS.** THEY CERTAINLY WEREN'T GOING TO SUDDENLY ACCEPT A **PRIESTESS...**

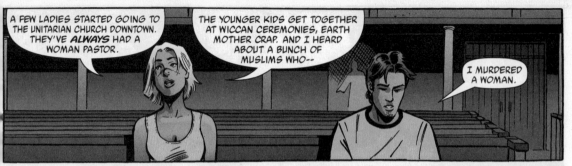

A FEW LADIES STARTED GOING TO THE UNITARIAN CHURCH DOWNTOWN. THEY'VE *ALWAYS* HAD A WOMAN PASTOR.

THE YOUNGER KIDS GET TOGETHER AT WICCAN CEREMONIES, EARTH MOTHER CRAP. AND I HEARD ABOUT A BUNCH OF MUSLIMS WHO--

I MURDERED A WOMAN.

...WHAT DID YOU SAY?

NOT EVEN A WOMAN...

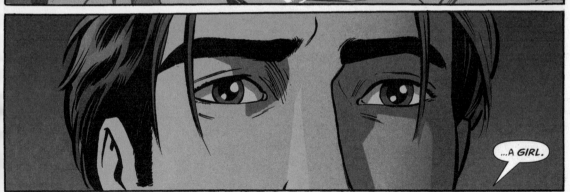

...A GIRL.

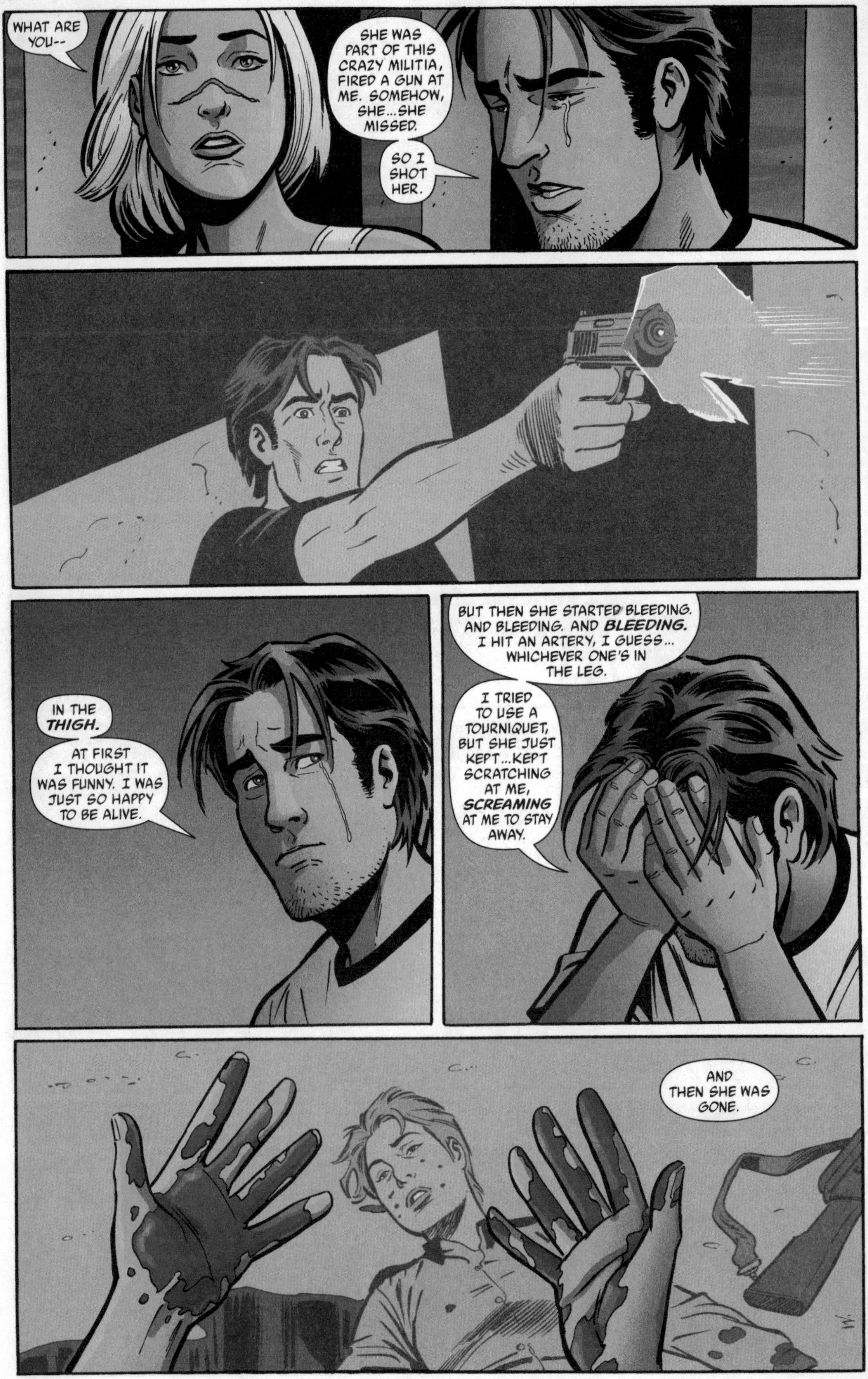
WHAT ARE YOU--
SHE WAS PART OF THIS CRAZY MILITIA, FIRED A GUN AT ME. SOMEHOW, SHE...SHE MISSED.
SO I SHOT HER.
IN THE THIGH.
AT FIRST I THOUGHT IT WAS FUNNY. I WAS JUST SO HAPPY TO BE ALIVE.
BUT THEN SHE STARTED BLEEDING. AND BLEEDING. AND BLEEDING. I HIT AN ARTERY, I GUESS... WHICHEVER ONE'S IN THE LEG.
I TRIED TO USE A TOURNIQUET, BUT SHE JUST KEPT...KEPT SCRATCHING AT ME, SCREAMING AT ME TO STAY AWAY.
AND THEN SHE WAS GONE.

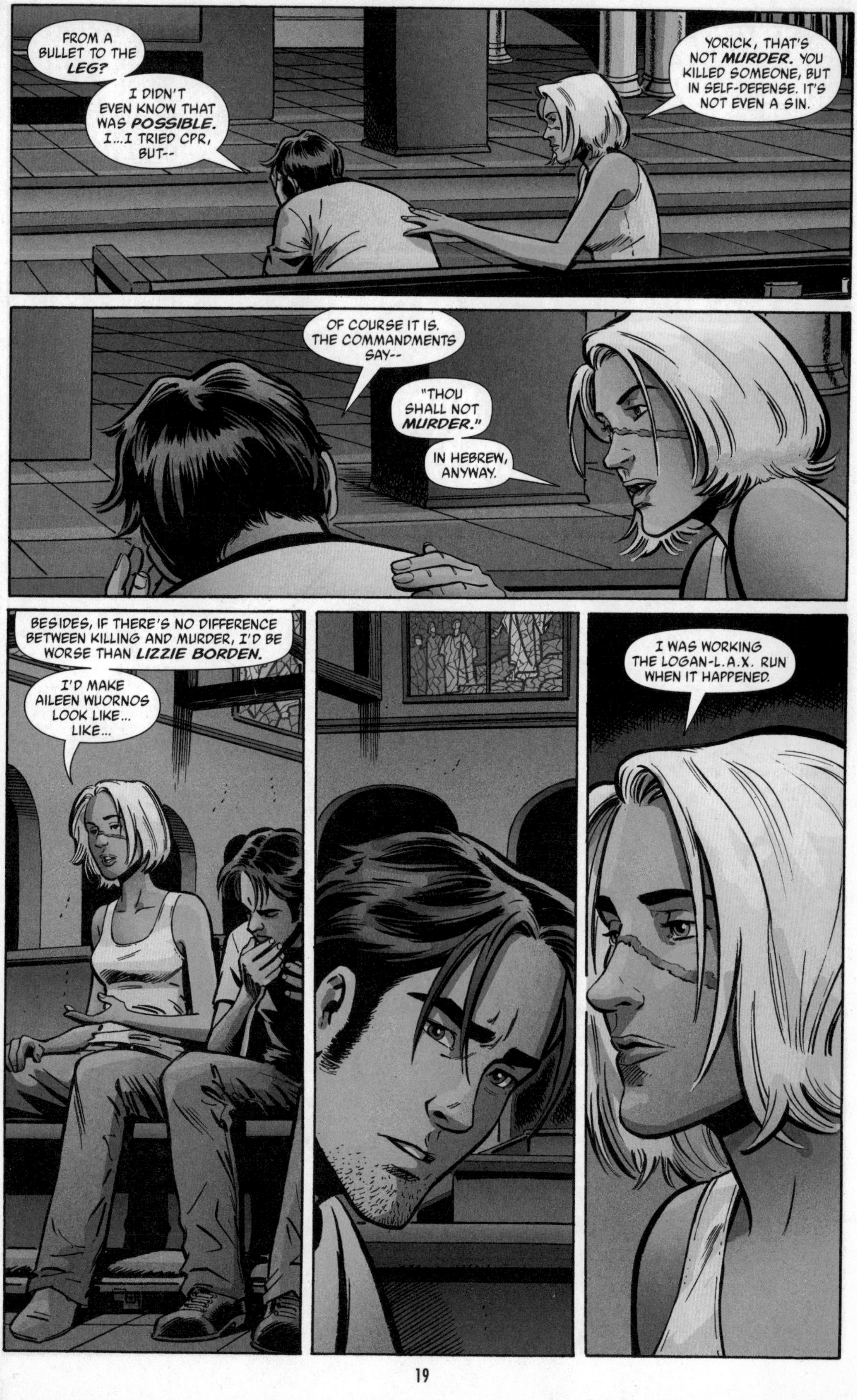
FROM A BULLET TO THE LEG?
I DIDN'T EVEN KNOW THAT WAS POSSIBLE. I...I TRIED CPR, BUT--
YORICK, THAT'S NOT MURDER. YOU KILLED SOMEONE, BUT IN SELF-DEFENSE. IT'S NOT EVEN A SIN.
OF COURSE IT IS. THE COMMANDMENTS SAY--
"THOU SHALL NOT MURDER."
IN HEBREW, ANYWAY.
BESIDES, IF THERE'S NO DIFFERENCE BETWEEN KILLING AND MURDER, I'D BE WORSE THAN LIZZIE BORDEN.
I'D MAKE AILEEN WUORNOS LOOK LIKE... LIKE...
I WAS WORKING THE LOGAN-L.A.X. RUN WHEN IT HAPPENED.

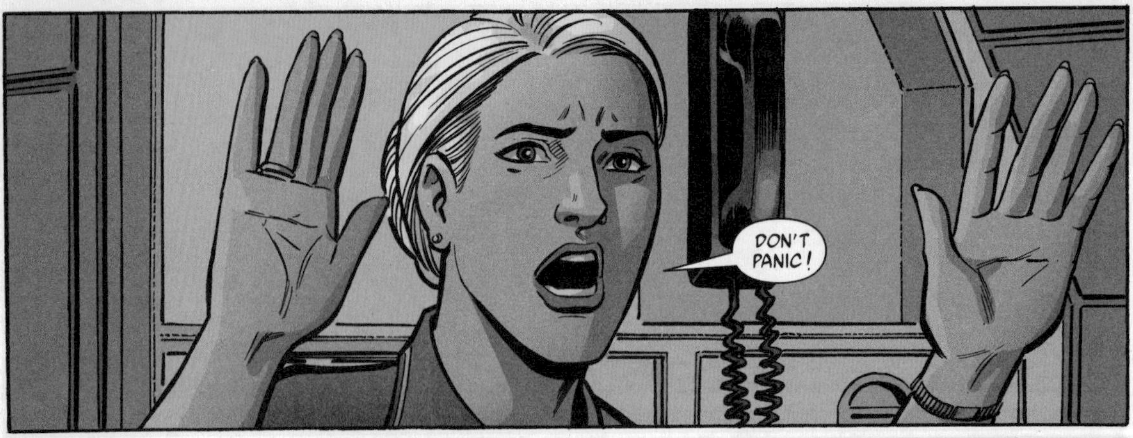
DON'T PANIC!

15,000 Feet Above Cooksfield
July 17, 2002

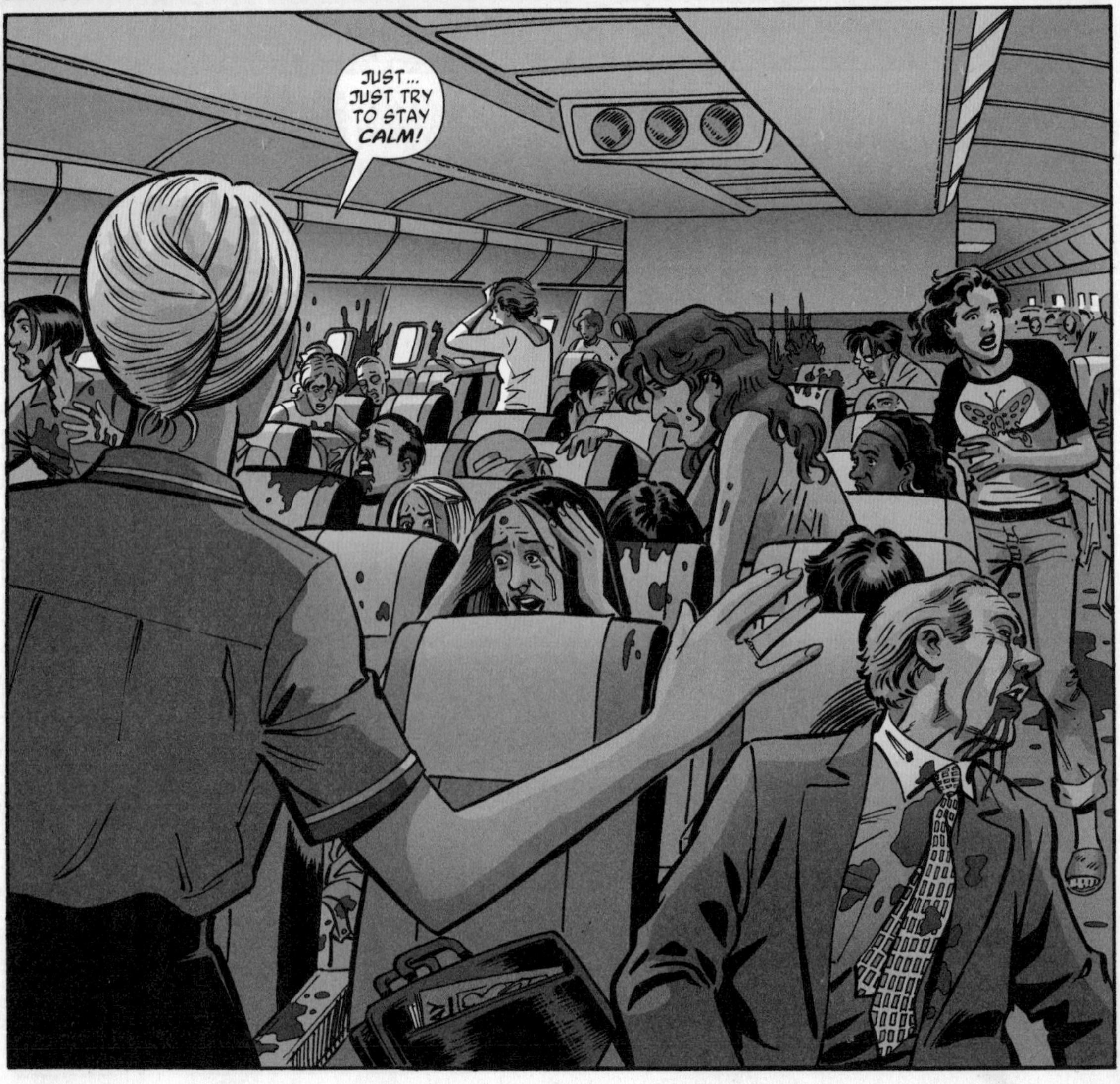
JUST... JUST TRY TO STAY CALM!

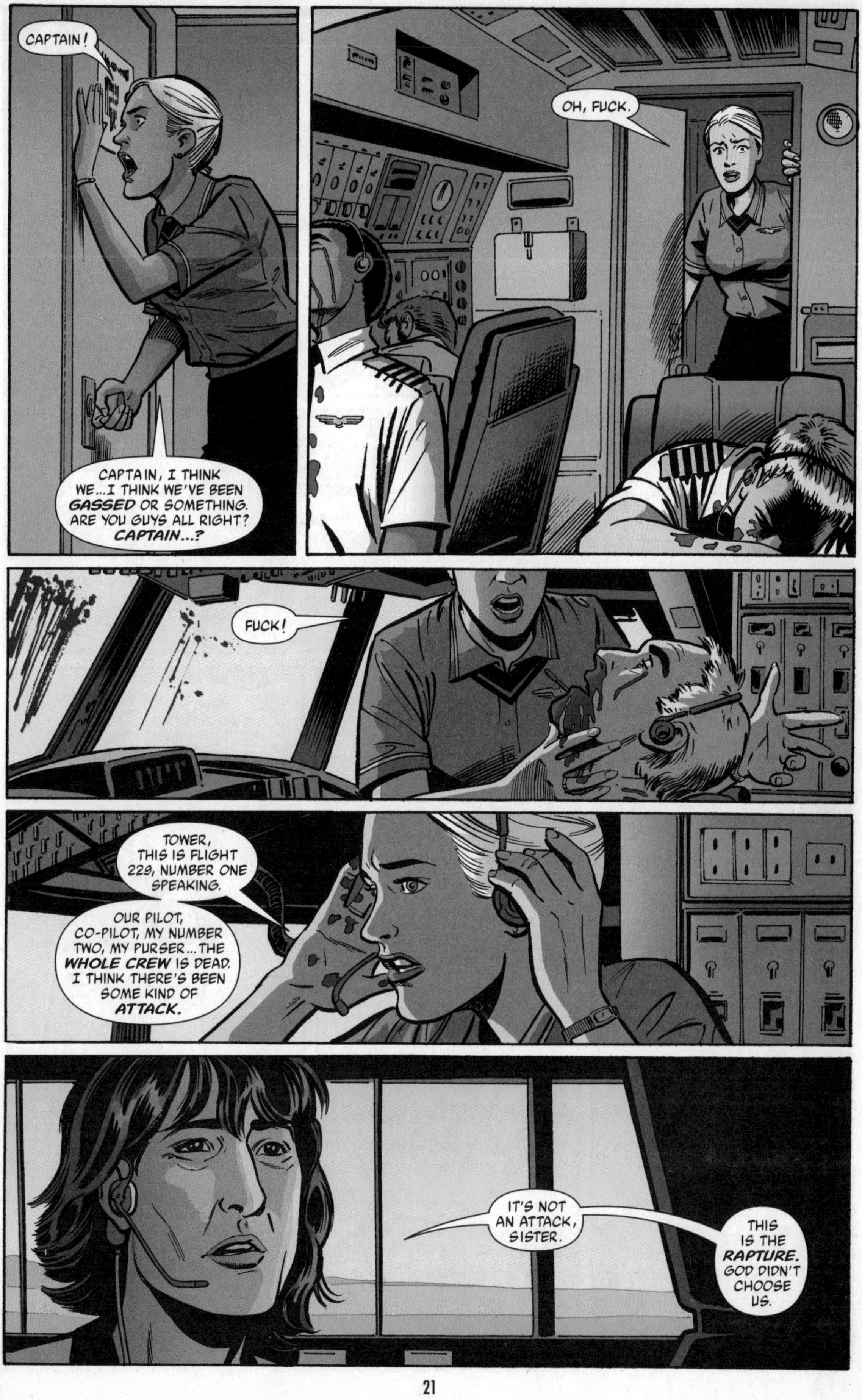
CAPTAIN!
CAPTAIN, I THINK WE...I THINK WE'VE BEEN **GASSED** OR SOMETHING. ARE YOU GUYS ALL RIGHT? **CAPTAIN...?**
OH, FUCK.
FUCK!
TOWER, THIS IS FLIGHT 229, NUMBER ONE SPEAKING.
OUR PILOT, CO-PILOT, MY NUMBER TWO, MY PURSER...THE **WHOLE CREW** IS DEAD. I THINK THERE'S BEEN SOME KIND OF **ATTACK.**
IT'S NOT AN ATTACK, SISTER.
THIS IS THE **RAPTURE.** GOD DIDN'T CHOOSE US.

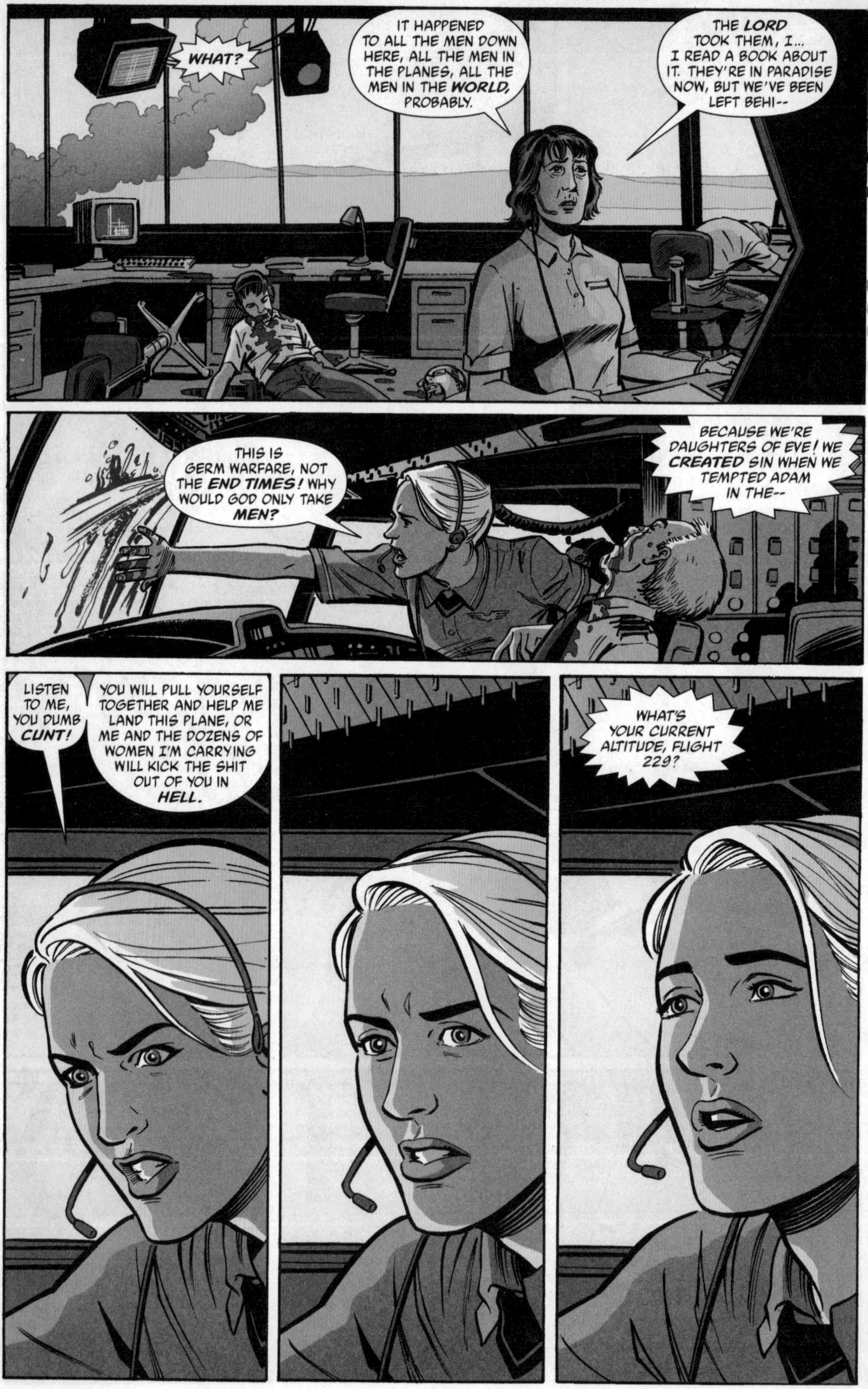
WHAT?
IT HAPPENED TO ALL THE MEN DOWN HERE, ALL THE MEN IN THE PLANES, ALL THE MEN IN THE WORLD, PROBABLY.
THE LORD TOOK THEM, I... I READ A BOOK ABOUT IT. THEY'RE IN PARADISE NOW, BUT WE'VE BEEN LEFT BEHI--
THIS IS GERM WARFARE, NOT THE END TIMES! WHY WOULD GOD ONLY TAKE MEN?
BECAUSE WE'RE DAUGHTERS OF EVE! WE CREATED SIN WHEN WE TEMPTED ADAM IN THE--
LISTEN TO ME, YOU DUMB CUNT!
YOU WILL PULL YOURSELF TOGETHER AND HELP ME LAND THIS PLANE, OR ME AND THE DOZENS OF WOMEN I'M CARRYING WILL KICK THE SHIT OUT OF YOU IN HELL.
WHAT'S YOUR CURRENT ALTITUDE, FLIGHT 229?

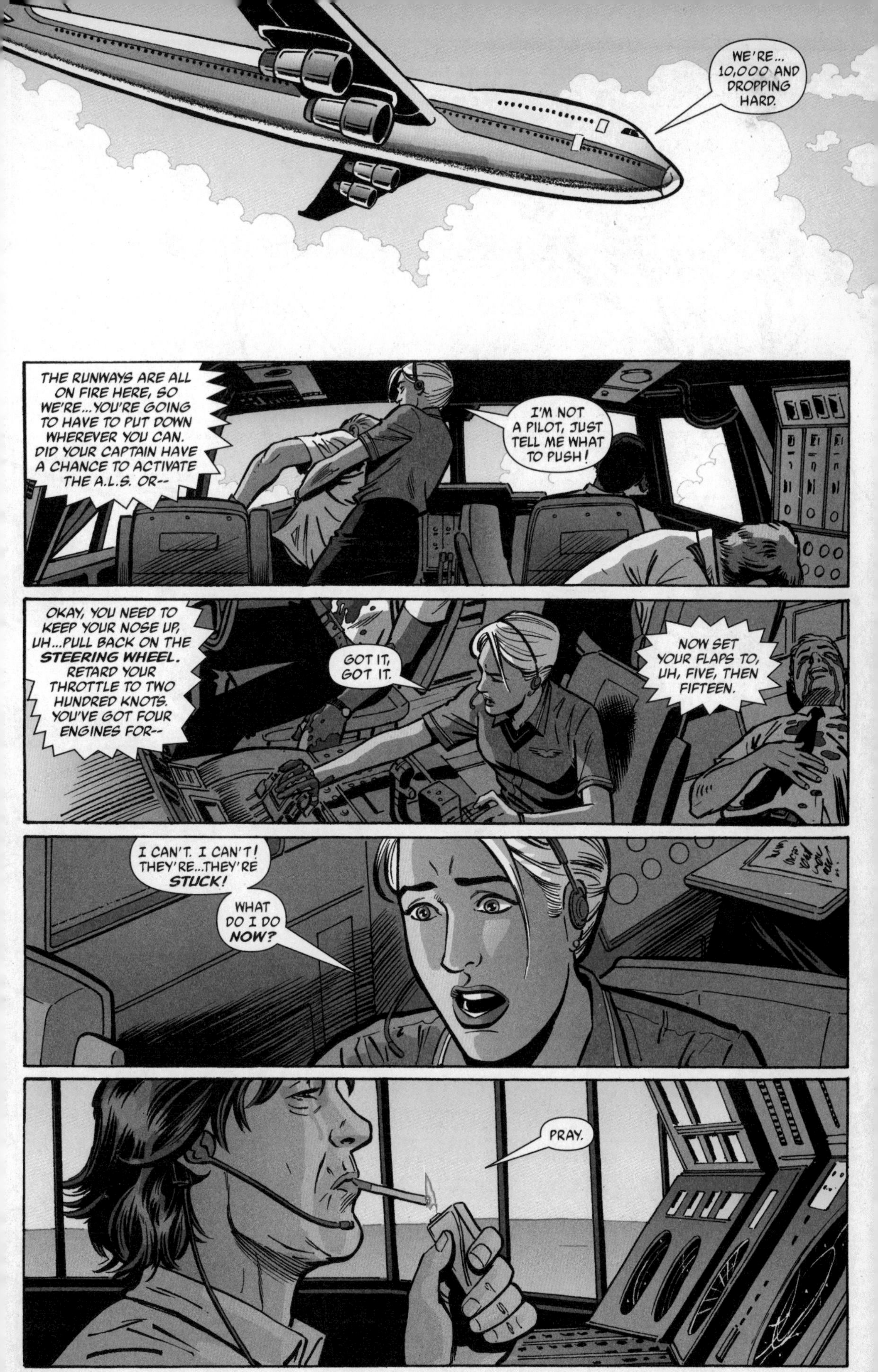
WE'RE... 10,000 AND DROPPING HARD.
THE RUNWAYS ARE ALL ON FIRE HERE, SO WE'RE...YOU'RE GOING TO HAVE TO PUT DOWN WHEREVER YOU CAN. DID YOUR CAPTAIN HAVE A CHANCE TO ACTIVATE THE A.L.S. OR--
I'M NOT A PILOT, JUST TELL ME WHAT TO PUSH!
OKAY, YOU NEED TO KEEP YOUR NOSE UP, UH...PULL BACK ON THE STEERING WHEEL. RETARD YOUR THROTTLE TO TWO HUNDRED KNOTS. YOU'VE GOT FOUR ENGINES FOR--
GOT IT, GOT IT.
NOW SET YOUR FLAPS TO, UH, FIVE, THEN FIFTEEN.
I CAN'T. I CAN'T! THEY'RE...THEY'RE STUCK!
WHAT DO I DO NOW?
PRAY.

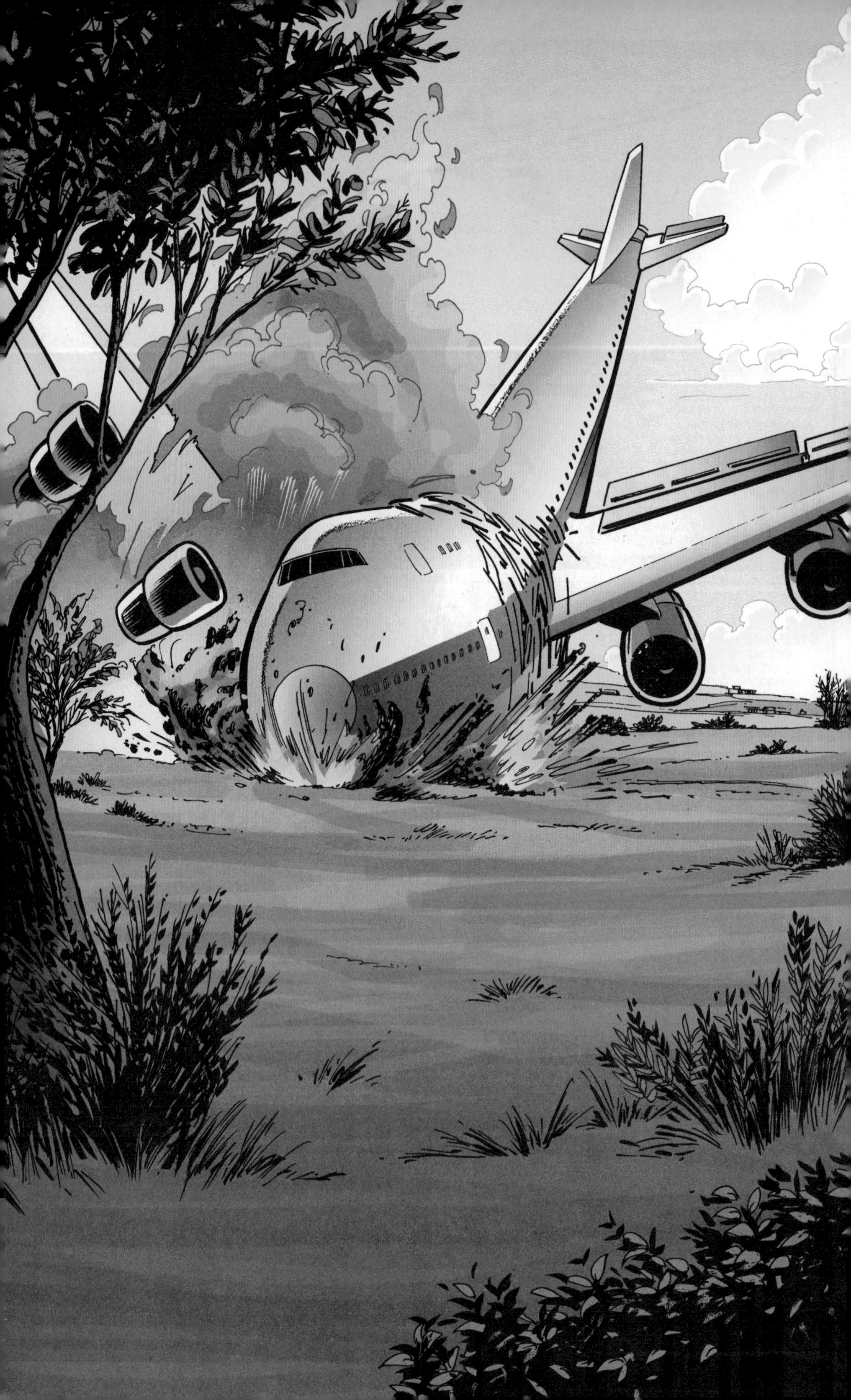

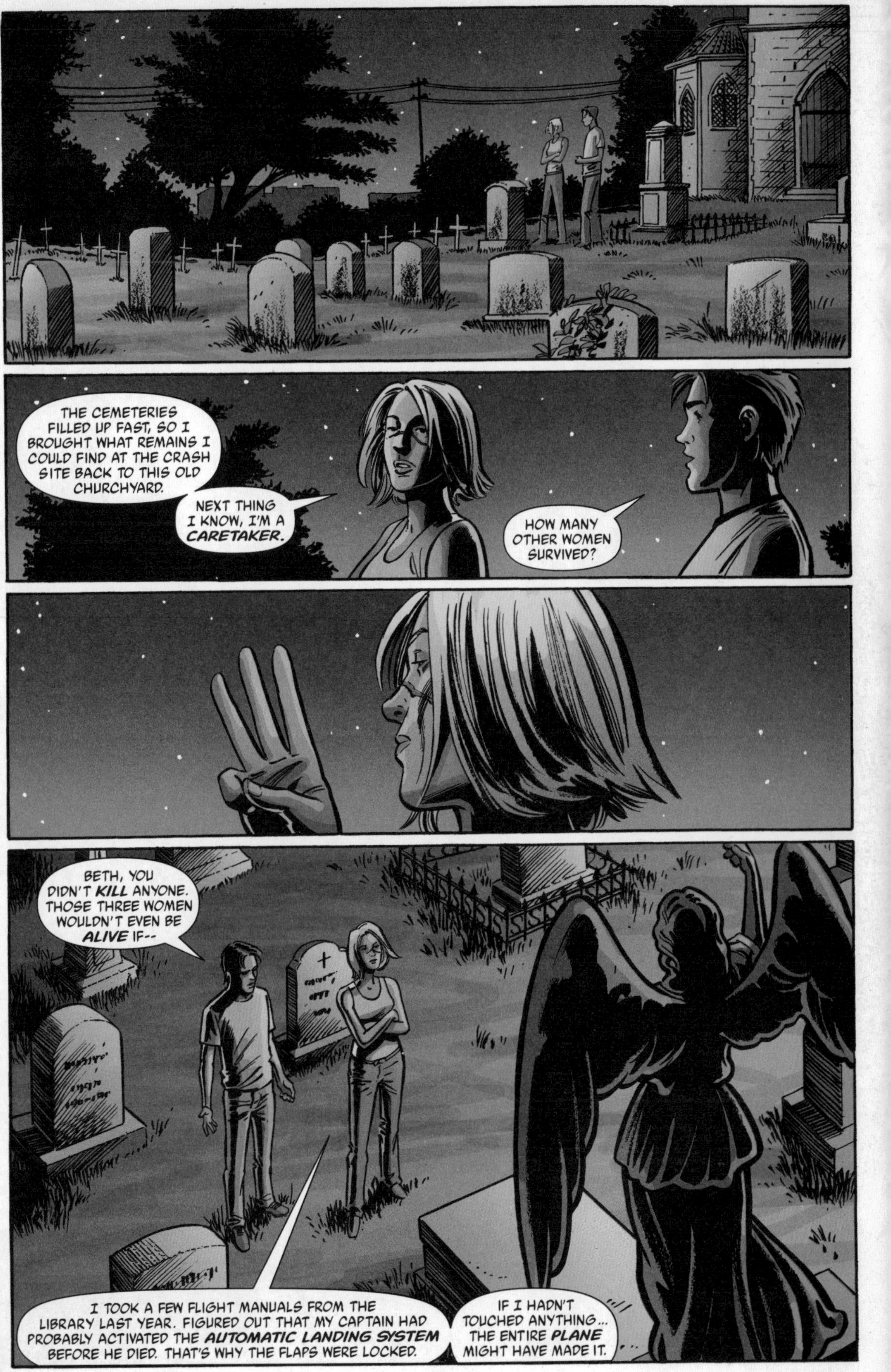

THE CEMETERIES FILLED UP FAST, SO I BROUGHT WHAT REMAINS I COULD FIND AT THE CRASH SITE BACK TO THIS OLD CHURCHYARD.
NEXT THING I KNOW, I'M A CARETAKER.
HOW MANY OTHER WOMEN SURVIVED?
BETH, YOU DIDN'T KILL ANYONE. THOSE THREE WOMEN WOULDN'T EVEN BE ALIVE IF--
I TOOK A FEW FLIGHT MANUALS FROM THE LIBRARY LAST YEAR. FIGURED OUT THAT MY CAPTAIN HAD PROBABLY ACTIVATED THE AUTOMATIC LANDING SYSTEM BEFORE HE DIED. THAT'S WHY THE FLAPS WERE LOCKED.
IF I HADN'T TOUCHED ANYTHING... THE ENTIRE PLANE MIGHT HAVE MADE IT.

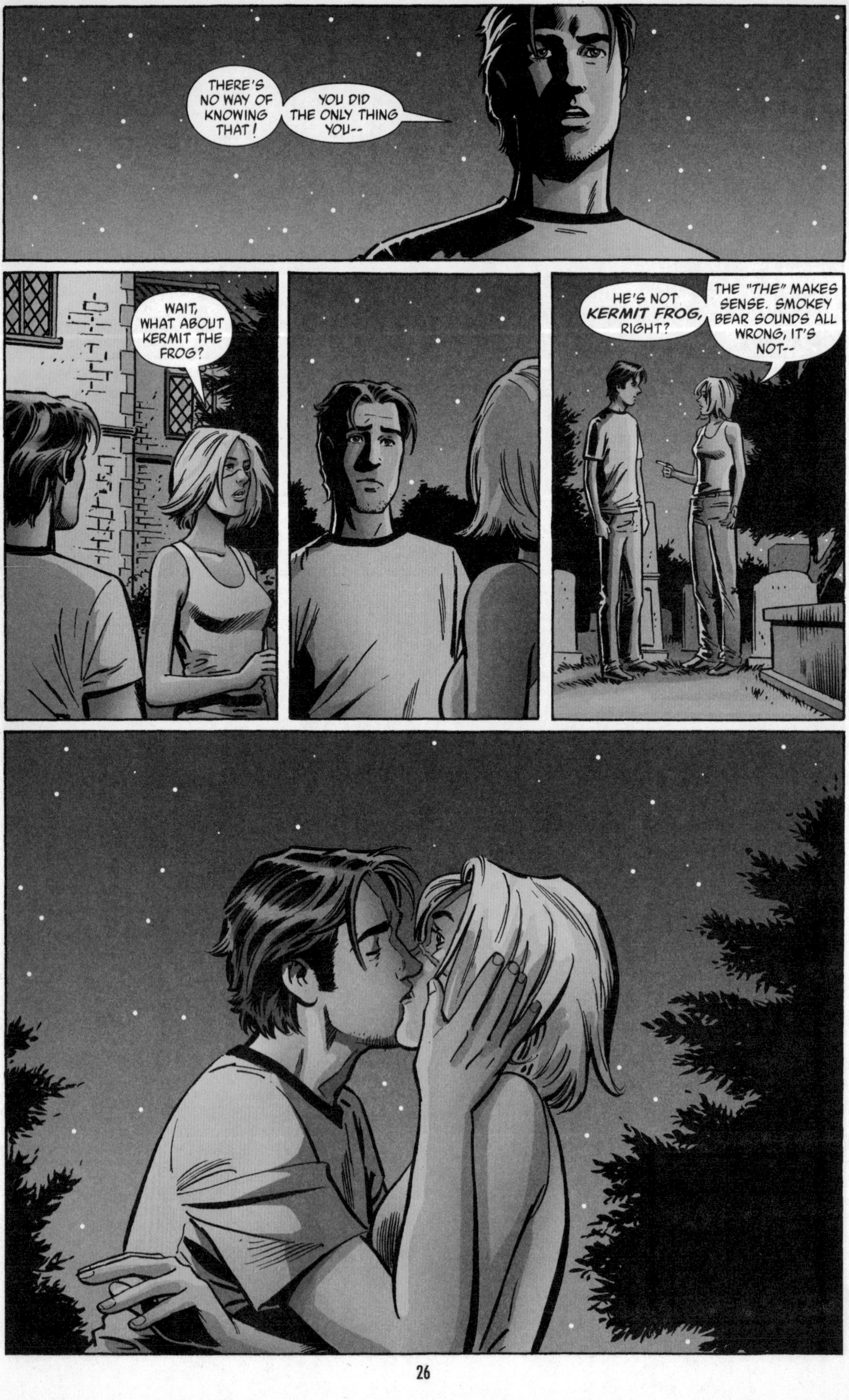
THERE'S NO WAY OF KNOWING THAT!
YOU DID THE ONLY THING YOU--
WAIT, WHAT ABOUT KERMIT THE FROG?
HE'S NOT KERMIT FROG, RIGHT?
THE "THE" MAKES SENSE. SMOKEY BEAR SOUNDS ALL WRONG, IT'S NOT--

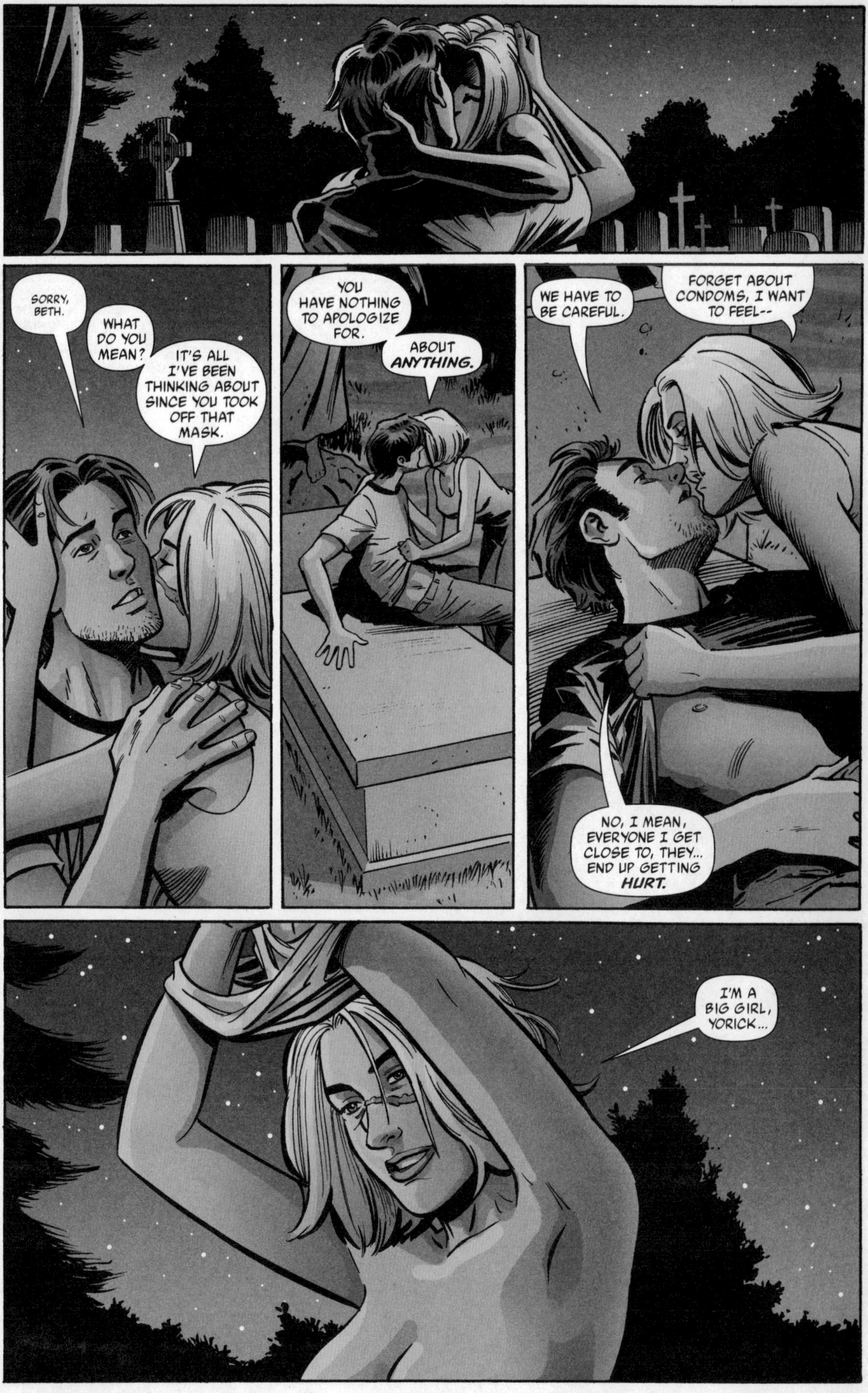
SORRY, BETH.
WHAT DO YOU MEAN?
IT'S ALL I'VE BEEN THINKING ABOUT SINCE YOU TOOK OFF THAT MASK.
YOU HAVE NOTHING TO APOLOGIZE FOR.
ABOUT ANYTHING.
WE HAVE TO BE CAREFUL.
FORGET ABOUT CONDOMS, I WANT TO FEEL--
NO, I MEAN, EVERYONE I GET CLOSE TO, THEY... END UP GETTING HURT.
I'M A BIG GIRL, YORICK...

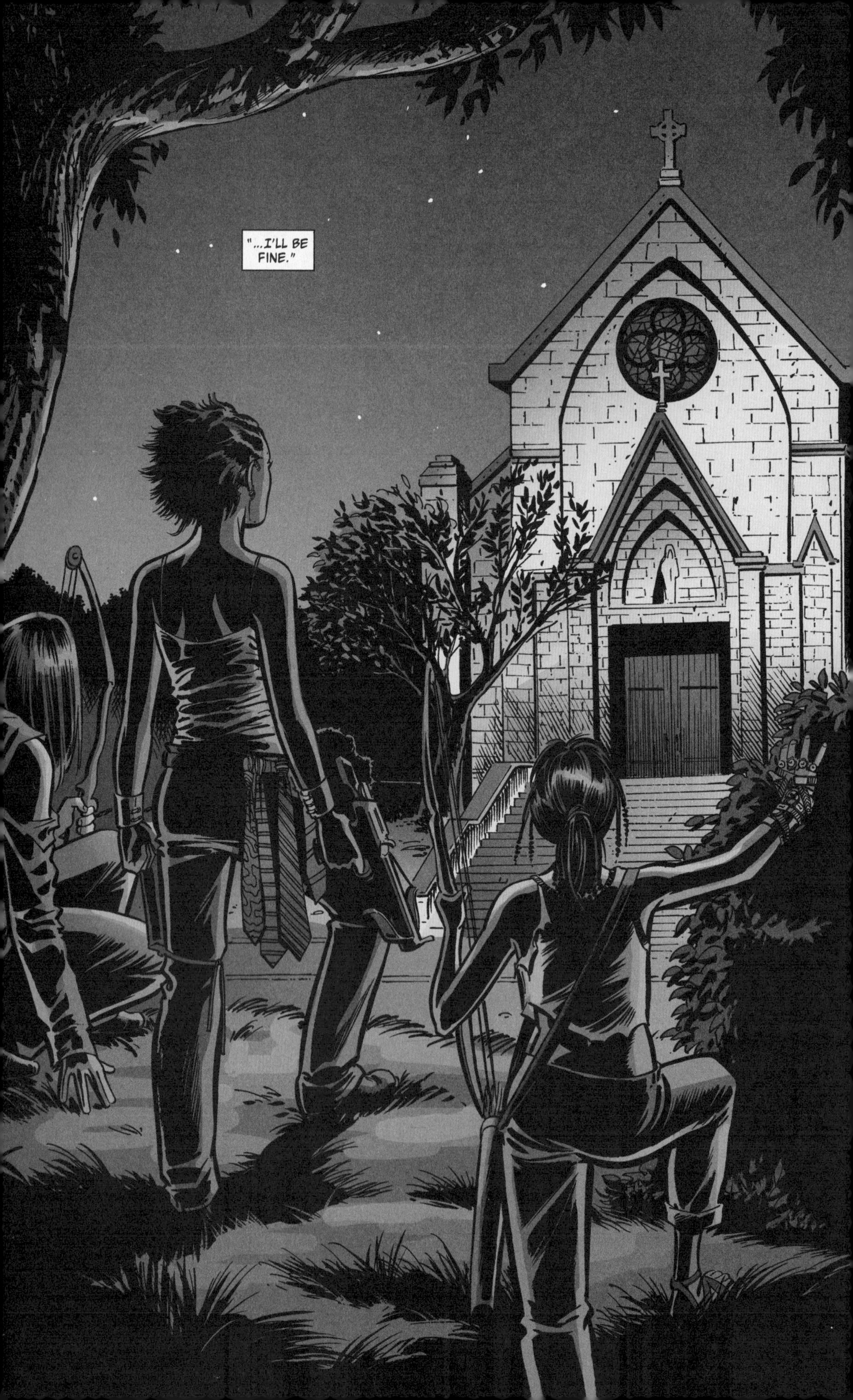
"...I'LL BE FINE."

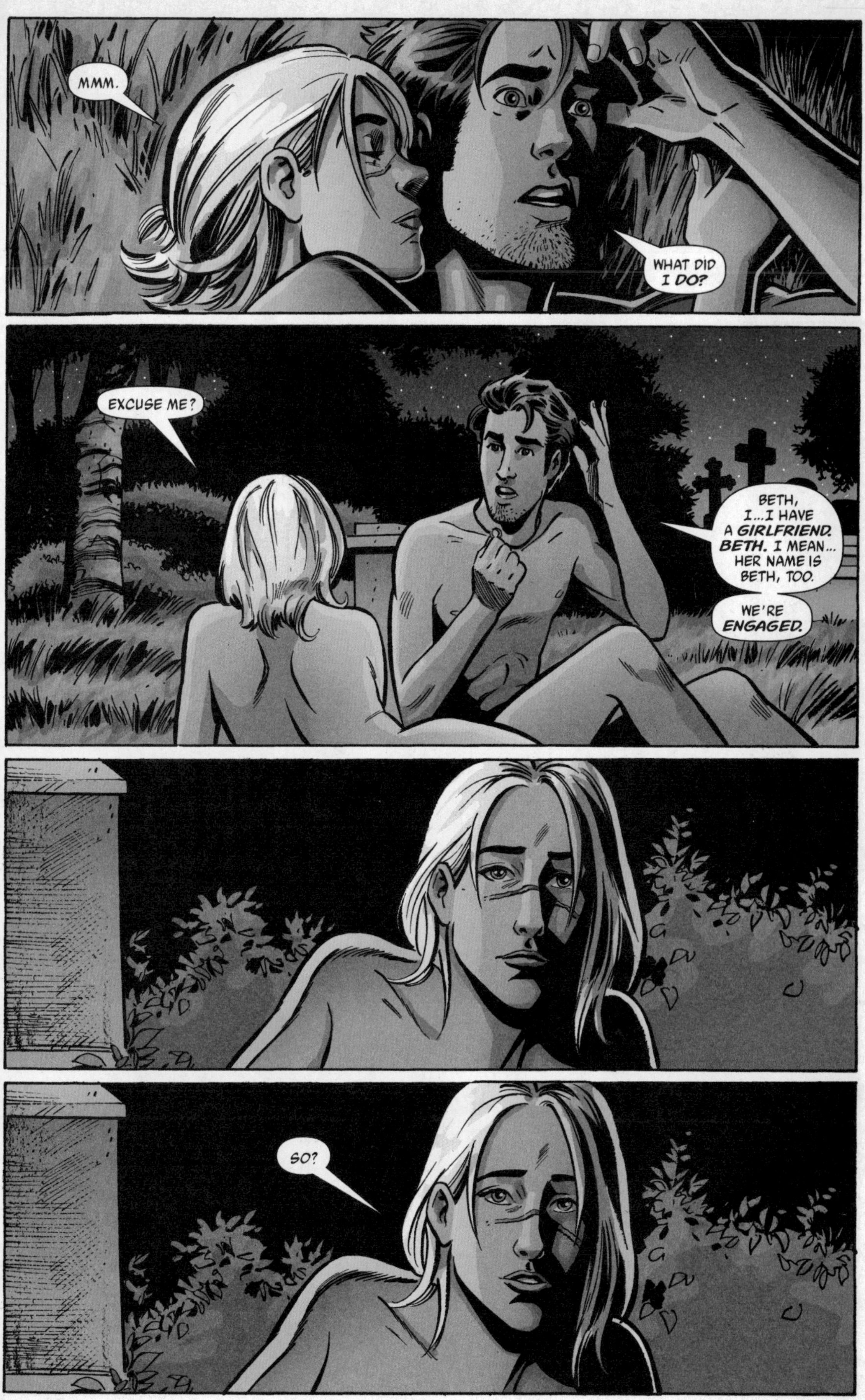
MMM.
WHAT DID I DO?
EXCUSE ME?
BETH, I...I HAVE A GIRLFRIEND. BETH. I MEAN... HER NAME IS BETH, TOO.
WE'RE ENGAGED.
SO?

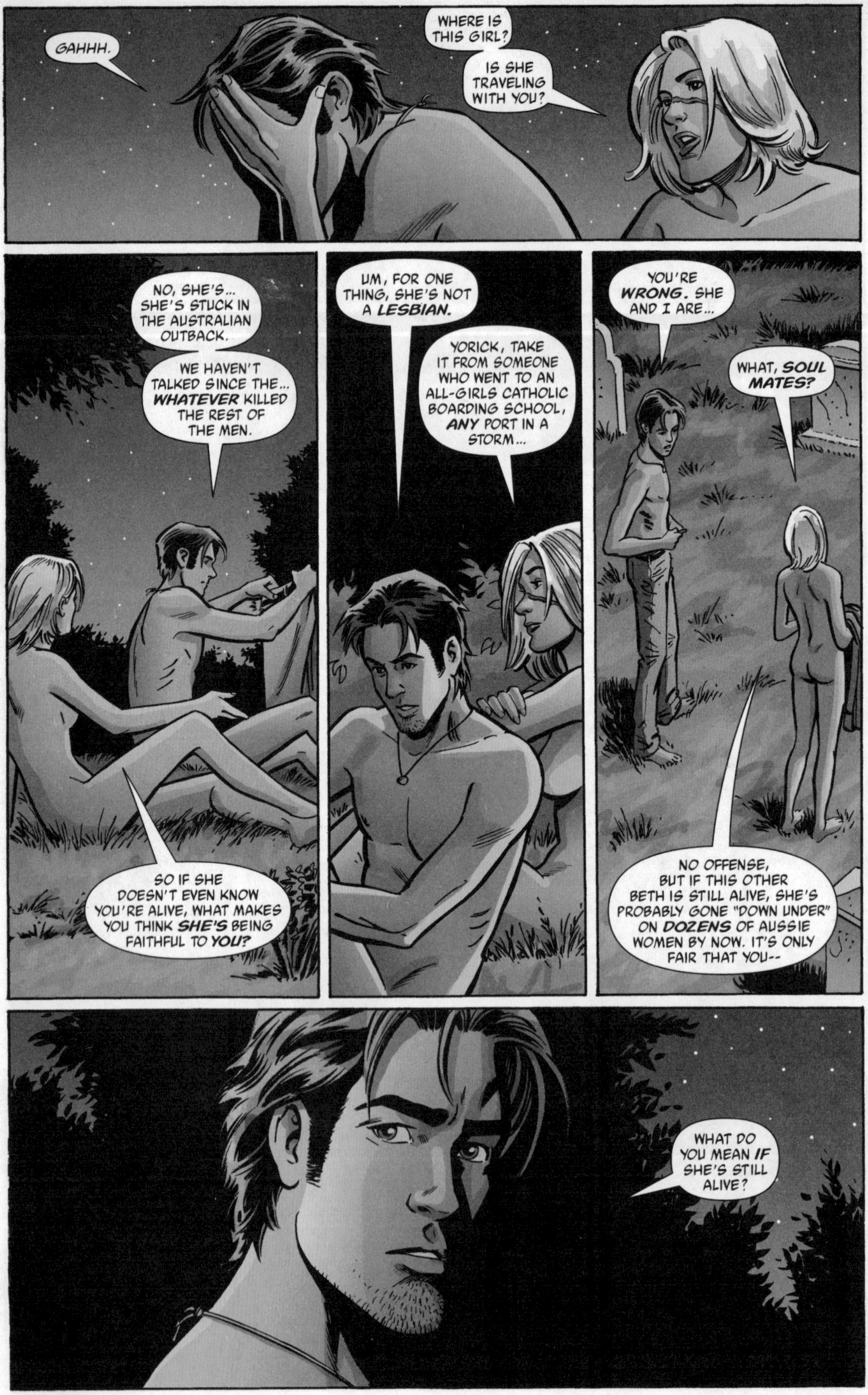
GAHHH.
WHERE IS THIS GIRL?
IS SHE TRAVELING WITH YOU?
NO, SHE'S... SHE'S STUCK IN THE AUSTRALIAN OUTBACK.
WE HAVEN'T TALKED SINCE THE... WHATEVER KILLED THE REST OF THE MEN.
SO IF SHE DOESN'T EVEN KNOW YOU'RE ALIVE, WHAT MAKES YOU THINK SHE'S BEING FAITHFUL TO YOU?
UM, FOR ONE THING, SHE'S NOT A LESBIAN.
YORICK, TAKE IT FROM SOMEONE WHO WENT TO AN ALL-GIRLS CATHOLIC BOARDING SCHOOL, ANY PORT IN A STORM...
YOU'RE WRONG. SHE AND I ARE...
WHAT, SOUL MATES?
NO OFFENSE, BUT IF THIS OTHER BETH IS STILL ALIVE, SHE'S PROBABLY GONE "DOWN UNDER" ON DOZENS OF AUSSIE WOMEN BY NOW. IT'S ONLY FAIR THAT YOU--
WHAT DO YOU MEAN IF SHE'S STILL ALIVE?

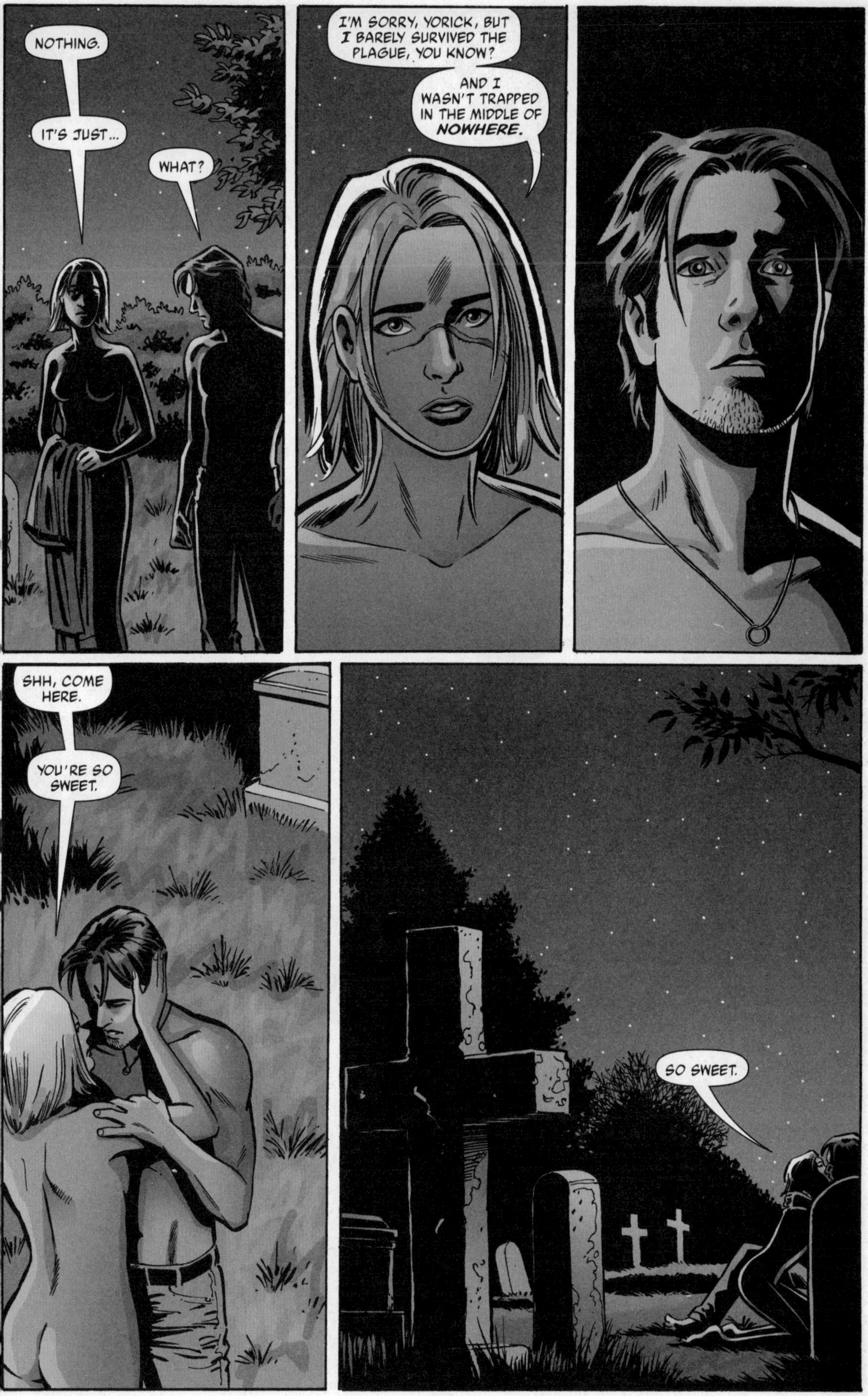
NOTHING.
IT'S JUST...
WHAT?
I'M SORRY, YORICK, BUT I BARELY SURVIVED THE PLAGUE, YOU KNOW?
AND I WASN'T TRAPPED IN THE MIDDLE OF NOWHERE.
SHH, COME HERE.
YOU'RE SO SWEET.
SO SWEET.

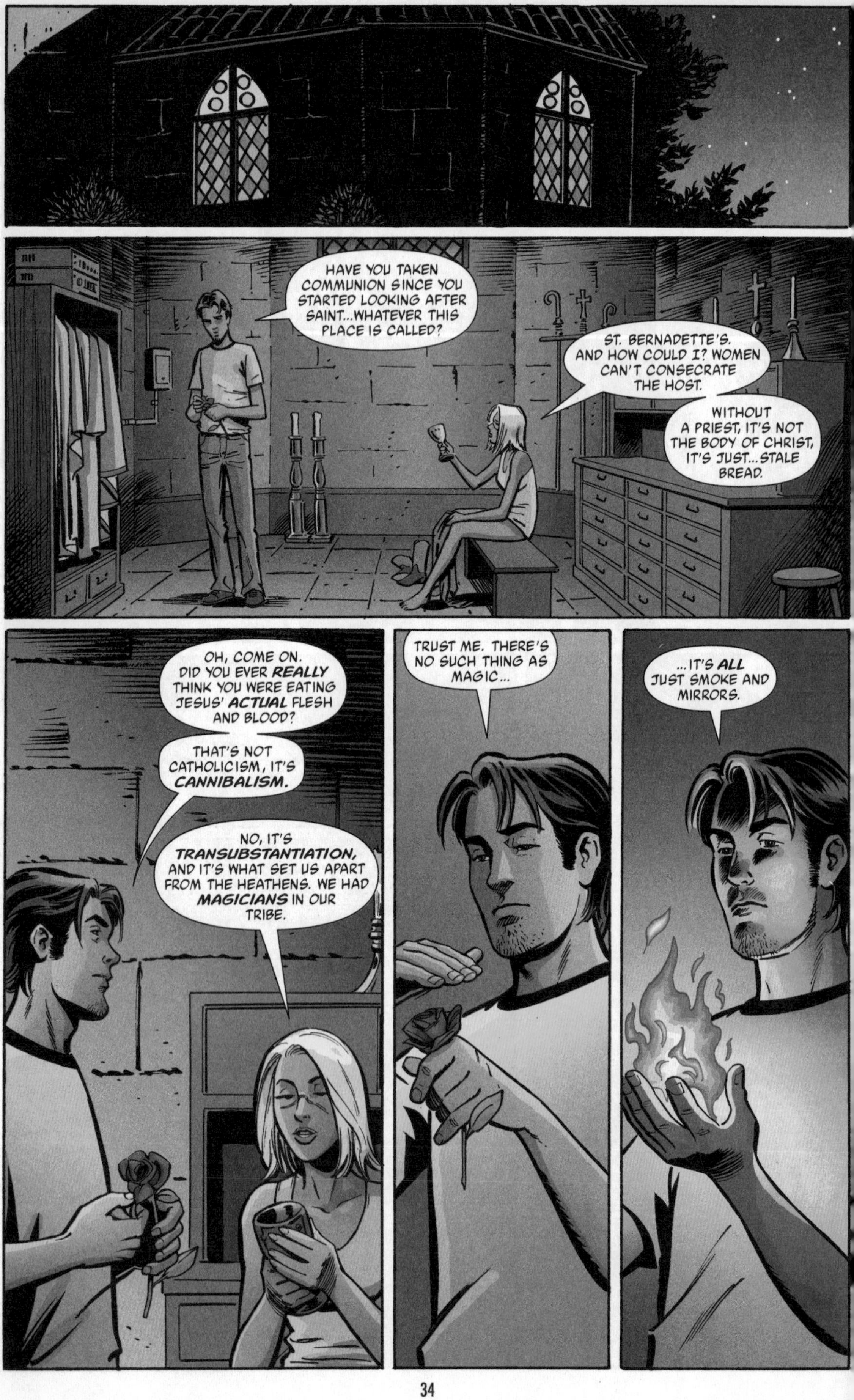
HAVE YOU TAKEN COMMUNION SINCE YOU STARTED LOOKING AFTER SAINT...WHATEVER THIS PLACE IS CALLED?
ST. BERNADETTE'S. AND HOW COULD I? WOMEN CAN'T CONSECRATE THE HOST.
WITHOUT A PRIEST, IT'S NOT THE BODY OF CHRIST, IT'S JUST...STALE BREAD.
OH, COME ON. DID YOU EVER REALLY THINK YOU WERE EATING JESUS' ACTUAL FLESH AND BLOOD?
THAT'S NOT CATHOLICISM, IT'S CANNIBALISM.
NO, IT'S TRANSUBSTANTIATION, AND IT'S WHAT SET US APART FROM THE HEATHENS. WE HAD MAGICIANS IN OUR TRIBE.
TRUST ME. THERE'S NO SUCH THING AS MAGIC...
...IT'S ALL JUST SMOKE AND MIRRORS.

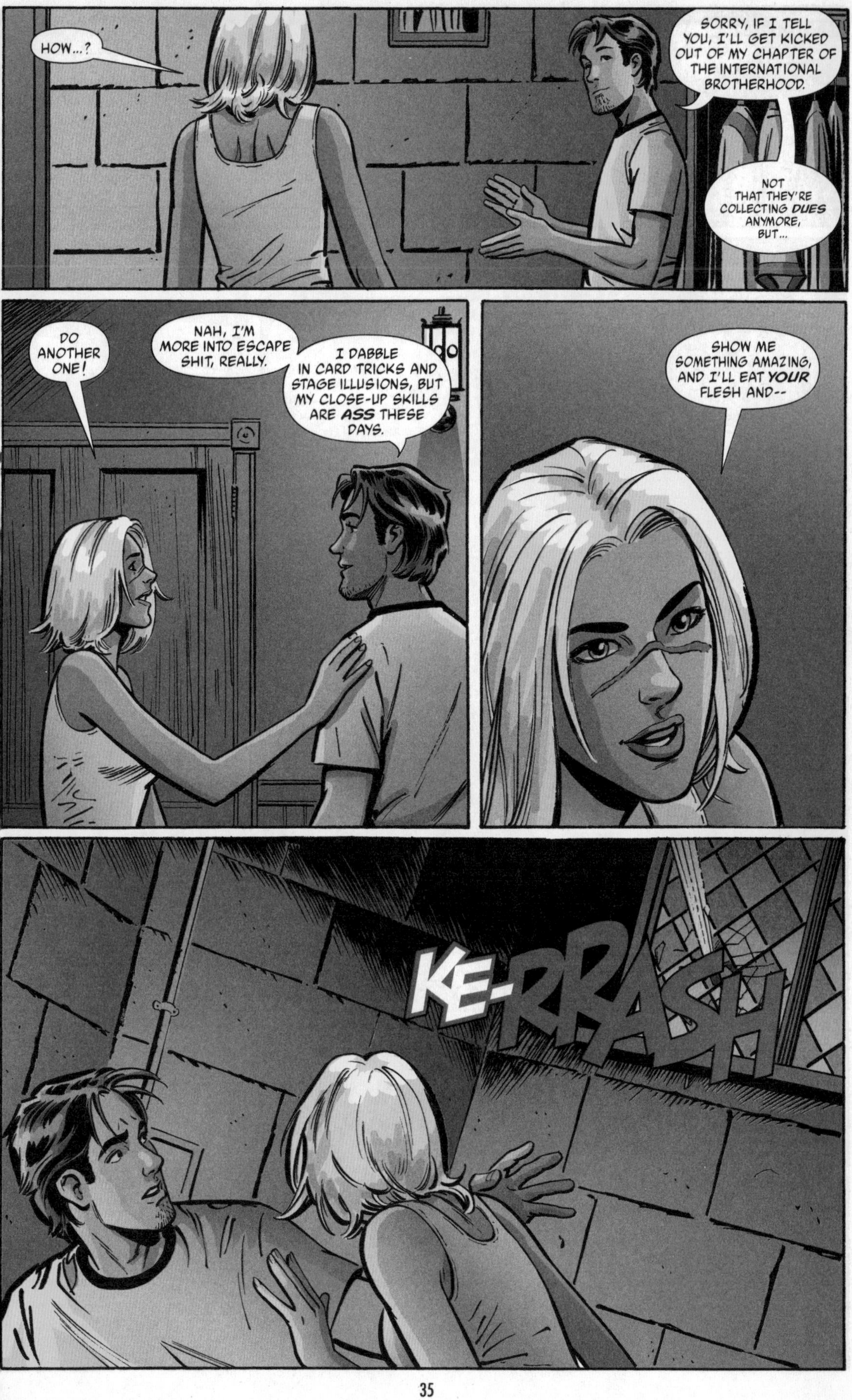
HOW...?
SORRY, IF I TELL YOU, I'LL GET KICKED OUT OF MY CHAPTER OF THE INTERNATIONAL BROTHERHOOD.
NOT THAT THEY'RE COLLECTING DUES ANYMORE, BUT...
DO ANOTHER ONE!
NAH, I'M MORE INTO ESCAPE SHIT, REALLY.
I DABBLE IN CARD TRICKS AND STAGE ILLUSIONS, BUT MY CLOSE-UP SKILLS ARE ASS THESE DAYS.
SHOW ME SOMETHING AMAZING, AND I'LL EAT YOUR FLESH AND--
KE-RRASH

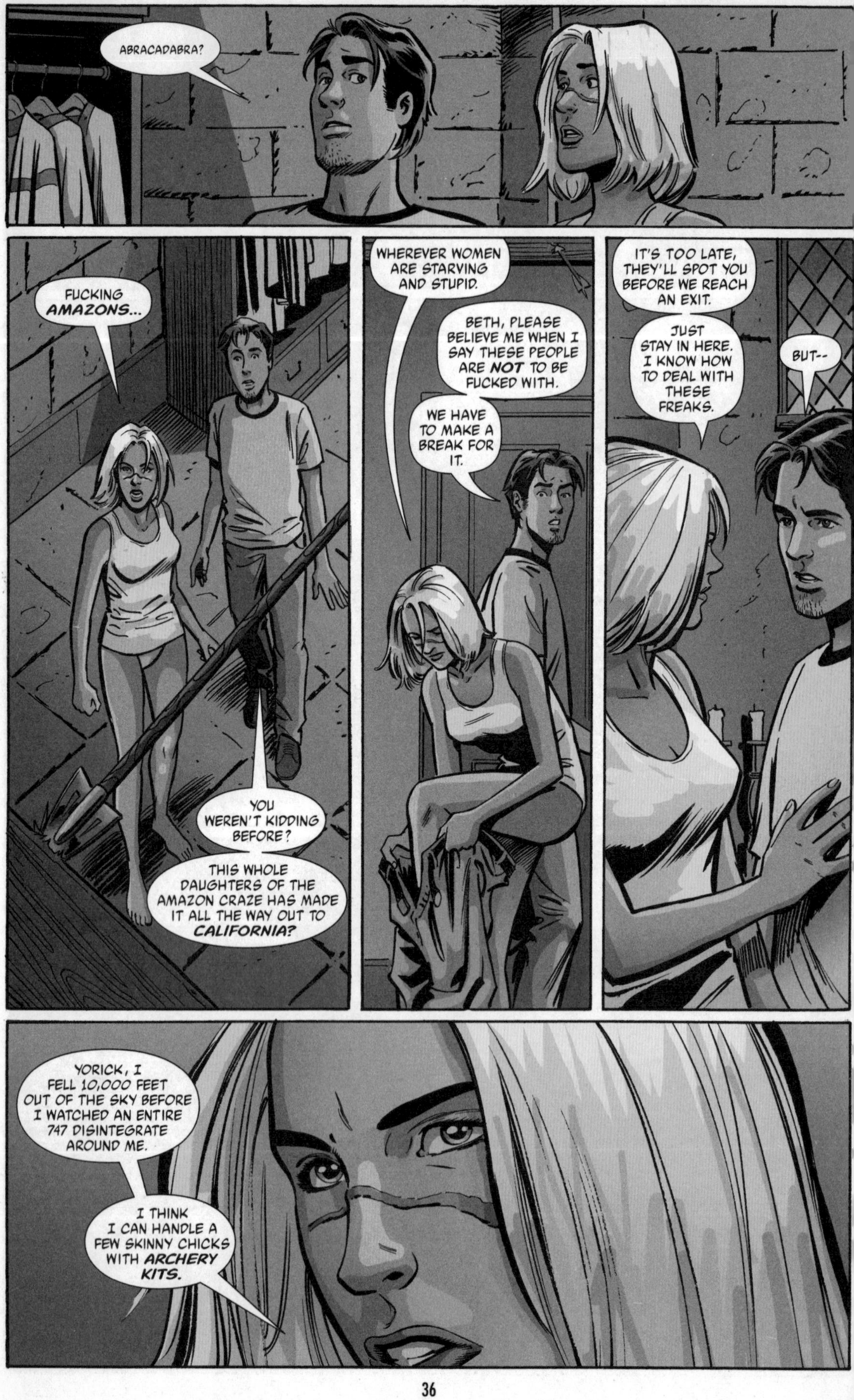

ABRACADABRA?
FUCKING AMAZONS...
YOU WEREN'T KIDDING BEFORE?
THIS WHOLE DAUGHTERS OF THE AMAZON CRAZE HAS MADE IT ALL THE WAY OUT TO CALIFORNIA?
WHEREVER WOMEN ARE STARVING AND STUPID.
BETH, PLEASE BELIEVE ME WHEN I SAY THESE PEOPLE ARE NOT TO BE FUCKED WITH.
WE HAVE TO MAKE A BREAK FOR IT.
IT'S TOO LATE, THEY'LL SPOT YOU BEFORE WE REACH AN EXIT.
JUST STAY IN HERE. I KNOW HOW TO DEAL WITH THESE FREAKS.
BUT--
YORICK, I FELL 10,000 FEET OUT OF THE SKY BEFORE I WATCHED AN ENTIRE 747 DISINTEGRATE AROUND ME.
I THINK I CAN HANDLE A FEW SKINNY CHICKS WITH ARCHERY KITS.

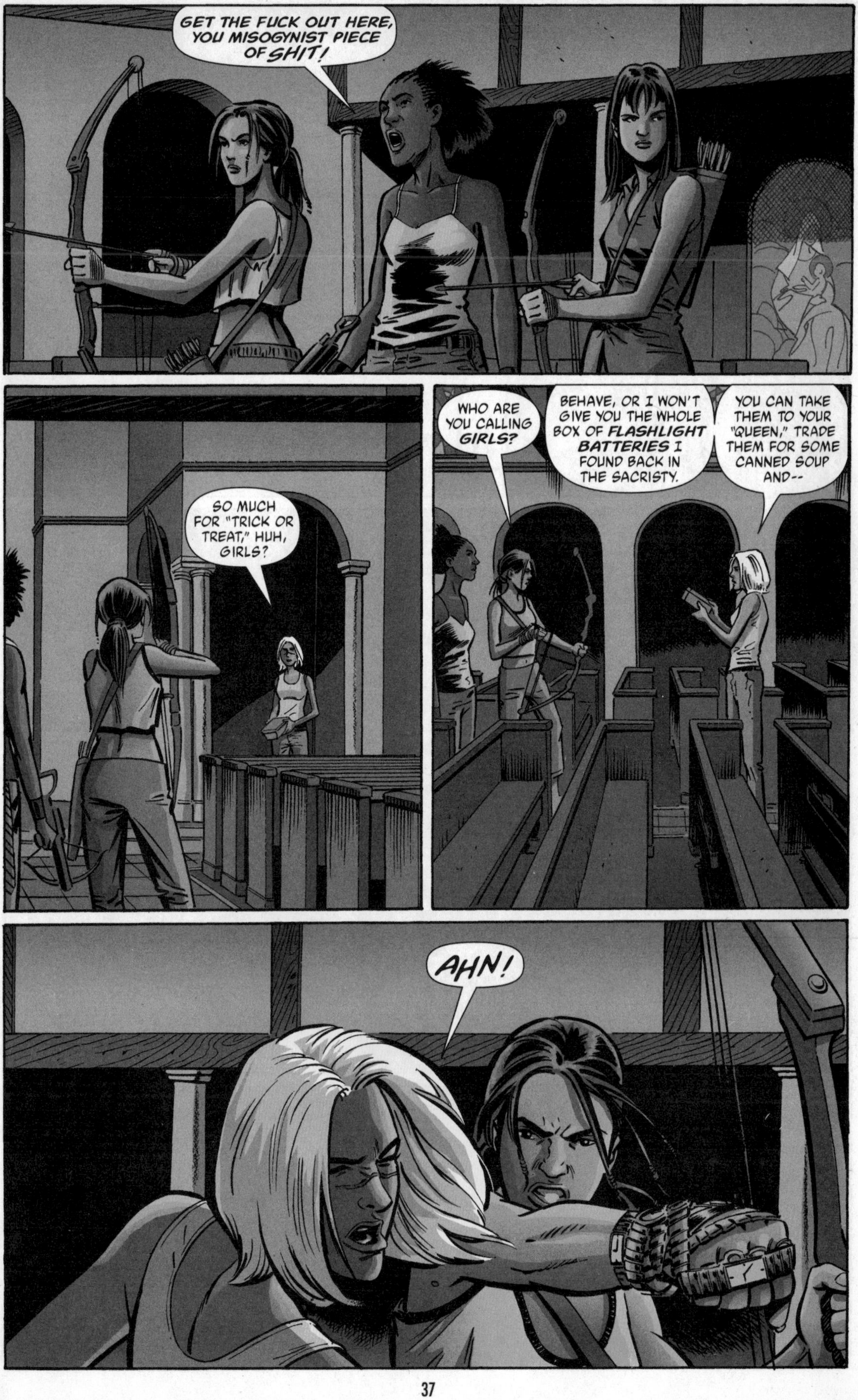
GET THE FUCK OUT HERE, YOU MISOGYNIST PIECE OF SHIT!
SO MUCH FOR "TRICK OR TREAT," HUH, GIRLS?
WHO ARE YOU CALLING GIRLS?
BEHAVE, OR I WON'T GIVE YOU THE WHOLE BOX OF FLASHLIGHT BATTERIES I FOUND BACK IN THE SACRISTY.
YOU CAN TAKE THEM TO YOUR "QUEEN," TRADE THEM FOR SOME CANNED SOUP AND--
AHN!

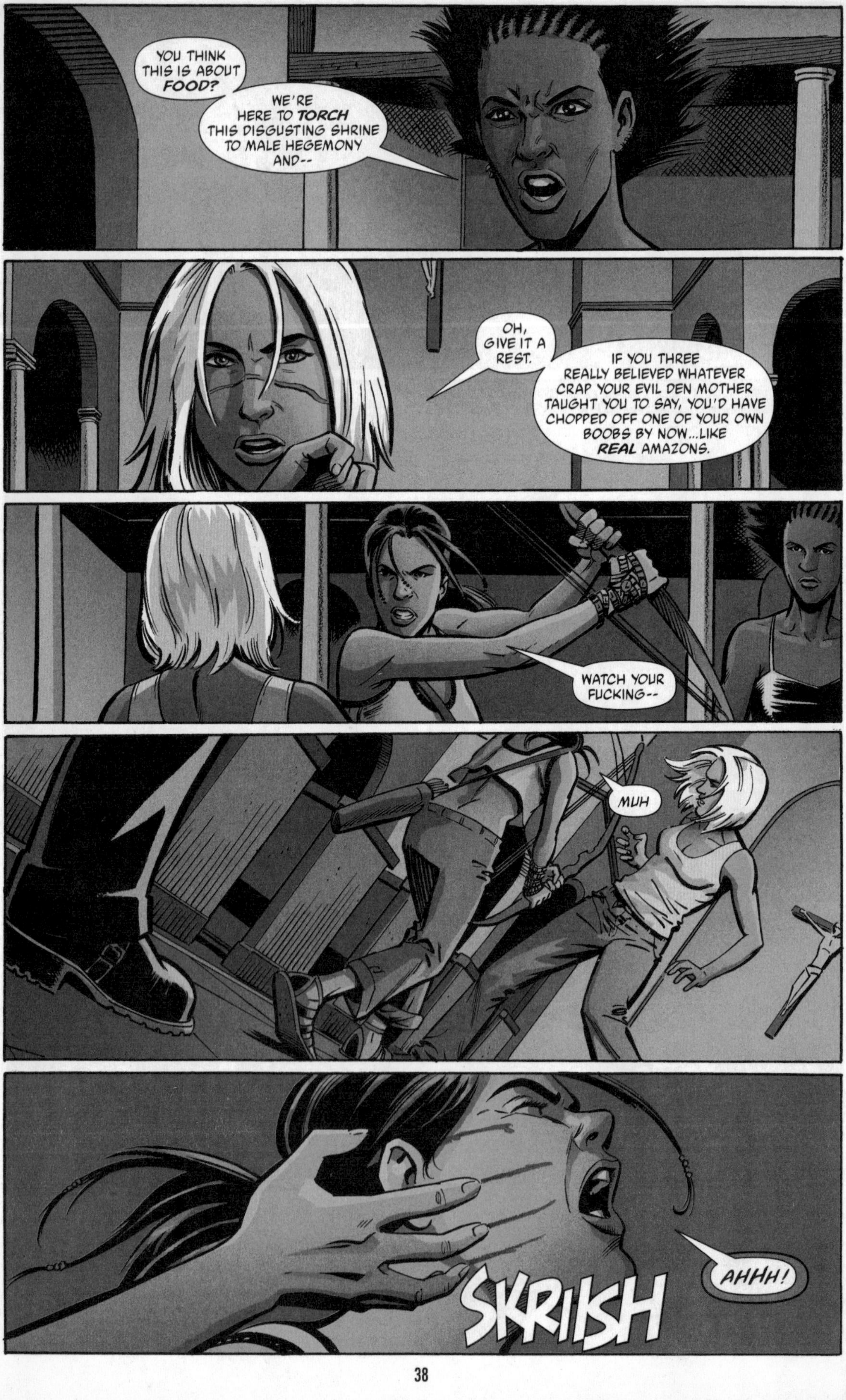
YOU THINK THIS IS ABOUT FOOD?
WE'RE HERE TO TORCH THIS DISGUSTING SHRINE TO MALE HEGEMONY AND--
OH, GIVE IT A REST.
IF YOU THREE REALLY BELIEVED WHATEVER CRAP YOUR EVIL DEN MOTHER TAUGHT YOU TO SAY, YOU'D HAVE CHOPPED OFF ONE OF YOUR OWN BOOBS BY NOW...LIKE REAL AMAZONS.
WATCH YOUR FUCKING--
MUH
AHHH!
SKRISH

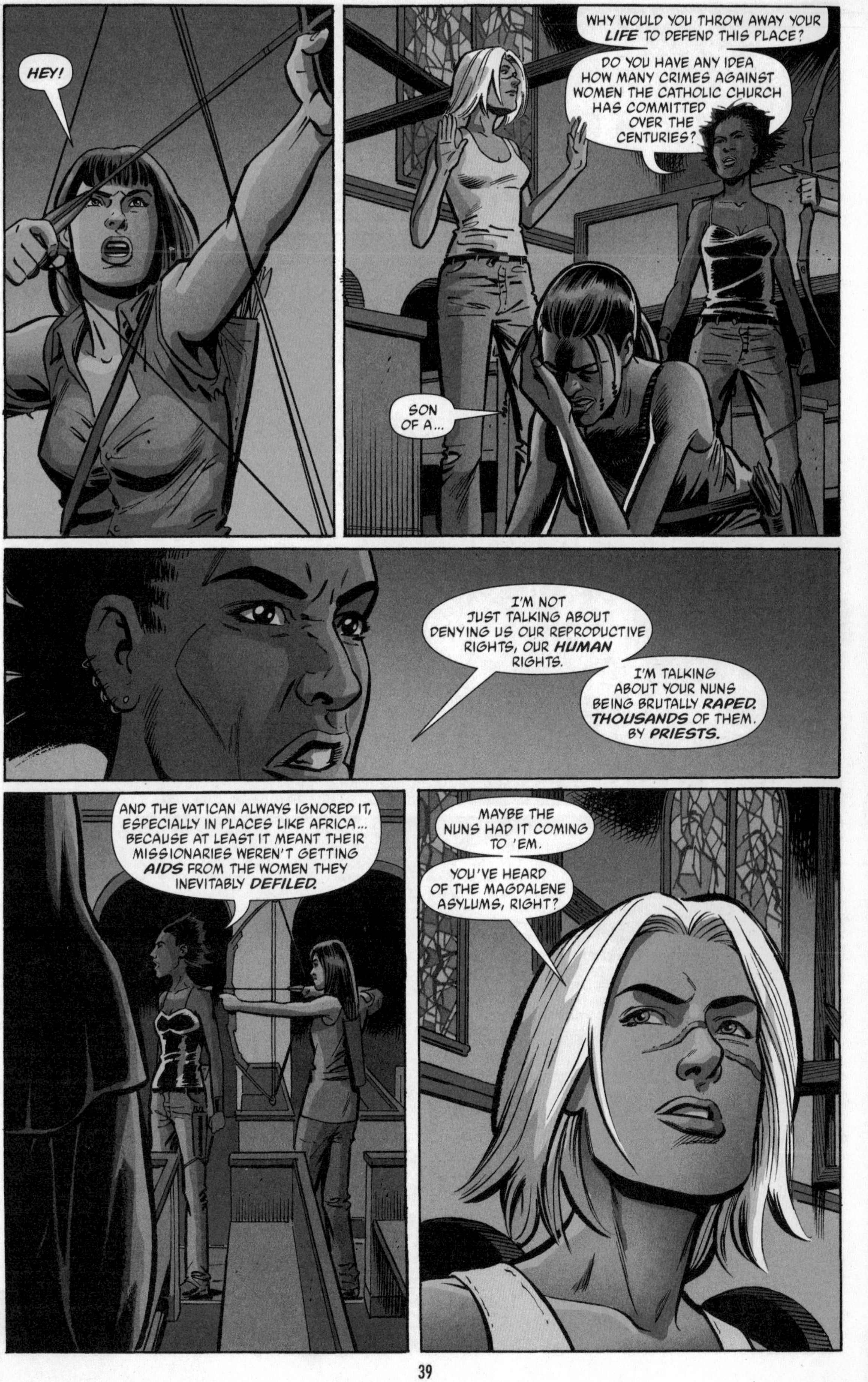
HEY!
WHY WOULD YOU THROW AWAY YOUR LIFE TO DEFEND THIS PLACE?
DO YOU HAVE ANY IDEA HOW MANY CRIMES AGAINST WOMEN THE CATHOLIC CHURCH HAS COMMITTED OVER THE CENTURIES?
SON OF A...
I'M NOT JUST TALKING ABOUT DENYING US OUR REPRODUCTIVE RIGHTS, OUR HUMAN RIGHTS.
I'M TALKING ABOUT YOUR NUNS BEING BRUTALLY RAPED. THOUSANDS OF THEM. BY PRIESTS.
AND THE VATICAN ALWAYS IGNORED IT, ESPECIALLY IN PLACES LIKE AFRICA... BECAUSE AT LEAST IT MEANT THEIR MISSIONARIES WEREN'T GETTING AIDS FROM THE WOMEN THEY INEVITABLY DEFILED.
MAYBE THE NUNS HAD IT COMING TO 'EM.
YOU'VE HEARD OF THE MAGDALENE ASYLUMS, RIGHT?

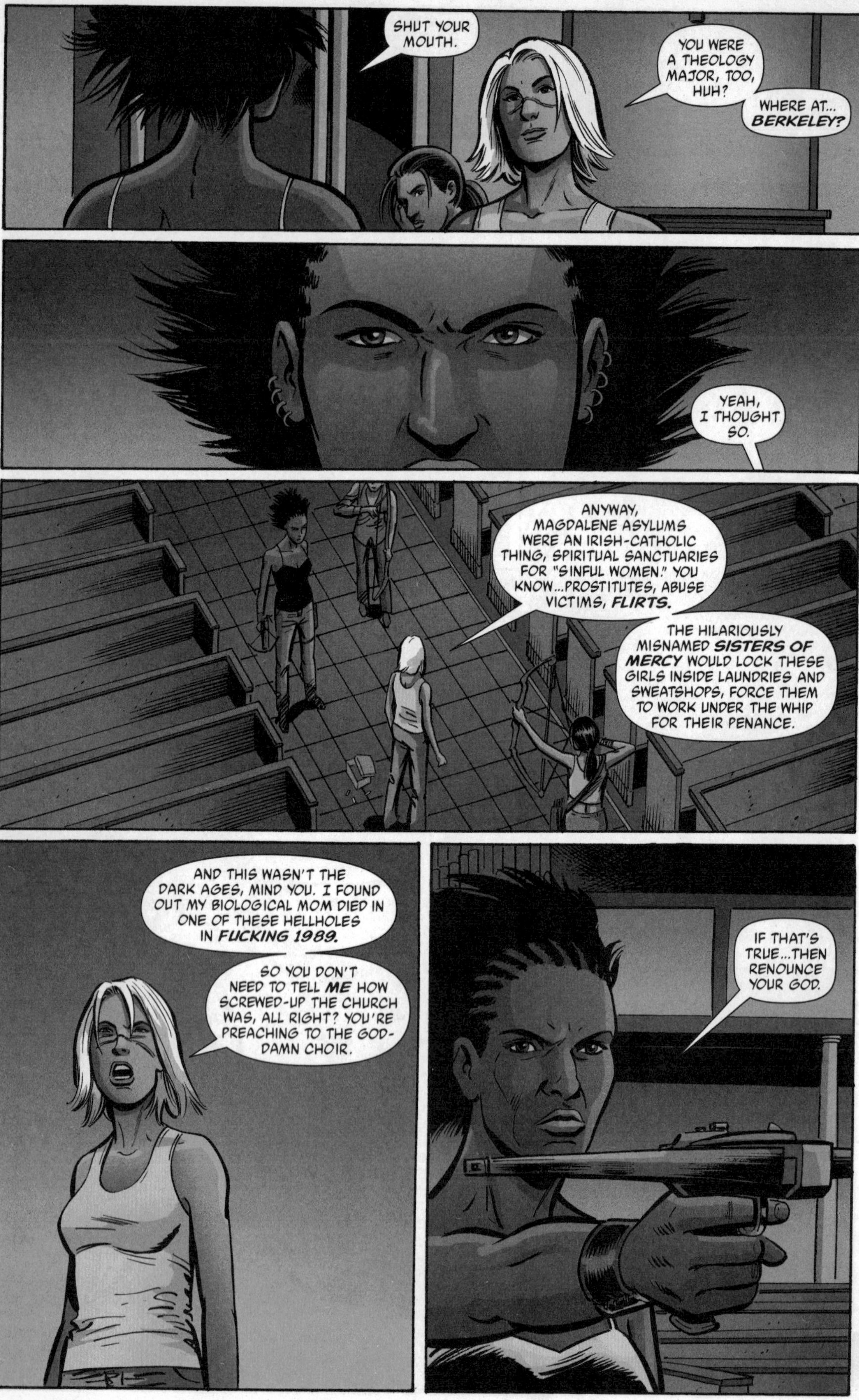
SHUT YOUR MOUTH.
YOU WERE A THEOLOGY MAJOR, TOO, HUH?
WHERE AT... **BERKELEY?**
YEAH, I THOUGHT SO.
ANYWAY, MAGDALENE ASYLUMS WERE AN IRISH-CATHOLIC THING, SPIRITUAL SANCTUARIES FOR "SINFUL WOMEN." YOU KNOW...PROSTITUTES, ABUSE VICTIMS, **FLIRTS.**
THE HILARIOUSLY MISNAMED **SISTERS OF MERCY** WOULD LOCK THESE GIRLS INSIDE LAUNDRIES AND SWEATSHOPS, FORCE THEM TO WORK UNDER THE WHIP FOR THEIR PENANCE.
AND THIS WASN'T THE DARK AGES, MIND YOU. I FOUND OUT MY BIOLOGICAL MOM DIED IN ONE OF THESE HELLHOLES IN **FUCKING 1989.**
SO YOU DON'T NEED TO TELL **ME** HOW SCREWED-UP THE CHURCH WAS, ALL RIGHT? YOU'RE PREACHING TO THE GOD-DAMN CHOIR.
IF THAT'S TRUE...THEN RENOUNCE YOUR GOD.

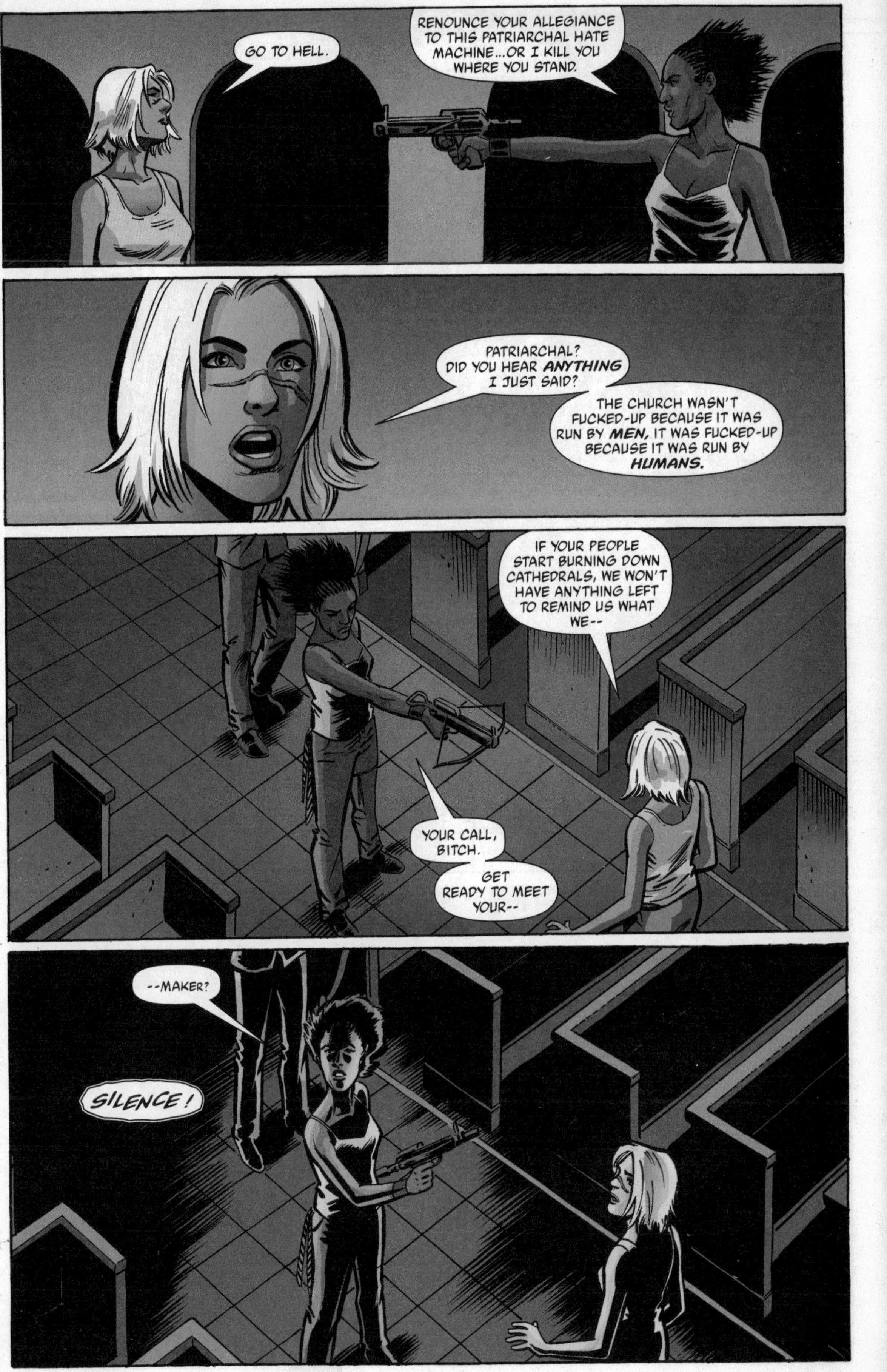

GO TO HELL.
RENOUNCE YOUR ALLEGIANCE TO THIS PATRIARCHAL HATE MACHINE...OR I KILL YOU WHERE YOU STAND.
PATRIARCHAL? DID YOU HEAR ANYTHING I JUST SAID?
THE CHURCH WASN'T FUCKED-UP BECAUSE IT WAS RUN BY MEN, IT WAS FUCKED-UP BECAUSE IT WAS RUN BY HUMANS.
IF YOUR PEOPLE START BURNING DOWN CATHEDRALS, WE WON'T HAVE ANYTHING LEFT TO REMIND US WHAT WE--
YOUR CALL, BITCH.
GET READY TO MEET YOUR--
--MAKER?
SILENCE!

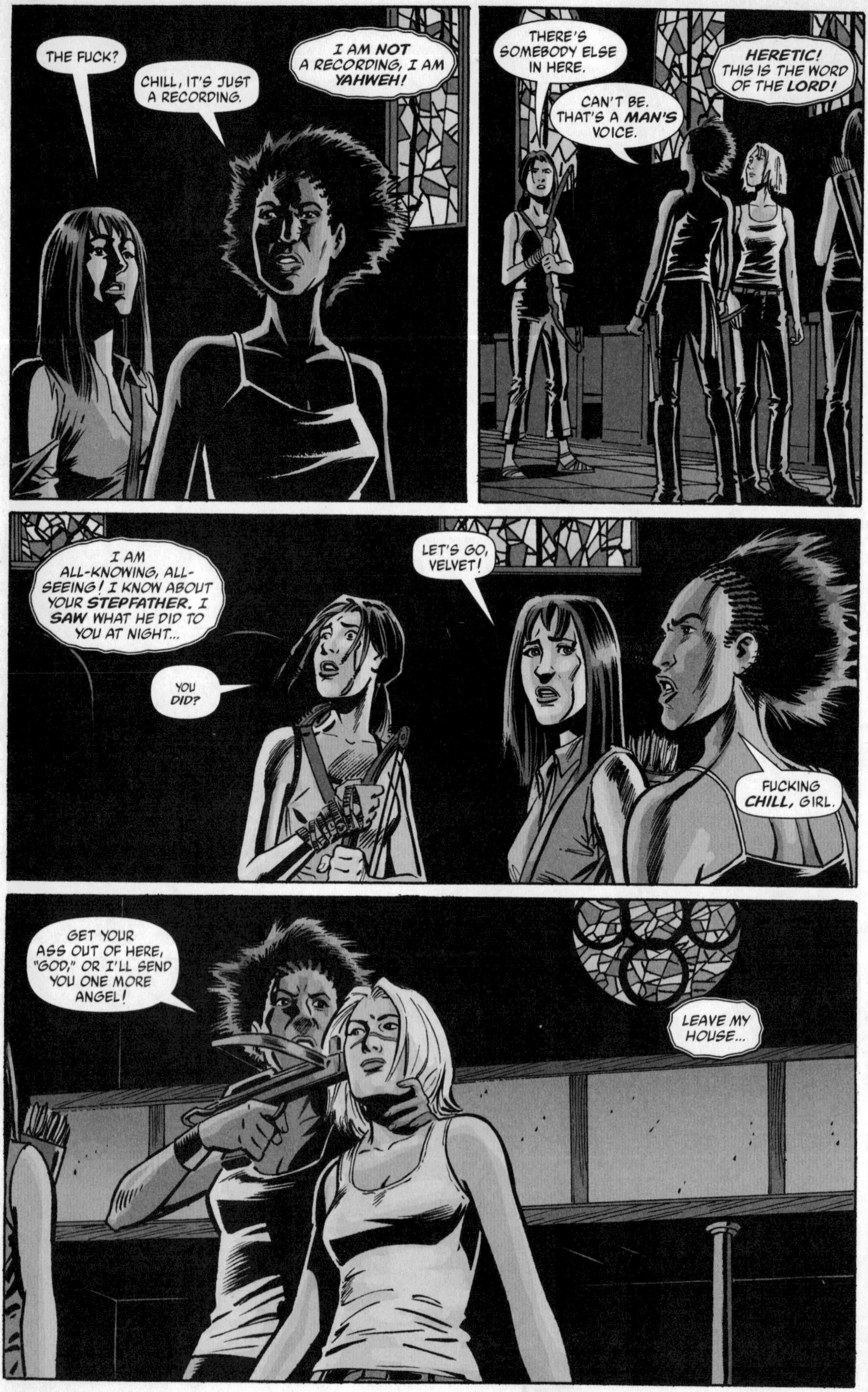
THE FUCK?
CHILL, IT'S JUST A RECORDING.
I AM NOT A RECORDING, I AM YAHWEH!
THERE'S SOMEBODY ELSE IN HERE.
CAN'T BE. THAT'S A MAN'S VOICE.
HERETIC! THIS IS THE WORD OF THE LORD!
I AM ALL-KNOWING, ALL-SEEING! I KNOW ABOUT YOUR STEPFATHER. I SAW WHAT HE DID TO YOU AT NIGHT...
YOU DID?
LET'S GO, VELVET!
FUCKING CHILL, GIRL.
GET YOUR ASS OUT OF HERE, "GOD," OR I'LL SEND YOU ONE MORE ANGEL!
LEAVE MY HOUSE...

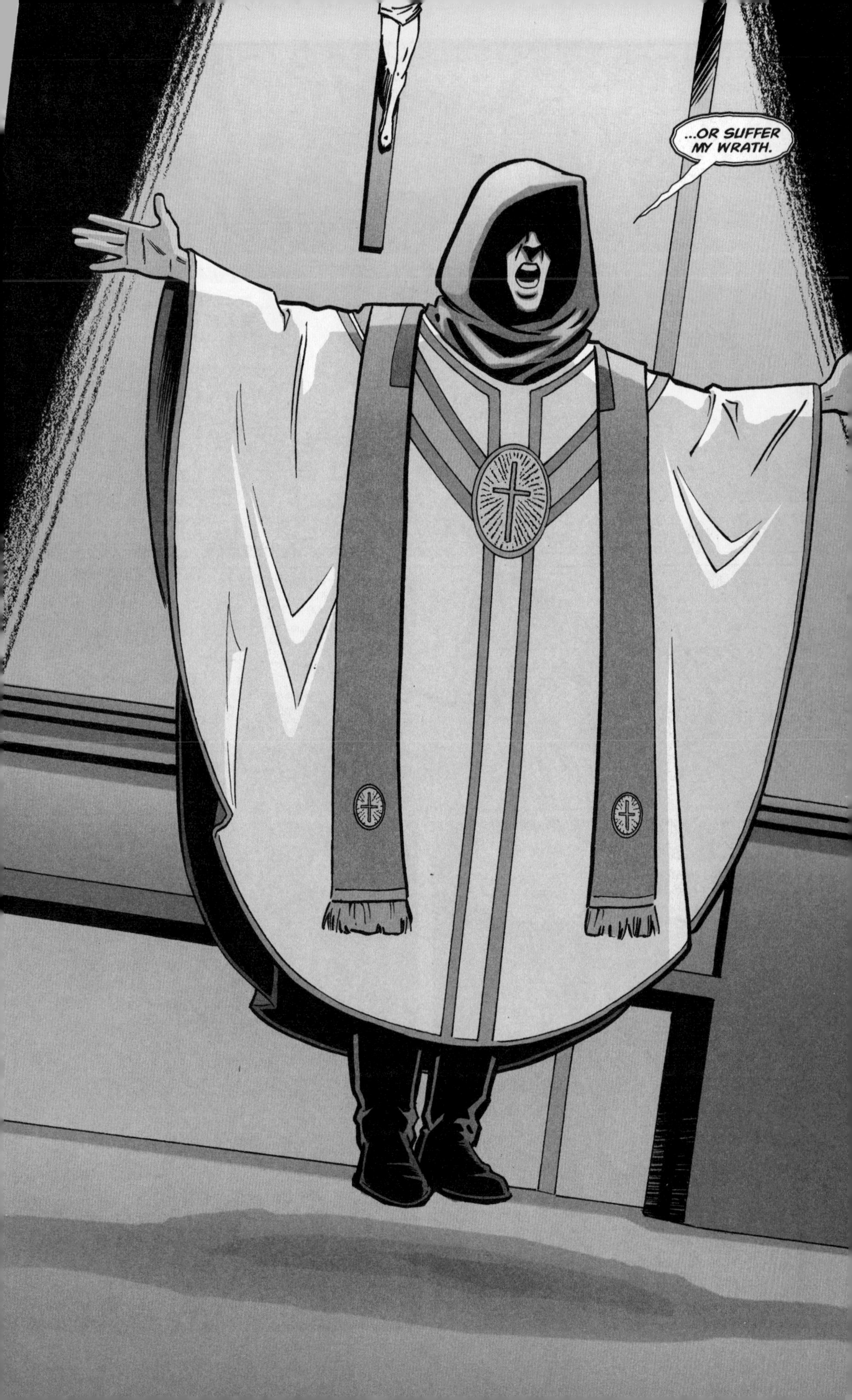
...OR SUFFER MY WRATH.

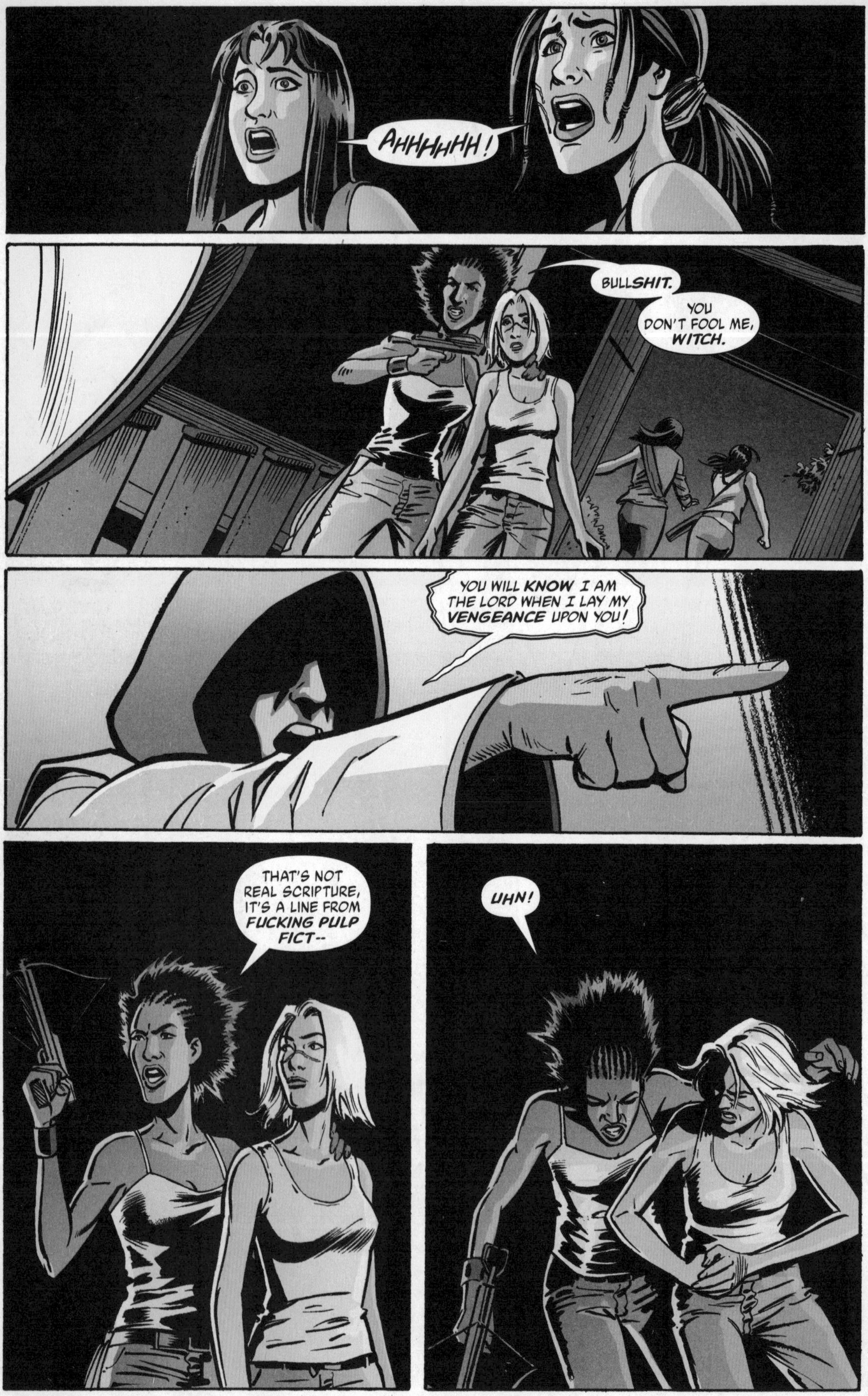
AHHHHHH!
BULLSHIT.
YOU DON'T FOOL ME, WITCH.
YOU WILL KNOW I AM THE LORD WHEN I LAY MY VENGEANCE UPON YOU!
THAT'S NOT REAL SCRIPTURE, IT'S A LINE FROM FUCKING PULP FICT--
UHN!

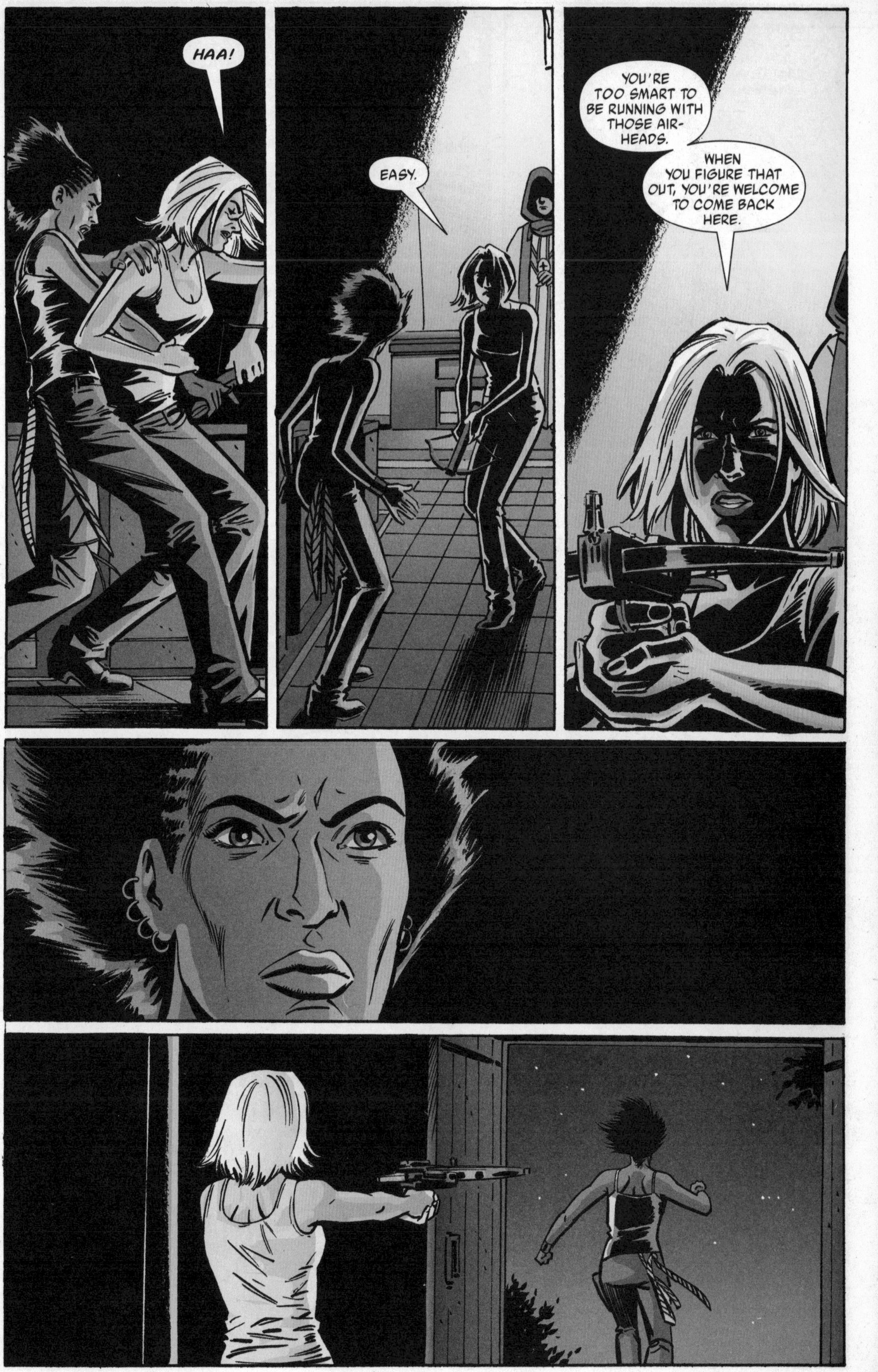
HAA!
EASY.
YOU'RE TOO SMART TO BE RUNNING WITH THOSE AIR-HEADS.
WHEN YOU FIGURE THAT OUT, YOU'RE WELCOME TO COME BACK HERE.

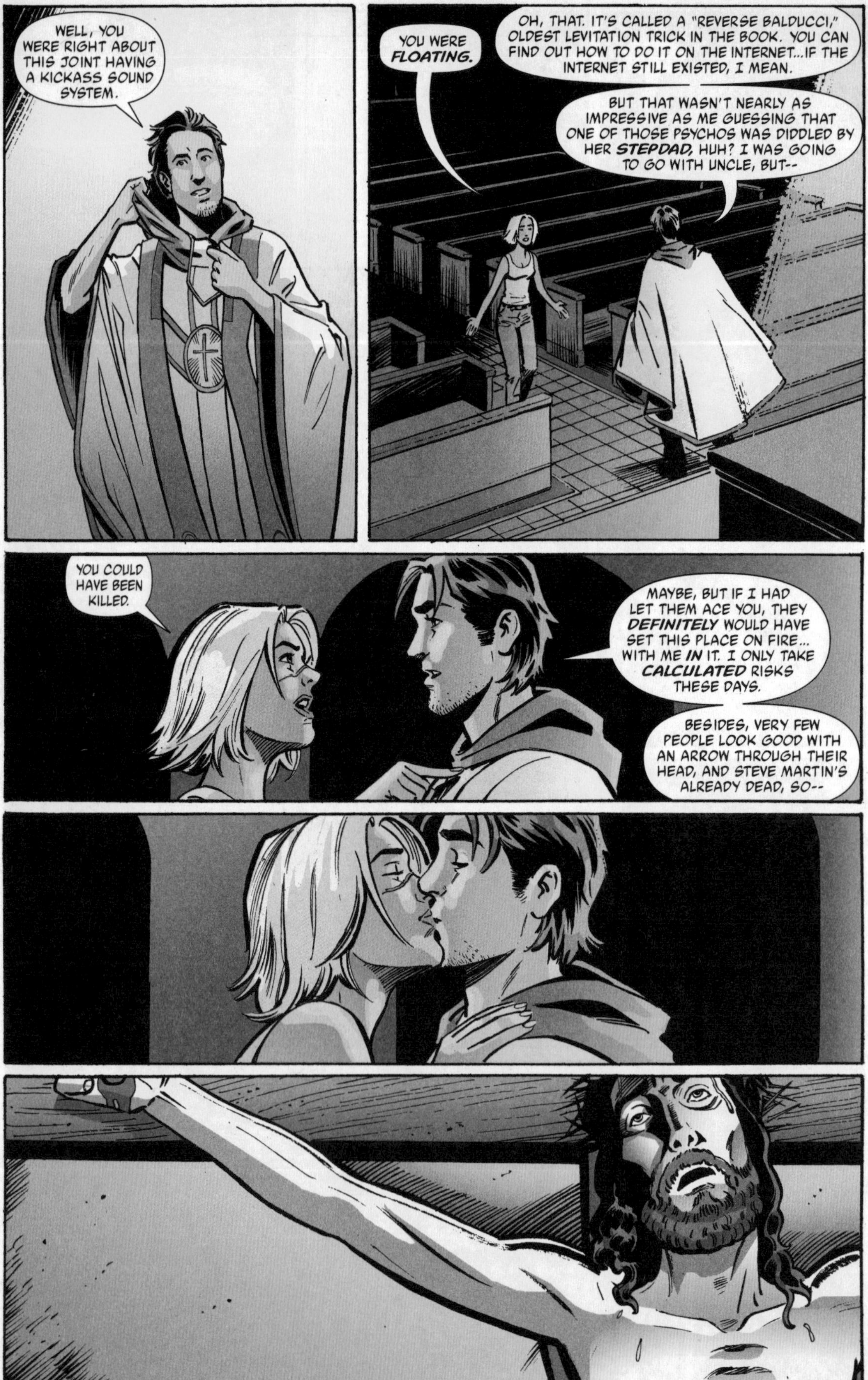
WELL, YOU WERE RIGHT ABOUT THIS JOINT HAVING A KICKASS SOUND SYSTEM.
YOU WERE FLOATING.
OH, THAT. IT'S CALLED A "REVERSE BALDUCCI," OLDEST LEVITATION TRICK IN THE BOOK. YOU CAN FIND OUT HOW TO DO IT ON THE INTERNET...IF THE INTERNET STILL EXISTED, I MEAN.
BUT THAT WASN'T NEARLY AS IMPRESSIVE AS ME GUESSING THAT ONE OF THOSE PSYCHOS WAS DIDDLED BY HER STEPDAD, HUH? I WAS GOING TO GO WITH UNCLE, BUT--
YOU COULD HAVE BEEN KILLED.
MAYBE, BUT IF I HAD LET THEM ACE YOU, THEY DEFINITELY WOULD HAVE SET THIS PLACE ON FIRE... WITH ME IN IT. I ONLY TAKE CALCULATED RISKS THESE DAYS.
BESIDES, VERY FEW PEOPLE LOOK GOOD WITH AN ARROW THROUGH THEIR HEAD, AND STEVE MARTIN'S ALREADY DEAD, SO--

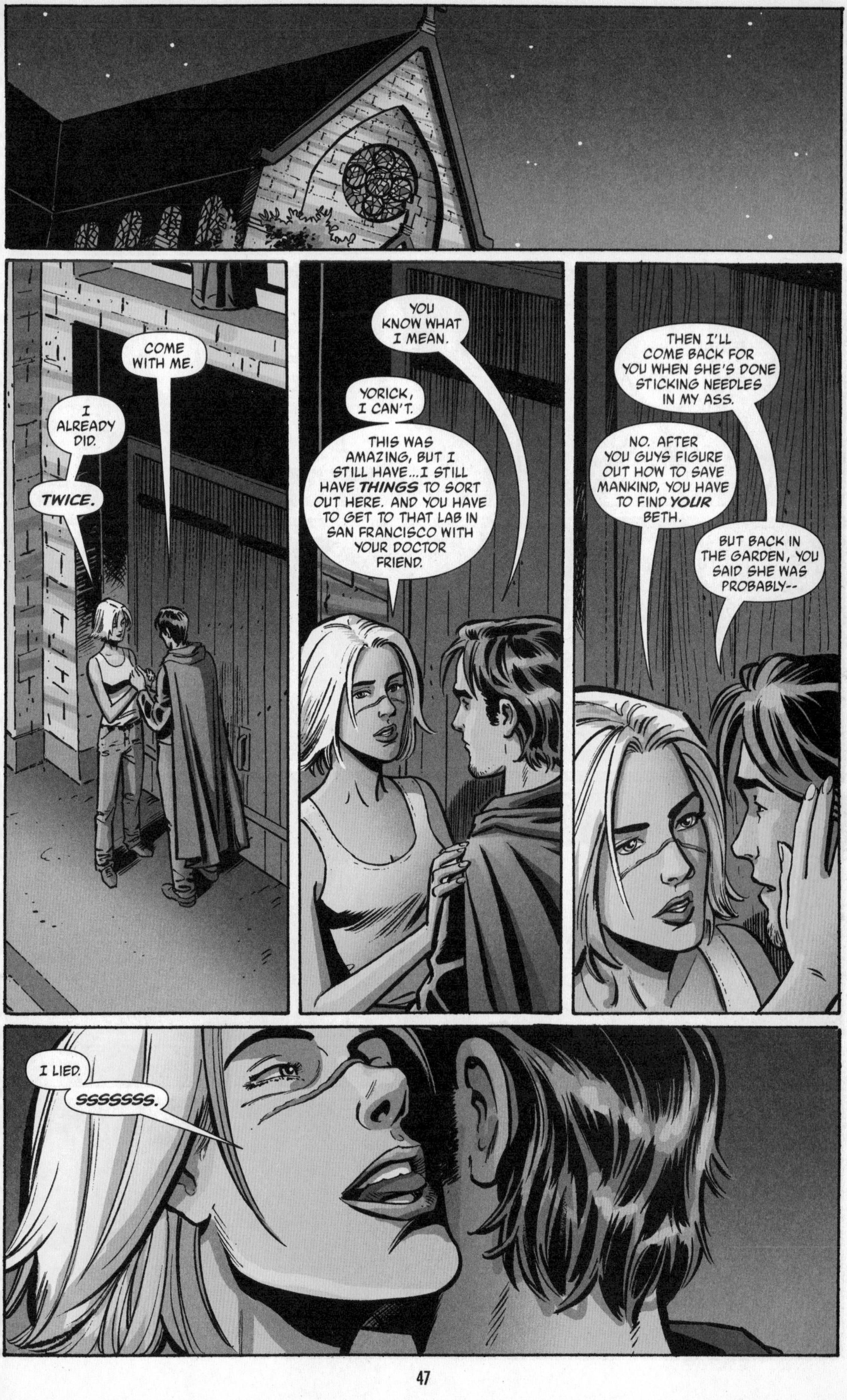
COME WITH ME.
I ALREADY DID.
TWICE.
YOU KNOW WHAT I MEAN.
YORICK, I CAN'T.
THIS WAS AMAZING, BUT I STILL HAVE...I STILL HAVE THINGS TO SORT OUT HERE. AND YOU HAVE TO GET TO THAT LAB IN SAN FRANCISCO WITH YOUR DOCTOR FRIEND.
THEN I'LL COME BACK FOR YOU WHEN SHE'S DONE STICKING NEEDLES IN MY ASS.
NO. AFTER YOU GUYS FIGURE OUT HOW TO SAVE MANKIND, YOU HAVE TO FIND YOUR BETH.
BUT BACK IN THE GARDEN, YOU SAID SHE WAS PROBABLY--
I LIED.
SSSSSSS.

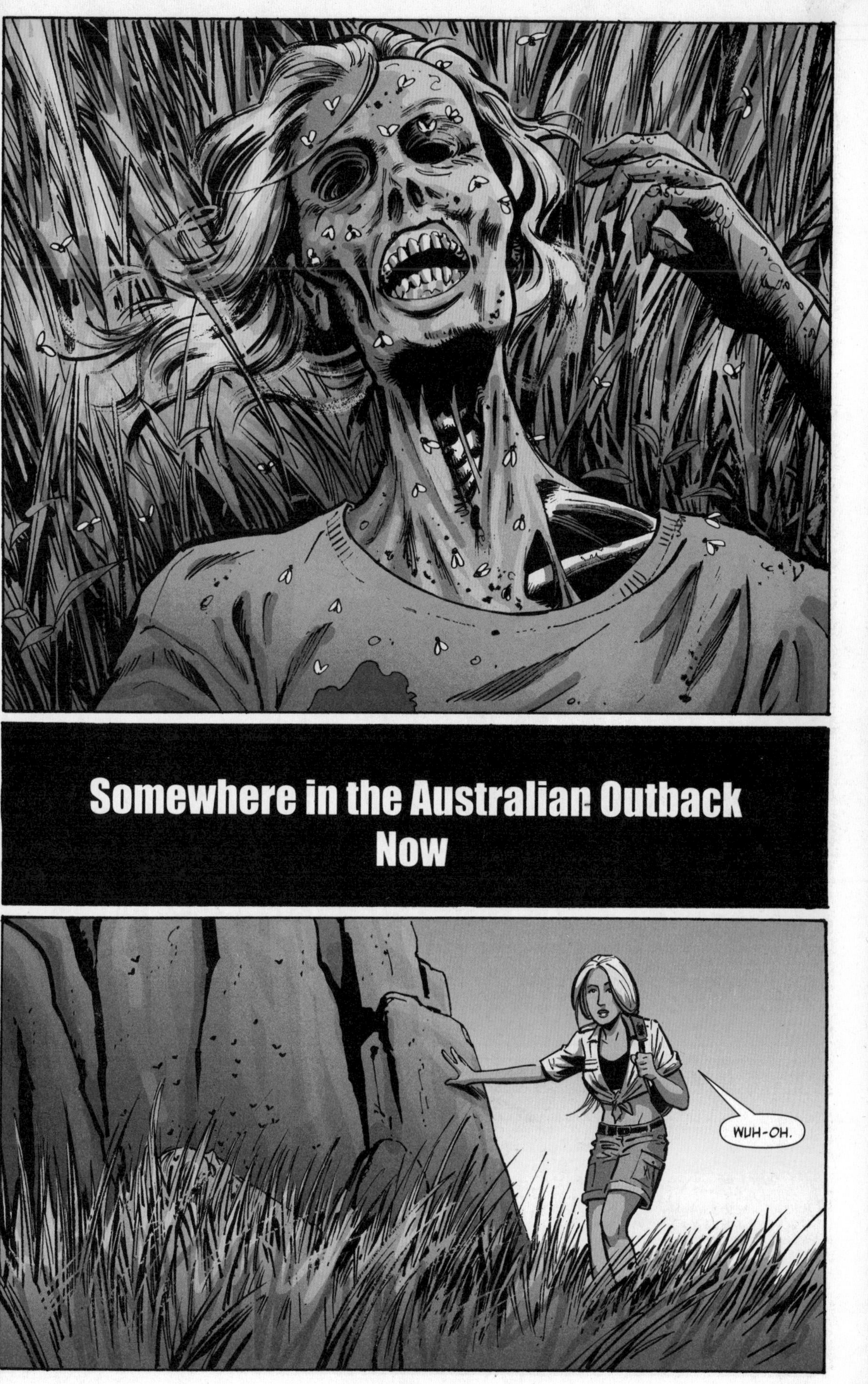
Somewhere in the Australian Outback
Now
WUH-OH.

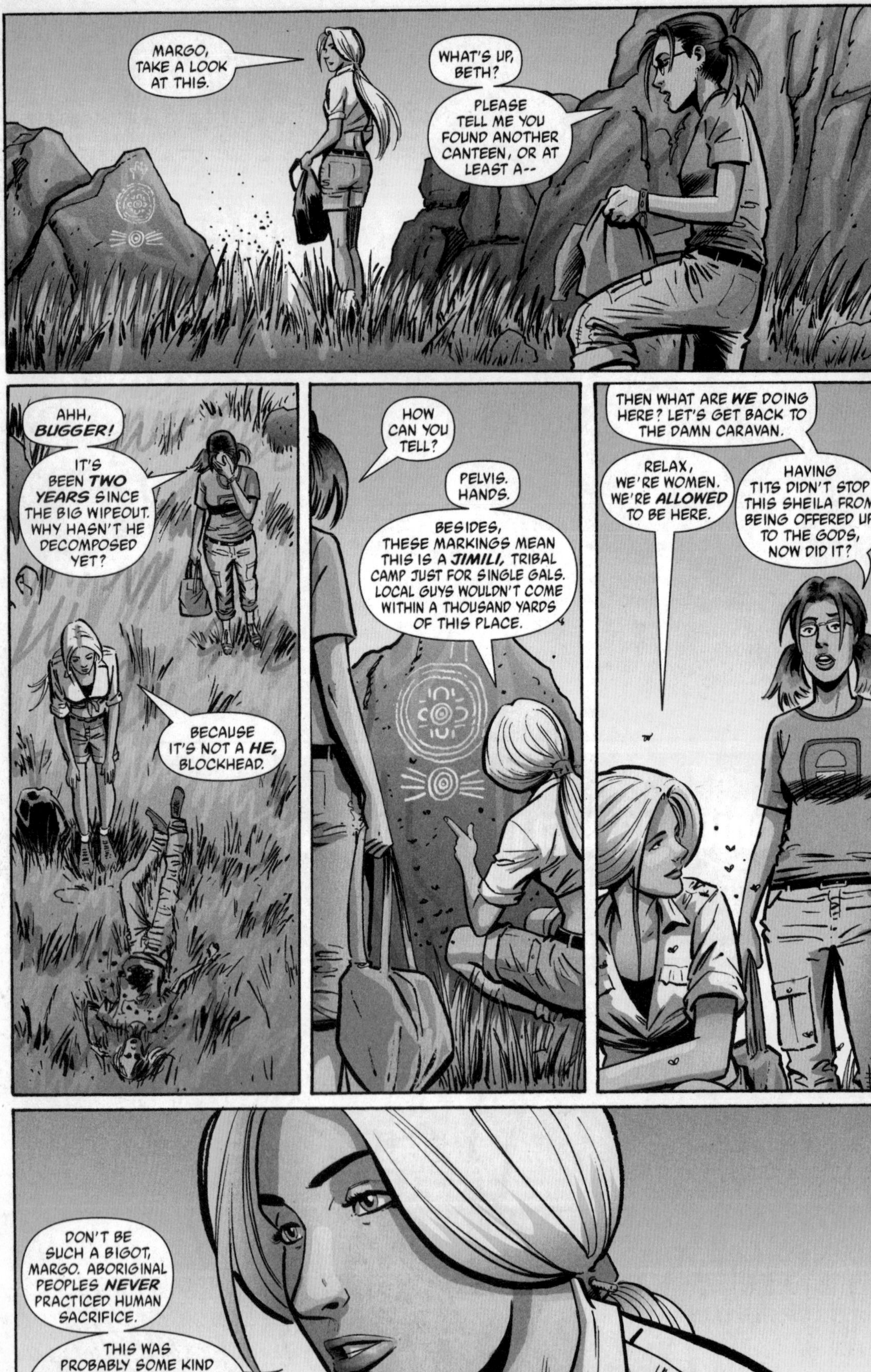
MARGO, TAKE A LOOK AT THIS.
WHAT'S UP, BETH?
PLEASE TELL ME YOU FOUND ANOTHER CANTEEN, OR AT LEAST A--
AHH, BUGGER!
IT'S BEEN TWO YEARS SINCE THE BIG WIPEOUT. WHY HASN'T HE DECOMPOSED YET?
BECAUSE IT'S NOT A HE, BLOCKHEAD.
HOW CAN YOU TELL?
PELVIS. HANDS.
BESIDES, THESE MARKINGS MEAN THIS IS A JIMILI, TRIBAL CAMP JUST FOR SINGLE GALS. LOCAL GUYS WOULDN'T COME WITHIN A THOUSAND YARDS OF THIS PLACE.
THEN WHAT ARE WE DOING HERE? LET'S GET BACK TO THE DAMN CARAVAN.
RELAX, WE'RE WOMEN. WE'RE ALLOWED TO BE HERE.
HAVING TITS DIDN'T STOP THIS SHEILA FROM BEING OFFERED UP TO THE GODS, NOW DID IT?
DON'T BE SUCH A BIGOT, MARGO. ABORIGINAL PEOPLES NEVER PRACTICED HUMAN SACRIFICE.
THIS WAS PROBABLY SOME KIND OF ACCIDENT. WE SHOULD TRY TO FIND THE ELDERS AND SEE IF THERE'S ANYTHING WE CAN DO TO HELP...

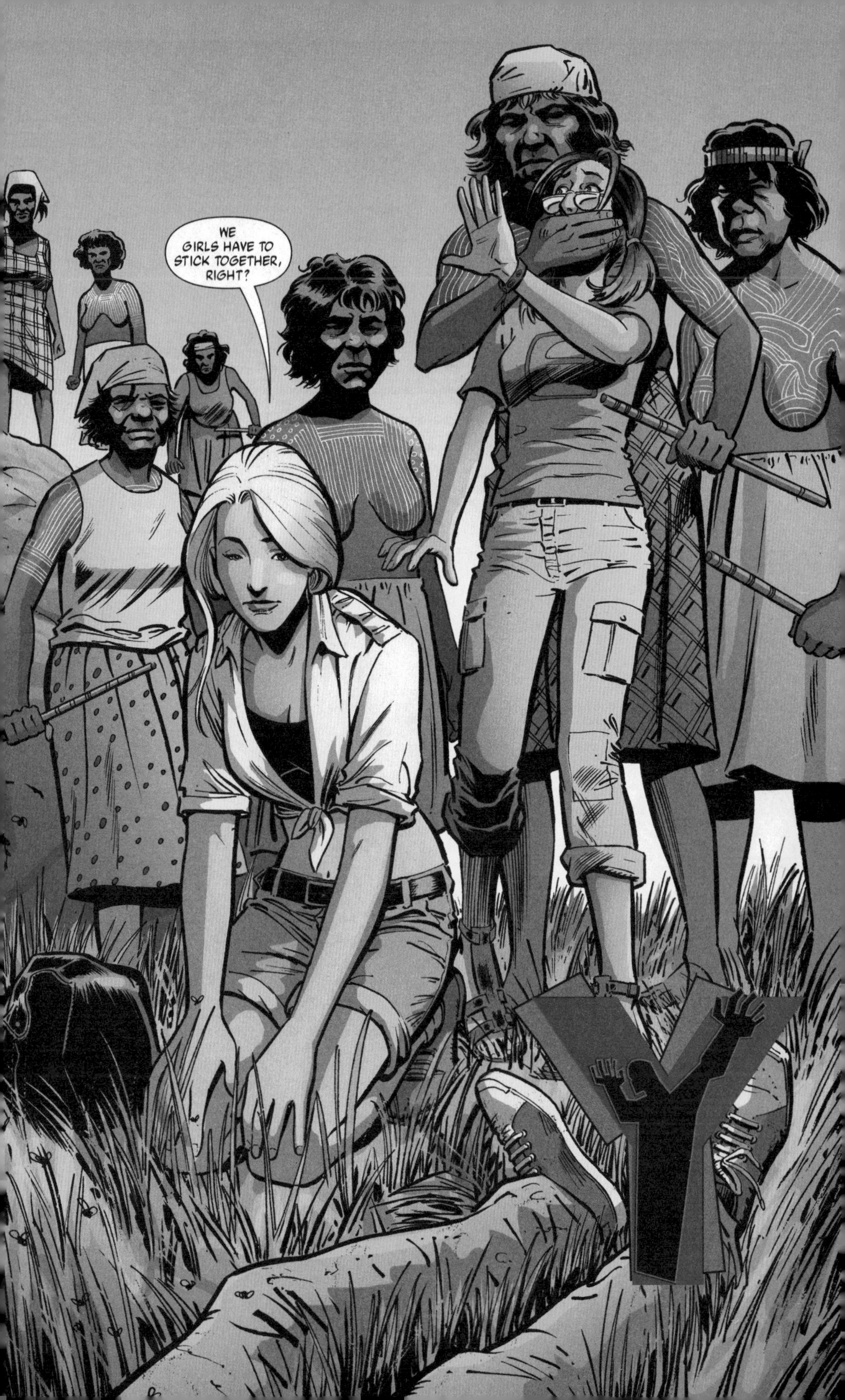
WE GIRLS HAVE TO STICK TOGETHER, RIGHT?

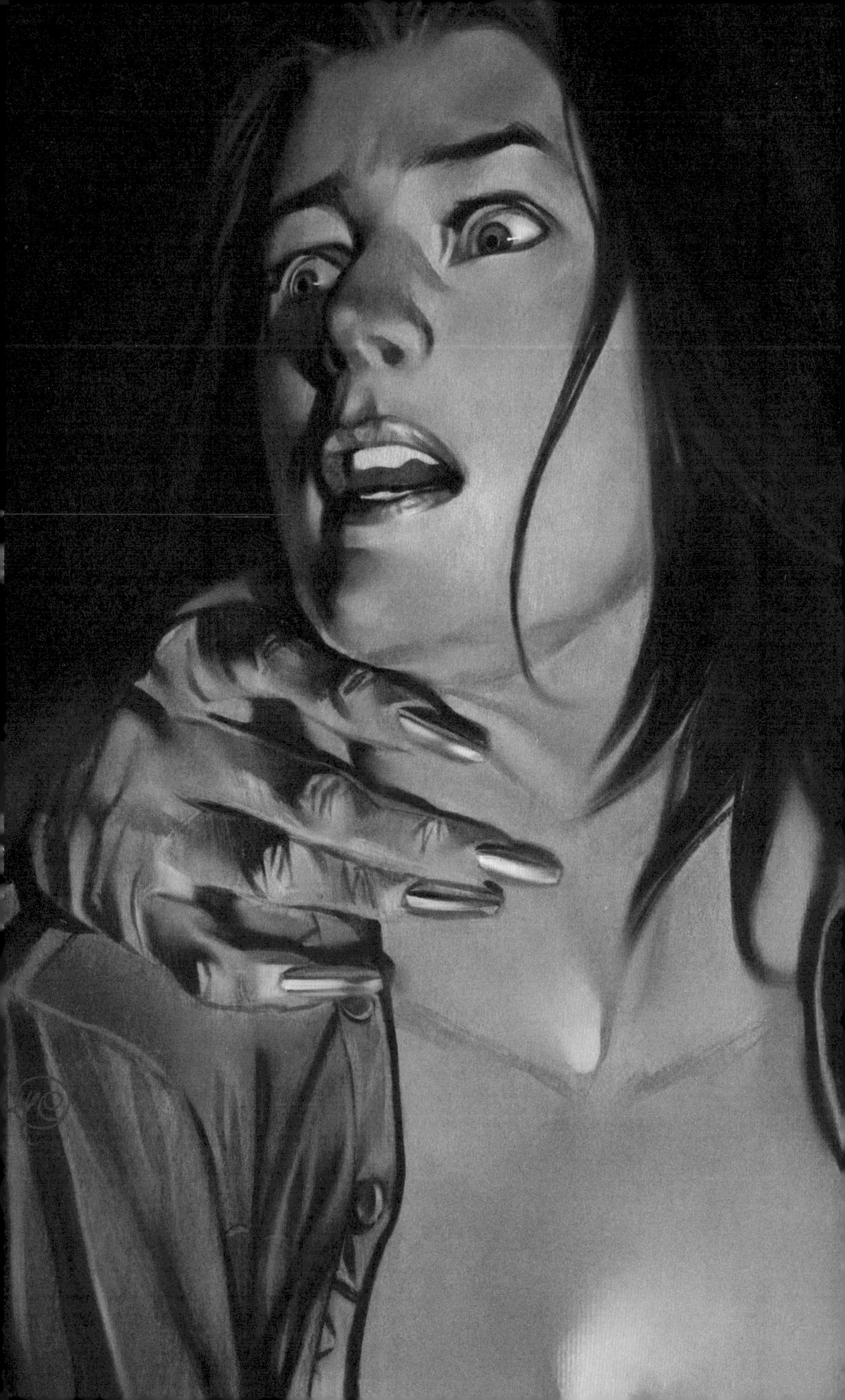

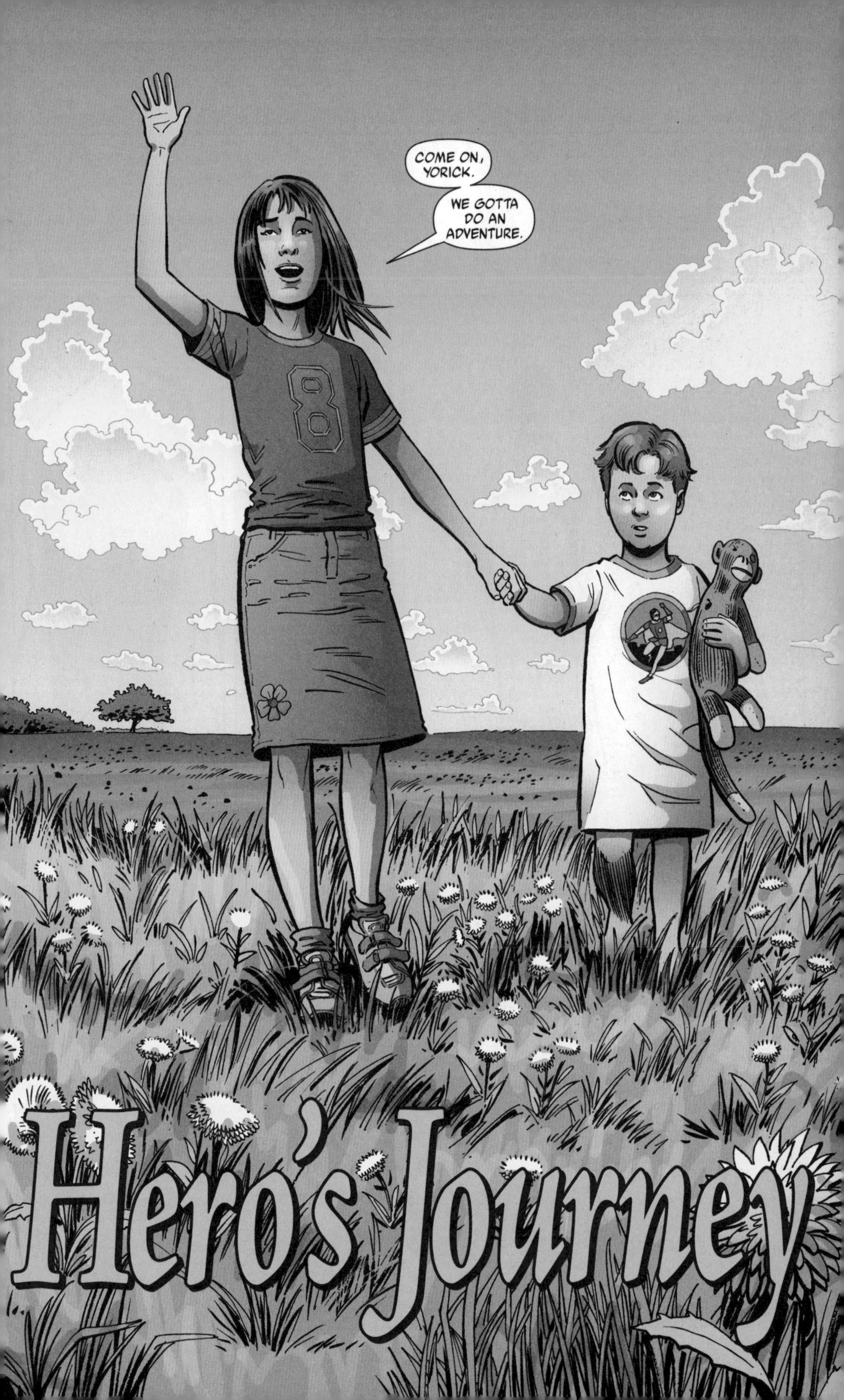
COME ON, YORICK.
WE GOTTA DO AN ADVENTURE.
Hero's Journey

WHY, HE-WO?

'CAUSE YOU HAVE TO MEET MY FRIEND.

HER NAME IS QUEEN VICTORIA.

HELLO, QUEEN VICTORIA.

HELLO, HERO! WHO'S THIS?

HE'S MY LITTLE BROTHER. HIS NAME IS YORICK. HE'S GONNA JOIN OUR DANDELION LEAGUE.

HELLO, YORICK! NICE TO MEET YOU!

HI.

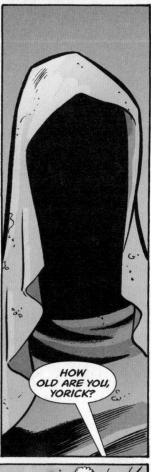

HOW OLD ARE YOU, YORICK?

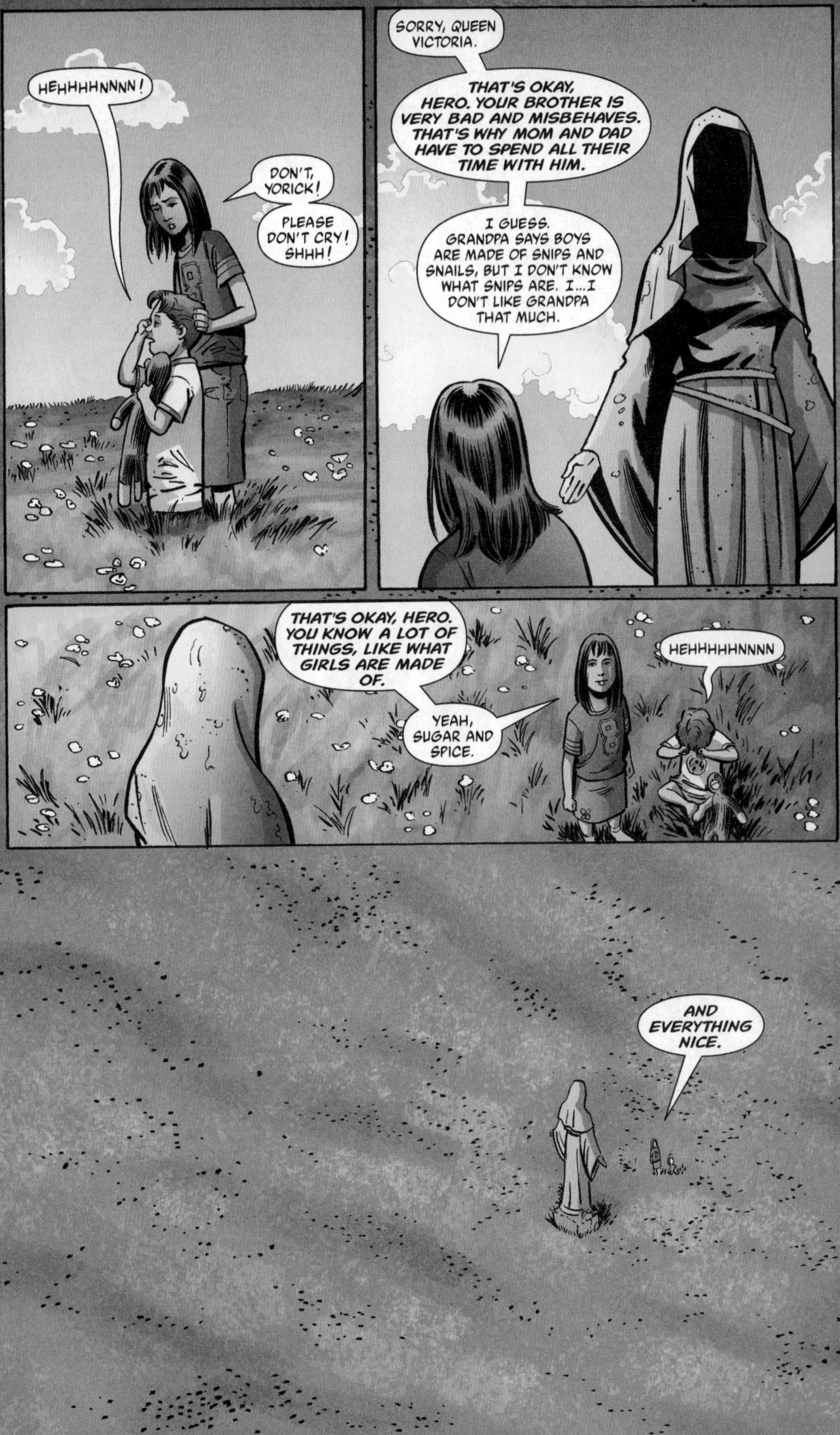
HEHHHHNNNN!
DON'T, YORICK!
PLEASE DON'T CRY! SHHH!
SORRY, QUEEN VICTORIA.
THAT'S OKAY, HERO. YOUR BROTHER IS VERY BAD AND MISBEHAVES. THAT'S WHY MOM AND DAD HAVE TO SPEND ALL THEIR TIME WITH HIM.
I GUESS. GRANDPA SAYS BOYS ARE MADE OF SNIPS AND SNAILS, BUT I DON'T KNOW WHAT SNIPS ARE. I...I DON'T LIKE GRANDPA THAT MUCH.
THAT'S OKAY, HERO. YOU KNOW A LOT OF THINGS, LIKE WHAT GIRLS ARE MADE OF.
YEAH, SUGAR AND SPICE.
HEHHHHHNNNN
AND EVERYTHING NICE.

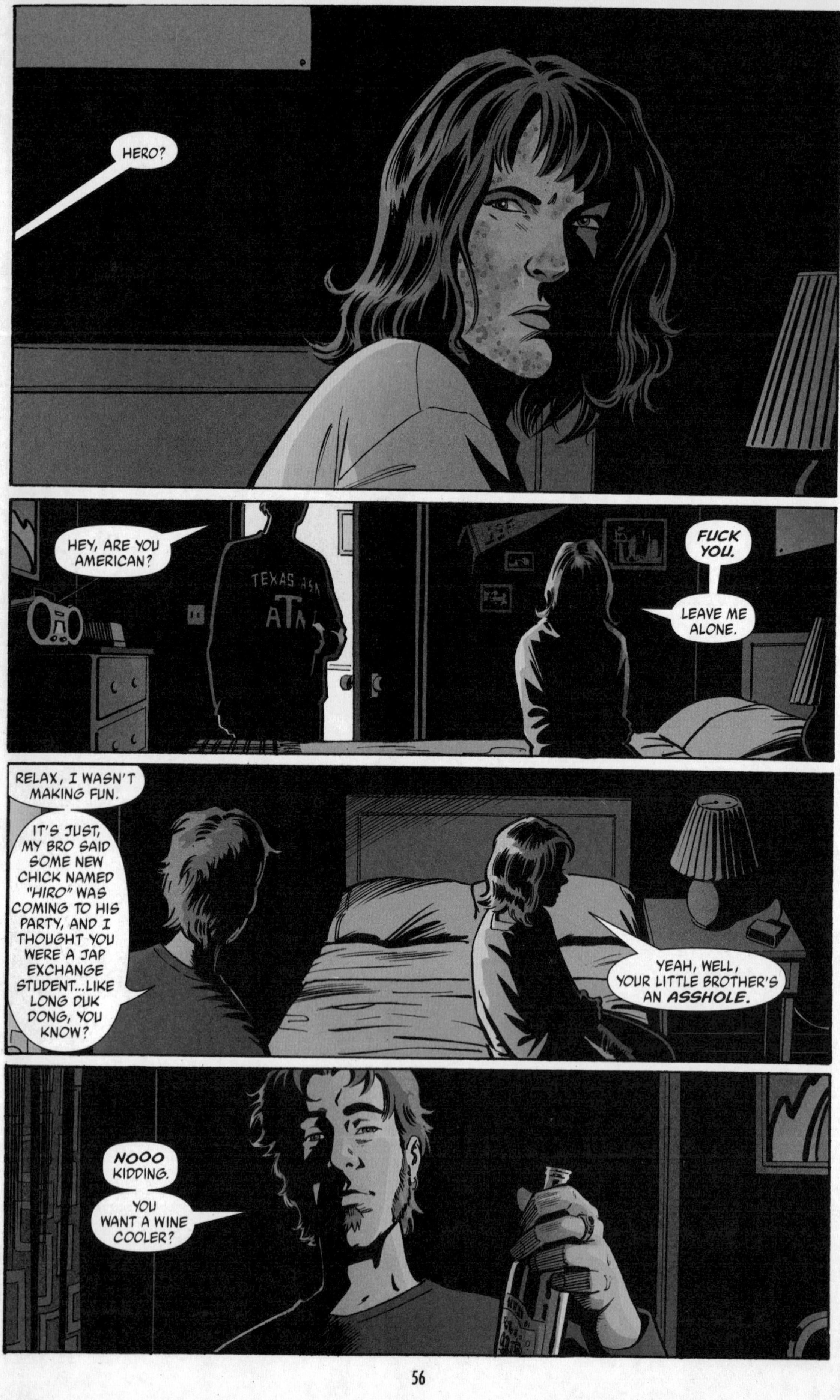
HERO?
HEY, ARE YOU AMERICAN?
FUCK YOU.
LEAVE ME ALONE.
RELAX, I WASN'T MAKING FUN.
IT'S JUST, MY BRO SAID SOME NEW CHICK NAMED "HIRO" WAS COMING TO HIS PARTY, AND I THOUGHT YOU WERE A JAP EXCHANGE STUDENT...LIKE LONG DUK DONG, YOU KNOW?
YEAH, WELL, YOUR LITTLE BROTHER'S AN ASSHOLE.
NOOO KIDDING.
YOU WANT A WINE COOLER?

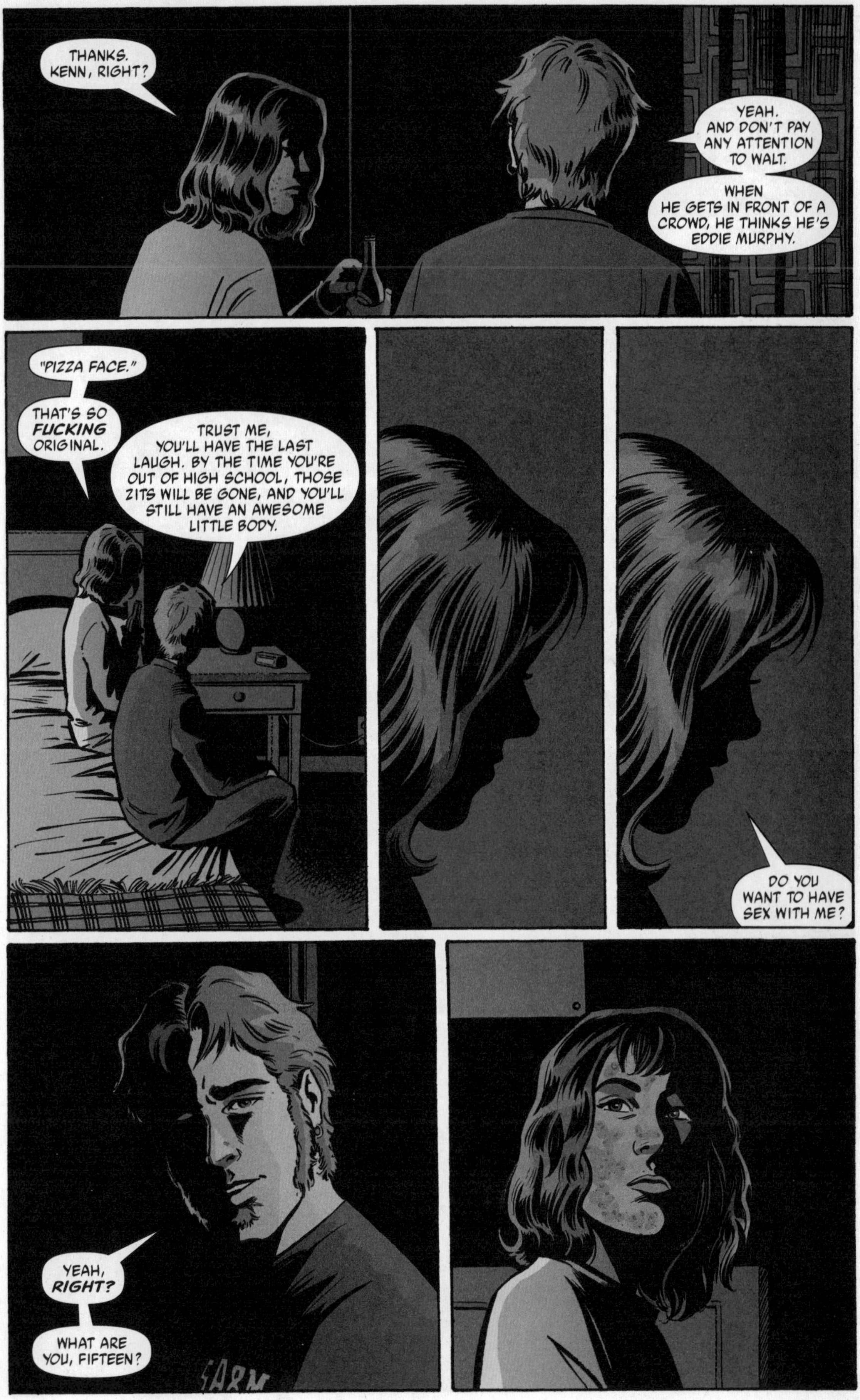
THANKS. KENN, RIGHT?
YEAH. AND DON'T PAY ANY ATTENTION TO WALT.
WHEN HE GETS IN FRONT OF A CROWD, HE THINKS HE'S EDDIE MURPHY.
"PIZZA FACE."
THAT'S SO **FUCKING** ORIGINAL.
TRUST ME, YOU'LL HAVE THE LAST LAUGH. BY THE TIME YOU'RE OUT OF HIGH SCHOOL, THOSE ZITS WILL BE GONE, AND YOU'LL STILL HAVE AN AWESOME LITTLE BODY.
DO YOU WANT TO HAVE SEX WITH ME?
YEAH, **RIGHT?**
WHAT ARE YOU, FIFTEEN?

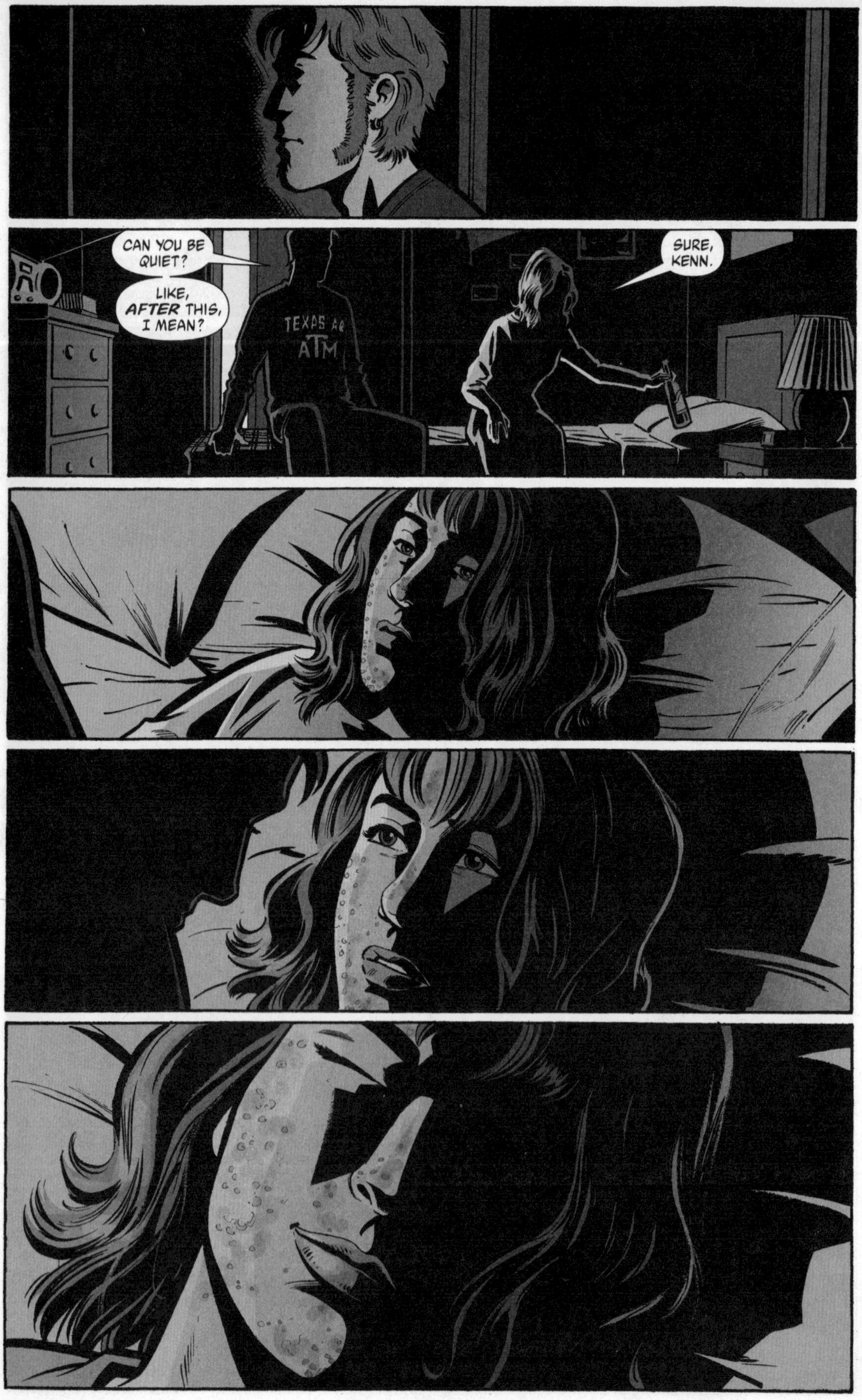
CAN YOU BE QUIET?
LIKE, AFTER THIS, I MEAN?
SURE, KENN.
TEXAS A&M

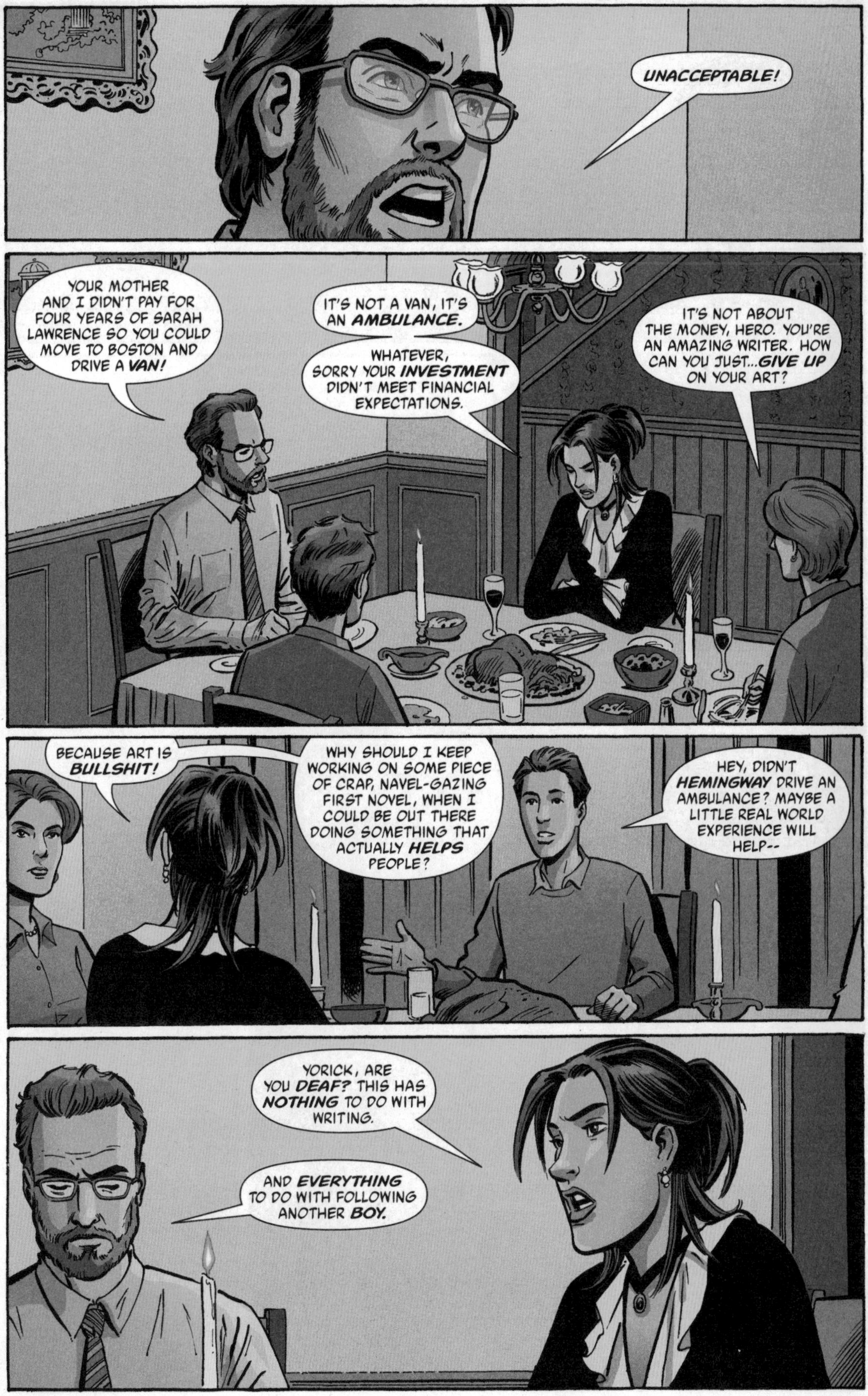
UNACCEPTABLE!
YOUR MOTHER AND I DIDN'T PAY FOR FOUR YEARS OF SARAH LAWRENCE SO YOU COULD MOVE TO BOSTON AND DRIVE A *VAN!*
IT'S NOT A VAN, IT'S AN *AMBULANCE.*
WHATEVER, SORRY YOUR *INVESTMENT* DIDN'T MEET FINANCIAL EXPECTATIONS.
IT'S NOT ABOUT THE MONEY, HERO. YOU'RE AN AMAZING WRITER. HOW CAN YOU JUST...*GIVE UP* ON YOUR ART?
BECAUSE ART IS *BULLSHIT!*
WHY SHOULD I KEEP WORKING ON SOME PIECE OF CRAP, NAVEL-GAZING FIRST NOVEL, WHEN I COULD BE OUT THERE DOING SOMETHING THAT ACTUALLY *HELPS* PEOPLE?
HEY, DIDN'T *HEMINGWAY* DRIVE AN AMBULANCE? MAYBE A LITTLE REAL WORLD EXPERIENCE WILL HELP--
YORICK, ARE YOU *DEAF?* THIS HAS *NOTHING* TO DO WITH WRITING.
AND *EVERYTHING* TO DO WITH FOLLOWING ANOTHER *BOY.*

JOE ISN'T "ANOTHER BOY," DAD.

HE RESPECTS ME FOR WHO I AM, WHICH IS MORE THAN I CAN SAY FOR ANY OF THE *OTHER* MEN IN MY LIFE.

DIAL IT DOWN, KIDDO. IT'S NOT LIKE WE'RE *MY* TOTALITARIAN PARENTS, TRYING TO FORCE YOU INTO THE FAMILY BUSINESS. YOUR FATHER JUST DOESN'T WANT YOU THROWING AWAY YOUR DREAMS OVER SOME *GUY* WHO DOESN'T EVEN--

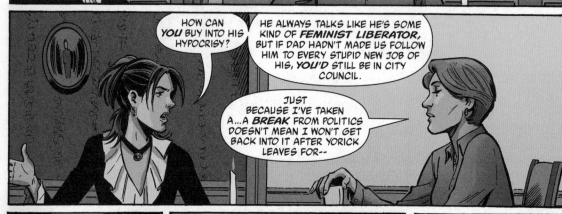

HOW CAN *YOU* BUY INTO HIS HYPOCRISY?

HE ALWAYS TALKS LIKE HE'S SOME KIND OF *FEMINIST LIBERATOR,* BUT IF DAD HADN'T MADE US FOLLOW HIM TO EVERY STUPID NEW JOB OF HIS, *YOU'D* STILL BE IN CITY COUNCIL.

JUST BECAUSE I'VE TAKEN A...A *BREAK* FROM POLITICS DOESN'T MEAN I WON'T GET BACK INTO IT AFTER YORICK LEAVES FOR--

FORGET IT!

I'M SO SICK OF THIS FAMILY'S *FICTION!*

IS IT JUST ME...OR IS CRANBERRY SAUCE *WAY* TOO AWESOME TO EAT JUST ONCE A YEAR?

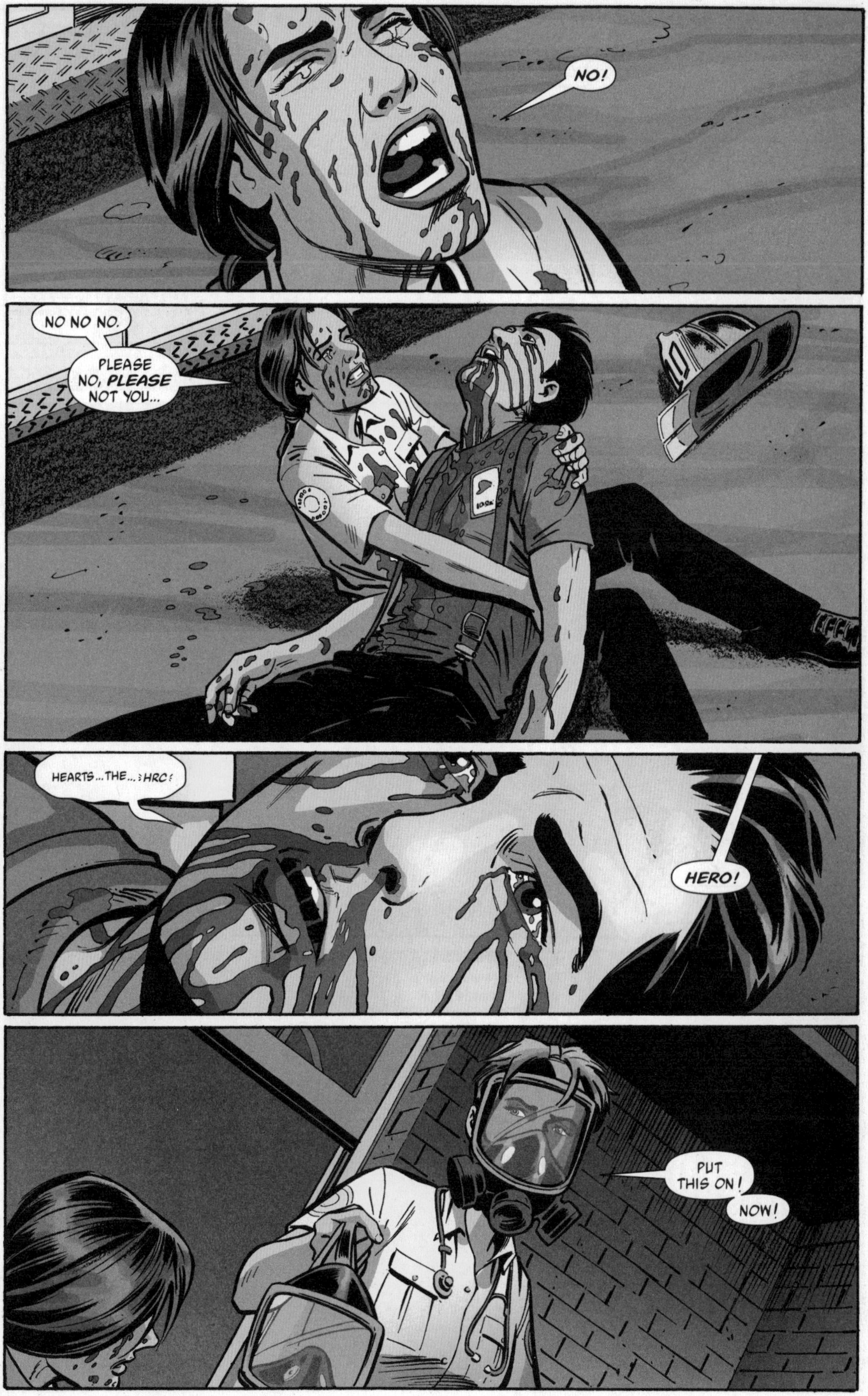
NO!
NO NO NO.
PLEASE NO, *PLEASE* NOT YOU...
HEARTS...THE...HRC
HERO!
PUT THIS ON!
NOW!

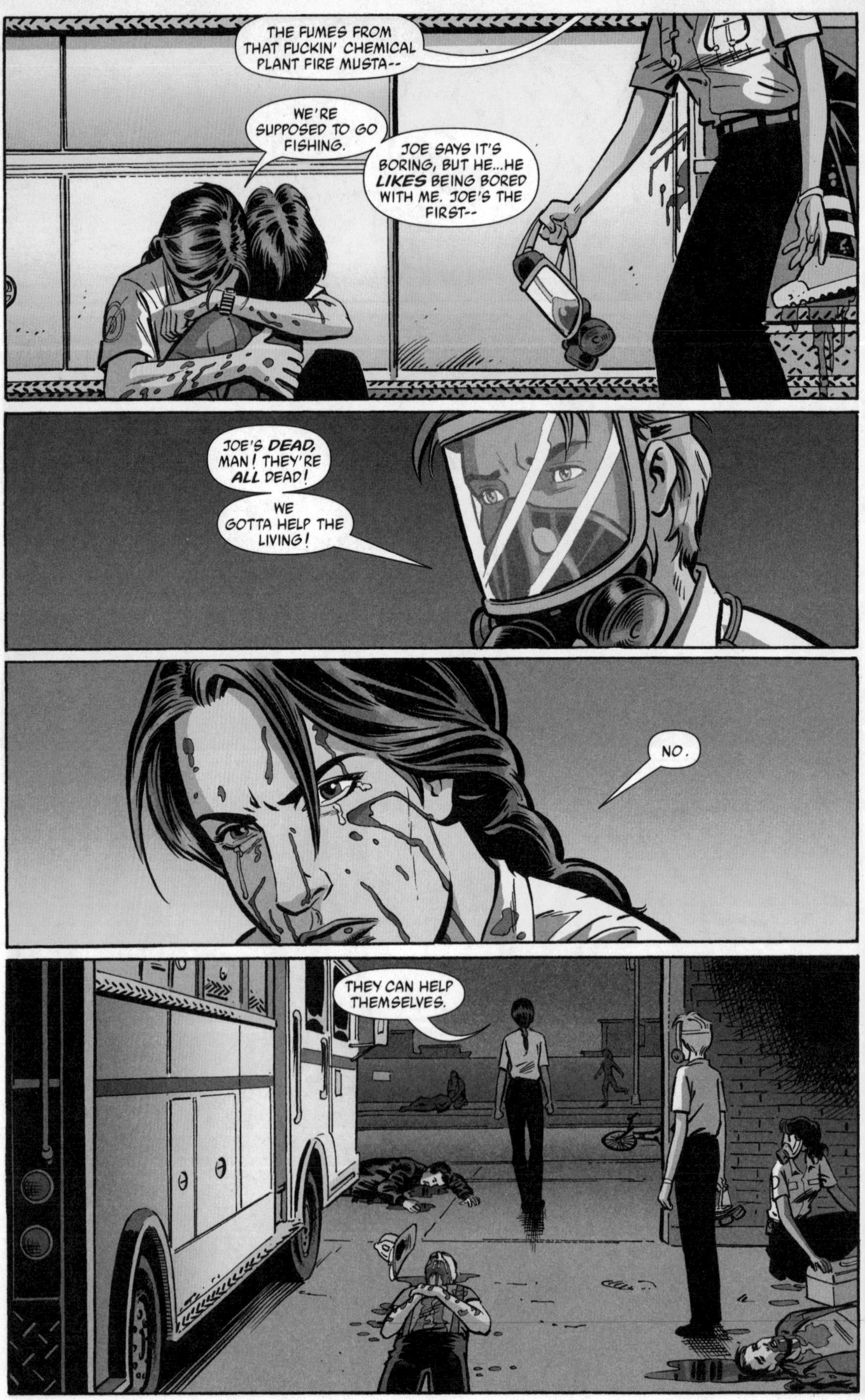
THE FUMES FROM THAT FUCKIN' CHEMICAL PLANT FIRE MUSTA--
WE'RE SUPPOSED TO GO FISHING.
JOE SAYS IT'S BORING, BUT HE...HE LIKES BEING BORED WITH ME. JOE'S THE FIRST--
JOE'S DEAD, MAN! THEY'RE ALL DEAD!
WE GOTTA HELP THE LIVING!
NO.
THEY CAN HELP THEMSELVES.

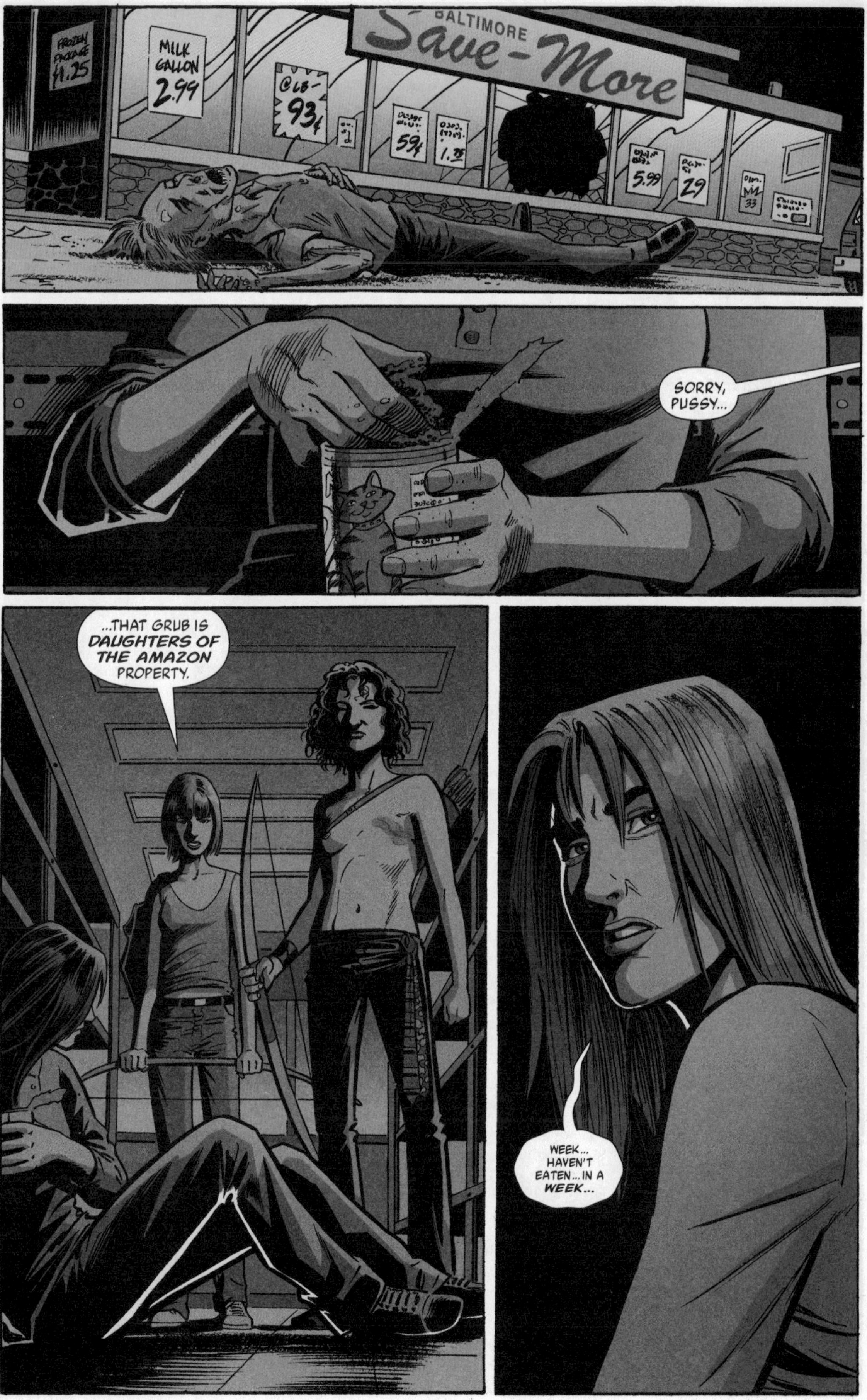
BALTIMORE
Save-More
MILK GALLON 2.99
FROZEN PACKAGE $1.25
@LB- 93¢
59¢
1.35
5.99
29
SORRY, PUSSY...
...THAT GRUB IS DAUGHTERS OF THE AMAZON PROPERTY.
WEEK... HAVEN'T EATEN... IN A WEEK...

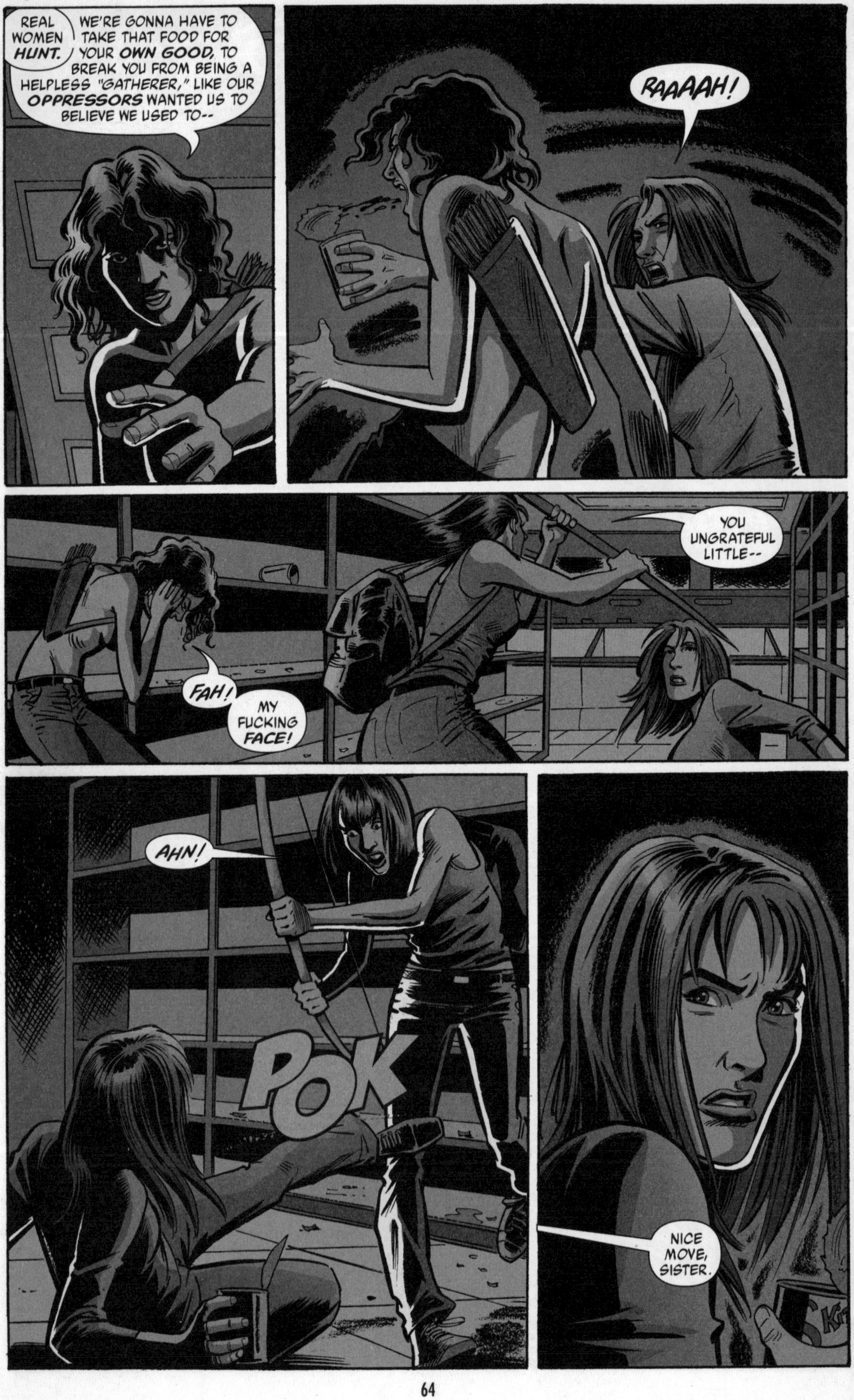
REAL WOMEN HUNT.
WE'RE GONNA HAVE TO TAKE THAT FOOD FOR YOUR OWN GOOD, TO BREAK YOU FROM BEING A HELPLESS "GATHERER," LIKE OUR OPPRESSORS WANTED US TO BELIEVE WE USED TO--
RAAAAH!
YOU UNGRATEFUL LITTLE--
FAH!
MY FUCKING FACE!
AHN!
POK
NICE MOVE, SISTER.

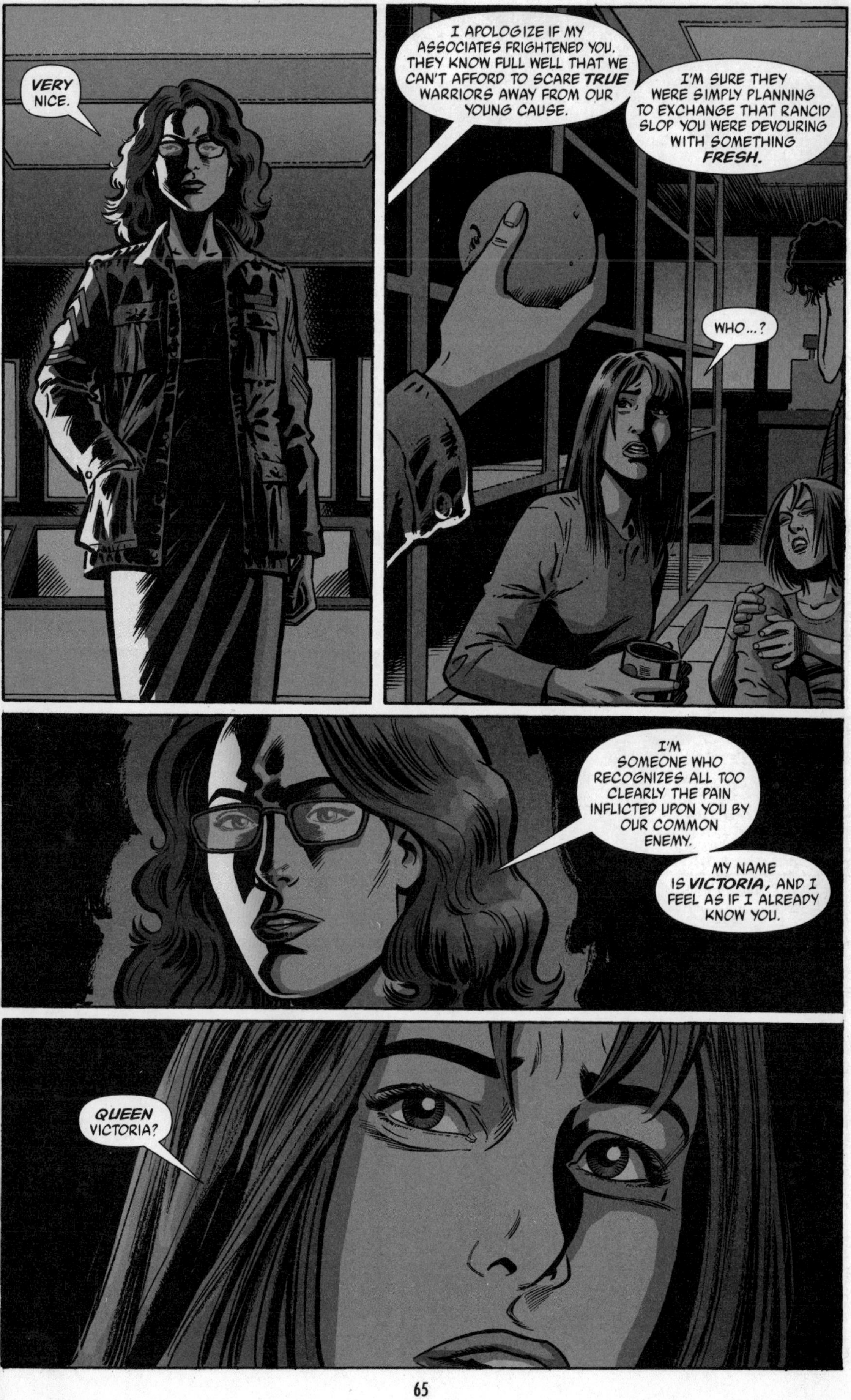
VERY NICE.
I APOLOGIZE IF MY ASSOCIATES FRIGHTENED YOU. THEY KNOW FULL WELL THAT WE CAN'T AFFORD TO SCARE TRUE WARRIORS AWAY FROM OUR YOUNG CAUSE.
I'M SURE THEY WERE SIMPLY PLANNING TO EXCHANGE THAT RANCID SLOP YOU WERE DEVOURING WITH SOMETHING FRESH.
WHO...?
I'M SOMEONE WHO RECOGNIZES ALL TOO CLEARLY THE PAIN INFLICTED UPON YOU BY OUR COMMON ENEMY.
MY NAME IS VICTORIA, AND I FEEL AS IF I ALREADY KNOW YOU.
QUEEN VICTORIA?

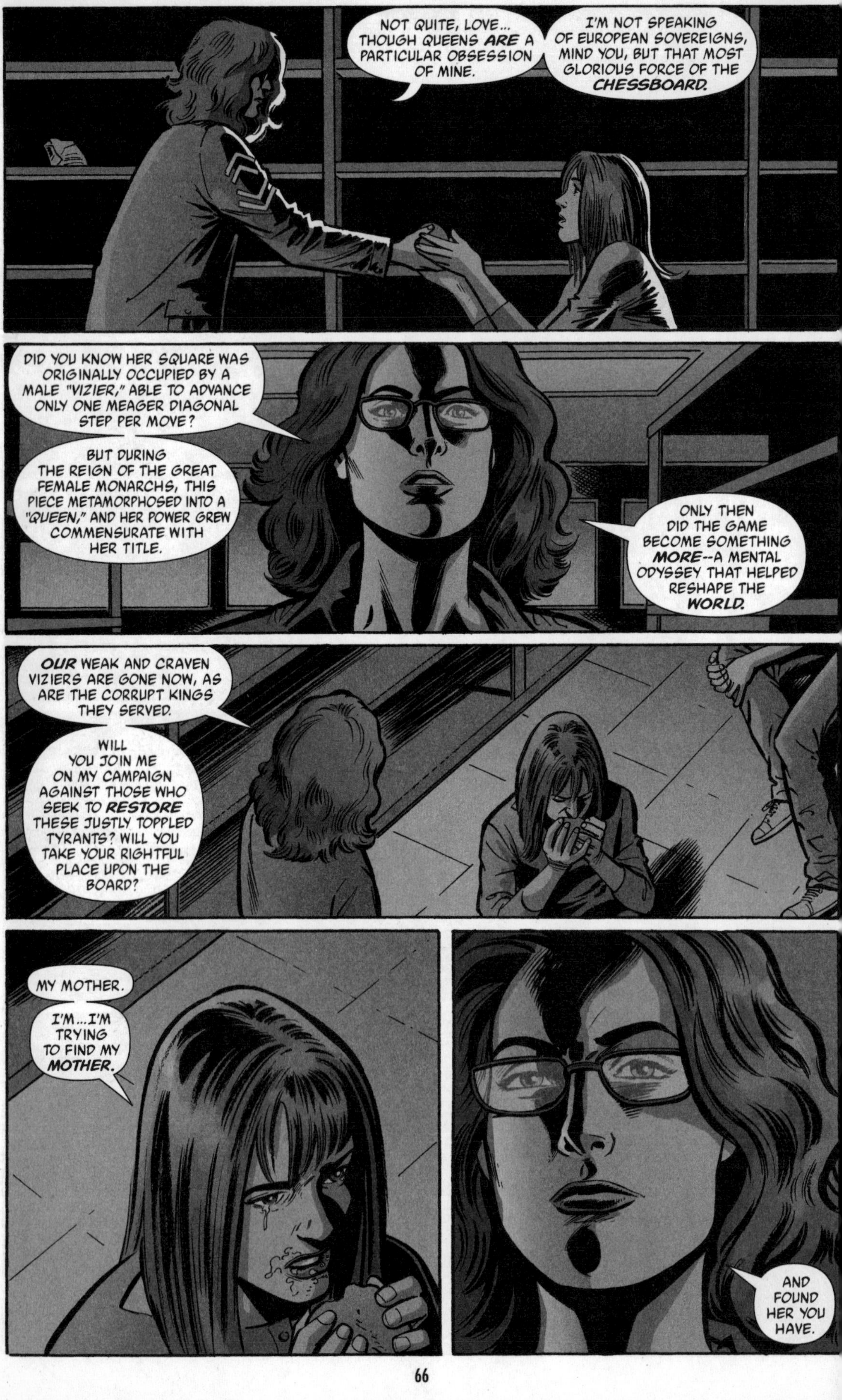
NOT QUITE, LOVE... THOUGH QUEENS ARE A PARTICULAR OBSESSION OF MINE.
I'M NOT SPEAKING OF EUROPEAN SOVEREIGNS, MIND YOU, BUT THAT MOST GLORIOUS FORCE OF THE CHESSBOARD.
DID YOU KNOW HER SQUARE WAS ORIGINALLY OCCUPIED BY A MALE "VIZIER," ABLE TO ADVANCE ONLY ONE MEAGER DIAGONAL STEP PER MOVE?
BUT DURING THE REIGN OF THE GREAT FEMALE MONARCHS, THIS PIECE METAMORPHOSED INTO A "QUEEN," AND HER POWER GREW COMMENSURATE WITH HER TITLE.
ONLY THEN DID THE GAME BECOME SOMETHING MORE--A MENTAL ODYSSEY THAT HELPED RESHAPE THE WORLD.
OUR WEAK AND CRAVEN VIZIERS ARE GONE NOW, AS ARE THE CORRUPT KINGS THEY SERVED.
WILL YOU JOIN ME ON MY CAMPAIGN AGAINST THOSE WHO SEEK TO RESTORE THESE JUSTLY TOPPLED TYRANTS? WILL YOU TAKE YOUR RIGHTFUL PLACE UPON THE BOARD?
MY MOTHER.
I'M...I'M TRYING TO FIND MY MOTHER.
AND FOUND HER YOU HAVE.

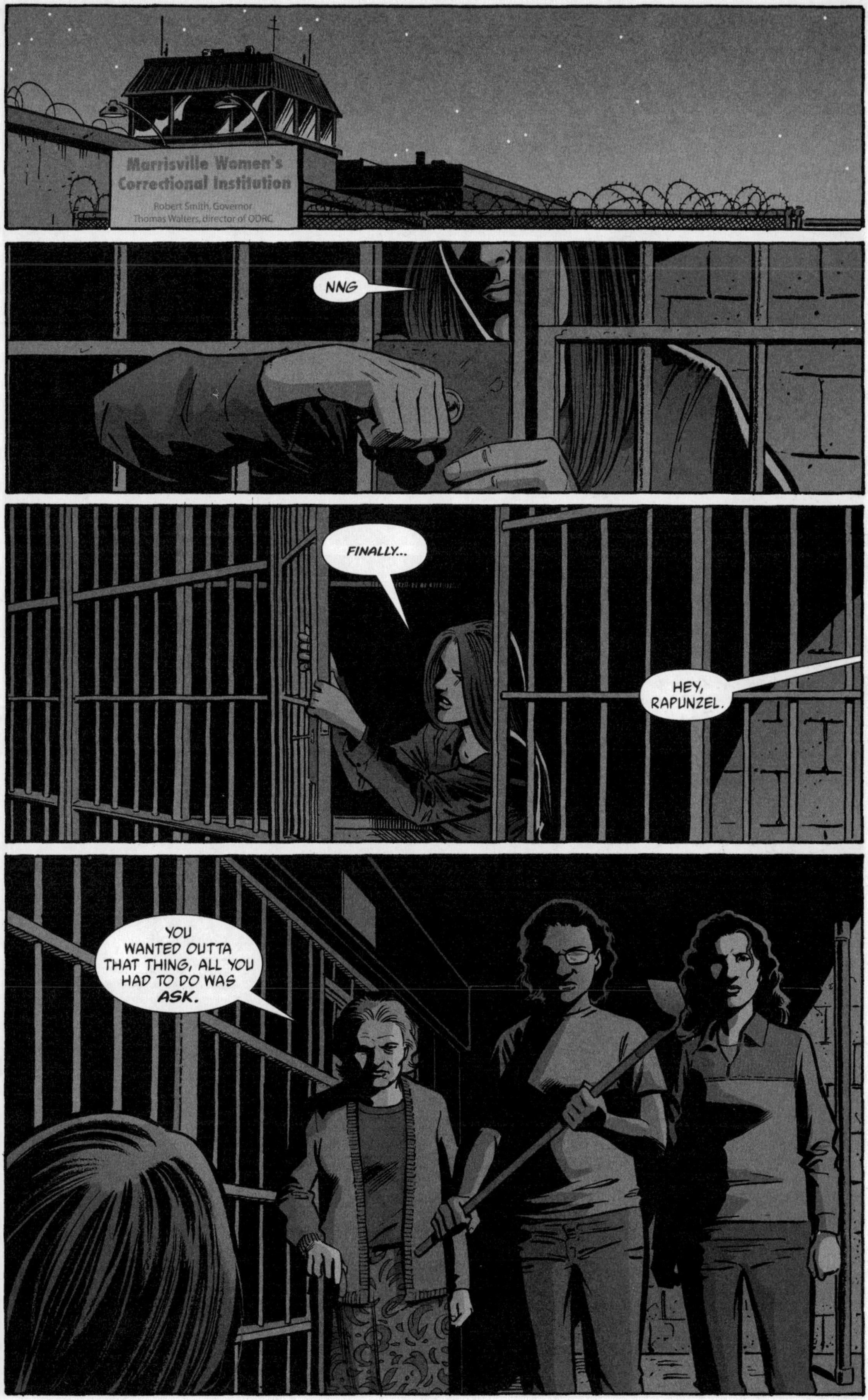
Marrisville Women's Correctional Institution
Robert Smith, Governor
Thomas Walters, director of ODRC
NNG
FINALLY...
HEY, RAPUNZEL.
YOU WANTED OUTTA THAT THING, ALL YOU HAD TO DO WAS ASK.

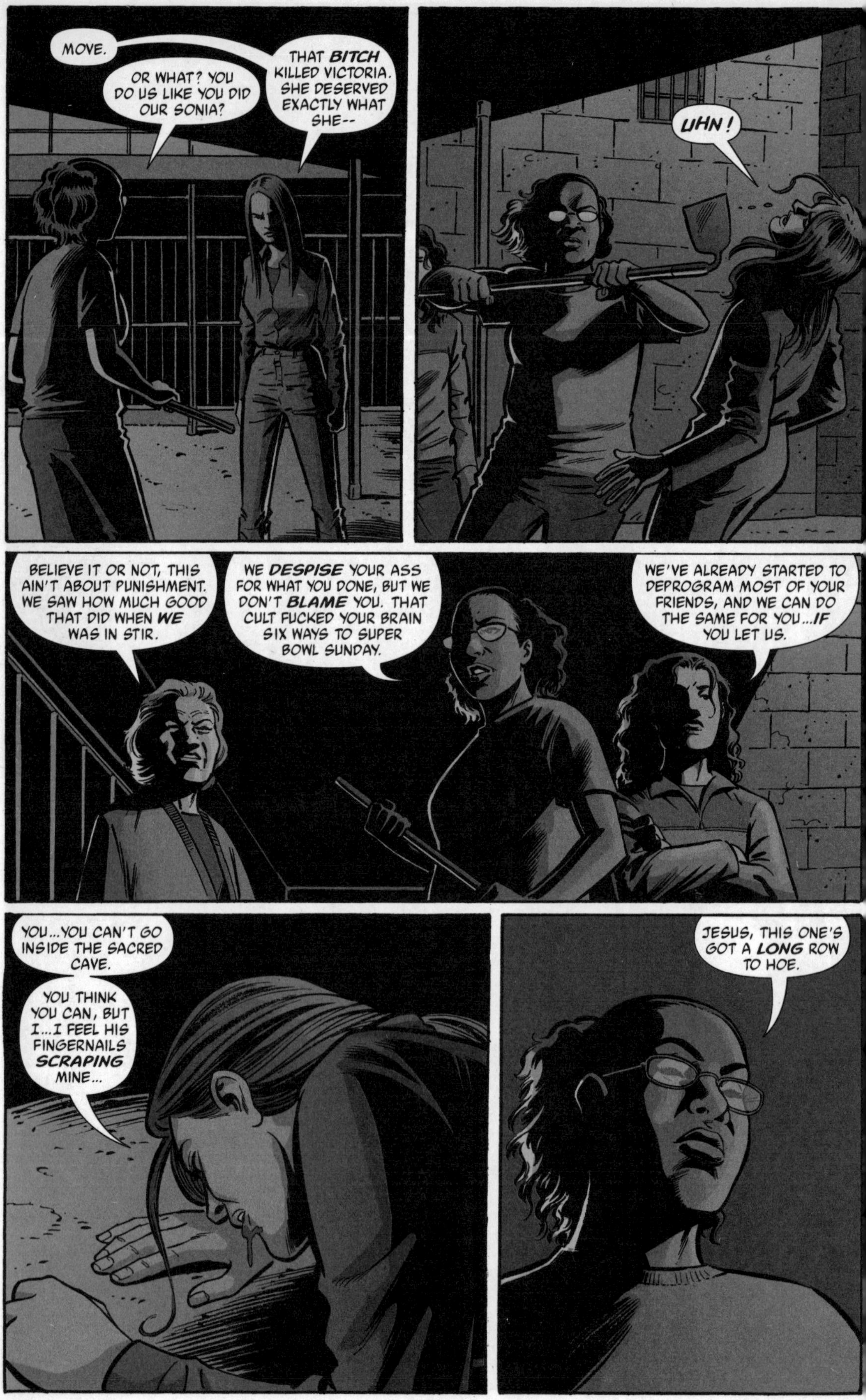
MOVE.
OR WHAT? YOU DO US LIKE YOU DID OUR SONIA?
THAT BITCH KILLED VICTORIA. SHE DESERVED EXACTLY WHAT SHE--
UHN!
BELIEVE IT OR NOT, THIS AIN'T ABOUT PUNISHMENT. WE SAW HOW MUCH GOOD THAT DID WHEN WE WAS IN STIR.
WE DESPISE YOUR ASS FOR WHAT YOU DONE, BUT WE DON'T BLAME YOU. THAT CULT FUCKED YOUR BRAIN SIX WAYS TO SUPER BOWL SUNDAY.
WE'VE ALREADY STARTED TO DEPROGRAM MOST OF YOUR FRIENDS, AND WE CAN DO THE SAME FOR YOU...IF YOU LET US.
YOU...YOU CAN'T GO INSIDE THE SACRED CAVE.
YOU THINK YOU CAN, BUT I...I FEEL HIS FINGERNAILS SCRAPING MINE...
JESUS, THIS ONE'S GOT A LONG ROW TO HOE.

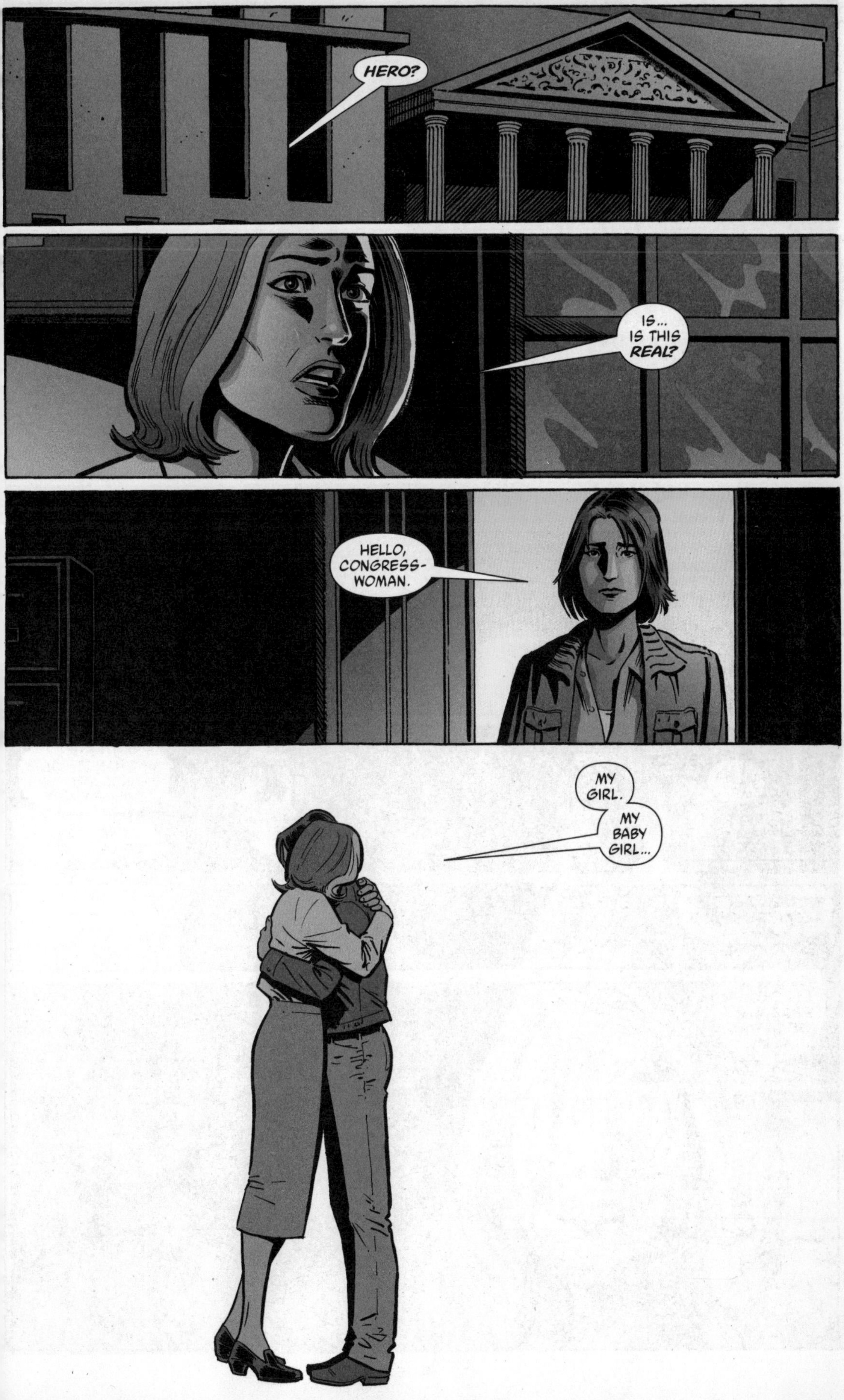
HERO?
IS... IS THIS REAL?
HELLO, CONGRESS-WOMAN.
MY GIRL.
MY BABY GIRL...

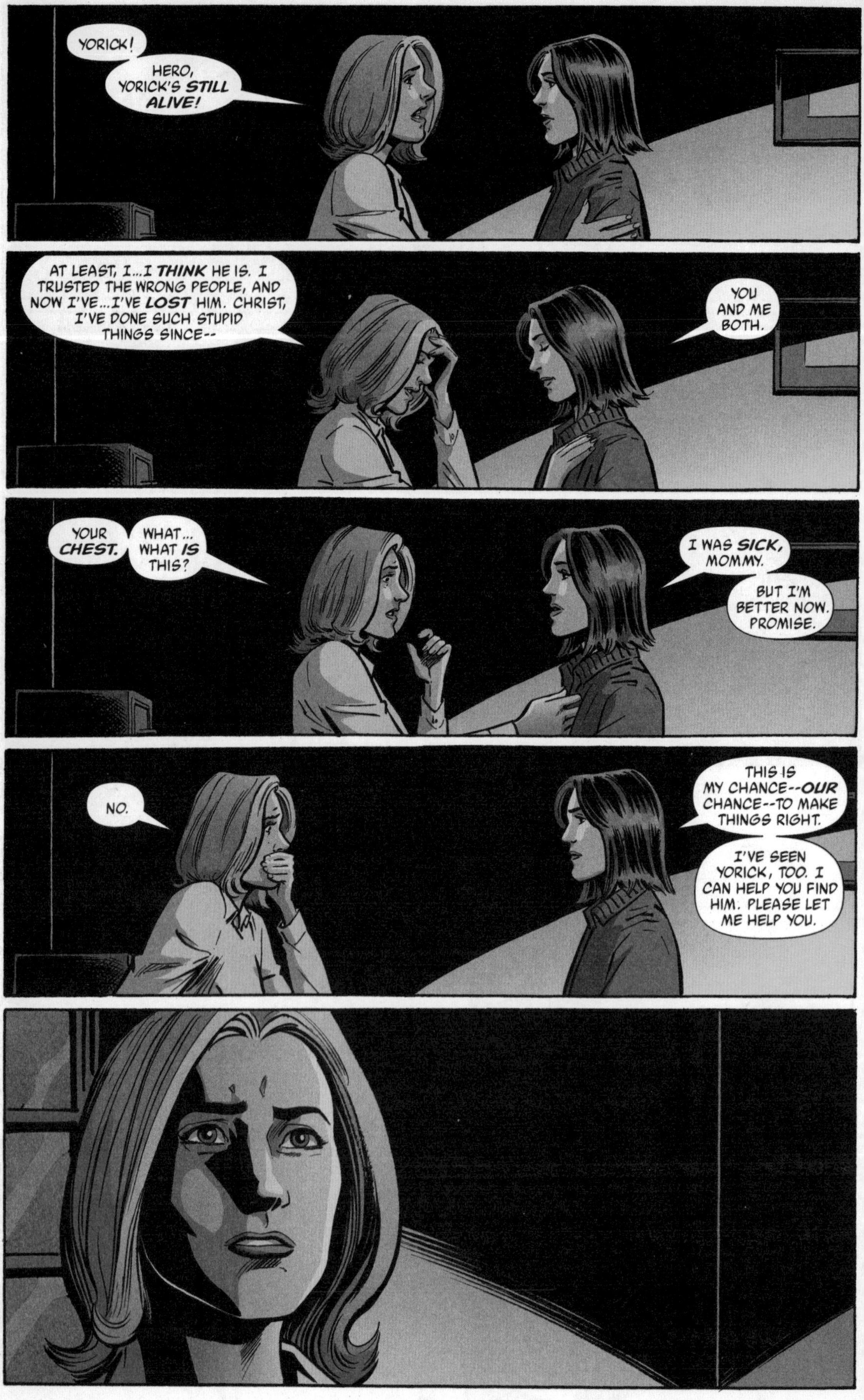
YORICK!
HERO, YORICK'S STILL ALIVE!
AT LEAST, I...I THINK HE IS. I TRUSTED THE WRONG PEOPLE, AND NOW I'VE...I'VE LOST HIM. CHRIST, I'VE DONE SUCH STUPID THINGS SINCE--
YOU AND ME BOTH.
YOUR CHEST.
WHAT... WHAT IS THIS?
I WAS SICK, MOMMY.
BUT I'M BETTER NOW. PROMISE.
NO.
THIS IS MY CHANCE--OUR CHANCE--TO MAKE THINGS RIGHT.
I'VE SEEN YORICK, TOO. I CAN HELP YOU FIND HIM. PLEASE LET ME HELP YOU.

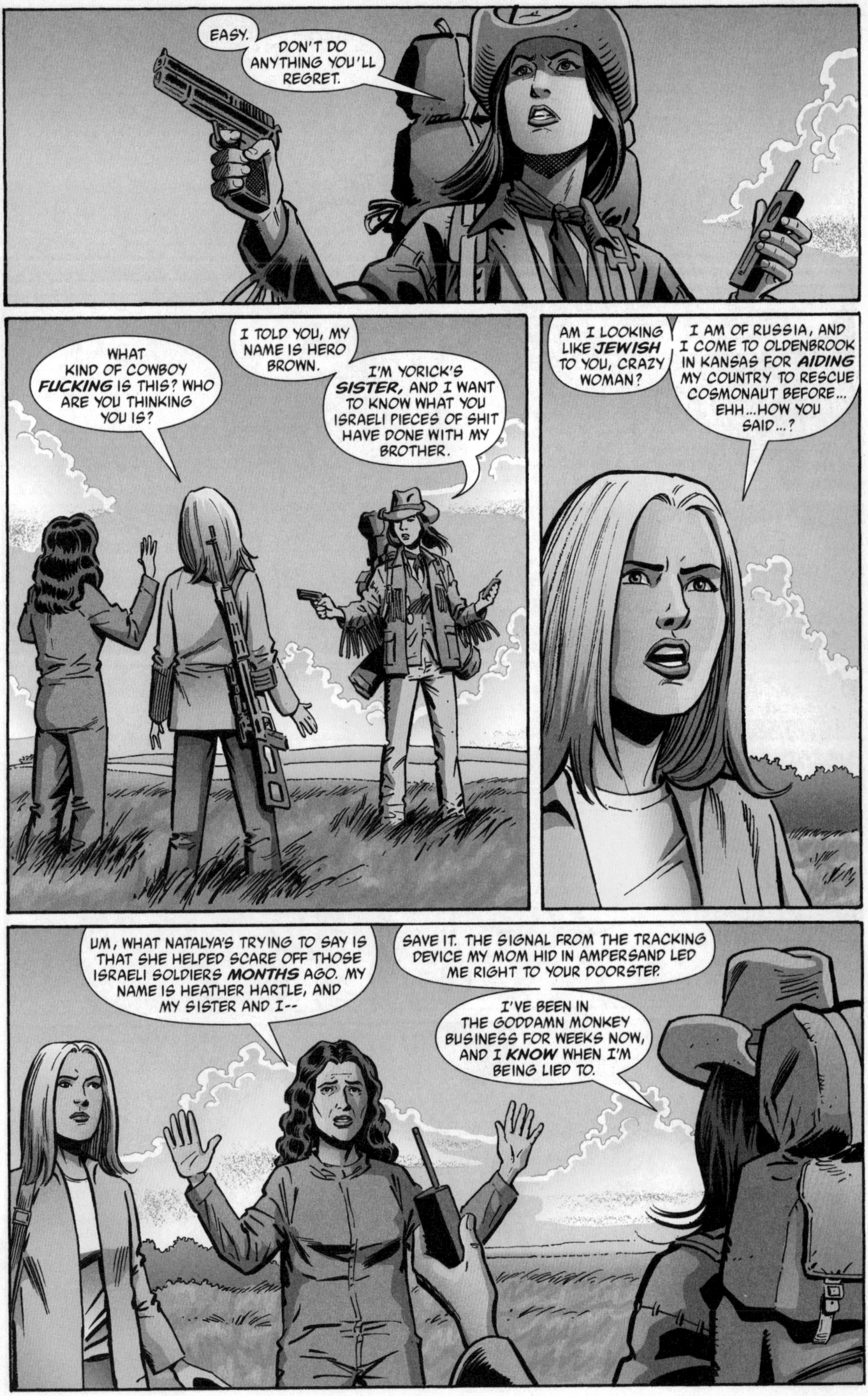
EASY.
DON'T DO ANYTHING YOU'LL REGRET.
WHAT KIND OF COWBOY FUCKING IS THIS? WHO ARE YOU THINKING YOU IS?
I TOLD YOU, MY NAME IS HERO BROWN.
I'M YORICK'S SISTER, AND I WANT TO KNOW WHAT YOU ISRAELI PIECES OF SHIT HAVE DONE WITH MY BROTHER.
AM I LOOKING LIKE JEWISH TO YOU, CRAZY WOMAN?
I AM OF RUSSIA, AND I COME TO OLDENBROOK IN KANSAS FOR AIDING MY COUNTRY TO RESCUE COSMONAUT BEFORE... EHH...HOW YOU SAID...?
UM, WHAT NATALYA'S TRYING TO SAY IS THAT SHE HELPED SCARE OFF THOSE ISRAELI SOLDIERS MONTHS AGO. MY NAME IS HEATHER HARTLE, AND MY SISTER AND I--
SAVE IT. THE SIGNAL FROM THE TRACKING DEVICE MY MOM HID IN AMPERSAND LED ME RIGHT TO YOUR DOORSTEP.
I'VE BEEN IN THE GODDAMN MONKEY BUSINESS FOR WEEKS NOW, AND I KNOW WHEN I'M BEING LIED TO.

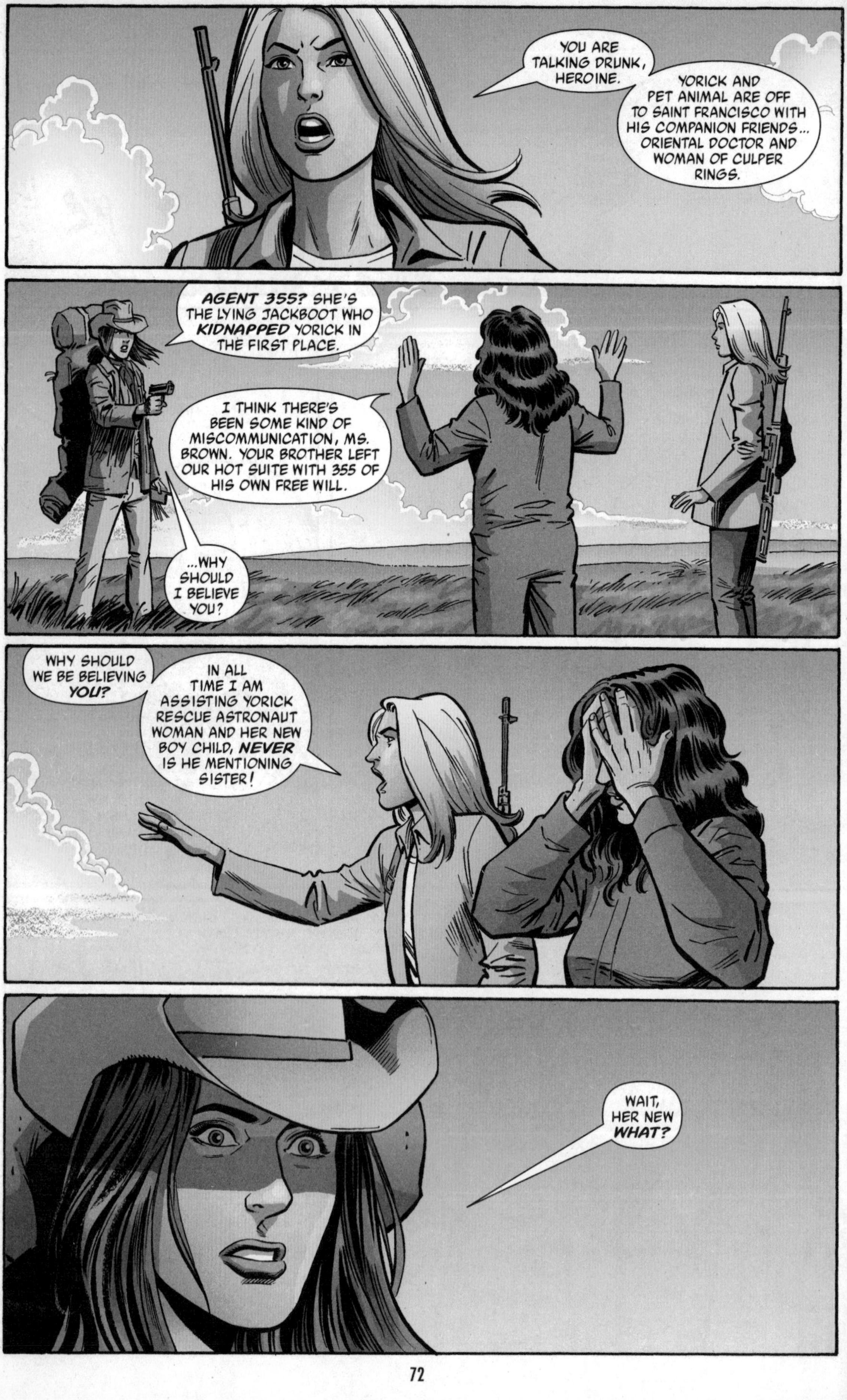
YOU ARE TALKING DRUNK, HEROINE.
YORICK AND PET ANIMAL ARE OFF TO SAINT FRANCISCO WITH HIS COMPANION FRIENDS... ORIENTAL DOCTOR AND WOMAN OF CULPER RINGS.
AGENT 355? SHE'S THE LYING JACKBOOT WHO KIDNAPPED YORICK IN THE FIRST PLACE.
I THINK THERE'S BEEN SOME KIND OF MISCOMMUNICATION, MS. BROWN. YOUR BROTHER LEFT OUR HOT SUITE WITH 355 OF HIS OWN FREE WILL.
...WHY SHOULD I BELIEVE YOU?
WHY SHOULD WE BE BELIEVING YOU?
IN ALL TIME I AM ASSISTING YORICK RESCUE ASTRONAUT WOMAN AND HER NEW BOY CHILD, NEVER IS HE MENTIONING SISTER!
WAIT, HER NEW WHAT?

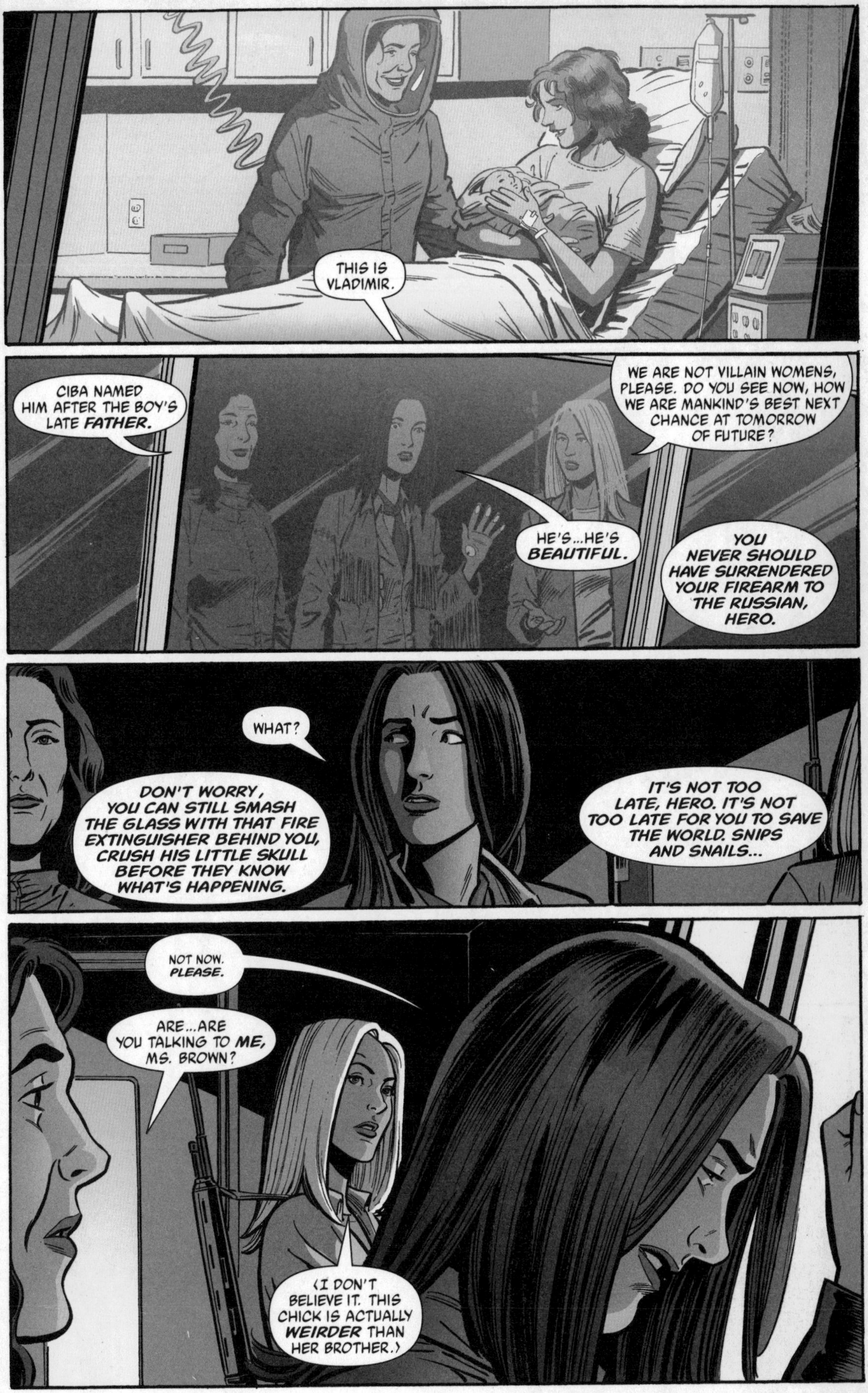
THIS IS VLADIMIR.
CIBA NAMED HIM AFTER THE BOY'S LATE FATHER.
WE ARE NOT VILLAIN WOMENS, PLEASE. DO YOU SEE NOW, HOW WE ARE MANKIND'S BEST NEXT CHANCE AT TOMORROW OF FUTURE?
HE'S...HE'S BEAUTIFUL.
YOU NEVER SHOULD HAVE SURRENDERED YOUR FIREARM TO THE RUSSIAN, HERO.
WHAT?
DON'T WORRY, YOU CAN STILL SMASH THE GLASS WITH THAT FIRE EXTINGUISHER BEHIND YOU, CRUSH HIS LITTLE SKULL BEFORE THEY KNOW WHAT'S HAPPENING.
IT'S NOT TOO LATE, HERO. IT'S NOT TOO LATE FOR YOU TO SAVE THE WORLD. SNIPS AND SNAILS...
NOT NOW. PLEASE.
ARE...ARE YOU TALKING TO ME, MS. BROWN?
‹I DON'T BELIEVE IT. THIS CHICK IS ACTUALLY WEIRDER THAN HER BROTHER.›

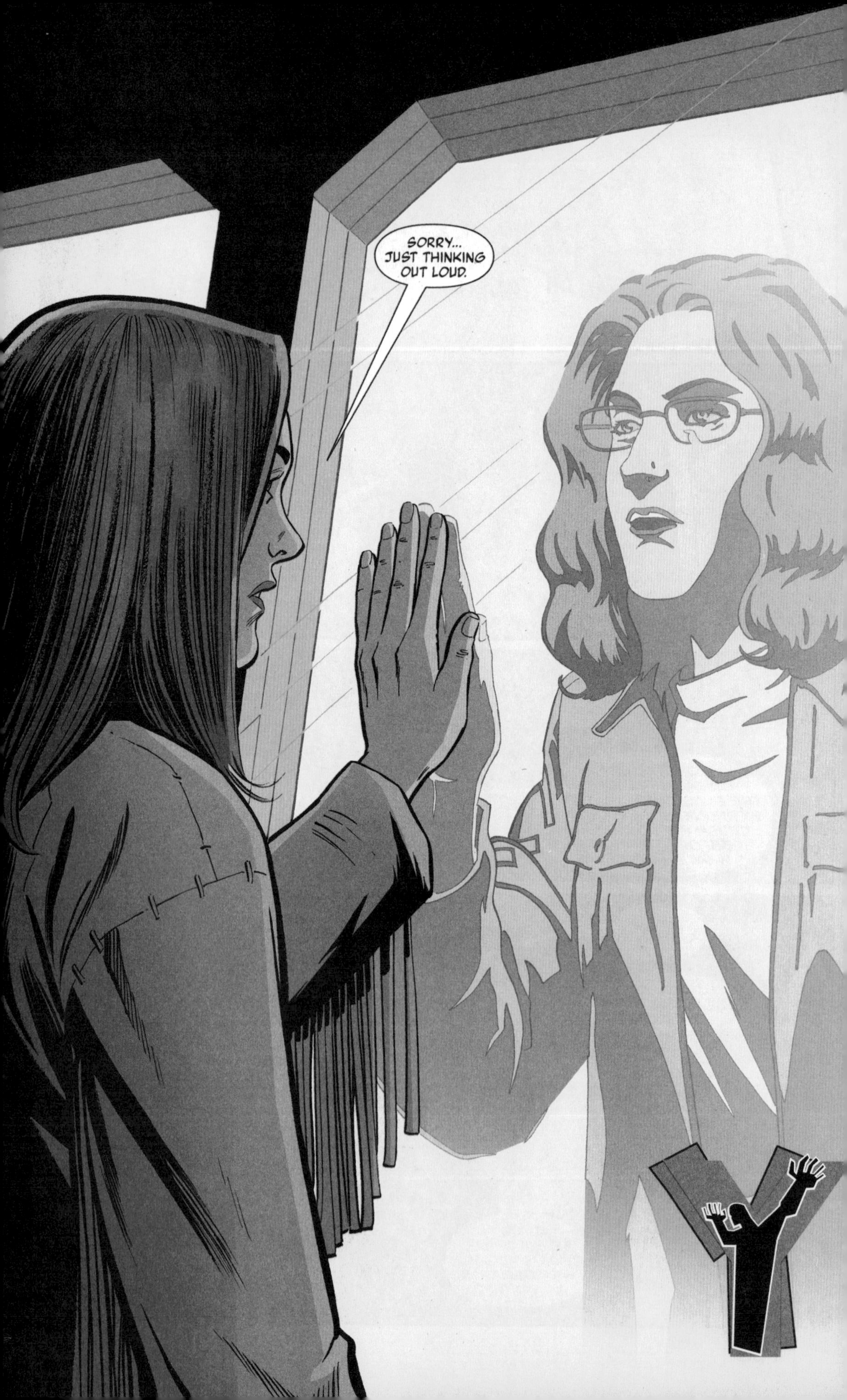
SORRY... JUST THINKING OUT LOUD.

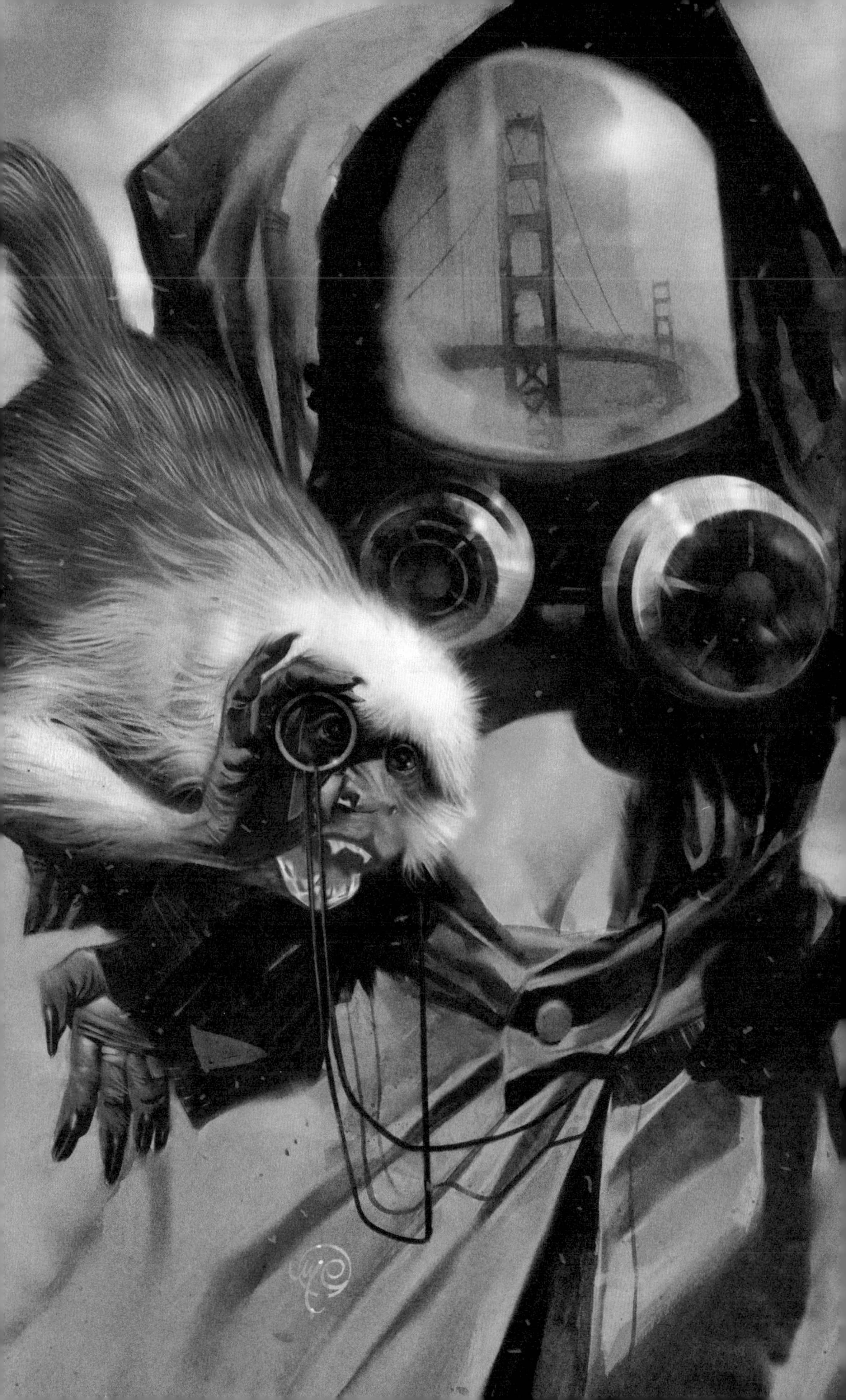

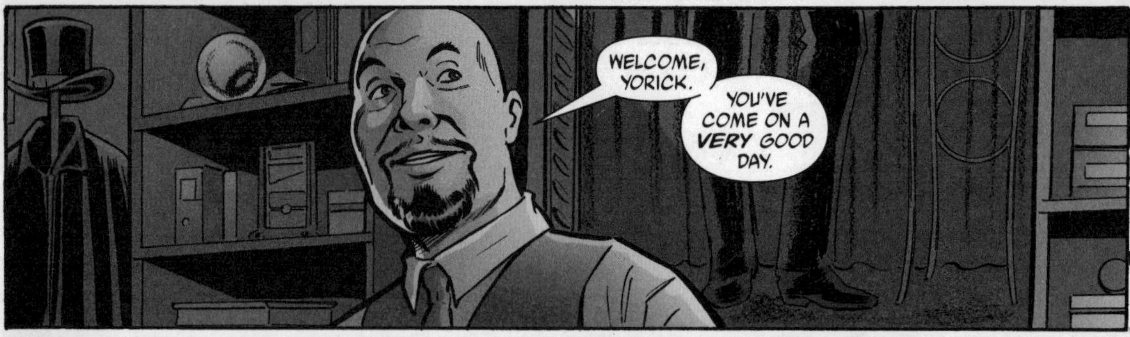
WELCOME, YORICK.
YOU'VE COME ON A VERY GOOD DAY.

New York City
July 17, 2002

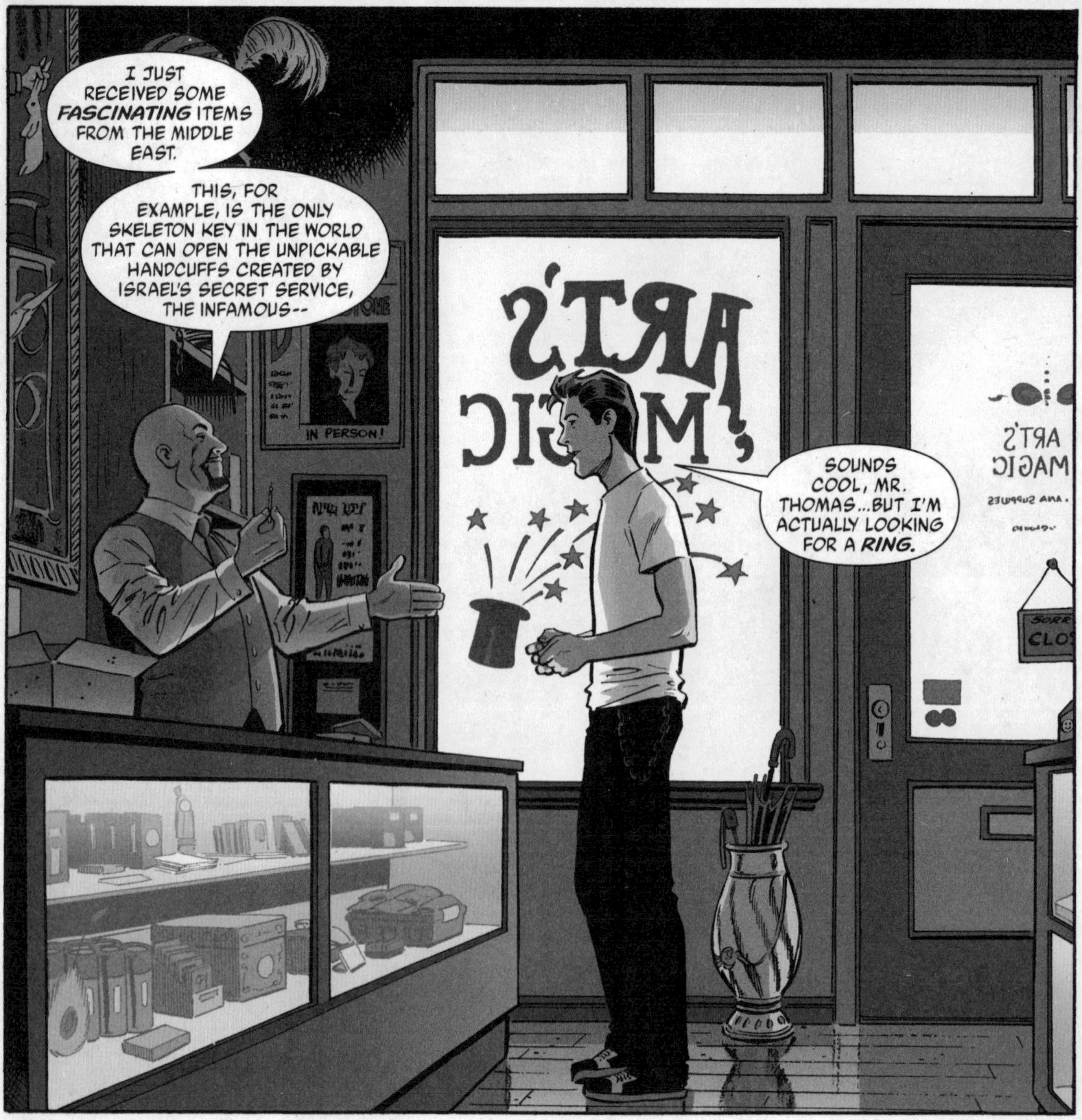
I JUST RECEIVED SOME FASCINATING ITEMS FROM THE MIDDLE EAST.
THIS, FOR EXAMPLE, IS THE ONLY SKELETON KEY IN THE WORLD THAT CAN OPEN THE UNPICKABLE HANDCUFFS CREATED BY ISRAEL'S SECRET SERVICE, THE INFAMOUS--
IN PERSON!
SOUNDS COOL, MR. THOMAS...BUT I'M ACTUALLY LOOKING FOR A RING.

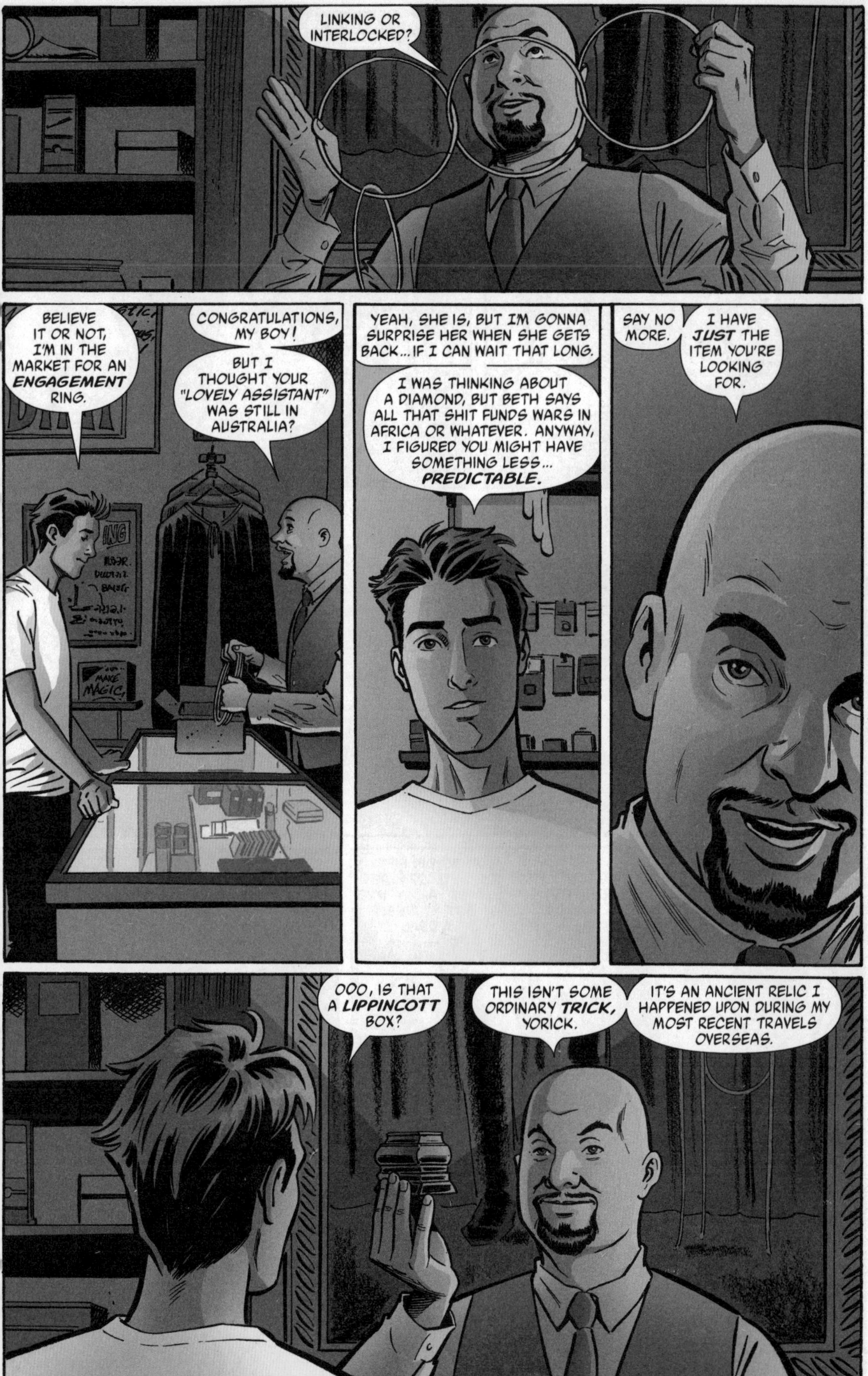
LINKING OR INTERLOCKED?
BELIEVE IT OR NOT, I'M IN THE MARKET FOR AN ENGAGEMENT RING.
CONGRATULATIONS, MY BOY!
BUT I THOUGHT YOUR "LOVELY ASSISTANT" WAS STILL IN AUSTRALIA?
MAKE MAGIC.
YEAH, SHE IS, BUT I'M GONNA SURPRISE HER WHEN SHE GETS BACK... IF I CAN WAIT THAT LONG.
I WAS THINKING ABOUT A DIAMOND, BUT BETH SAYS ALL THAT SHIT FUNDS WARS IN AFRICA OR WHATEVER. ANYWAY, I FIGURED YOU MIGHT HAVE SOMETHING LESS... PREDICTABLE.
SAY NO MORE.
I HAVE JUST THE ITEM YOU'RE LOOKING FOR.
OOO, IS THAT A LIPPINCOTT BOX?
THIS ISN'T SOME ORDINARY TRICK, YORICK.
IT'S AN ANCIENT RELIC I HAPPENED UPON DURING MY MOST RECENT TRAVELS OVERSEAS.

OH, SAVE THE OLD MAN FROM GREMLINS ROUTINE, MR. T.

IT'S TRUE! DO YOU SEE HOW THE RING GLISTENS LIKE GOLD IN ONE LIGHT...

...AND SILVER IN THE NEXT? THIS REPRESENTS THE MALE AND FEMALE SIDES WHICH ALL OF US POSSESS.

MANY CULTURES BELIEVE THAT MEN AND WOMEN ARE *REVERSED* AT THE MOMENT OF PROPOSAL. THE YOUNG LADY'S FINGER IS TRANSFORMED INTO A SYMBOLIC *PHALLUS*, WHILE THE GENTLEMAN PRESENTING THE RING--

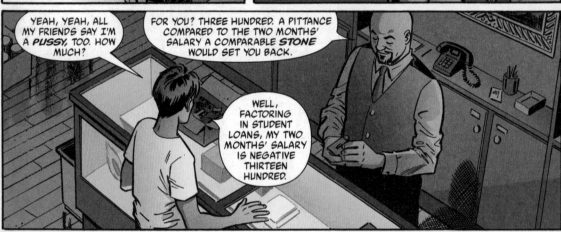

YEAH, YEAH, ALL MY FRIENDS SAY I'M A *PUSSY*, TOO. HOW MUCH?

FOR YOU? THREE HUNDRED. A PITTANCE COMPARED TO THE TWO MONTHS' SALARY A COMPARABLE *STONE* WOULD SET YOU BACK.

WELL, FACTORING IN STUDENT LOANS, MY TWO MONTHS' SALARY IS NEGATIVE THIRTEEN HUNDRED.

OF COURSE, IF YOU'D LIKE SOMETHING LESS *DISTINCTIVE* FOR YOUR BRIDE...

NO! NO, THAT ONE...THAT ONE FEELS *RIGHT*.

THROW IN FIFTY SHEETS OF FLASH PAPER, AND YOU'VE GOT YOURSELF A DEAL.

MAGIC ARTS

CLOSED

YOU, YOUNG MAN, ARE WISE BEYOND YOUR YEARS.

ABSOLUTELY NO REFUNDS

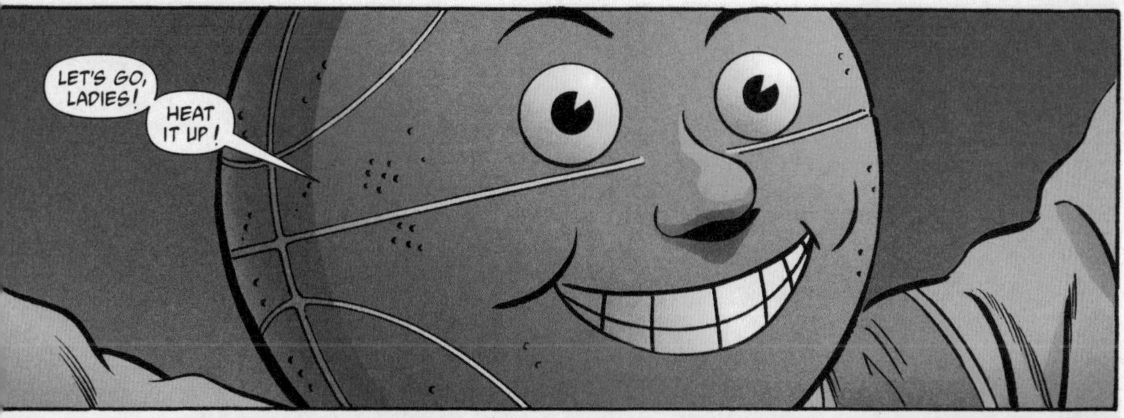
LET'S GO, LADIES!
HEAT IT UP!

San Francisco, California
Now

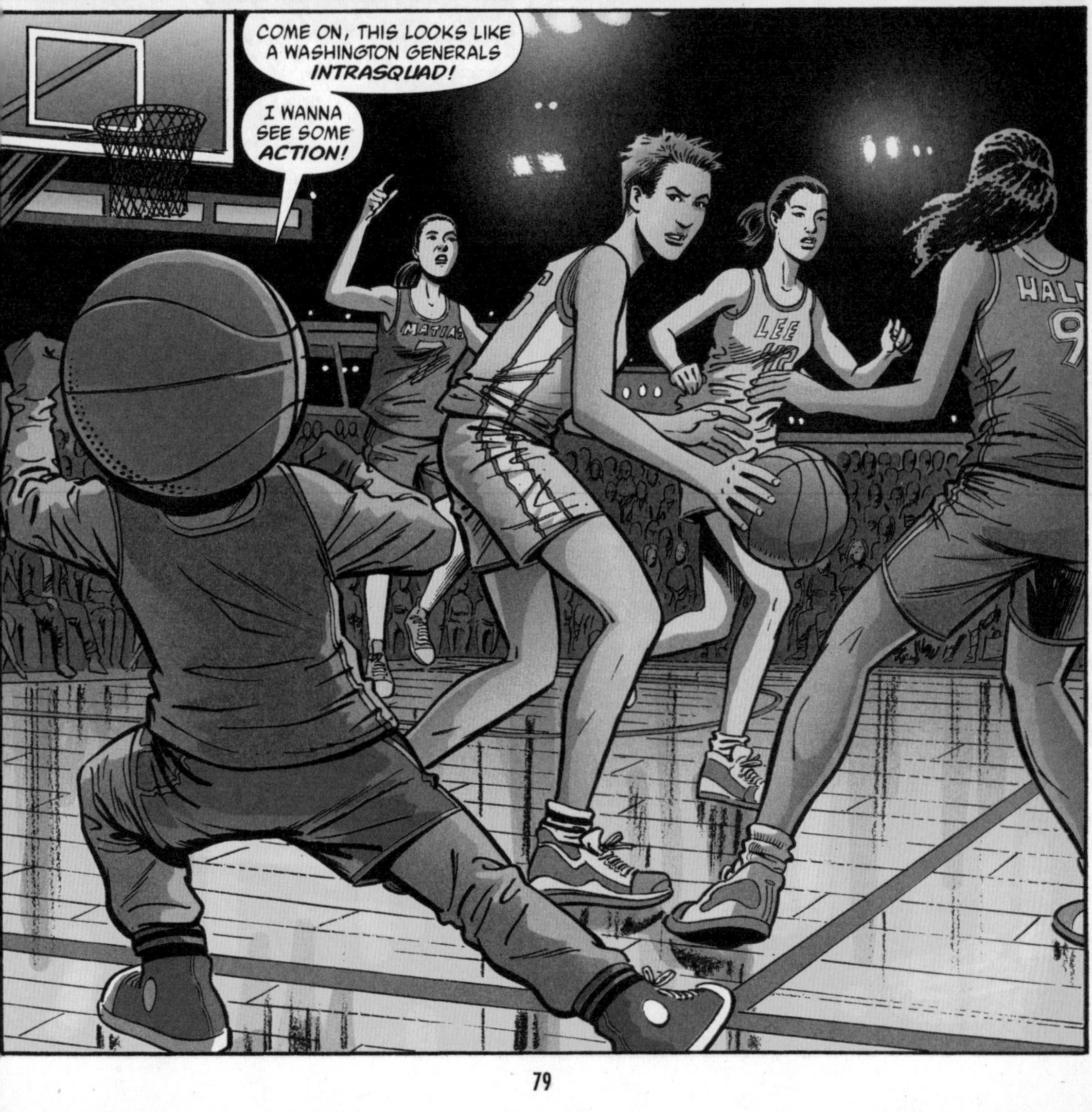
COME ON, THIS LOOKS LIKE A WASHINGTON GENERALS *INTRASQUAD!*
I WANNA SEE SOME *ACTION!*

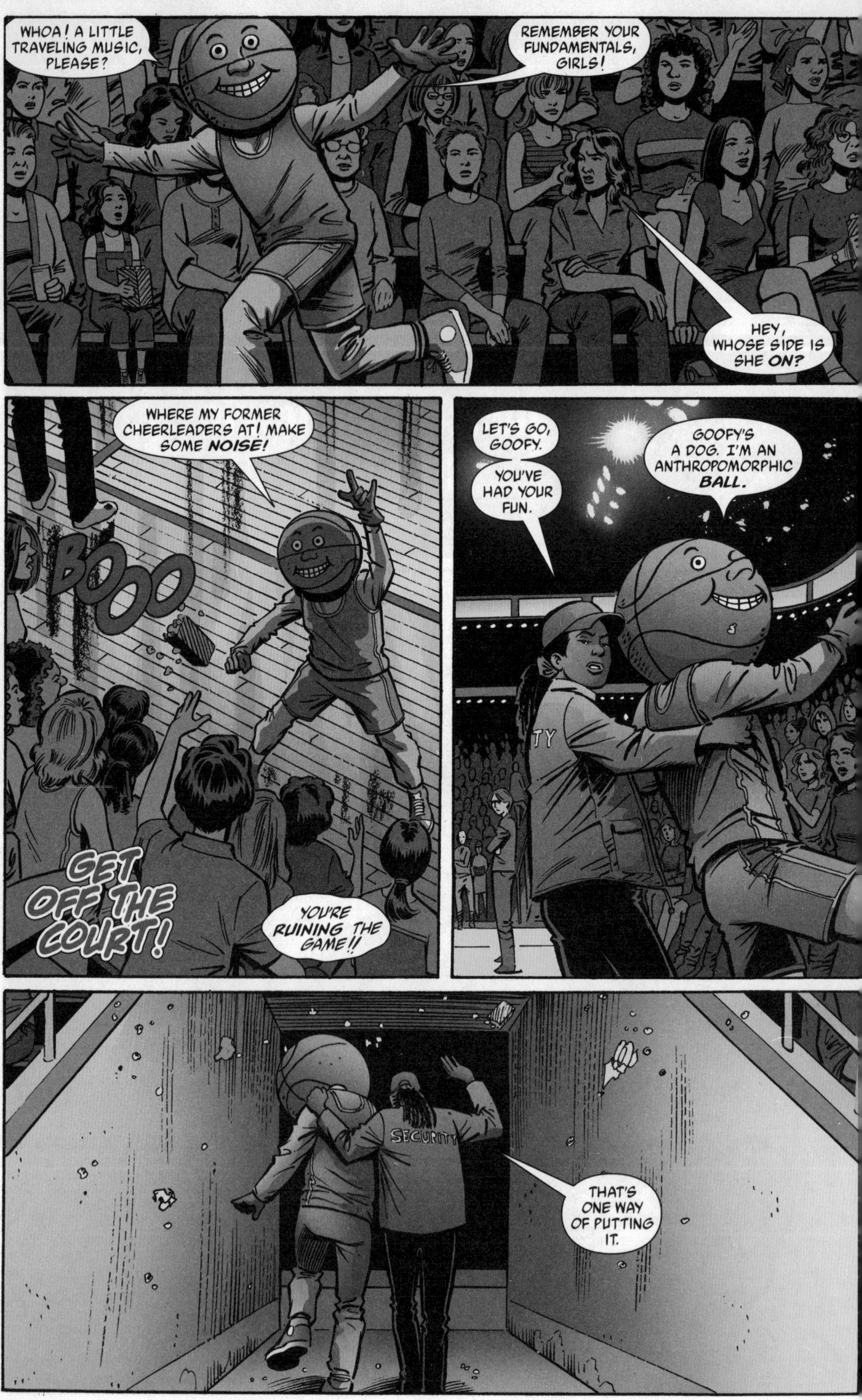
WHOA! A LITTLE TRAVELING MUSIC, PLEASE?
REMEMBER YOUR FUNDAMENTALS, GIRLS!
HEY, WHOSE SIDE IS SHE *ON?*
WHERE MY FORMER CHEERLEADERS AT! MAKE SOME *NOISE!*
BOOO
GET OFF THE COURT!
YOU'RE *RUINING* THE GAME!!
LET'S GO, GOOFY.
YOU'VE HAD YOUR FUN.
GOOFY'S A DOG. I'M AN ANTHROPOMORPHIC *BALL.*
SECURITY
THAT'S ONE WAY OF PUTTING IT.

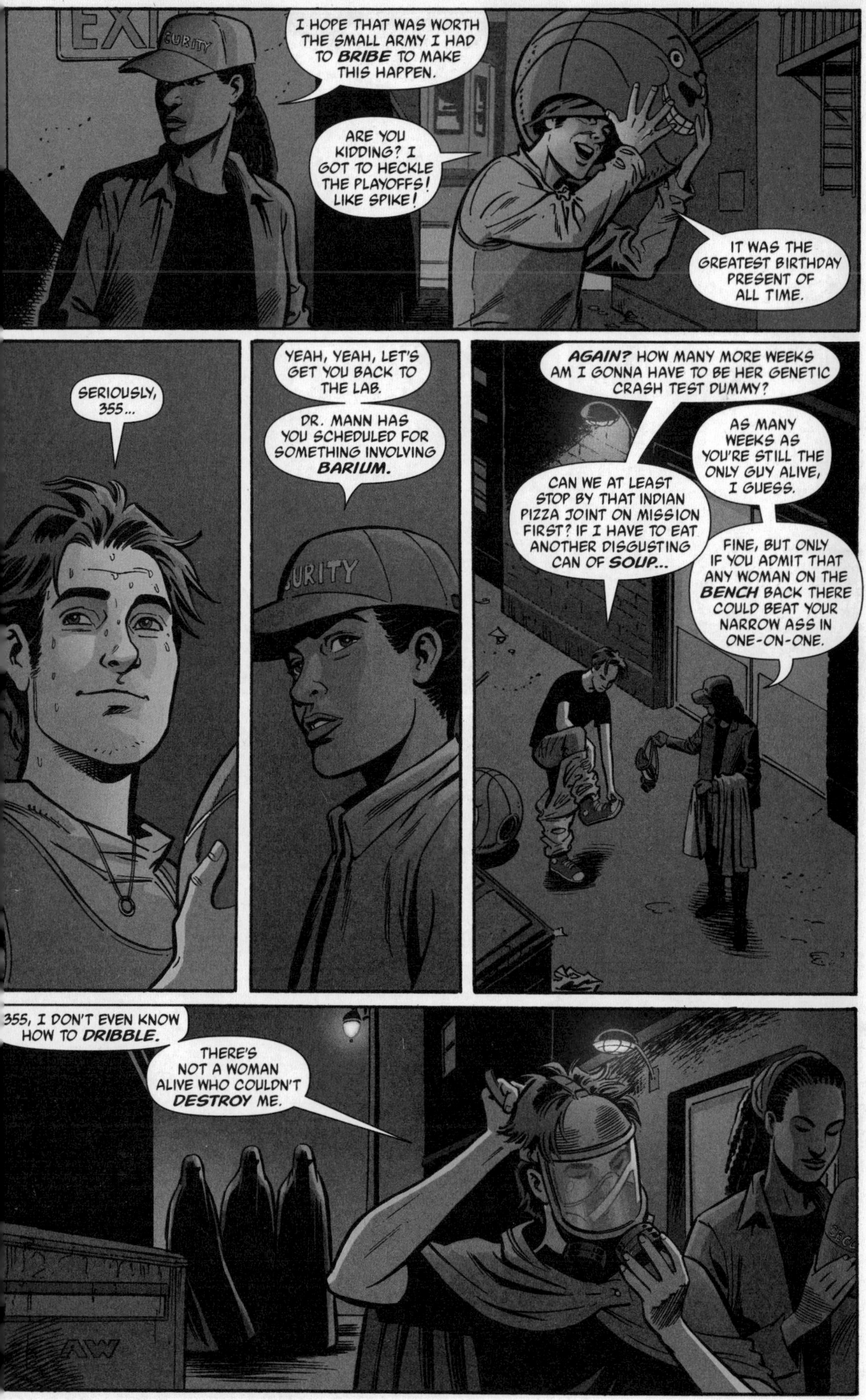

EXIT
SECURITY
I HOPE THAT WAS WORTH THE SMALL ARMY I HAD TO BRIBE TO MAKE THIS HAPPEN.
ARE YOU KIDDING? I GOT TO HECKLE THE PLAYOFFS! LIKE SPIKE!
IT WAS THE GREATEST BIRTHDAY PRESENT OF ALL TIME.
SERIOUSLY, 355...
YEAH, YEAH, LET'S GET YOU BACK TO THE LAB.
DR. MANN HAS YOU SCHEDULED FOR SOMETHING INVOLVING BARIUM.
SECURITY
AGAIN? HOW MANY MORE WEEKS AM I GONNA HAVE TO BE HER GENETIC CRASH TEST DUMMY?
AS MANY WEEKS AS YOU'RE STILL THE ONLY GUY ALIVE, I GUESS.
CAN WE AT LEAST STOP BY THAT INDIAN PIZZA JOINT ON MISSION FIRST? IF I HAVE TO EAT ANOTHER DISGUSTING CAN OF SOUP...
FINE, BUT ONLY IF YOU ADMIT THAT ANY WOMAN ON THE BENCH BACK THERE COULD BEAT YOUR NARROW ASS IN ONE-ON-ONE.
355, I DON'T EVEN KNOW HOW TO DRIBBLE.
THERE'S NOT A WOMAN ALIVE WHO COULDN'T DESTROY ME.

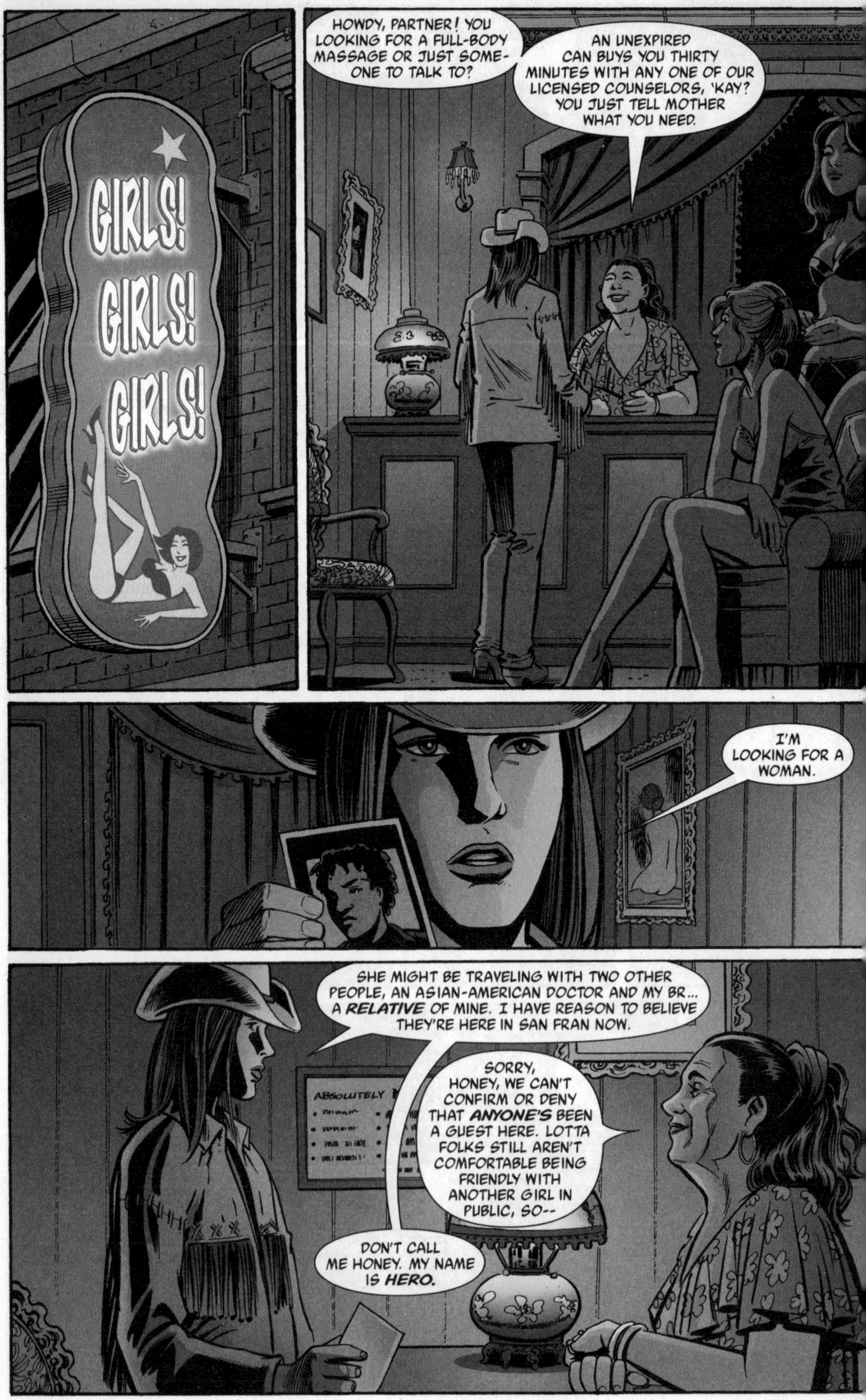
GIRLS! GIRLS! GIRLS!
HOWDY, PARTNER! YOU LOOKING FOR A FULL-BODY MASSAGE OR JUST SOMEONE TO TALK TO?
AN UNEXPIRED CAN BUYS YOU THIRTY MINUTES WITH ANY ONE OF OUR LICENSED COUNSELORS, 'KAY? YOU JUST TELL MOTHER WHAT YOU NEED.
I'M LOOKING FOR A WOMAN.
SHE MIGHT BE TRAVELING WITH TWO OTHER PEOPLE, AN ASIAN-AMERICAN DOCTOR AND MY BR... A *RELATIVE* OF MINE. I HAVE REASON TO BELIEVE THEY'RE HERE IN SAN FRAN NOW.
ABSOLUTELY
SORRY, HONEY, WE CAN'T CONFIRM OR DENY THAT *ANYONE'S* BEEN A GUEST HERE. LOTTA FOLKS STILL AREN'T COMFORTABLE BEING FRIENDLY WITH ANOTHER GIRL IN PUBLIC, SO--
DON'T CALL ME HONEY. MY NAME IS *HERO*.

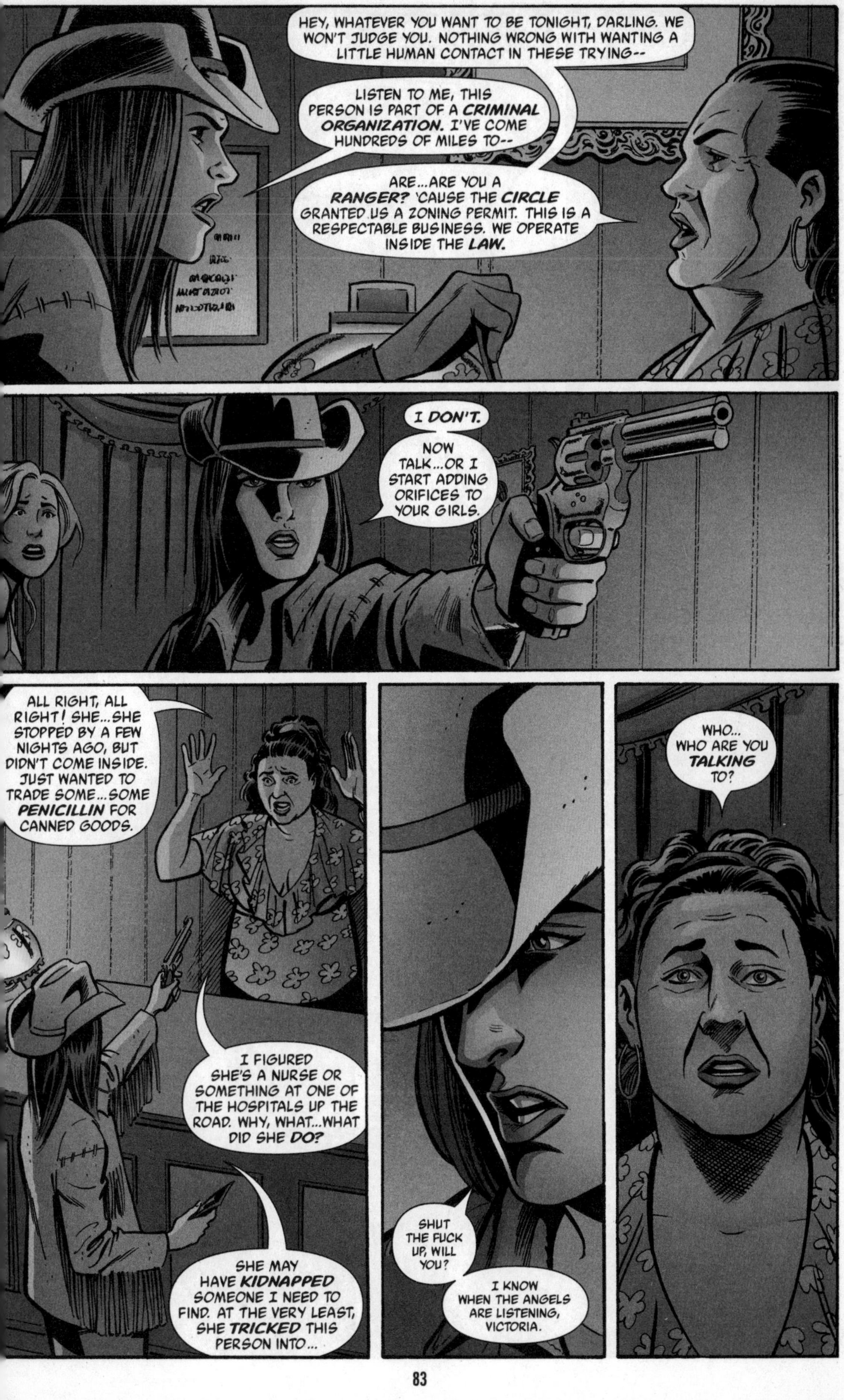
HEY, WHATEVER YOU WANT TO BE TONIGHT, DARLING. WE WON'T JUDGE YOU. NOTHING WRONG WITH WANTING A LITTLE HUMAN CONTACT IN THESE TRYING--
LISTEN TO ME, THIS PERSON IS PART OF A CRIMINAL ORGANIZATION. I'VE COME HUNDREDS OF MILES TO--
ARE...ARE YOU A RANGER? 'CAUSE THE CIRCLE GRANTED US A ZONING PERMIT. THIS IS A RESPECTABLE BUSINESS. WE OPERATE INSIDE THE LAW.
I DON'T.
NOW TALK...OR I START ADDING ORIFICES TO YOUR GIRLS.
ALL RIGHT, ALL RIGHT! SHE...SHE STOPPED BY A FEW NIGHTS AGO, BUT DIDN'T COME INSIDE. JUST WANTED TO TRADE SOME...SOME PENICILLIN FOR CANNED GOODS.
I FIGURED SHE'S A NURSE OR SOMETHING AT ONE OF THE HOSPITALS UP THE ROAD. WHY, WHAT...WHAT DID SHE DO?
SHE MAY HAVE KIDNAPPED SOMEONE I NEED TO FIND. AT THE VERY LEAST, SHE TRICKED THIS PERSON INTO...
SHUT THE FUCK UP, WILL YOU?
I KNOW WHEN THE ANGELS ARE LISTENING, VICTORIA.
WHO... WHO ARE YOU TALKING TO?

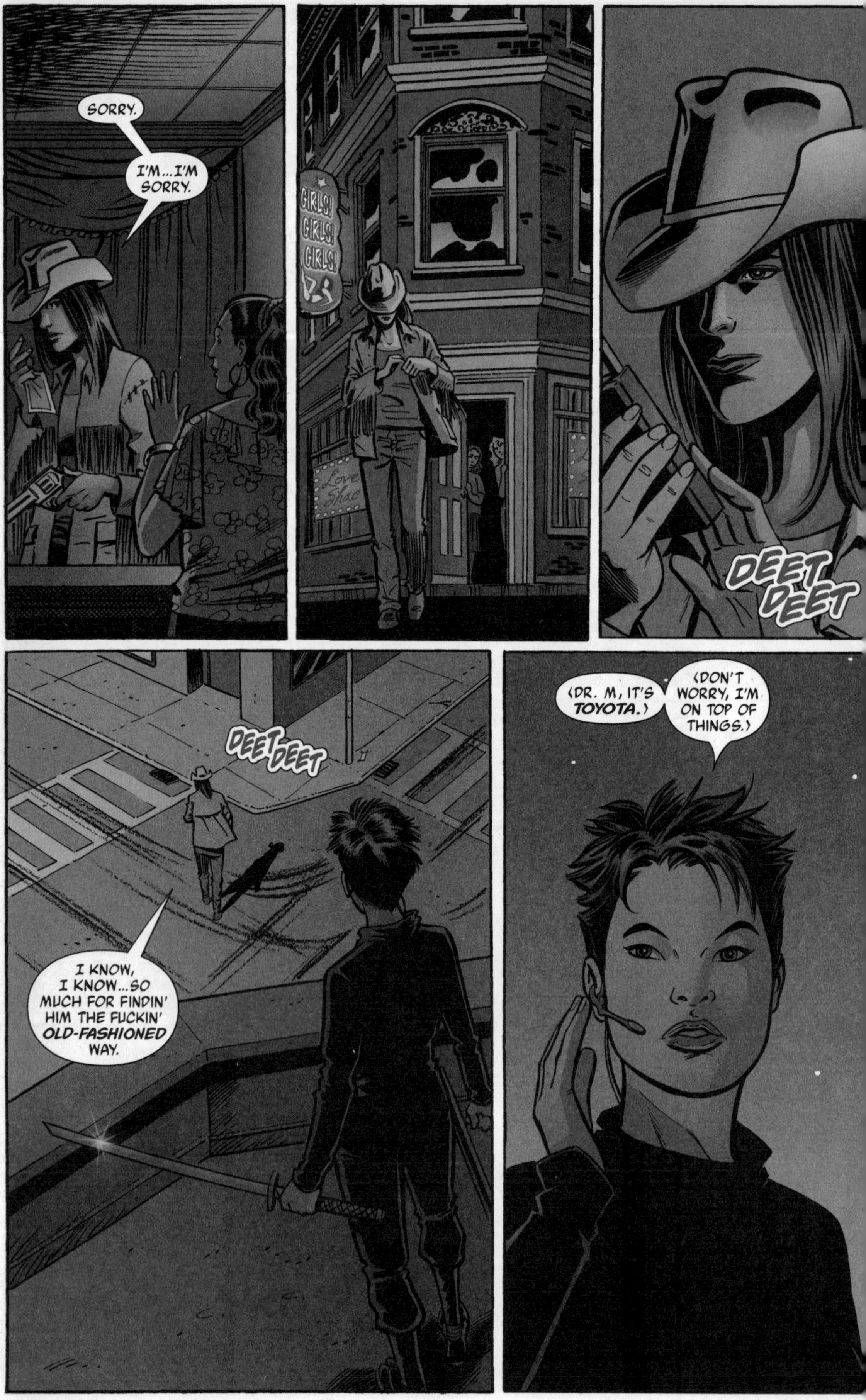

SORRY.
I'M...I'M SORRY.
GIRLS! GIRLS! GIRLS!
Love Shac
DEET DEET
DEET DEET
I KNOW, I KNOW...SO MUCH FOR FINDIN' HIM THE FUCKIN' OLD-FASHIONED WAY.
‹DR. M, IT'S TOYOTA.›
‹DON'T WORRY, I'M ON TOP OF THINGS.›

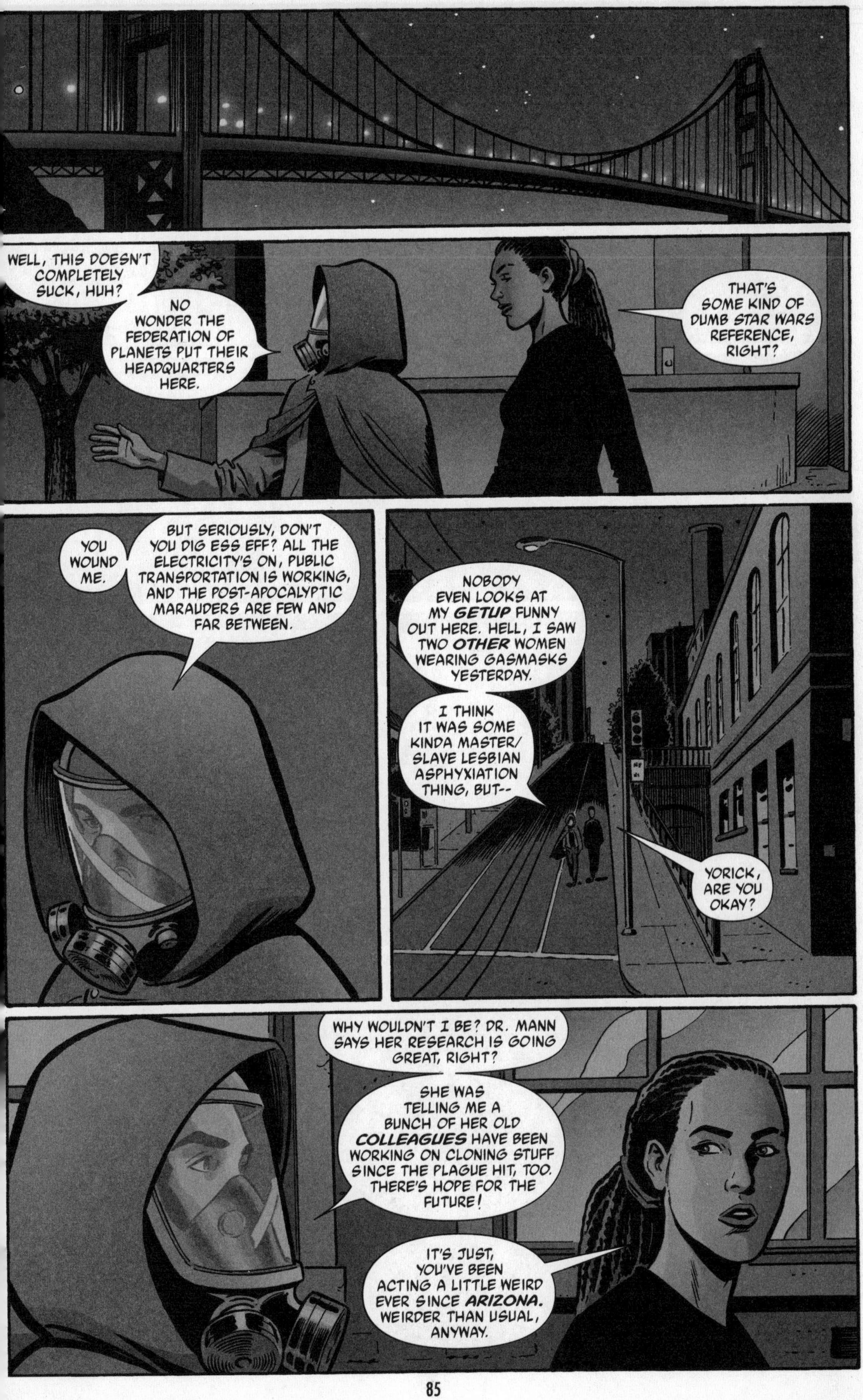

WELL, THIS DOESN'T COMPLETELY SUCK, HUH?
NO WONDER THE FEDERATION OF PLANETS PUT THEIR HEADQUARTERS HERE.
THAT'S SOME KIND OF DUMB STAR WARS REFERENCE, RIGHT?
YOU WOUND ME.
BUT SERIOUSLY, DON'T YOU DIG ESS EFF? ALL THE ELECTRICITY'S ON, PUBLIC TRANSPORTATION IS WORKING, AND THE POST-APOCALYPTIC MARAUDERS ARE FEW AND FAR BETWEEN.
NOBODY EVEN LOOKS AT MY GETUP FUNNY OUT HERE. HELL, I SAW TWO OTHER WOMEN WEARING GASMASKS YESTERDAY.
I THINK IT WAS SOME KINDA MASTER/ SLAVE LESBIAN ASPHYXIATION THING, BUT--
YORICK, ARE YOU OKAY?
WHY WOULDN'T I BE? DR. MANN SAYS HER RESEARCH IS GOING GREAT, RIGHT?
SHE WAS TELLING ME A BUNCH OF HER OLD COLLEAGUES HAVE BEEN WORKING ON CLONING STUFF SINCE THE PLAGUE HIT, TOO. THERE'S HOPE FOR THE FUTURE!
IT'S JUST, YOU'VE BEEN ACTING A LITTLE WEIRD EVER SINCE ARIZONA. WEIRDER THAN USUAL, ANYWAY.

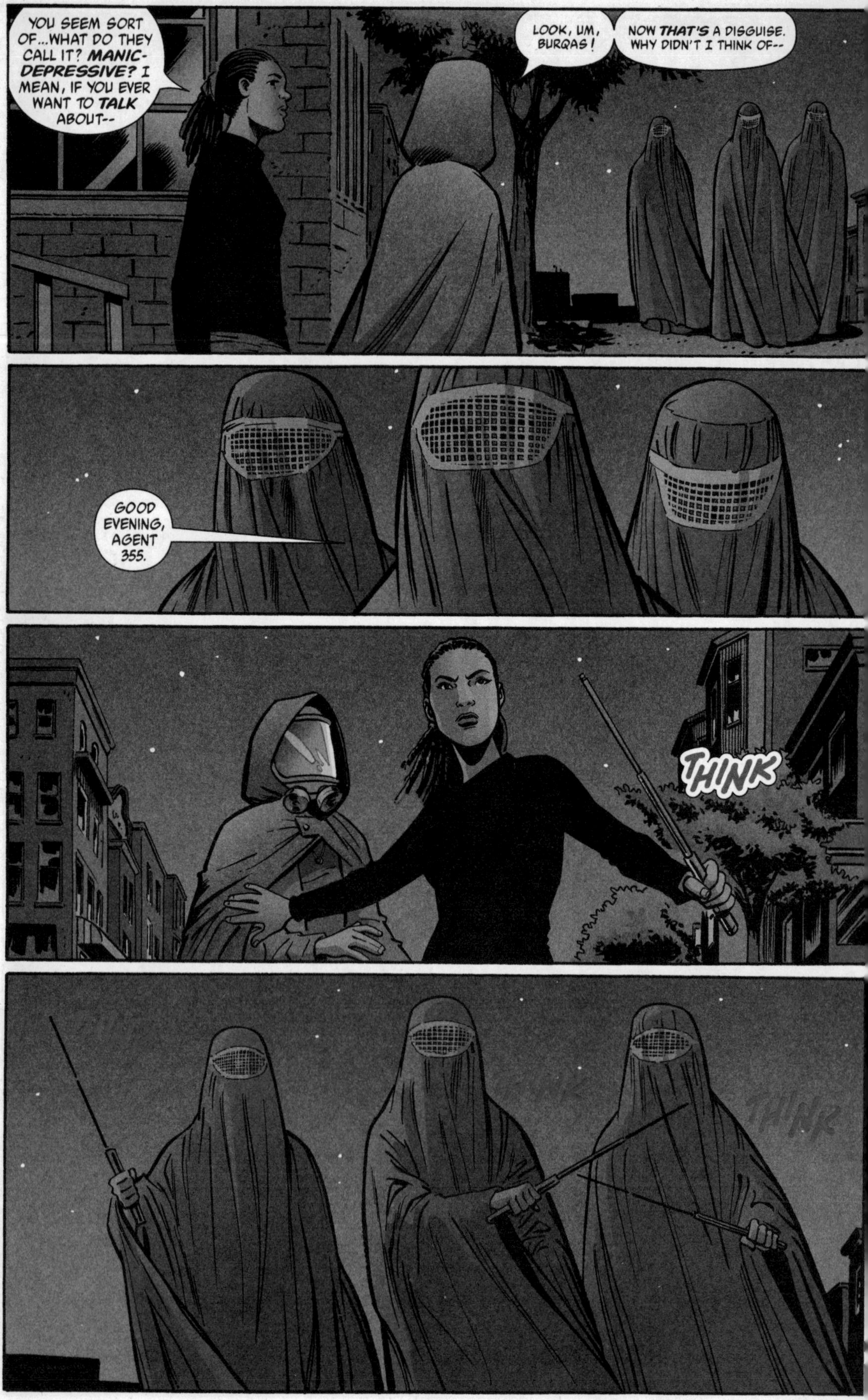
YOU SEEM SORT OF...WHAT DO THEY CALL IT? MANIC-DEPRESSIVE? I MEAN, IF YOU EVER WANT TO TALK ABOUT--
LOOK, UM, BURQAS!
NOW THAT'S A DISGUISE. WHY DIDN'T I THINK OF--
GOOD EVENING, AGENT 355.
THINK
THINK

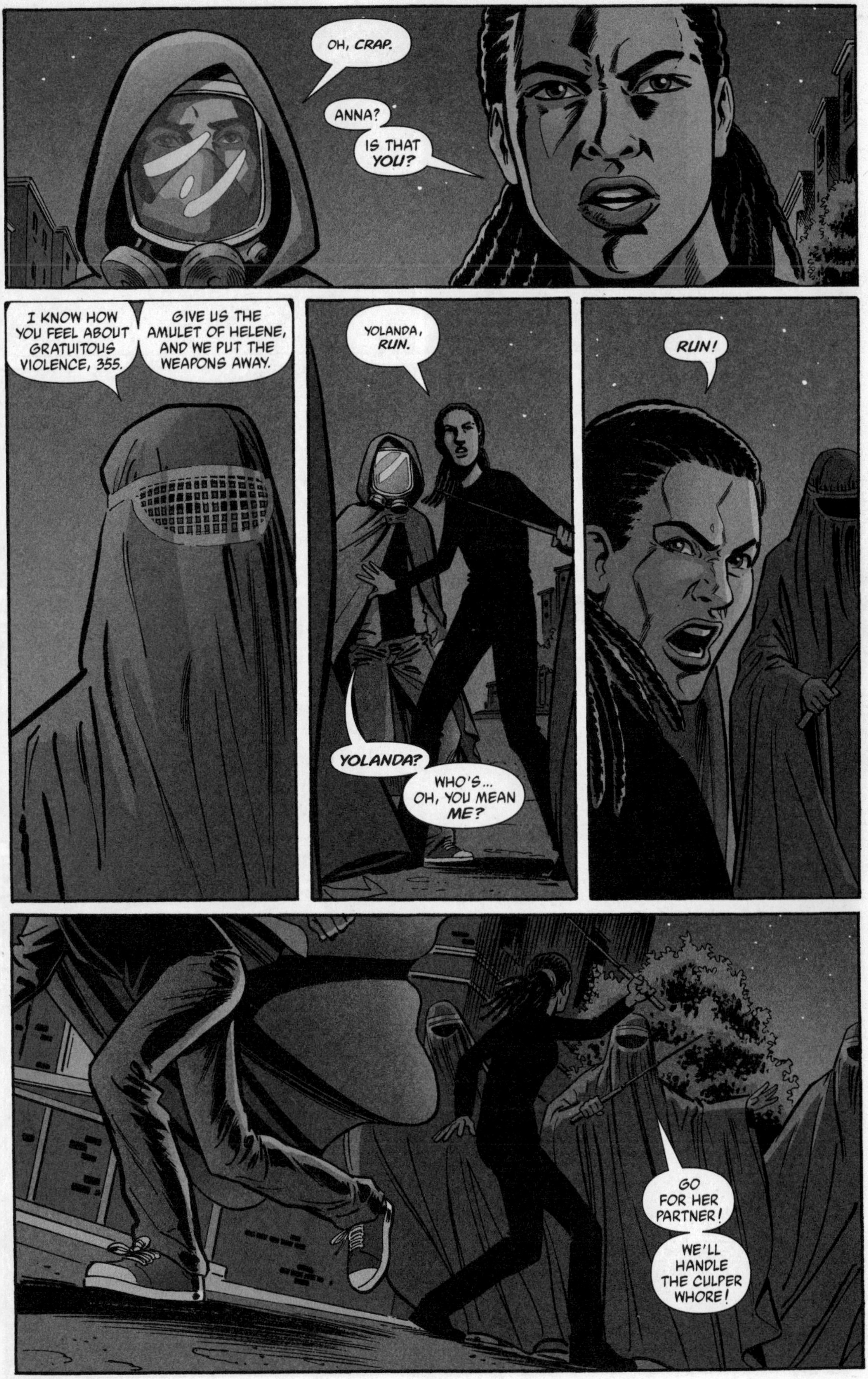
OH, CRAP.
ANNA?
IS THAT YOU?
I KNOW HOW YOU FEEL ABOUT GRATUITOUS VIOLENCE, 355.
GIVE US THE AMULET OF HELENE, AND WE PUT THE WEAPONS AWAY.
YOLANDA, RUN.
YOLANDA?
WHO'S... OH, YOU MEAN ME?
RUN!
GO FOR HER PARTNER!
WE'LL HANDLE THE CULPER WHORE!

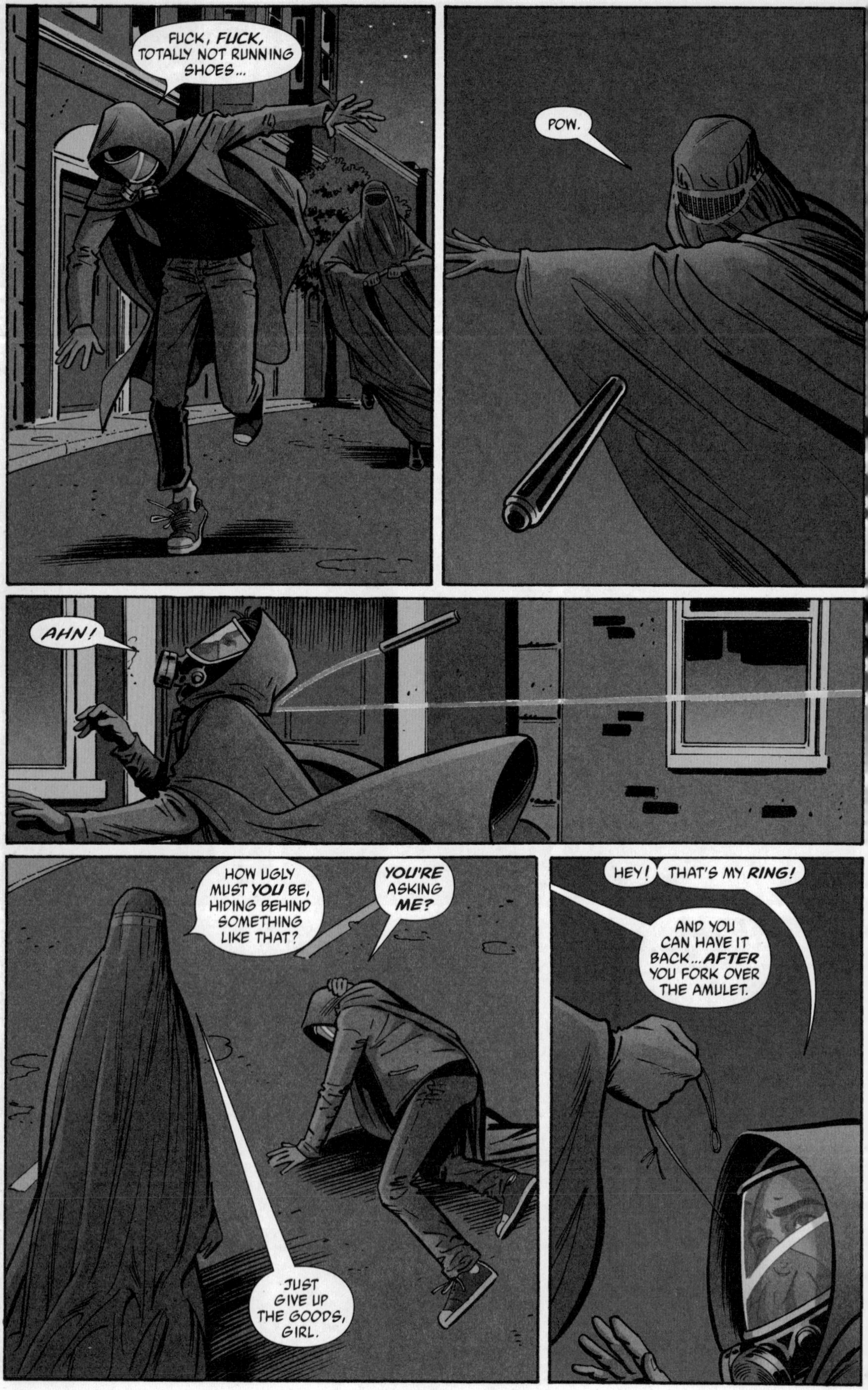
FUCK, FUCK, TOTALLY NOT RUNNING SHOES...
POW.
AHN!
HOW UGLY MUST YOU BE, HIDING BEHIND SOMETHING LIKE THAT?
YOU'RE ASKING ME?
JUST GIVE UP THE GOODS, GIRL.
HEY!
THAT'S MY RING!
AND YOU CAN HAVE IT BACK... AFTER YOU FORK OVER THE AMULET.

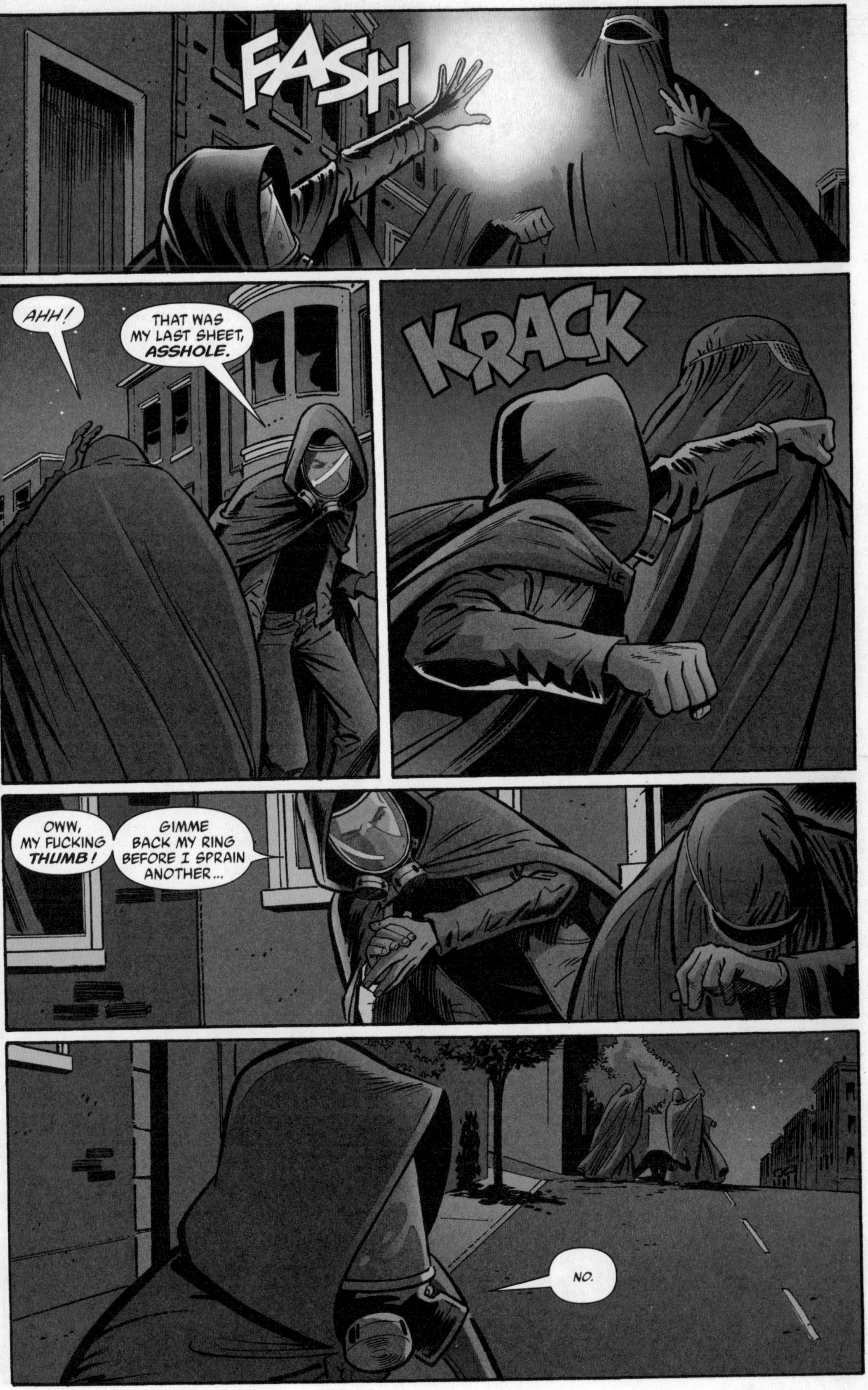
FASH
AHH!
THAT WAS MY LAST SHEET, ASSHOLE.
KRACK
OWW, MY FUCKING THUMB!
GIMME BACK MY RING BEFORE I SPRAIN ANOTHER...
NO.

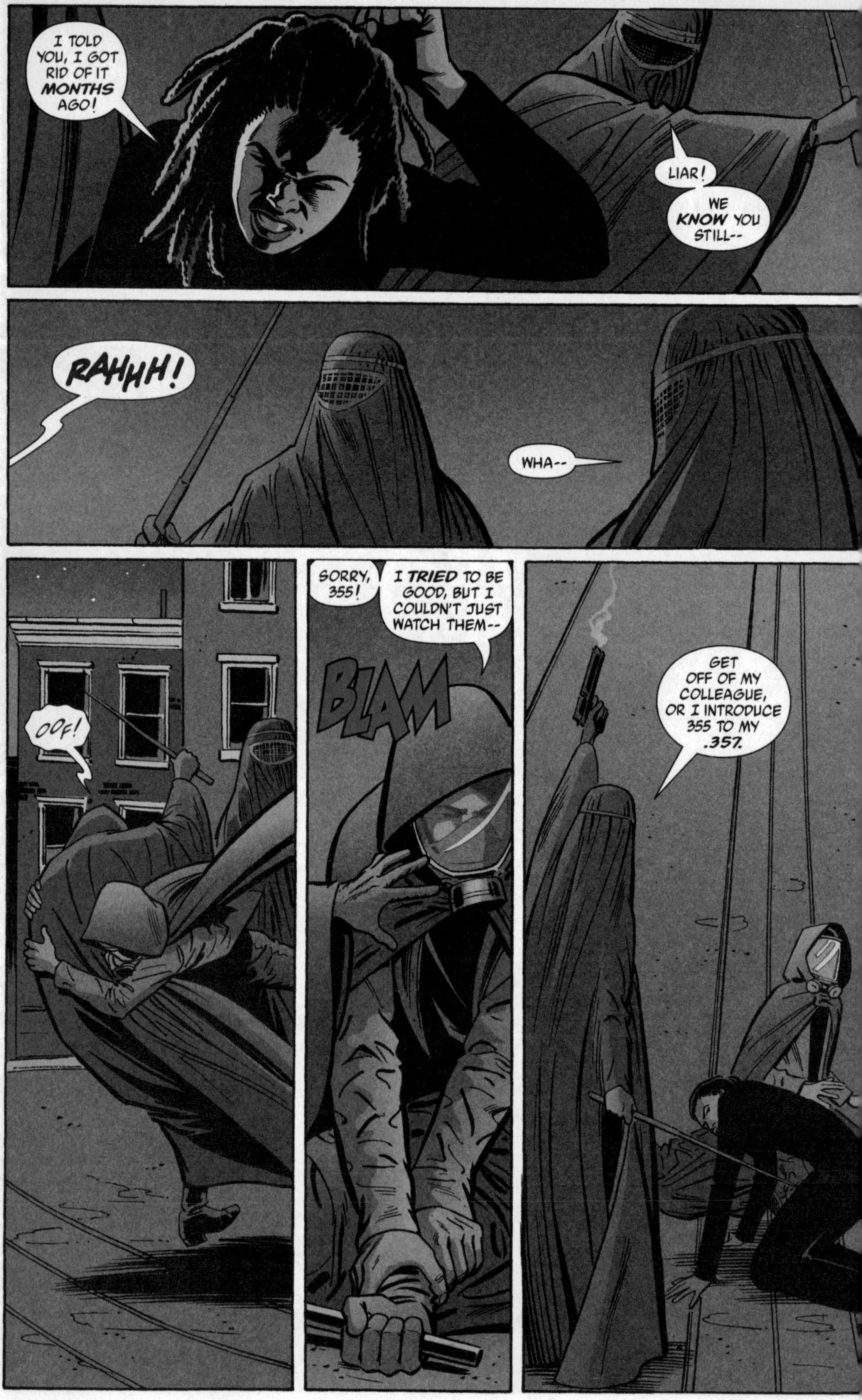
I TOLD YOU, I GOT RID OF IT MONTHS AGO!
LIAR!
WE KNOW YOU STILL--
RAHHH!
WHA--
OOF!
SORRY, 355!
I TRIED TO BE GOOD, BUT I COULDN'T JUST WATCH THEM--
BLAM
GET OFF OF MY COLLEAGUE, OR I INTRODUCE 355 TO MY .357.

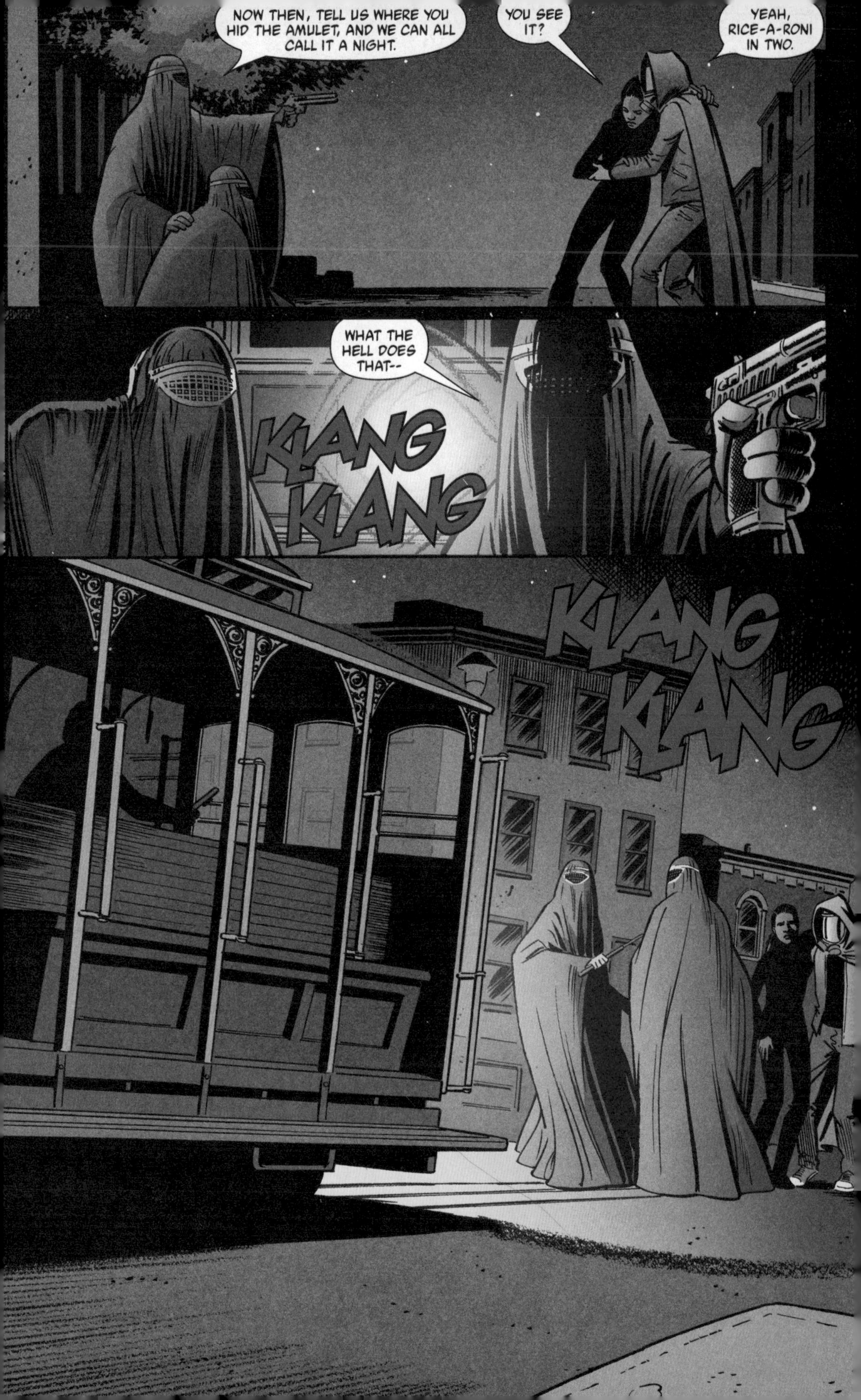
NOW THEN, TELL US WHERE YOU HID THE AMULET, AND WE CAN ALL CALL IT A NIGHT.
YOU SEE IT?
YEAH, RICE-A-RONI IN TWO.
WHAT THE HELL DOES THAT--
KLANG KLANG
KLANG KLANG

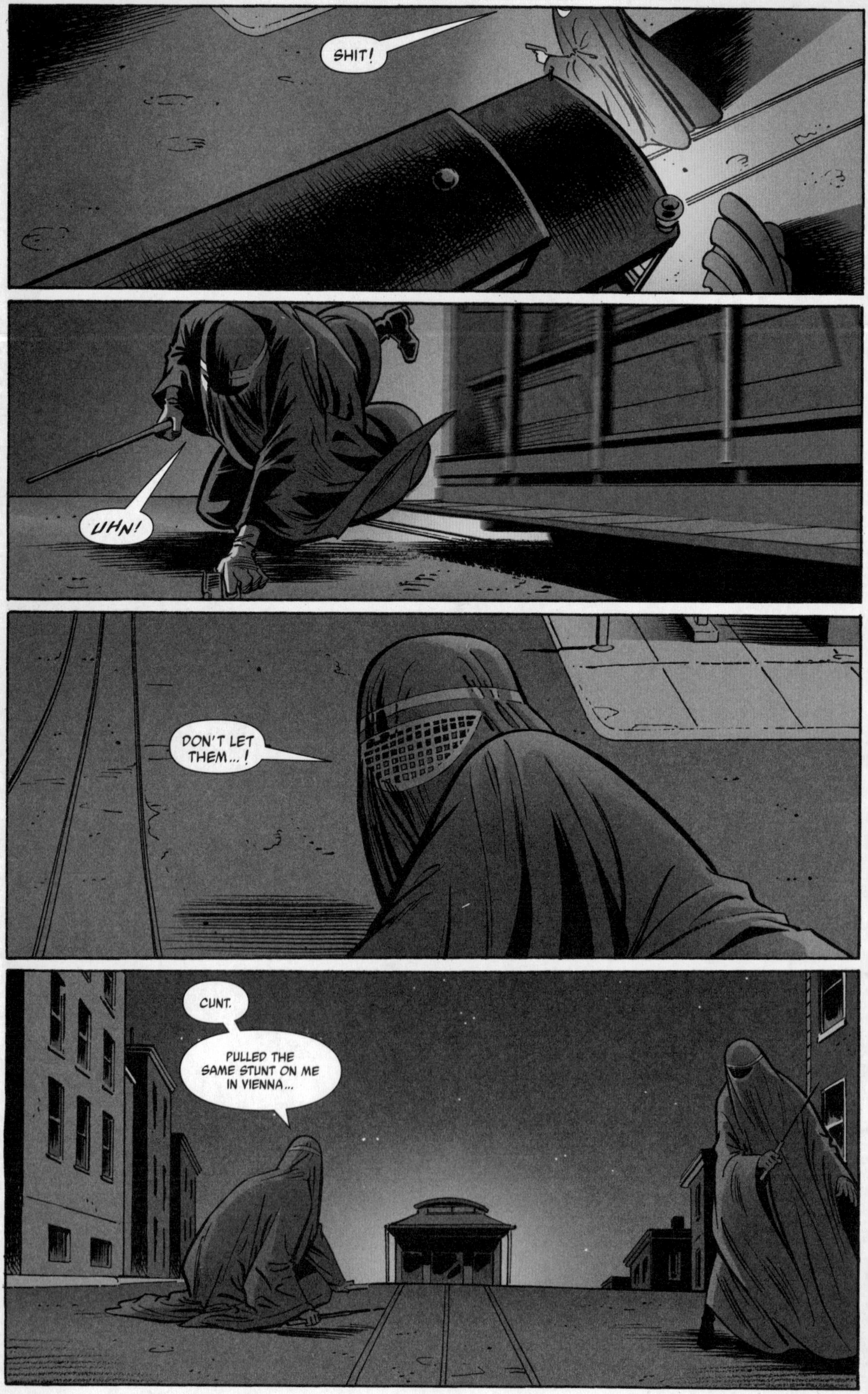
SHIT!
UHN!
DON'T LET THEM...!
CUNT.
PULLED THE SAME STUNT ON ME IN VIENNA...

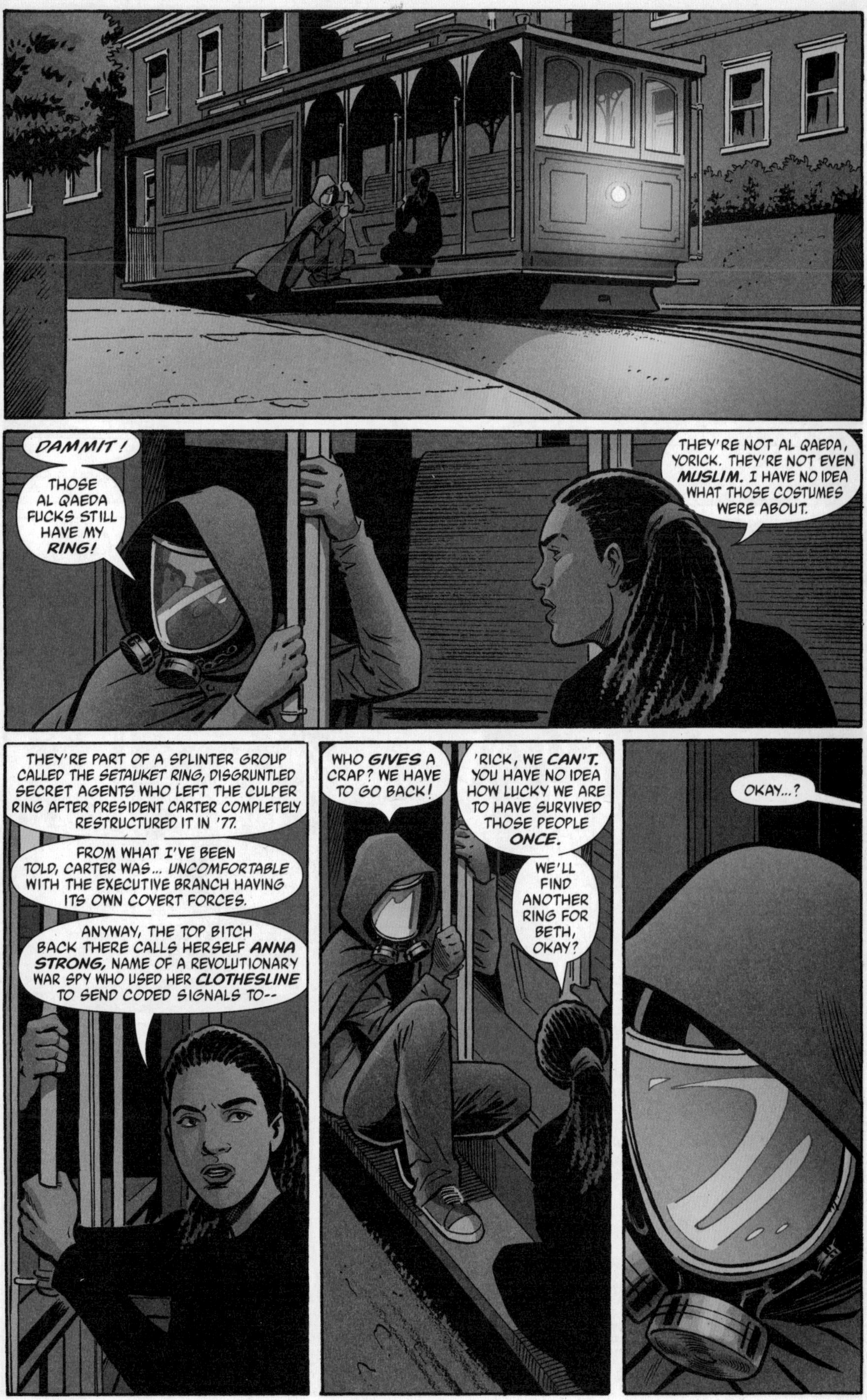
DAMMIT!
THOSE AL QAEDA FUCKS STILL HAVE MY RING!
THEY'RE NOT AL QAEDA, YORICK. THEY'RE NOT EVEN MUSLIM. I HAVE NO IDEA WHAT THOSE COSTUMES WERE ABOUT.
THEY'RE PART OF A SPLINTER GROUP CALLED THE SETAUKET RING, DISGRUNTLED SECRET AGENTS WHO LEFT THE CULPER RING AFTER PRESIDENT CARTER COMPLETELY RESTRUCTURED IT IN '77.
FROM WHAT I'VE BEEN TOLD, CARTER WAS... UNCOMFORTABLE WITH THE EXECUTIVE BRANCH HAVING ITS OWN COVERT FORCES.
ANYWAY, THE TOP BITCH BACK THERE CALLS HERSELF ANNA STRONG, NAME OF A REVOLUTIONARY WAR SPY WHO USED HER CLOTHESLINE TO SEND CODED SIGNALS TO--
WHO GIVES A CRAP? WE HAVE TO GO BACK!
'RICK, WE CAN'T. YOU HAVE NO IDEA HOW LUCKY WE ARE TO HAVE SURVIVED THOSE PEOPLE ONCE.
WE'LL FIND ANOTHER RING FOR BETH, OKAY?
OKAY...?

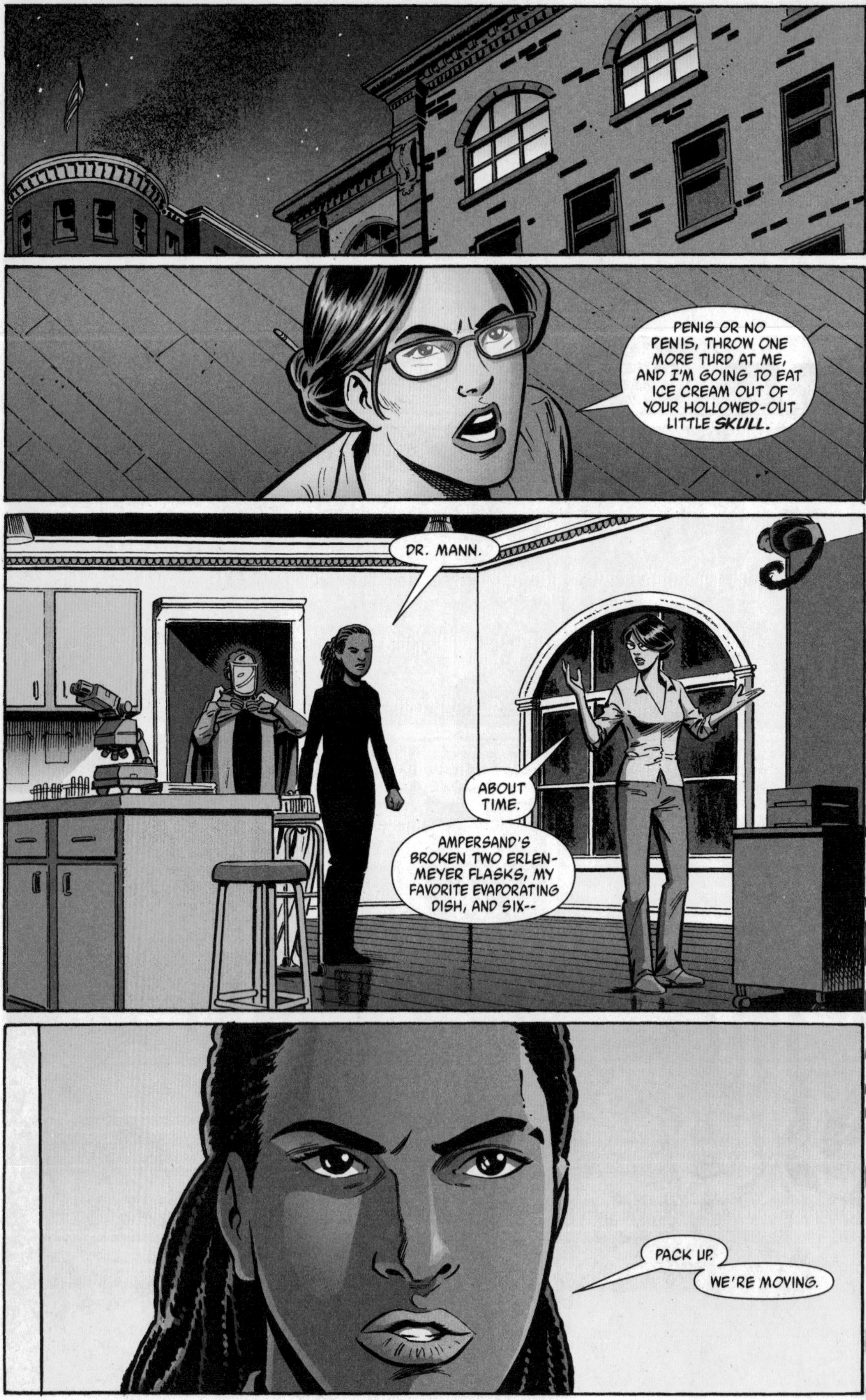
PENIS OR NO PENIS, THROW ONE MORE TURD AT ME, AND I'M GOING TO EAT ICE CREAM OUT OF YOUR HOLLOWED-OUT LITTLE SKULL.
DR. MANN.
ABOUT TIME.
AMPERSAND'S BROKEN TWO ERLEN-MEYER FLASKS, MY FAVORITE EVAPORATING DISH, AND SIX--
PACK UP.
WE'RE MOVING.

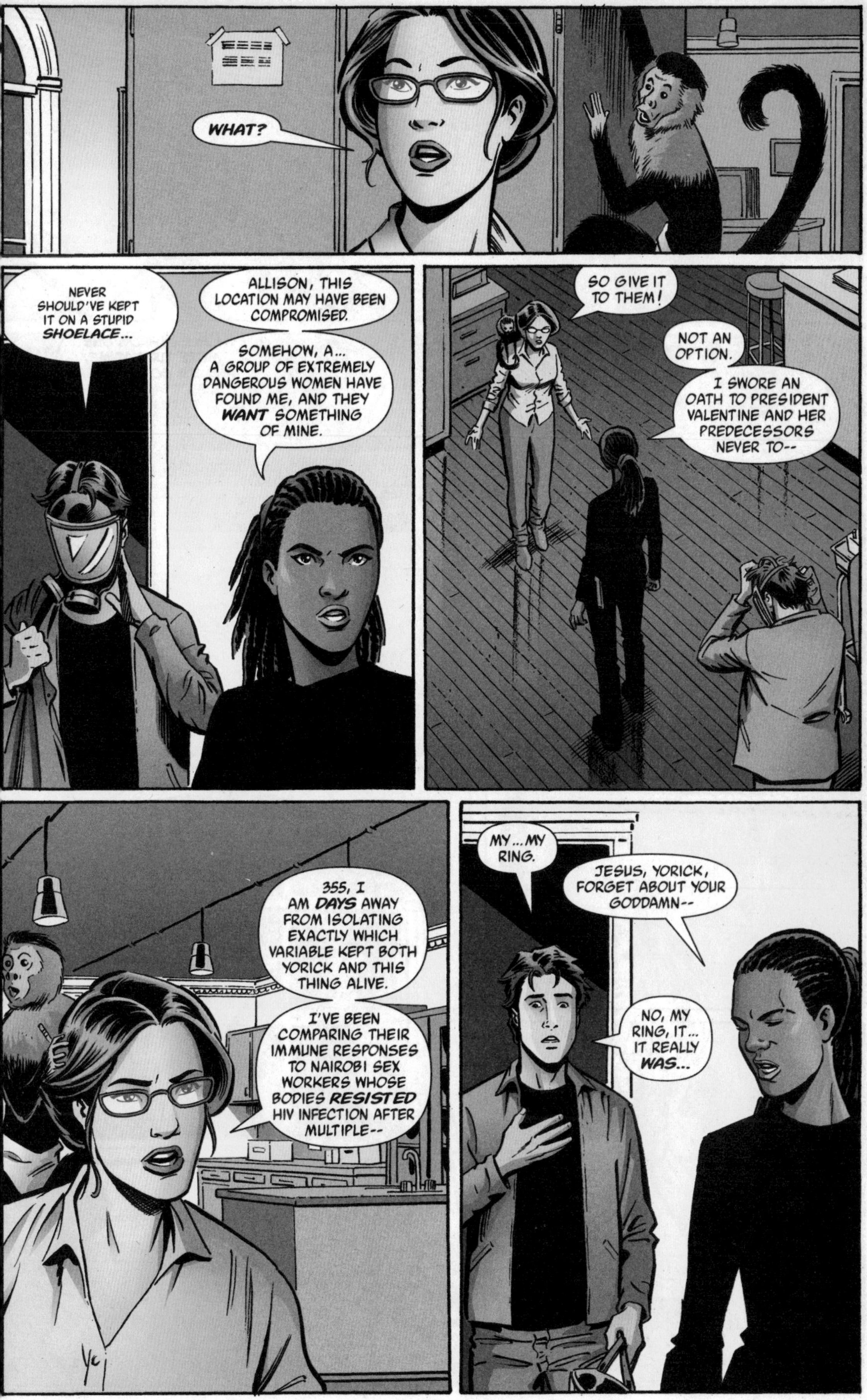
WHAT?
NEVER SHOULD'VE KEPT IT ON A STUPID SHOELACE...
ALLISON, THIS LOCATION MAY HAVE BEEN COMPROMISED.
SOMEHOW, A... A GROUP OF EXTREMELY DANGEROUS WOMEN HAVE FOUND ME, AND THEY WANT SOMETHING OF MINE.
SO GIVE IT TO THEM!
NOT AN OPTION.
I SWORE AN OATH TO PRESIDENT VALENTINE AND HER PREDECESSORS NEVER TO--
355, I AM DAYS AWAY FROM ISOLATING EXACTLY WHICH VARIABLE KEPT BOTH YORICK AND THIS THING ALIVE.
I'VE BEEN COMPARING THEIR IMMUNE RESPONSES TO NAIROBI SEX WORKERS WHOSE BODIES RESISTED HIV INFECTION AFTER MULTIPLE--
MY... MY RING.
JESUS, YORICK, FORGET ABOUT YOUR GODDAMN--
NO, MY RING, IT... IT REALLY WAS...

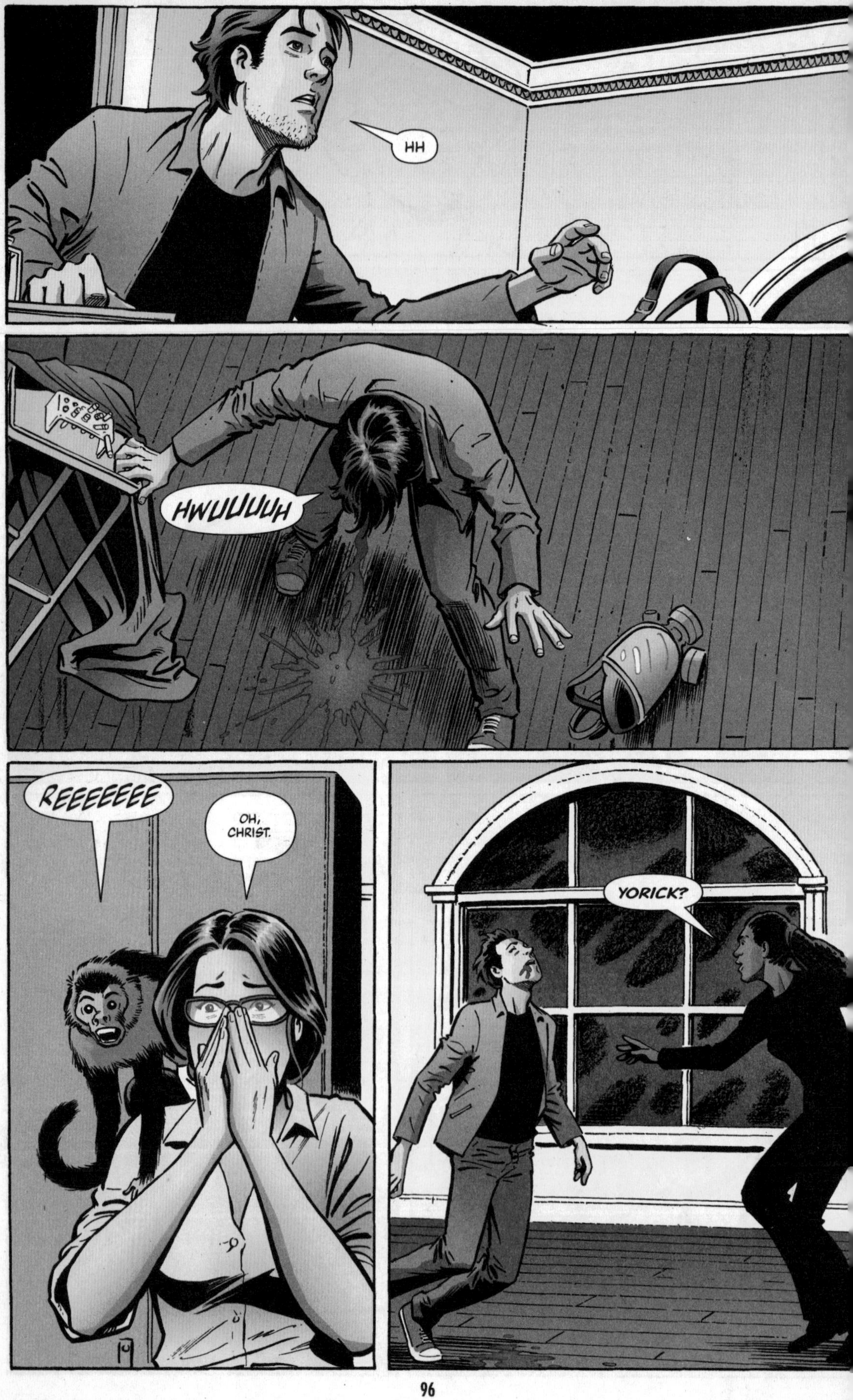
HH
HWUUUUH
REEEEEEE
OH, CHRIST.
YORICK?

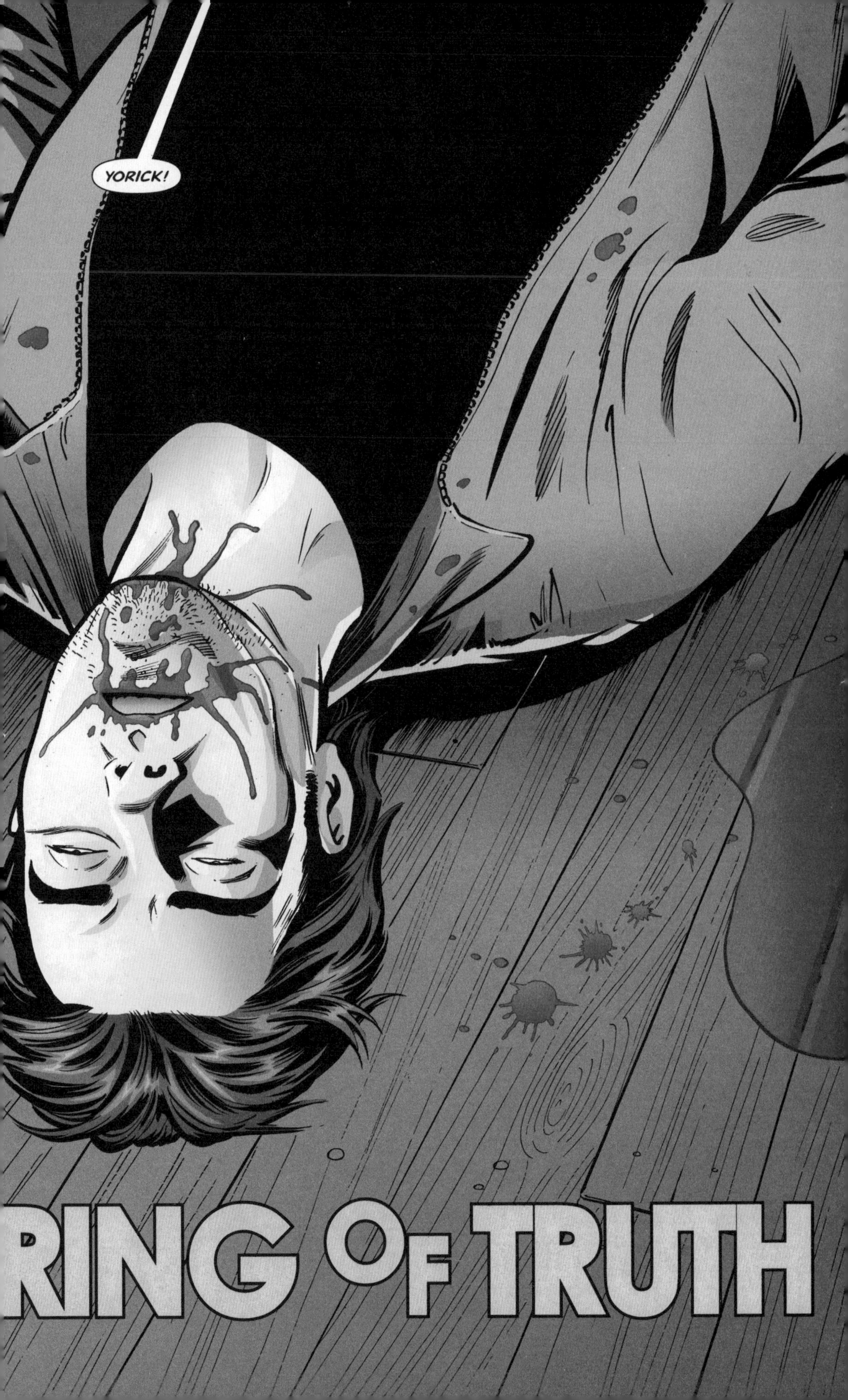
YORICK!
RING OF TRUTH

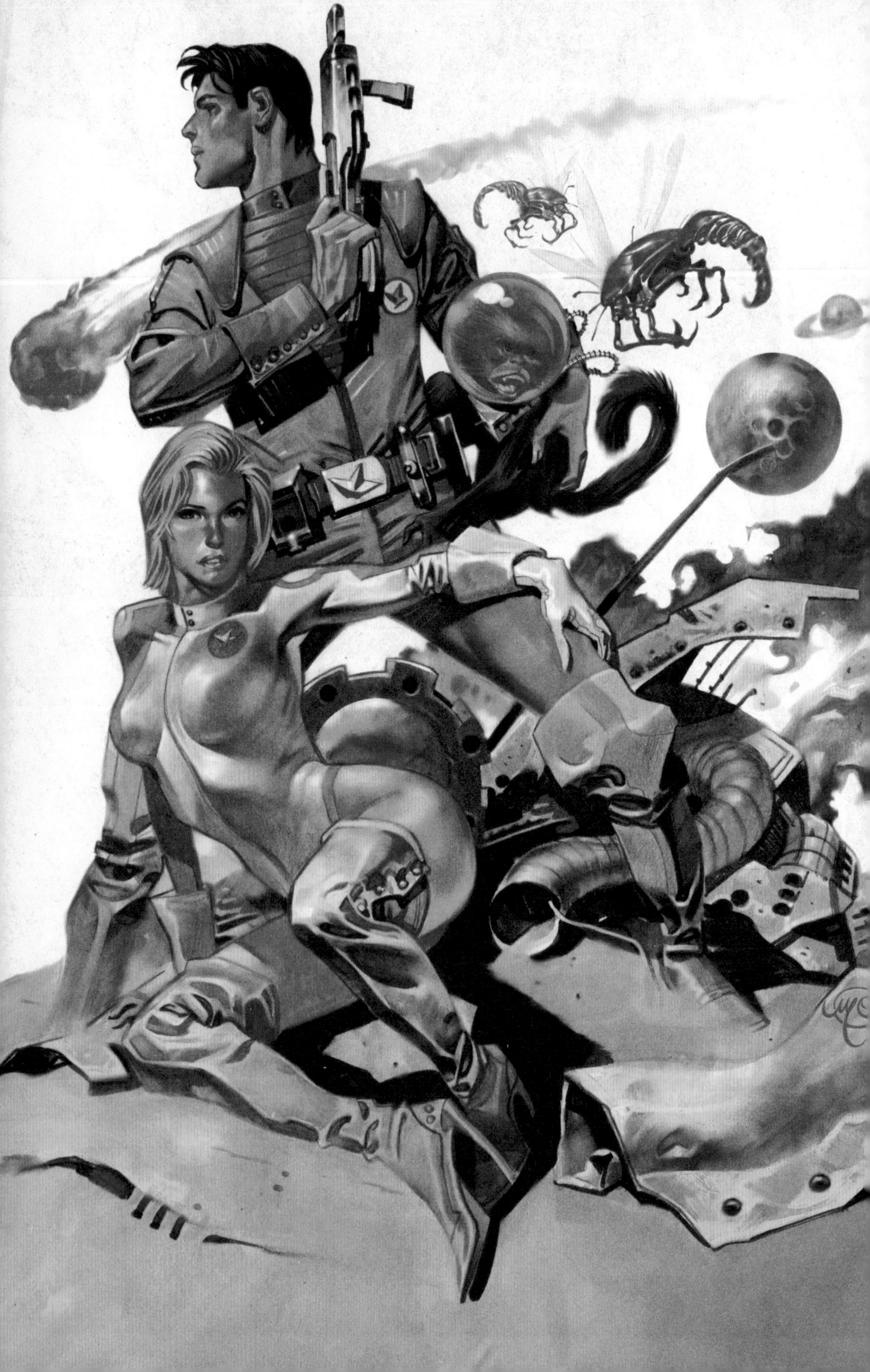

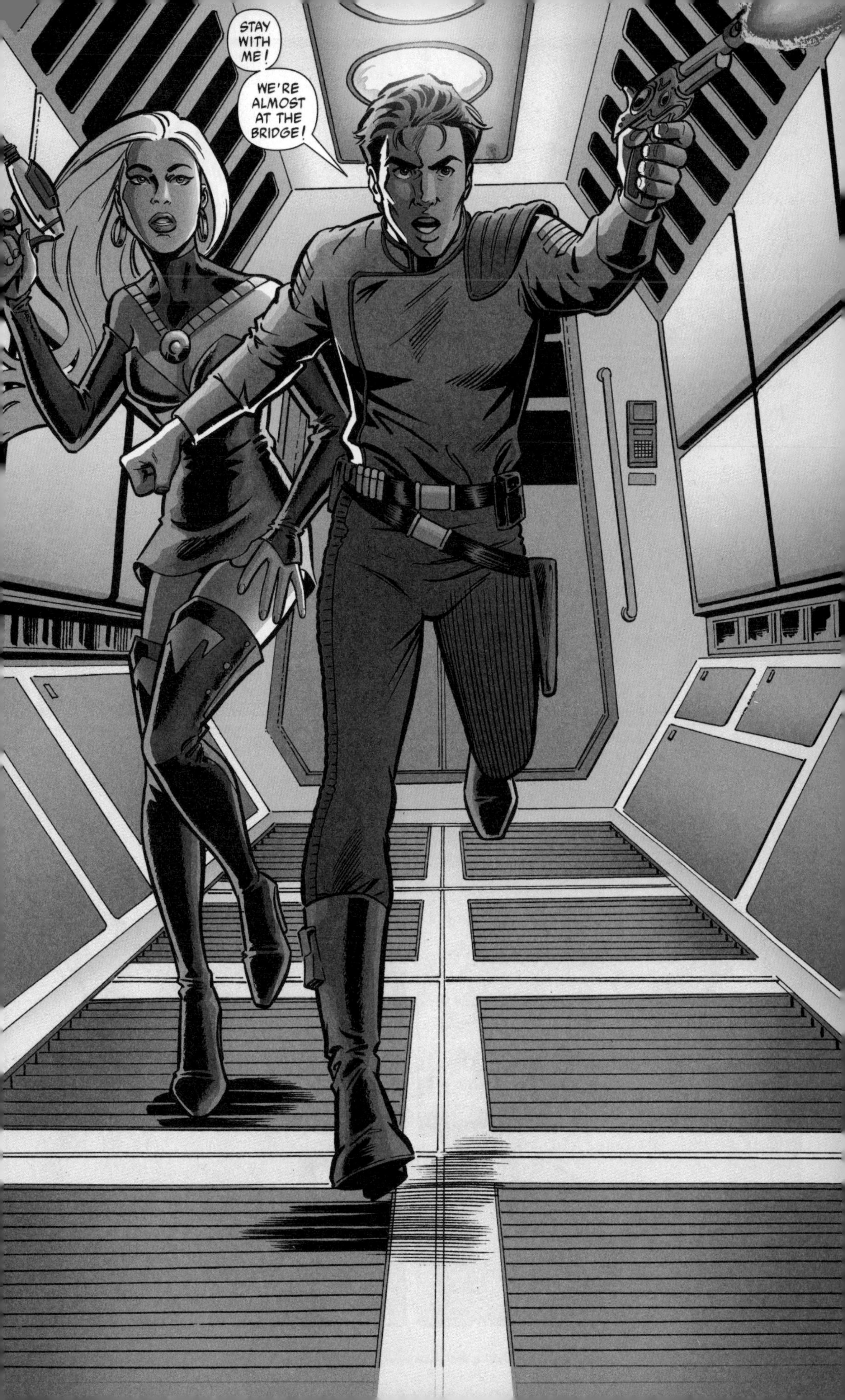
STAY WITH ME!
WE'RE ALMOST AT THE BRIDGE!

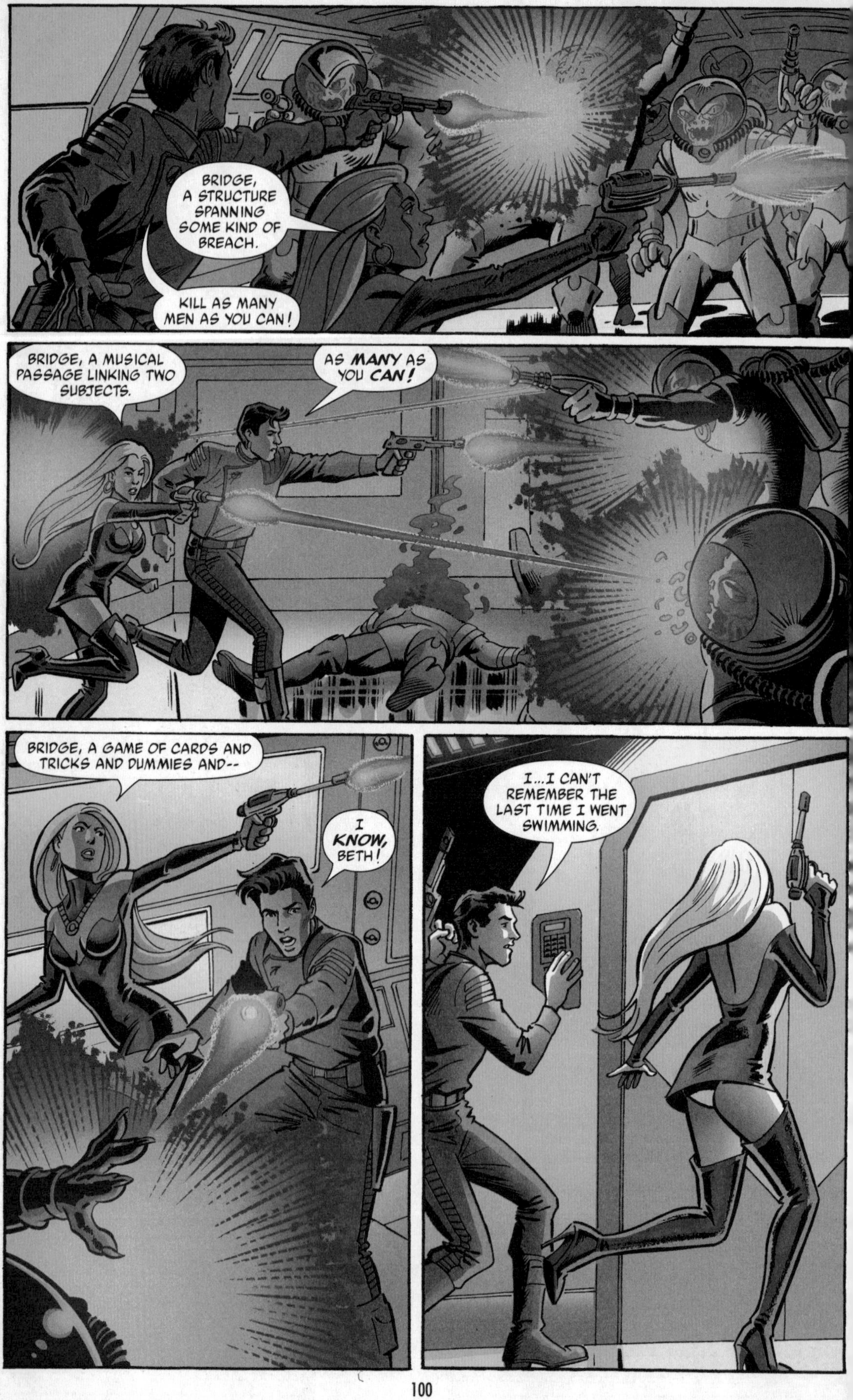
BRIDGE, A STRUCTURE SPANNING SOME KIND OF BREACH.
KILL AS MANY MEN AS YOU CAN!
BRIDGE, A MUSICAL PASSAGE LINKING TWO SUBJECTS.
AS MANY AS YOU CAN!
BRIDGE, A GAME OF CARDS AND TRICKS AND DUMMIES AND--
I KNOW, BETH!
I...I CAN'T REMEMBER THE LAST TIME I WENT SWIMMING.

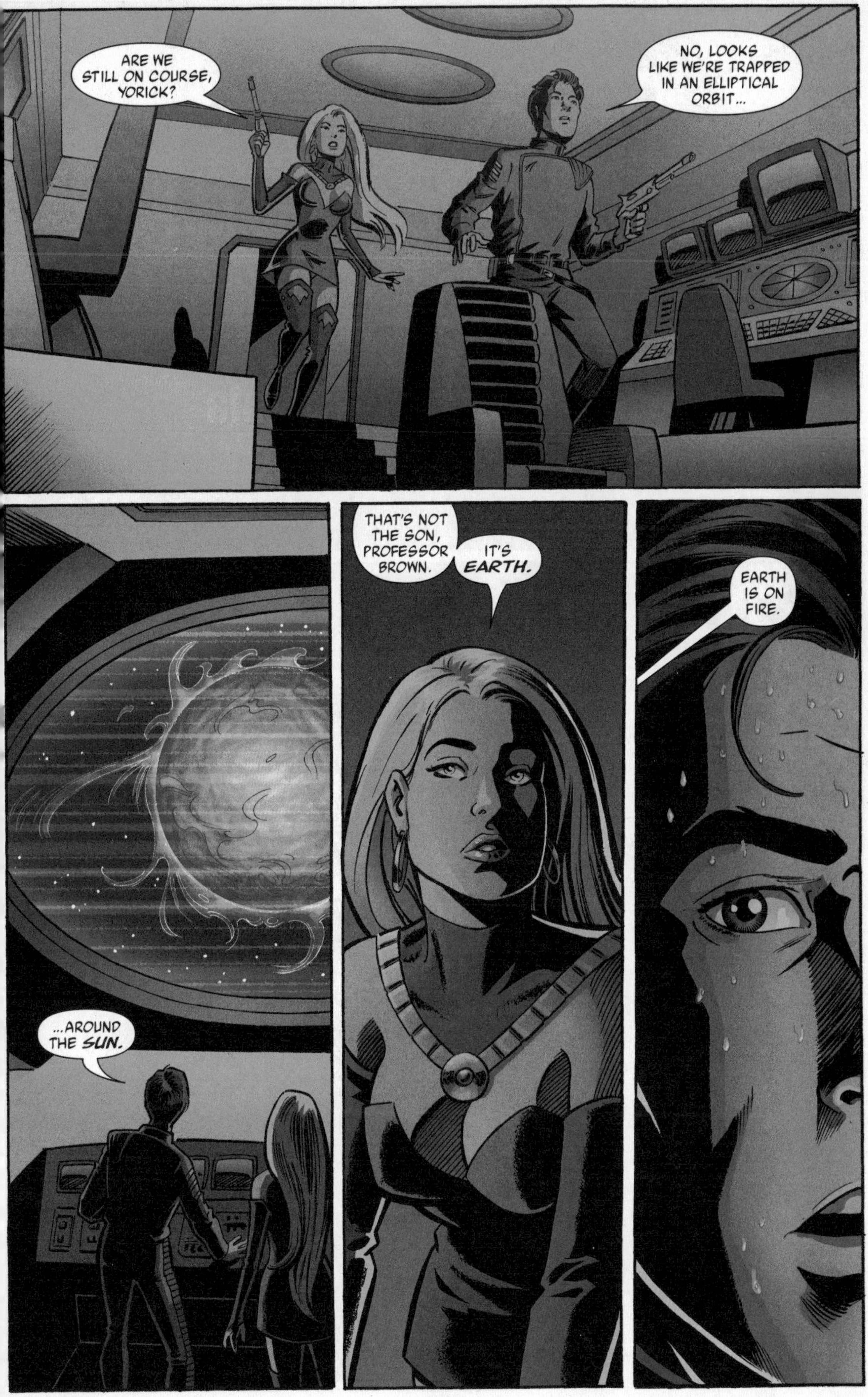
ARE WE STILL ON COURSE, YORICK?
NO, LOOKS LIKE WE'RE TRAPPED IN AN ELLIPTICAL ORBIT...
...AROUND THE SUN.
THAT'S NOT THE SON, PROFESSOR BROWN.
IT'S EARTH.
EARTH IS ON FIRE.

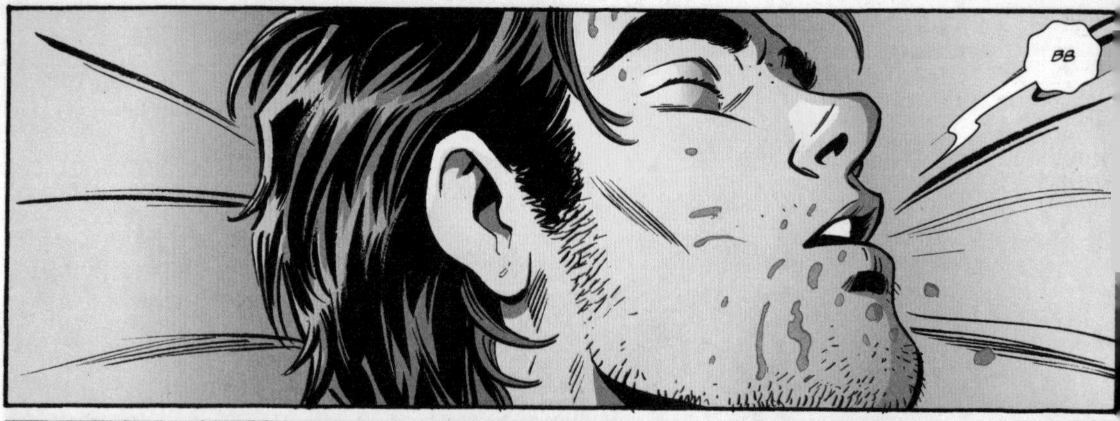
BB

San Francisco, California
Now

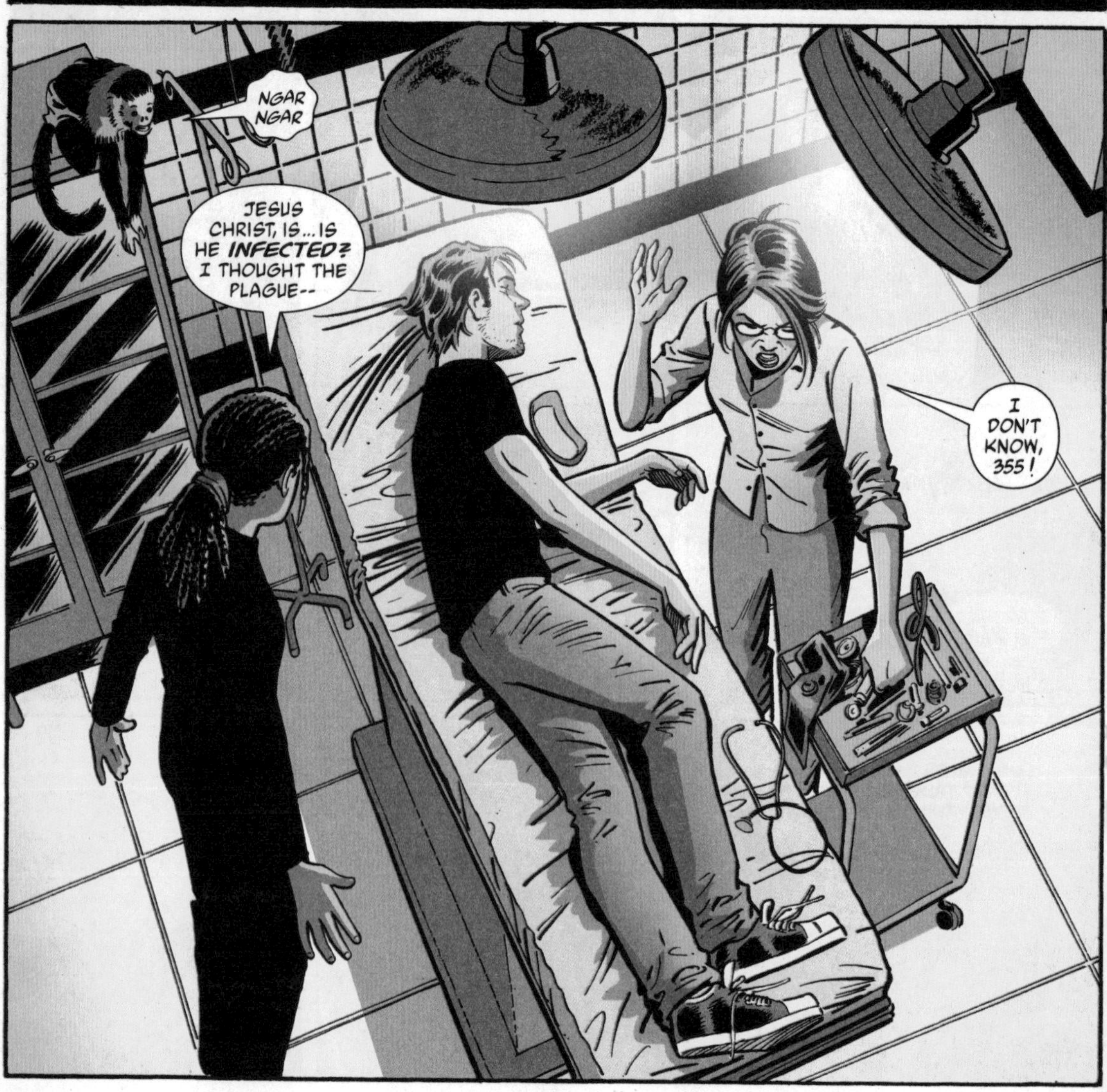
NGAR NGAR
JESUS CHRIST, IS...IS HE *INFECTED?* I THOUGHT THE PLAGUE--
I DON'T KNOW, 355!

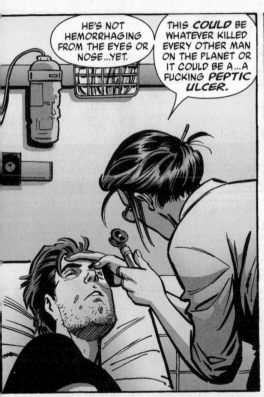

HE'S NOT HEMORRHAGING FROM THE EYES OR NOSE...YET.

THIS *COULD* BE WHATEVER KILLED EVERY OTHER MAN ON THE PLANET OR IT COULD BE A...A FUCKING *PEPTIC ULCER*.

EITHER WAY, HE'S PROBABLY GOING TO NEED BLOOD.

USE MINE. YORICK AND I ARE BOTH *O* POSITIVE. HIS MOTHER TOLD ME BACK IN--

NO, I'LL AUTO-TRANSFUSE, IF AND WHEN. I'VE GOT ENOUGH IN STORAGE, AND I DON'T WANT AN OUTSIDE SPECIMEN CONTAMINATING HIS--

HE'S NOT A GODDAMN *EXPERIMENT*, ALLISON!

JUST SAVE HIM!

RING...RING AROUND THE...

DON'T TRY TO TALK, 'RICK. EVERYTHING'S GOING TO BE--

HE'S RIGHT, YOU KNOW.

YOU *HAVE* TO FIND HIS RING.

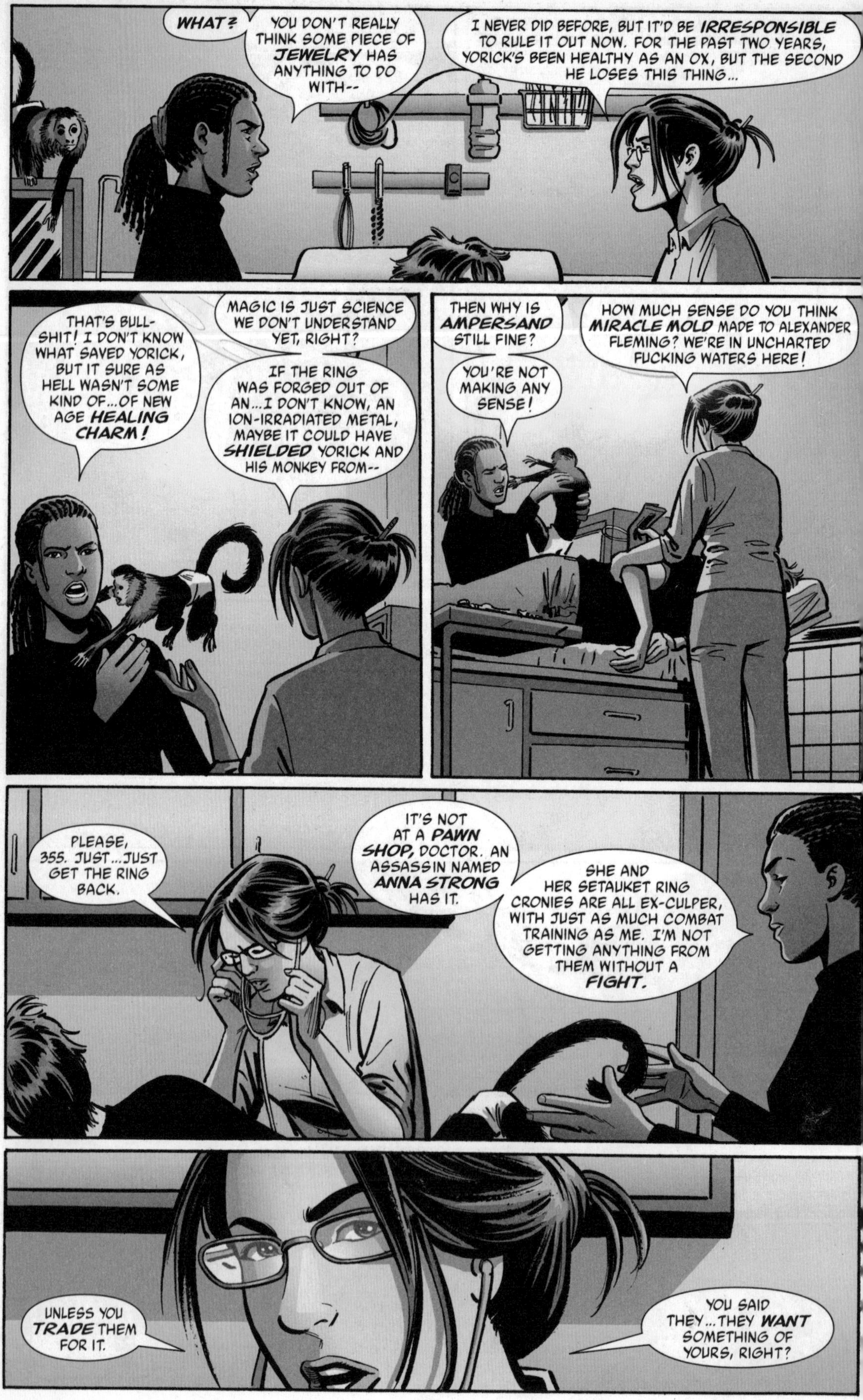
WHAT?
YOU DON'T REALLY THINK SOME PIECE OF JEWELRY HAS ANYTHING TO DO WITH--
I NEVER DID BEFORE, BUT IT'D BE IRRESPONSIBLE TO RULE IT OUT NOW. FOR THE PAST TWO YEARS, YORICK'S BEEN HEALTHY AS AN OX, BUT THE SECOND HE LOSES THIS THING...
THAT'S BULL-SHIT! I DON'T KNOW WHAT SAVED YORICK, BUT IT SURE AS HELL WASN'T SOME KIND OF...OF NEW AGE HEALING CHARM!
MAGIC IS JUST SCIENCE WE DON'T UNDERSTAND YET, RIGHT?
IF THE RING WAS FORGED OUT OF AN...I DON'T KNOW, AN ION-IRRADIATED METAL, MAYBE IT COULD HAVE SHIELDED YORICK AND HIS MONKEY FROM--
THEN WHY IS AMPERSAND STILL FINE?
YOU'RE NOT MAKING ANY SENSE!
HOW MUCH SENSE DO YOU THINK MIRACLE MOLD MADE TO ALEXANDER FLEMING? WE'RE IN UNCHARTED FUCKING WATERS HERE!
PLEASE, 355. JUST...JUST GET THE RING BACK.
IT'S NOT AT A PAWN SHOP, DOCTOR. AN ASSASSIN NAMED ANNA STRONG HAS IT.
SHE AND HER SETAUKET RING CRONIES ARE ALL EX-CULPER, WITH JUST AS MUCH COMBAT TRAINING AS ME. I'M NOT GETTING ANYTHING FROM THEM WITHOUT A FIGHT.
YOU SAID THEY...THEY WANT SOMETHING OF YOURS, RIGHT?
UNLESS YOU TRADE THEM FOR IT.

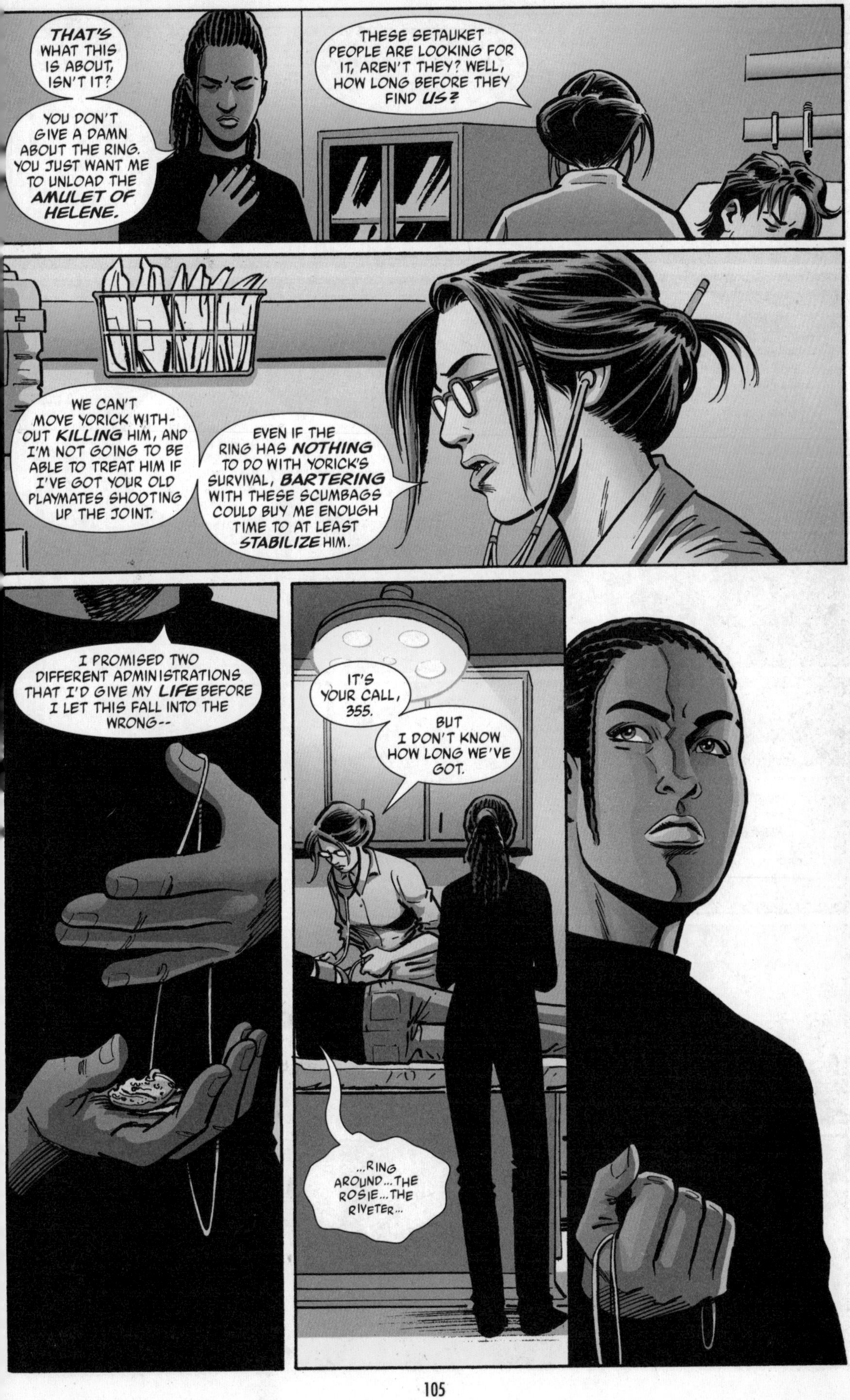
THAT'S WHAT THIS IS ABOUT, ISN'T IT?
YOU DON'T GIVE A DAMN ABOUT THE RING. YOU JUST WANT ME TO UNLOAD THE AMULET OF HELENE.
THESE SETAUKET PEOPLE ARE LOOKING FOR IT, AREN'T THEY? WELL, HOW LONG BEFORE THEY FIND US?
WE CAN'T MOVE YORICK WITHOUT KILLING HIM, AND I'M NOT GOING TO BE ABLE TO TREAT HIM IF I'VE GOT YOUR OLD PLAYMATES SHOOTING UP THE JOINT.
EVEN IF THE RING HAS NOTHING TO DO WITH YORICK'S SURVIVAL, BARTERING WITH THESE SCUMBAGS COULD BUY ME ENOUGH TIME TO AT LEAST STABILIZE HIM.
I PROMISED TWO DIFFERENT ADMINISTRATIONS THAT I'D GIVE MY LIFE BEFORE I LET THIS FALL INTO THE WRONG--
IT'S YOUR CALL, 355.
BUT I DON'T KNOW HOW LONG WE'VE GOT.
...RING AROUND...THE ROSIE...THE RIVETER...

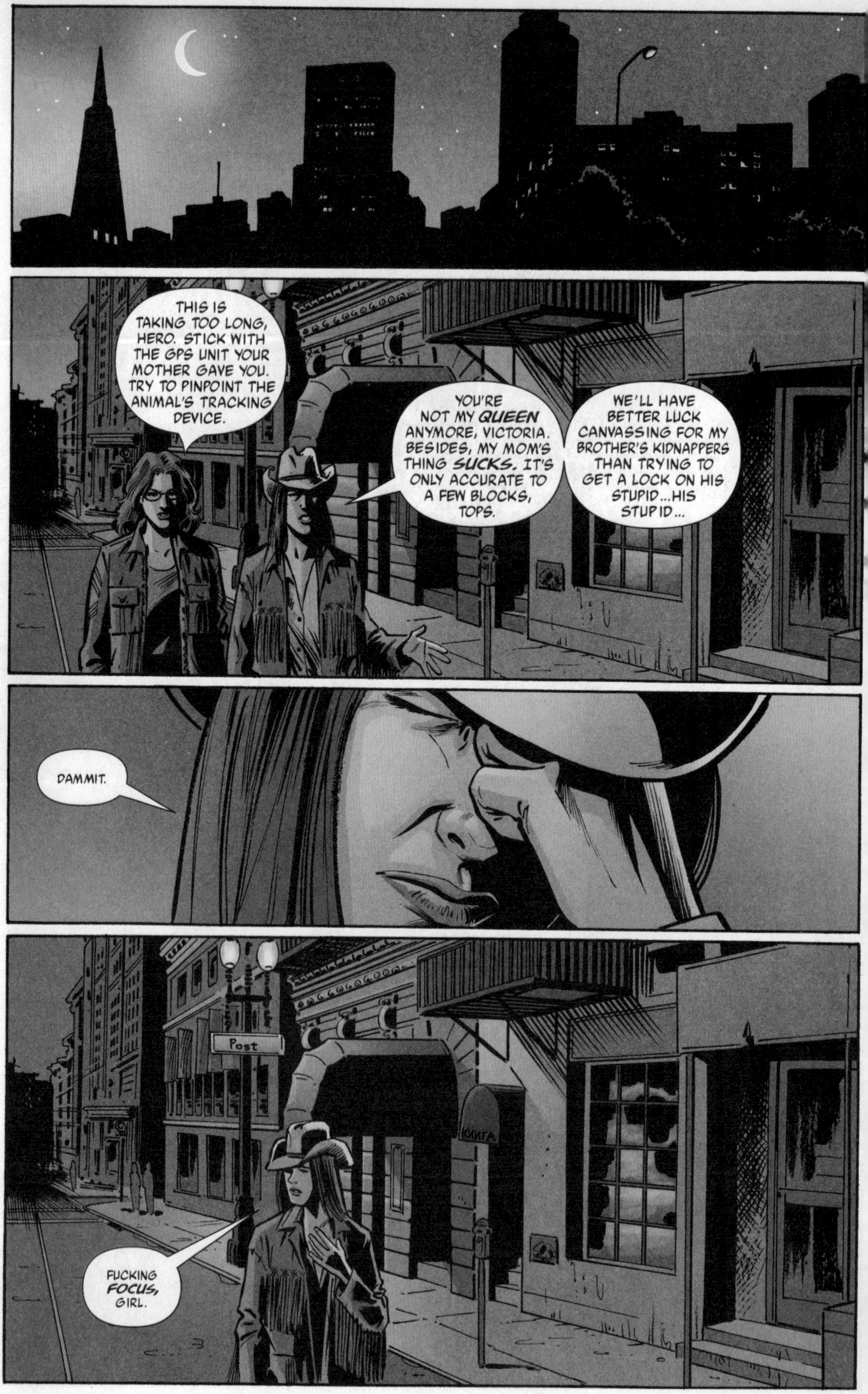
THIS IS TAKING TOO LONG, HERO. STICK WITH THE GPS UNIT YOUR MOTHER GAVE YOU. TRY TO PINPOINT THE ANIMAL'S TRACKING DEVICE.
YOU'RE NOT MY QUEEN ANYMORE, VICTORIA. BESIDES, MY MOM'S THING SUCKS. IT'S ONLY ACCURATE TO A FEW BLOCKS, TOPS.
WE'LL HAVE BETTER LUCK CANVASSING FOR MY BROTHER'S KIDNAPPERS THAN TRYING TO GET A LOCK ON HIS STUPID...HIS STUPID...
DAMMIT.
Post
FUCKING FOCUS, GIRL.

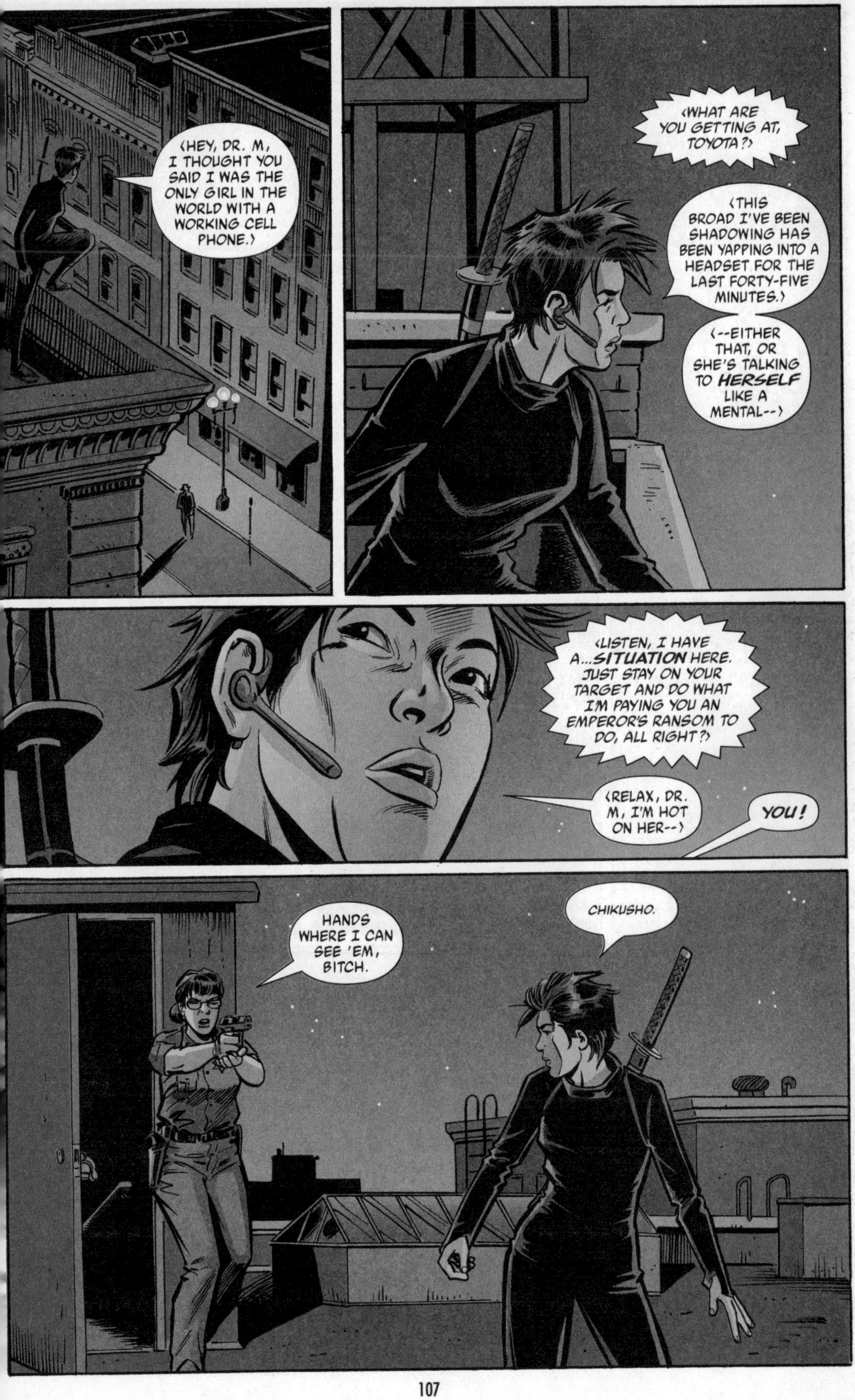
‹HEY, DR. M, I THOUGHT YOU SAID I WAS THE ONLY GIRL IN THE WORLD WITH A WORKING CELL PHONE.›
‹WHAT ARE YOU GETTING AT, TOYOTA?›
‹THIS BROAD I'VE BEEN SHADOWING HAS BEEN YAPPING INTO A HEADSET FOR THE LAST FORTY-FIVE MINUTES.›
‹--EITHER THAT, OR SHE'S TALKING TO **HERSELF** LIKE A MENTAL--›
‹LISTEN, I HAVE A...**SITUATION** HERE. JUST STAY ON YOUR TARGET AND DO WHAT I'M PAYING YOU AN EMPEROR'S RANSOM TO DO, ALL RIGHT?›
‹RELAX, DR. M, I'M HOT ON HER--›
YOU!
HANDS WHERE I CAN SEE 'EM, BITCH.
CHIKUSHO.

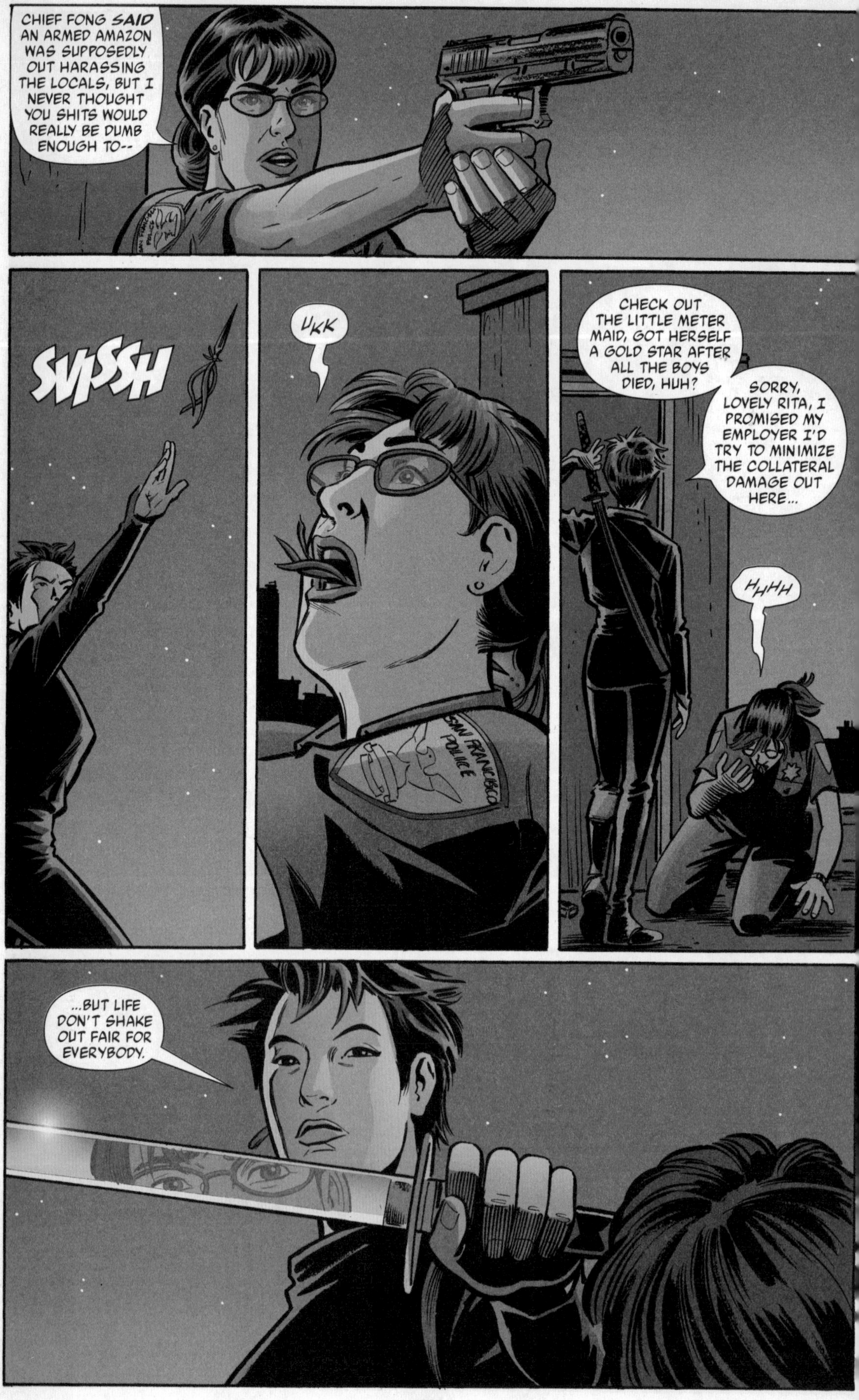
CHIEF FONG SAID AN ARMED AMAZON WAS SUPPOSEDLY OUT HARASSING THE LOCALS, BUT I NEVER THOUGHT YOU SHITS WOULD REALLY BE DUMB ENOUGH TO--
SVISSH
UKK
CHECK OUT THE LITTLE METER MAID, GOT HERSELF A GOLD STAR AFTER ALL THE BOYS DIED, HUH?
SORRY, LOVELY RITA, I PROMISED MY EMPLOYER I'D TRY TO MINIMIZE THE COLLATERAL DAMAGE OUT HERE...
HHHH
...BUT LIFE DON'T SHAKE OUT FAIR FOR EVERYBODY.

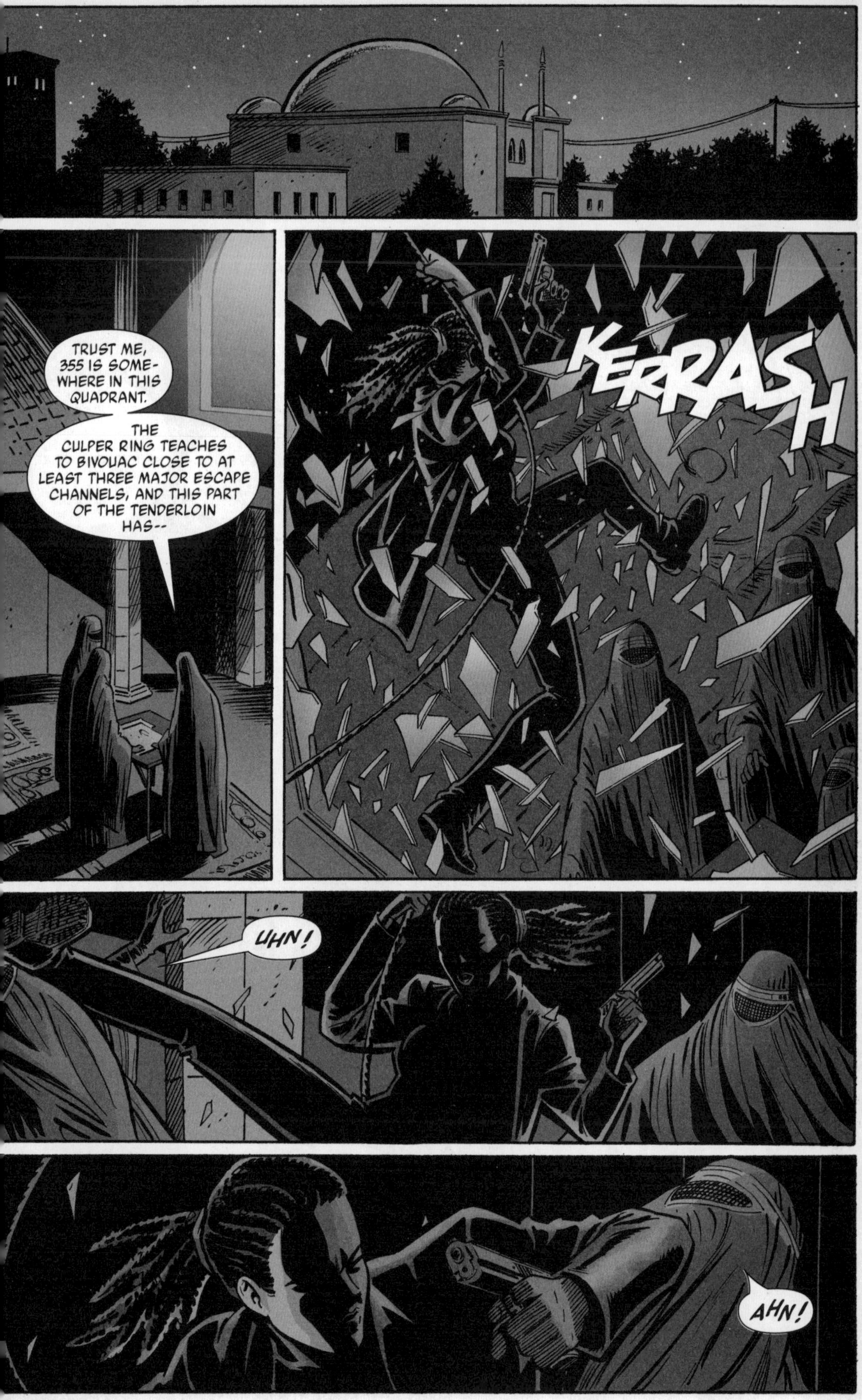
TRUST ME, 355 IS SOMEWHERE IN THIS QUADRANT.
THE CULPER RING TEACHES TO BIVOUAC CLOSE TO AT LEAST THREE MAJOR ESCAPE CHANNELS, AND THIS PART OF THE TENDERLOIN HAS--
KERRASH
UHN!
AHN!

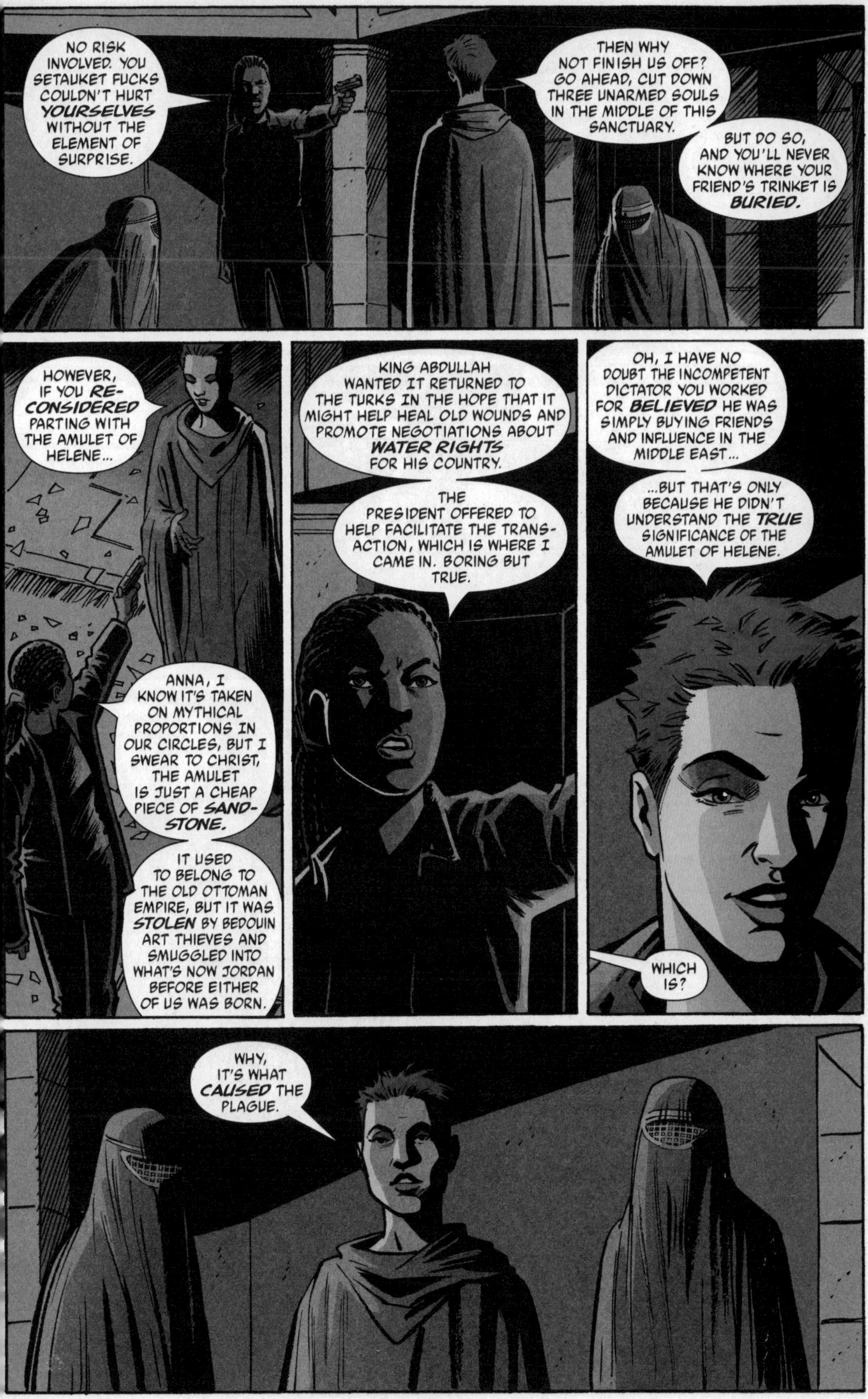
NO RISK INVOLVED. YOU SETAUKET FUCKS COULDN'T HURT YOURSELVES WITHOUT THE ELEMENT OF SURPRISE.
THEN WHY NOT FINISH US OFF? GO AHEAD, CUT DOWN THREE UNARMED SOULS IN THE MIDDLE OF THIS SANCTUARY.
BUT DO SO, AND YOU'LL NEVER KNOW WHERE YOUR FRIEND'S TRINKET IS BURIED.
HOWEVER, IF YOU RE-CONSIDERED PARTING WITH THE AMULET OF HELENE...
ANNA, I KNOW IT'S TAKEN ON MYTHICAL PROPORTIONS IN OUR CIRCLES, BUT I SWEAR TO CHRIST, THE AMULET IS JUST A CHEAP PIECE OF SAND-STONE.
IT USED TO BELONG TO THE OLD OTTOMAN EMPIRE, BUT IT WAS STOLEN BY BEDOUIN ART THIEVES AND SMUGGLED INTO WHAT'S NOW JORDAN BEFORE EITHER OF US WAS BORN.
KING ABDULLAH WANTED IT RETURNED TO THE TURKS IN THE HOPE THAT IT MIGHT HELP HEAL OLD WOUNDS AND PROMOTE NEGOTIATIONS ABOUT WATER RIGHTS FOR HIS COUNTRY.
THE PRESIDENT OFFERED TO HELP FACILITATE THE TRANS-ACTION, WHICH IS WHERE I CAME IN. BORING BUT TRUE.
OH, I HAVE NO DOUBT THE INCOMPETENT DICTATOR YOU WORKED FOR BELIEVED HE WAS SIMPLY BUYING FRIENDS AND INFLUENCE IN THE MIDDLE EAST...
...BUT THAT'S ONLY BECAUSE HE DIDN'T UNDERSTAND THE TRUE SIGNIFICANCE OF THE AMULET OF HELENE.
WHICH IS?
WHY, IT'S WHAT CAUSED THE PLAGUE.

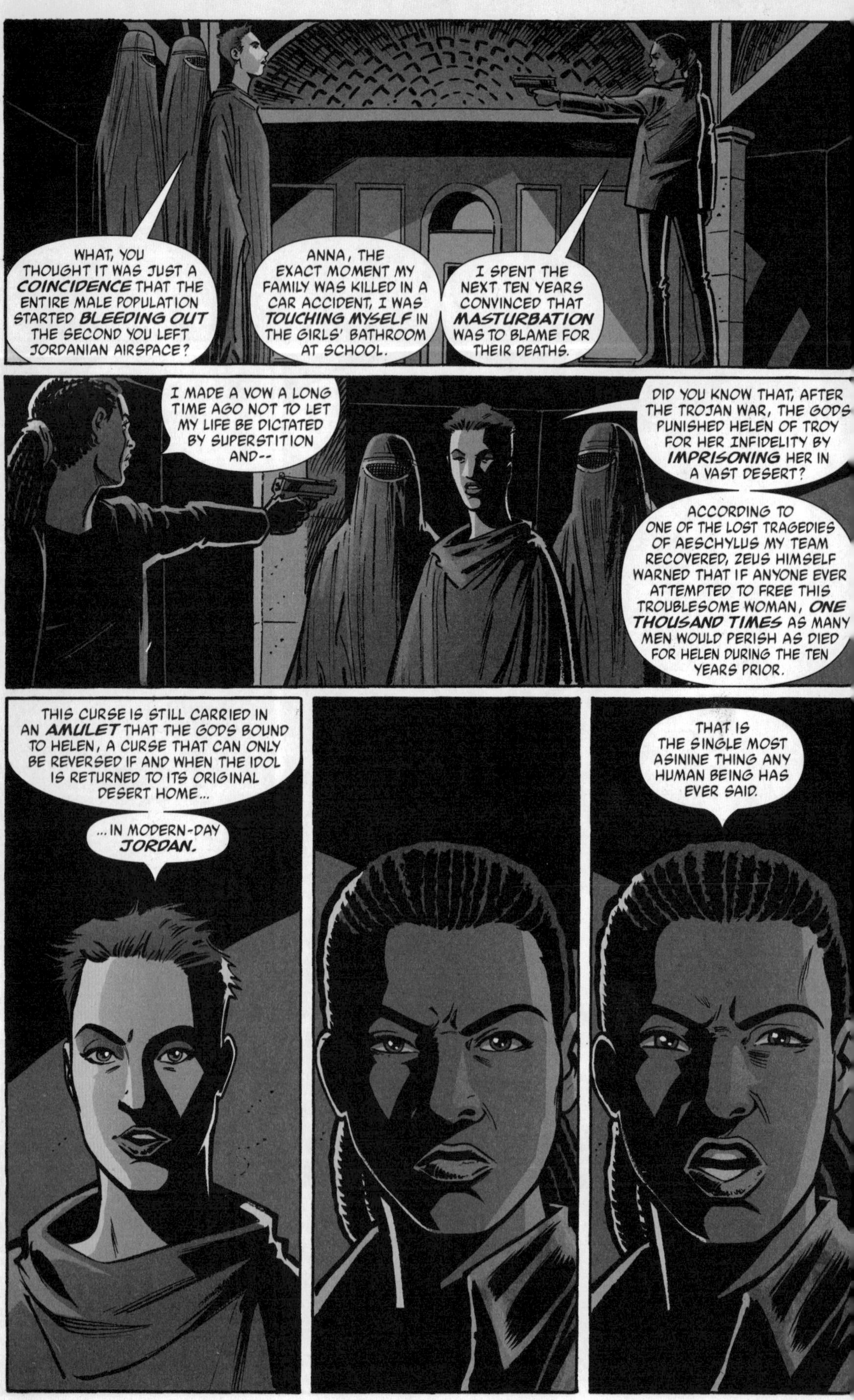
WHAT, YOU THOUGHT IT WAS JUST A COINCIDENCE THAT THE ENTIRE MALE POPULATION STARTED BLEEDING OUT THE SECOND YOU LEFT JORDANIAN AIRSPACE?
ANNA, THE EXACT MOMENT MY FAMILY WAS KILLED IN A CAR ACCIDENT, I WAS TOUCHING MYSELF IN THE GIRLS' BATHROOM AT SCHOOL.
I SPENT THE NEXT TEN YEARS CONVINCED THAT MASTURBATION WAS TO BLAME FOR THEIR DEATHS.
I MADE A VOW A LONG TIME AGO NOT TO LET MY LIFE BE DICTATED BY SUPERSTITION AND--
DID YOU KNOW THAT, AFTER THE TROJAN WAR, THE GODS PUNISHED HELEN OF TROY FOR HER INFIDELITY BY IMPRISONING HER IN A VAST DESERT?
ACCORDING TO ONE OF THE LOST TRAGEDIES OF AESCHYLUS MY TEAM RECOVERED, ZEUS HIMSELF WARNED THAT IF ANYONE EVER ATTEMPTED TO FREE THIS TROUBLESOME WOMAN, ONE THOUSAND TIMES AS MANY MEN WOULD PERISH AS DIED FOR HELEN DURING THE TEN YEARS PRIOR.
THIS CURSE IS STILL CARRIED IN AN AMULET THAT THE GODS BOUND TO HELEN, A CURSE THAT CAN ONLY BE REVERSED IF AND WHEN THE IDOL IS RETURNED TO ITS ORIGINAL DESERT HOME...
...IN MODERN-DAY JORDAN.
THAT IS THE SINGLE MOST ASININE THING ANY HUMAN BEING HAS EVER SAID.

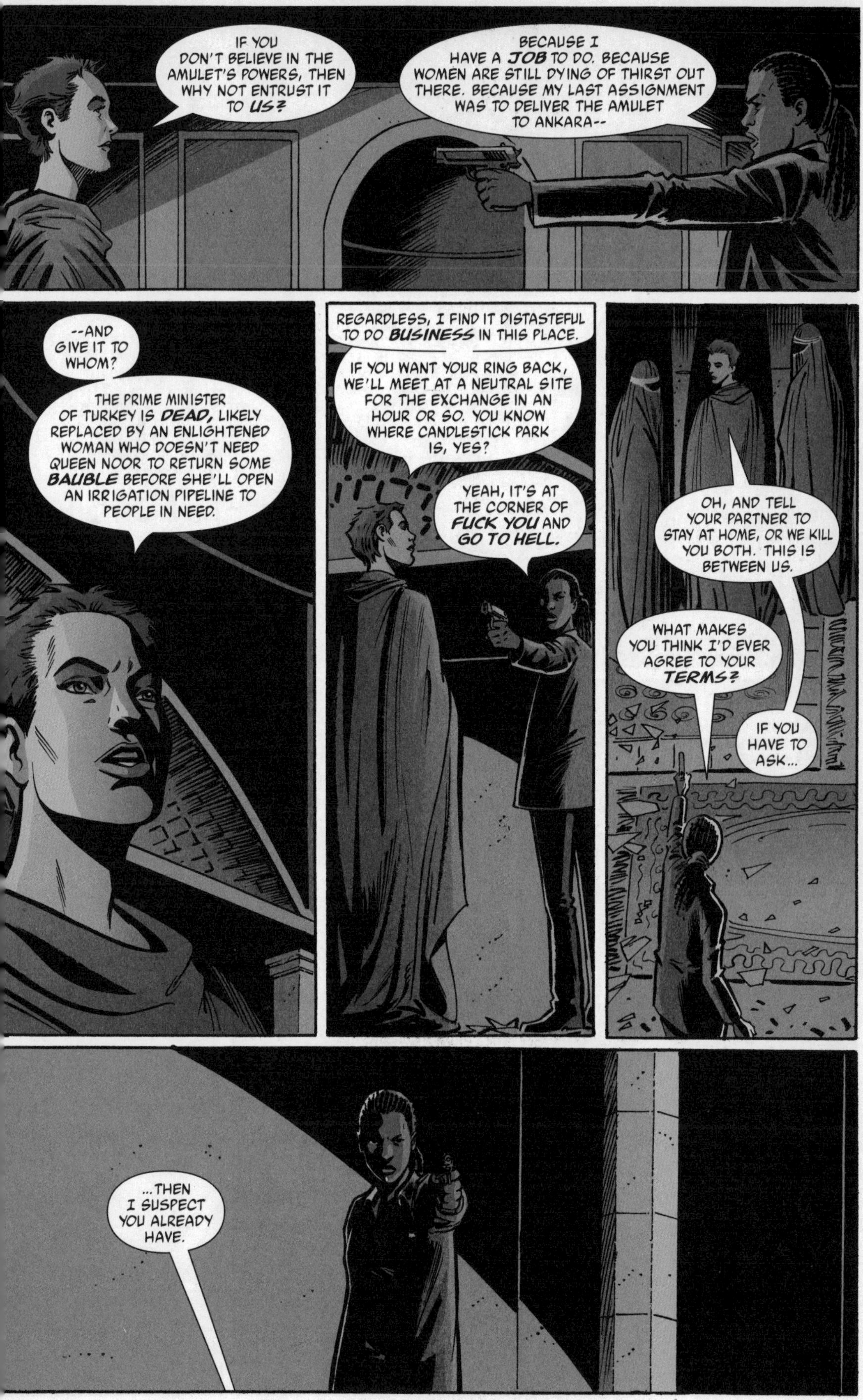
IF YOU DON'T BELIEVE IN THE AMULET'S POWERS, THEN WHY NOT ENTRUST IT TO US?
BECAUSE I HAVE A JOB TO DO. BECAUSE WOMEN ARE STILL DYING OF THIRST OUT THERE. BECAUSE MY LAST ASSIGNMENT WAS TO DELIVER THE AMULET TO ANKARA--
--AND GIVE IT TO WHOM?
THE PRIME MINISTER OF TURKEY IS DEAD, LIKELY REPLACED BY AN ENLIGHTENED WOMAN WHO DOESN'T NEED QUEEN NOOR TO RETURN SOME BAUBLE BEFORE SHE'LL OPEN AN IRRIGATION PIPELINE TO PEOPLE IN NEED.
REGARDLESS, I FIND IT DISTASTEFUL TO DO BUSINESS IN THIS PLACE.
IF YOU WANT YOUR RING BACK, WE'LL MEET AT A NEUTRAL SITE FOR THE EXCHANGE IN AN HOUR OR SO. YOU KNOW WHERE CANDLESTICK PARK IS, YES?
YEAH, IT'S AT THE CORNER OF FUCK YOU AND GO TO HELL.
OH, AND TELL YOUR PARTNER TO STAY AT HOME, OR WE KILL YOU BOTH. THIS IS BETWEEN US.
WHAT MAKES YOU THINK I'D EVER AGREE TO YOUR TERMS?
IF YOU HAVE TO ASK...
...THEN I SUSPECT YOU ALREADY HAVE.

DOC...
DOCTOR...
MANN...?

I'M RIGHT HERE, YORICK.

I WAS, UH, JUST PUTTING AMP IN ISOLATION. DON'T WANT YOU CATCHING *MONKEYPOX*, TOO.

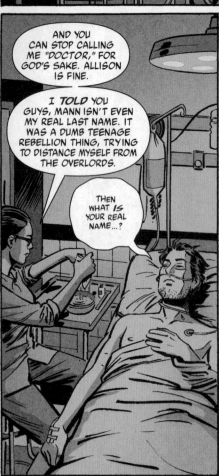

AND YOU CAN STOP CALLING ME "DOCTOR," FOR GOD'S SAKE. ALLISON IS FINE.

I *TOLD* YOU GUYS, MANN ISN'T EVEN MY REAL LAST NAME. IT WAS A DUMB TEENAGE REBELLION THING, TRYING TO DISTANCE MYSELF FROM THE OVERLORDS.

THEN WHAT *IS* YOUR REAL NAME...?

SORRY, SICKLY.

IT'S GONNA TAKE MORE THAN YOU PUKING UP YOUR SPLEEN TO GET THAT OUT OF ME.

COME ON...BACK IN 'ZONA... YOU SAID YOU'D ALWAYS TELL ME...THE *TRUTH*...

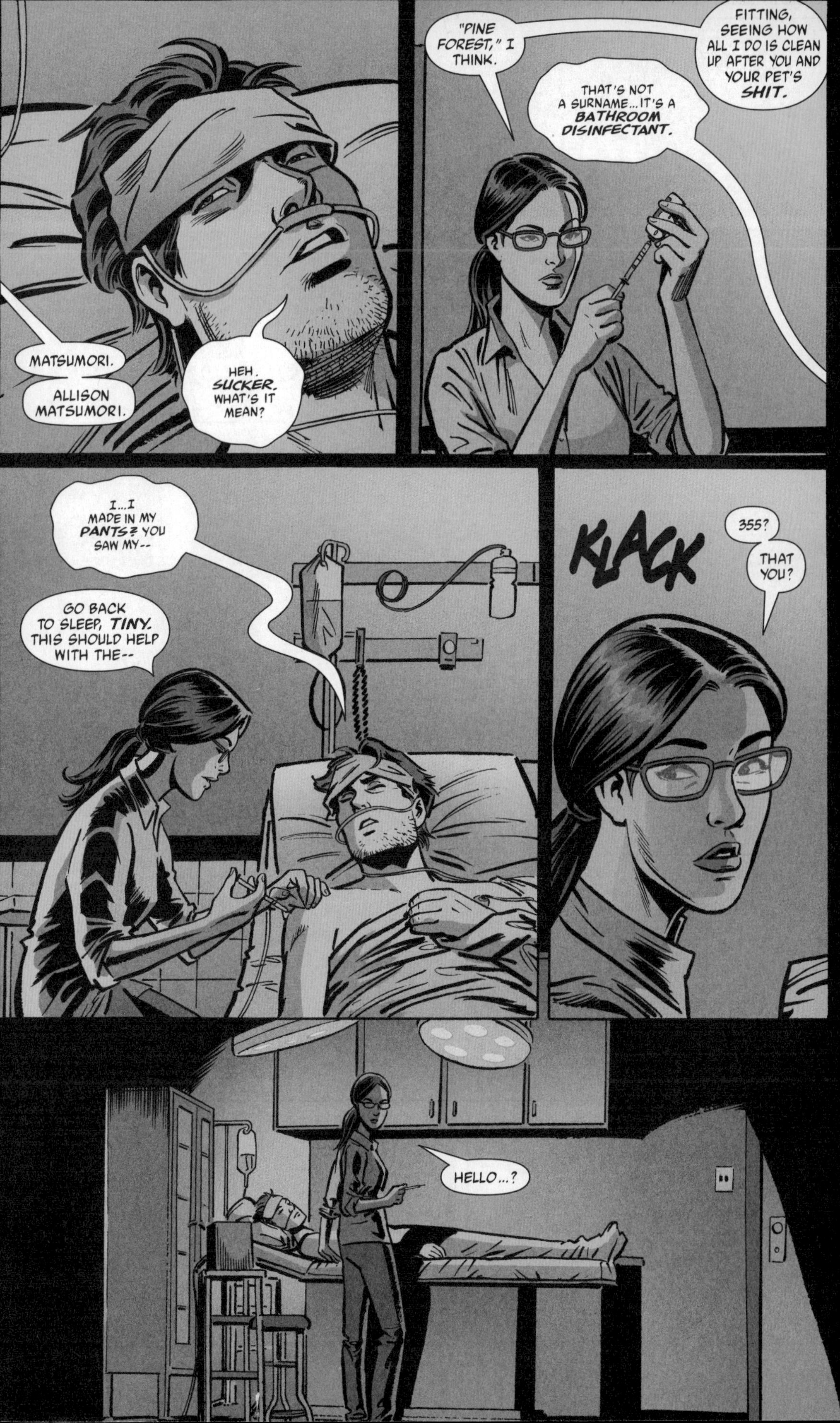
MATSUMORI.
ALLISON MATSUMORI.
HEH. SUCKER. WHAT'S IT MEAN?
"PINE FOREST," I THINK.
THAT'S NOT A SURNAME... IT'S A BATHROOM DISINFECTANT.
FITTING, SEEING HOW ALL I DO IS CLEAN UP AFTER YOU AND YOUR PET'S SHIT.
I...I MADE IN MY PANTS? YOU SAW MY--
GO BACK TO SLEEP, TINY. THIS SHOULD HELP WITH THE--
KLACK
355?
THAT YOU?
HELLO...?

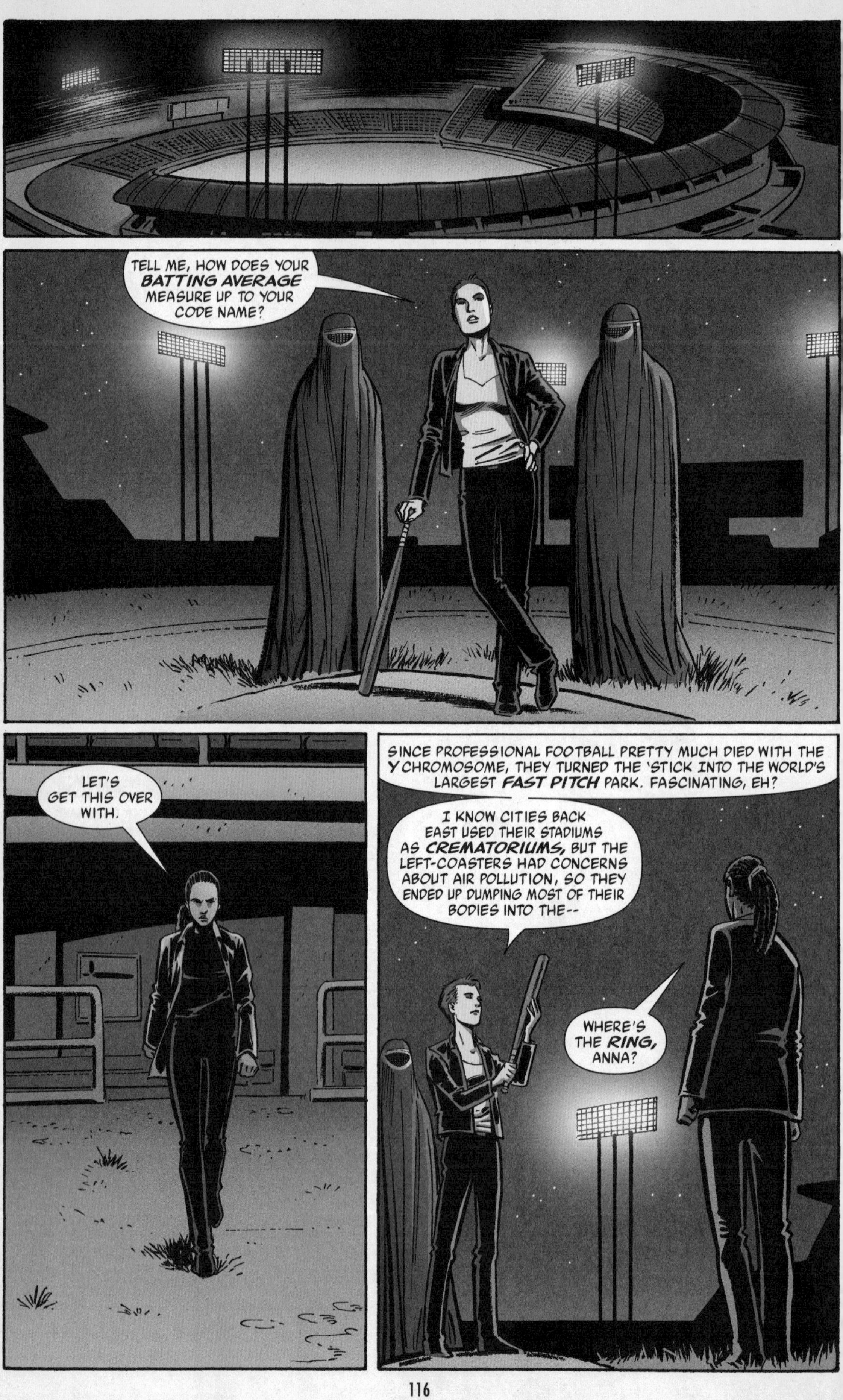
TELL ME, HOW DOES YOUR BATTING AVERAGE MEASURE UP TO YOUR CODE NAME?
LET'S GET THIS OVER WITH.
SINCE PROFESSIONAL FOOTBALL PRETTY MUCH DIED WITH THE Y CHROMOSOME, THEY TURNED THE 'STICK INTO THE WORLD'S LARGEST FAST PITCH PARK. FASCINATING, EH?
I KNOW CITIES BACK EAST USED THEIR STADIUMS AS CREMATORIUMS, BUT THE LEFT-COASTERS HAD CONCERNS ABOUT AIR POLLUTION, SO THEY ENDED UP DUMPING MOST OF THEIR BODIES INTO THE--
WHERE'S THE RING, ANNA?

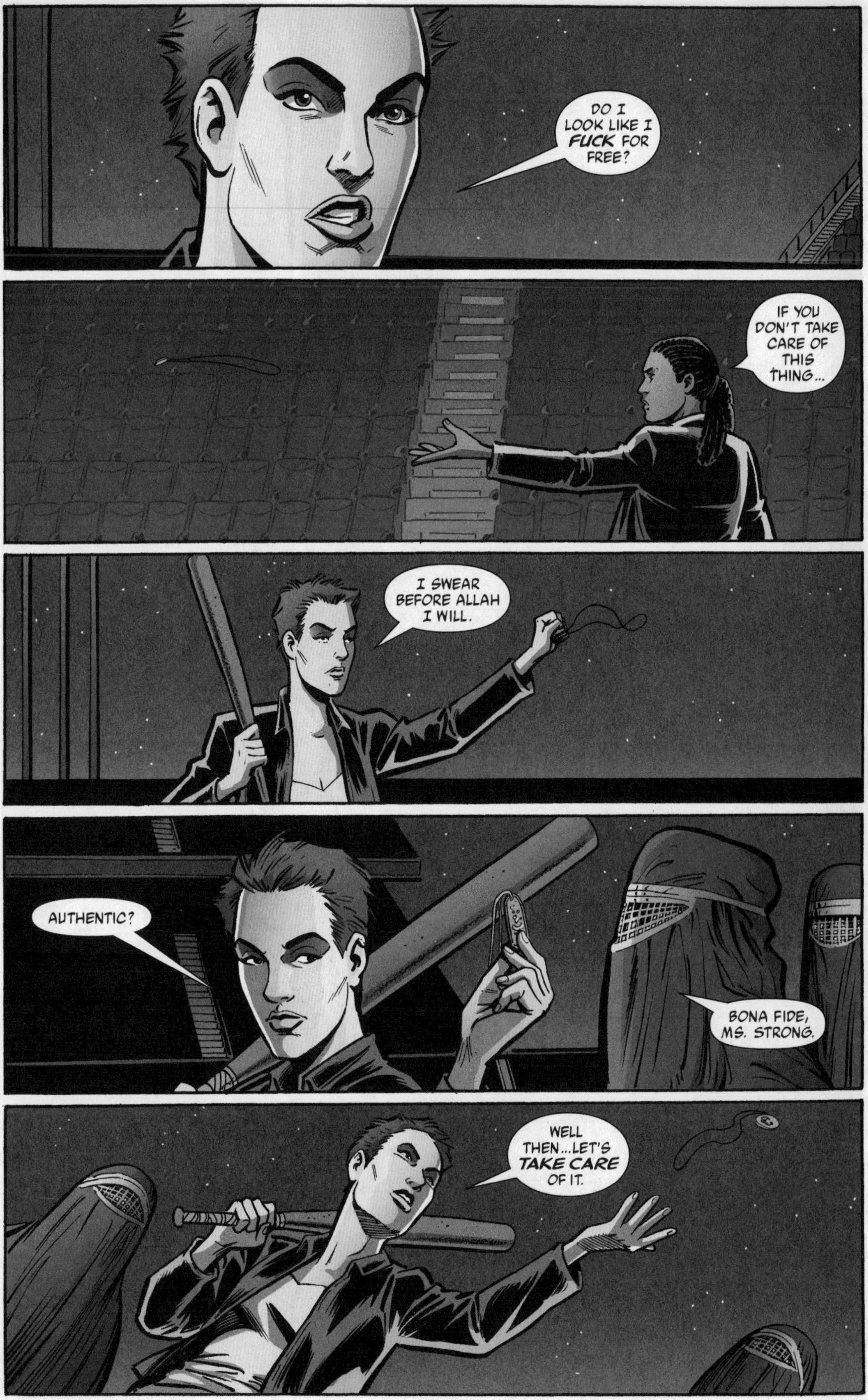
DO I LOOK LIKE I FUCK FOR FREE?
IF YOU DON'T TAKE CARE OF THIS THING...
I SWEAR BEFORE ALLAH I WILL.
AUTHENTIC?
BONA FIDE, MS. STRONG.
WELL THEN...LET'S TAKE CARE OF IT.

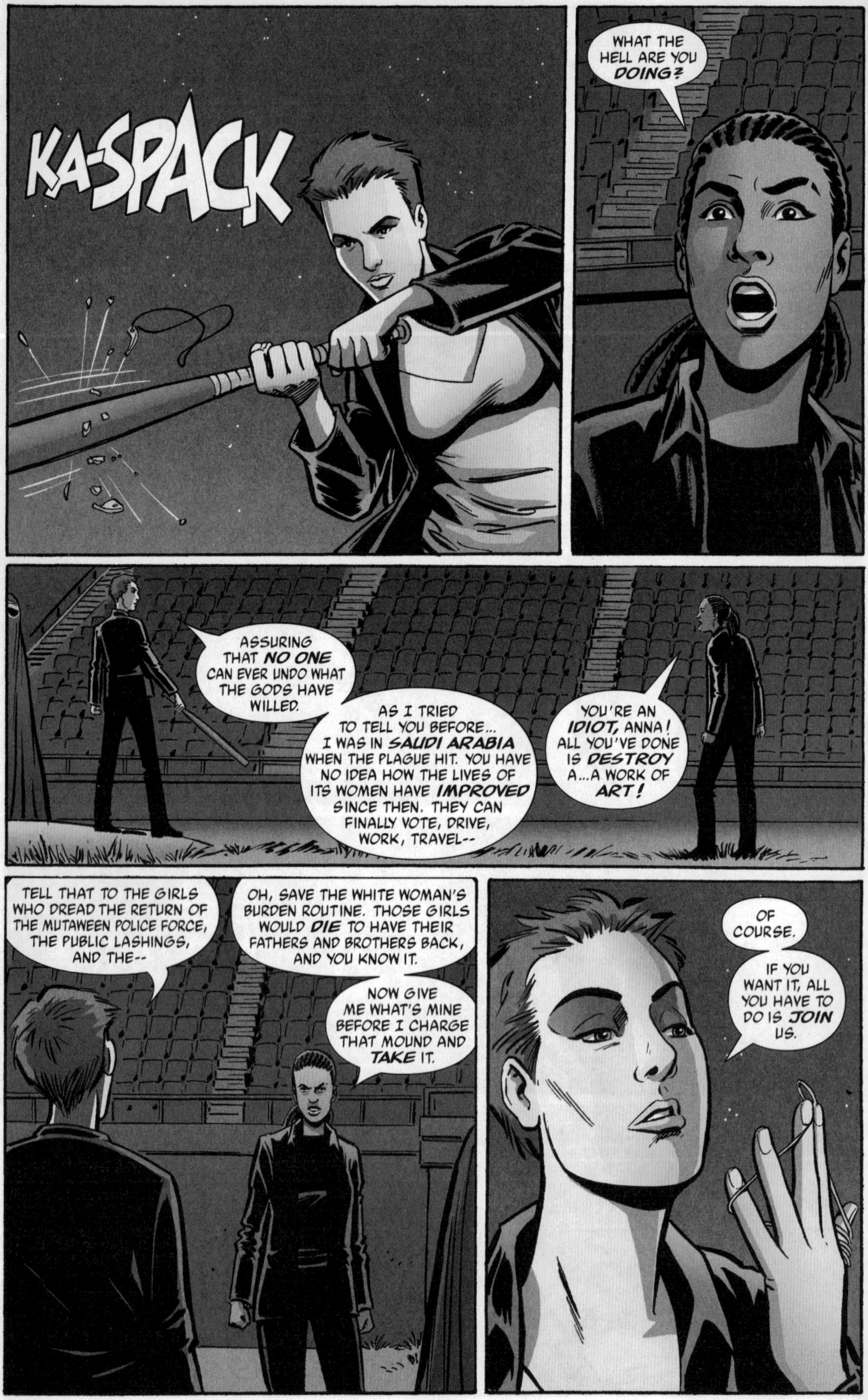
KA-SPACK
WHAT THE HELL ARE YOU DOING?
ASSURING THAT NO ONE CAN EVER UNDO WHAT THE GODS HAVE WILLED.
AS I TRIED TO TELL YOU BEFORE... I WAS IN SAUDI ARABIA WHEN THE PLAGUE HIT. YOU HAVE NO IDEA HOW THE LIVES OF ITS WOMEN HAVE IMPROVED SINCE THEN. THEY CAN FINALLY VOTE, DRIVE, WORK, TRAVEL--
YOU'RE AN IDIOT, ANNA! ALL YOU'VE DONE IS DESTROY A...A WORK OF ART!
TELL THAT TO THE GIRLS WHO DREAD THE RETURN OF THE MUTAWEEN POLICE FORCE, THE PUBLIC LASHINGS, AND THE--
OH, SAVE THE WHITE WOMAN'S BURDEN ROUTINE. THOSE GIRLS WOULD DIE TO HAVE THEIR FATHERS AND BROTHERS BACK, AND YOU KNOW IT.
NOW GIVE ME WHAT'S MINE BEFORE I CHARGE THAT MOUND AND TAKE IT.
OF COURSE.
IF YOU WANT IT, ALL YOU HAVE TO DO IS JOIN US.

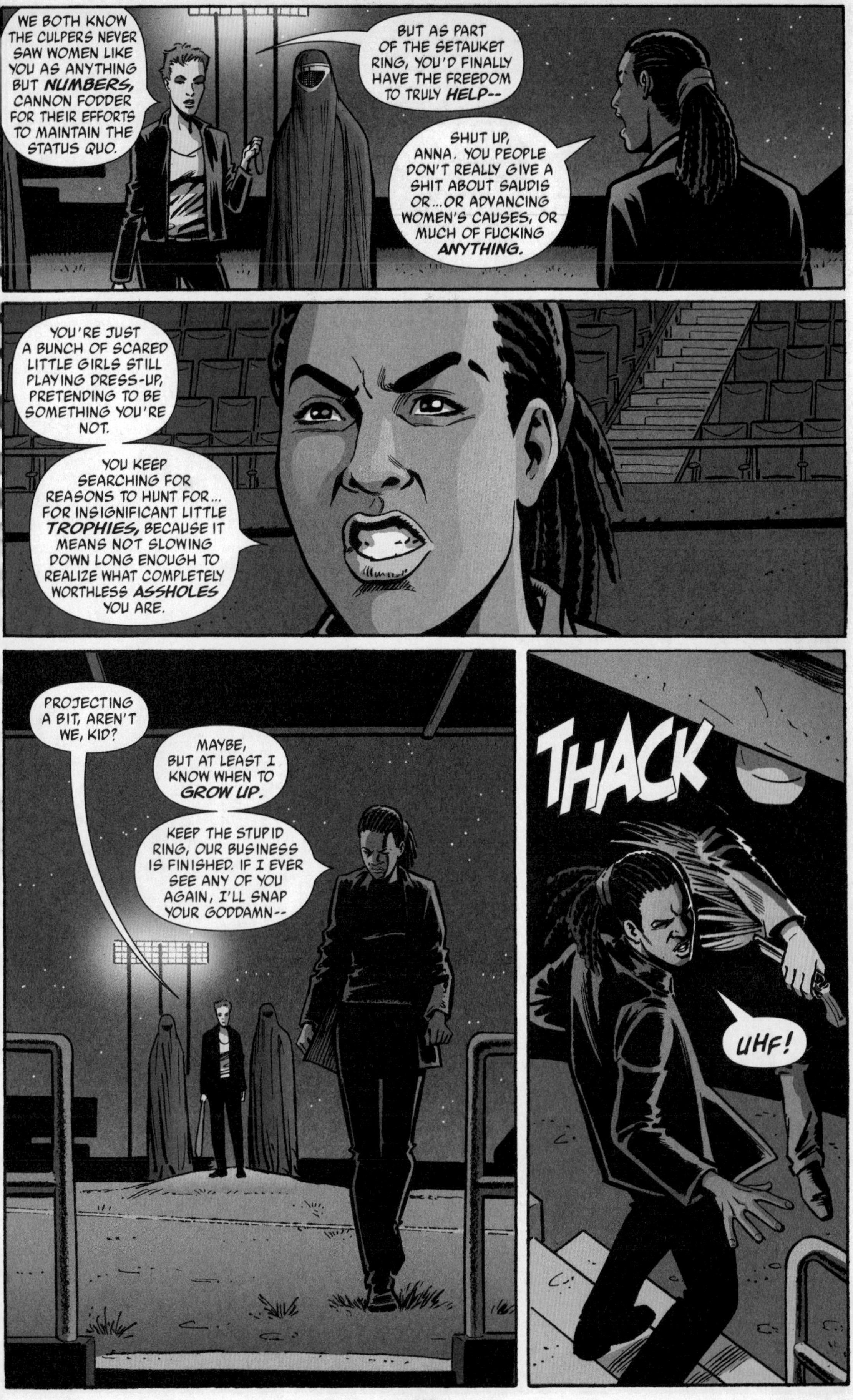
WE BOTH KNOW THE CULPERS NEVER SAW WOMEN LIKE YOU AS ANYTHING BUT NUMBERS, CANNON FODDER FOR THEIR EFFORTS TO MAINTAIN THE STATUS QUO.
BUT AS PART OF THE SETAUKET RING, YOU'D FINALLY HAVE THE FREEDOM TO TRULY HELP--
SHUT UP, ANNA. YOU PEOPLE DON'T REALLY GIVE A SHIT ABOUT SAUDIS OR...OR ADVANCING WOMEN'S CAUSES, OR MUCH OF FUCKING ANYTHING.
YOU'RE JUST A BUNCH OF SCARED LITTLE GIRLS STILL PLAYING DRESS-UP, PRETENDING TO BE SOMETHING YOU'RE NOT.
YOU KEEP SEARCHING FOR REASONS TO HUNT FOR... FOR INSIGNIFICANT LITTLE TROPHIES, BECAUSE IT MEANS NOT SLOWING DOWN LONG ENOUGH TO REALIZE WHAT COMPLETELY WORTHLESS ASSHOLES YOU ARE.
PROJECTING A BIT, AREN'T WE, KID?
MAYBE, BUT AT LEAST I KNOW WHEN TO GROW UP.
KEEP THE STUPID RING, OUR BUSINESS IS FINISHED. IF I EVER SEE ANY OF YOU AGAIN, I'LL SNAP YOUR GODDAMN--
THACK
UHF!

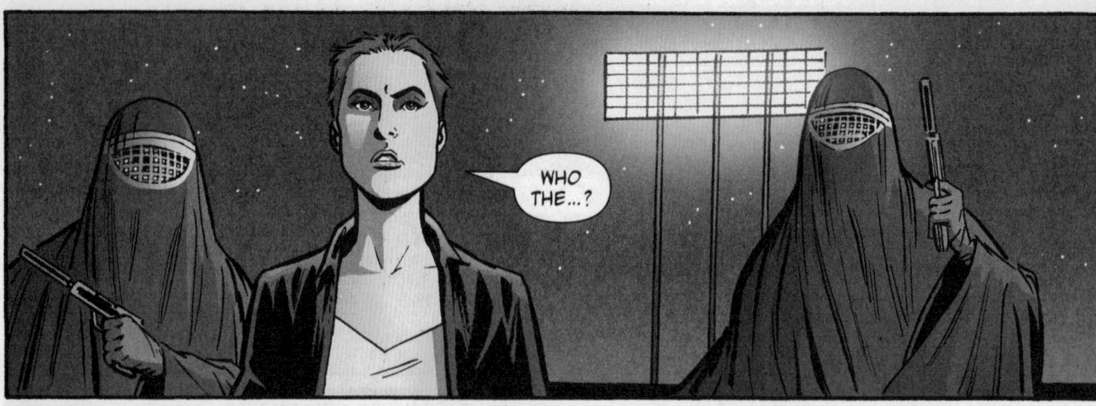
WHO THE...?
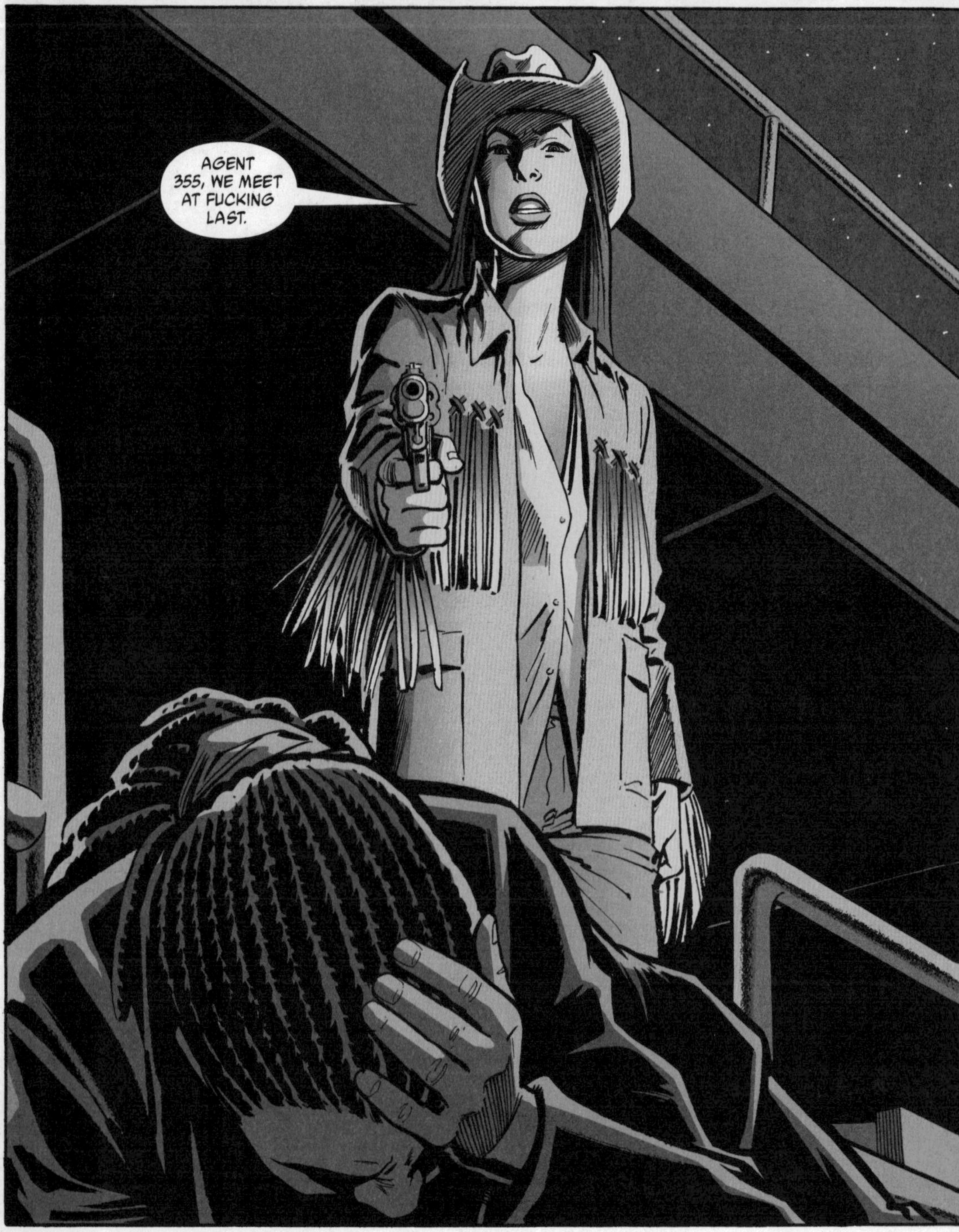
AGENT 355, WE MEET AT FUCKING LAST.

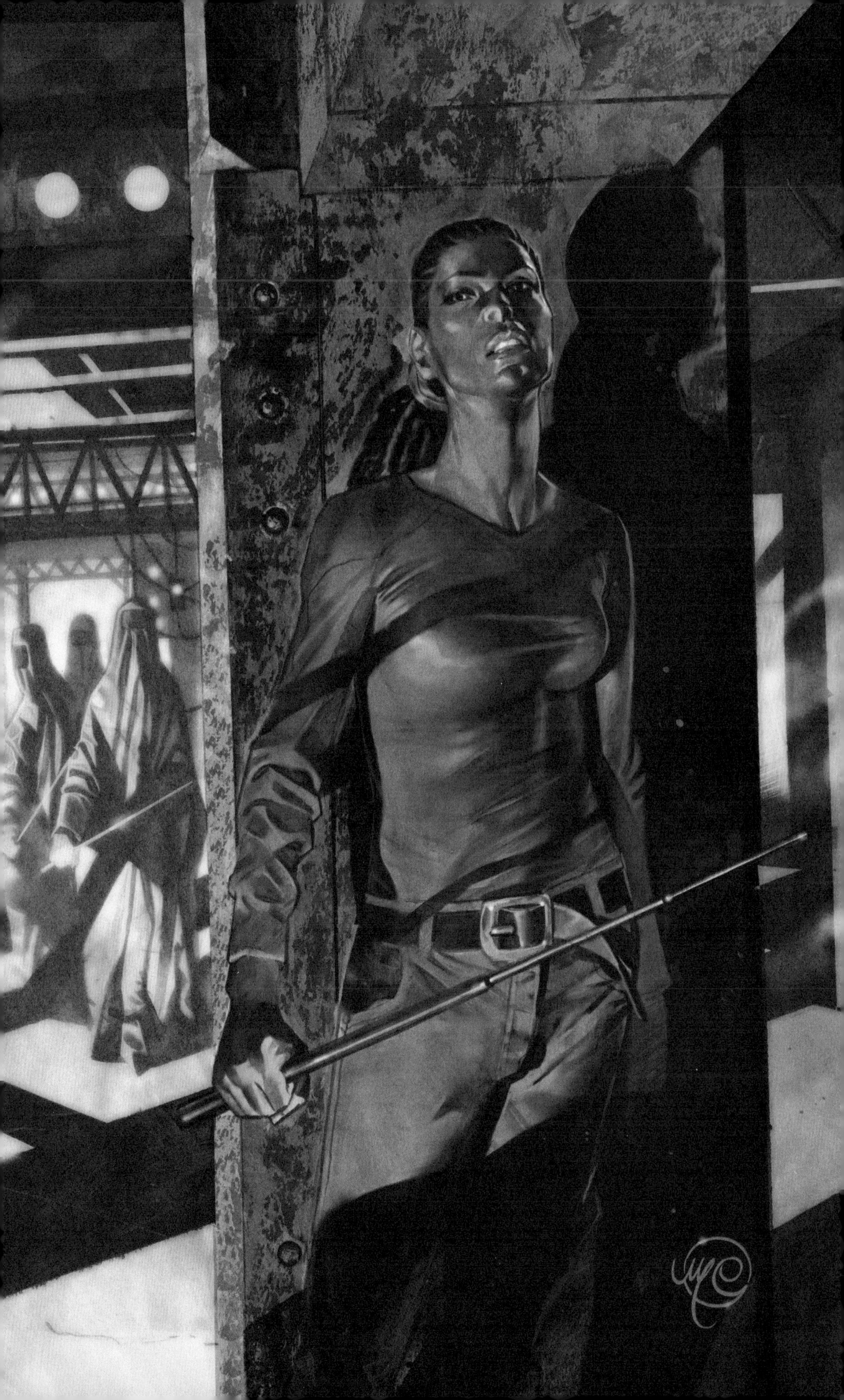

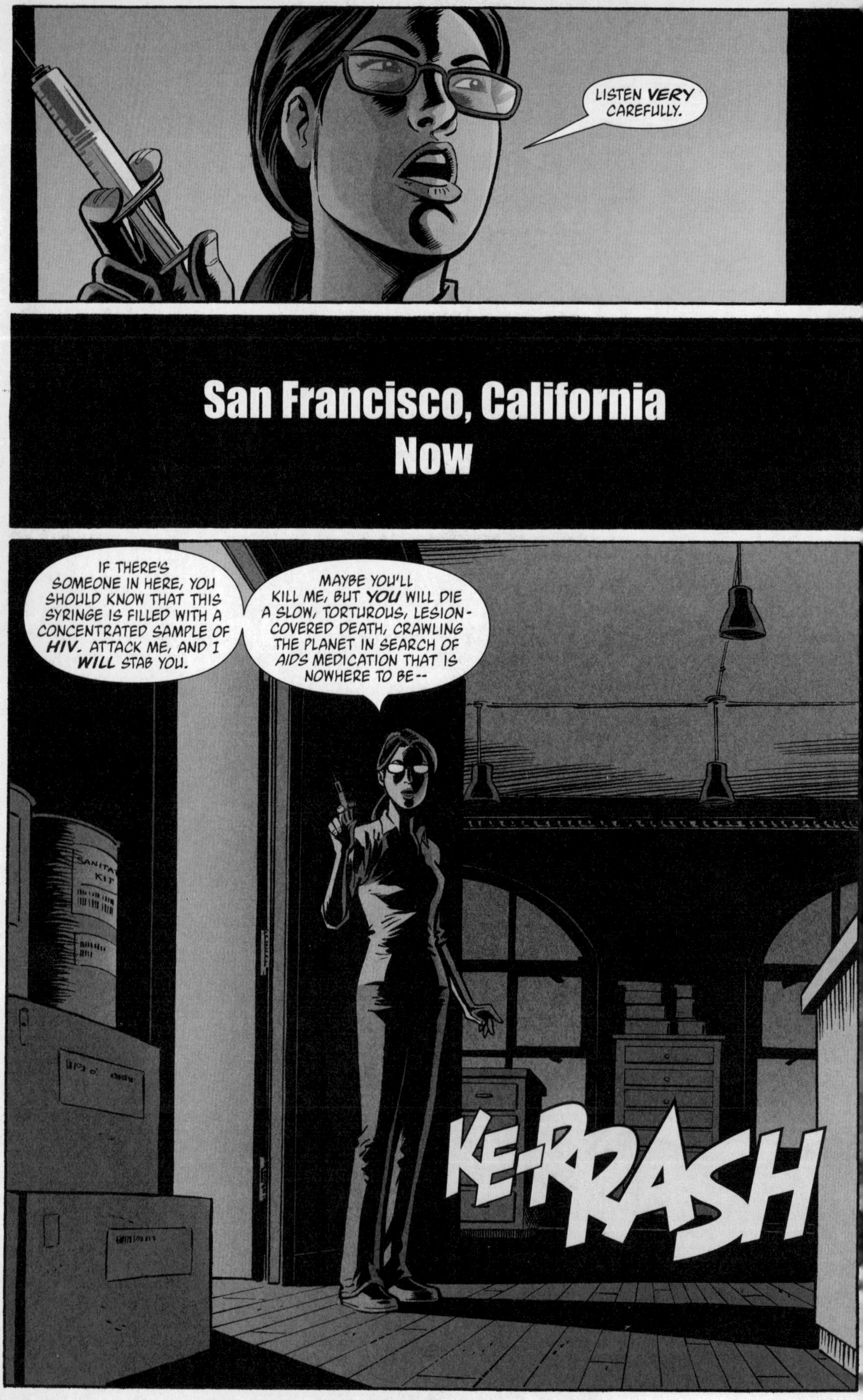
LISTEN VERY CAREFULLY.
San Francisco, California
Now
IF THERE'S SOMEONE IN HERE, YOU SHOULD KNOW THAT THIS SYRINGE IS FILLED WITH A CONCENTRATED SAMPLE OF HIV. ATTACK ME, AND I WILL STAB YOU.
MAYBE YOU'LL KILL ME, BUT YOU WILL DIE A SLOW, TORTUROUS, LESION-COVERED DEATH, CRAWLING THE PLANET IN SEARCH OF AIDS MEDICATION THAT IS NOWHERE TO BE--
KE-RRASH

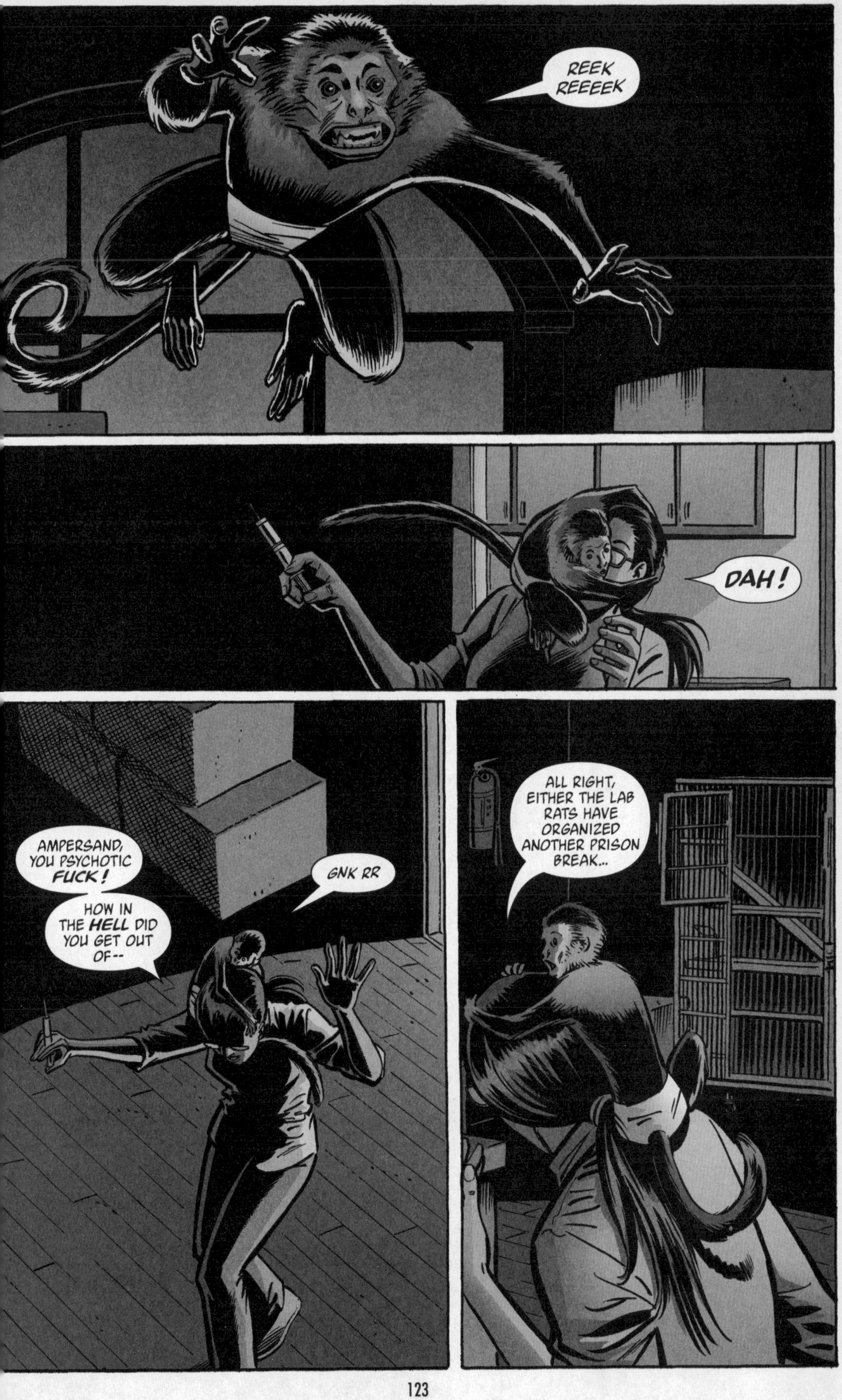
REEK REEEEK
DAH!
AMPERSAND, YOU PSYCHOTIC FUCK!
HOW IN THE HELL DID YOU GET OUT OF--
GNK RR
ALL RIGHT, EITHER THE LAB RATS HAVE ORGANIZED ANOTHER PRISON BREAK...

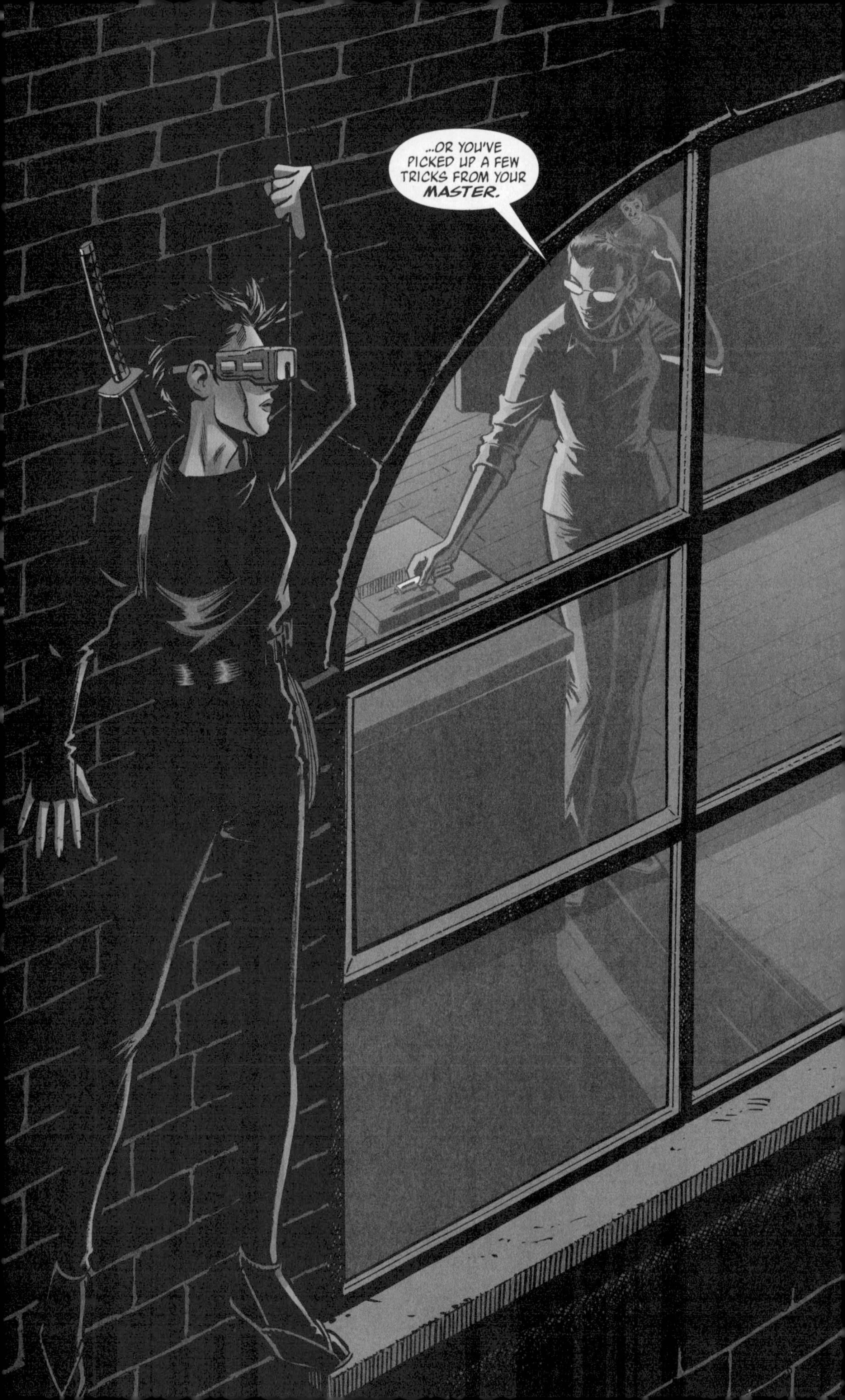
...OR YOU'VE PICKED UP A FEW TRICKS FROM YOUR MASTER.

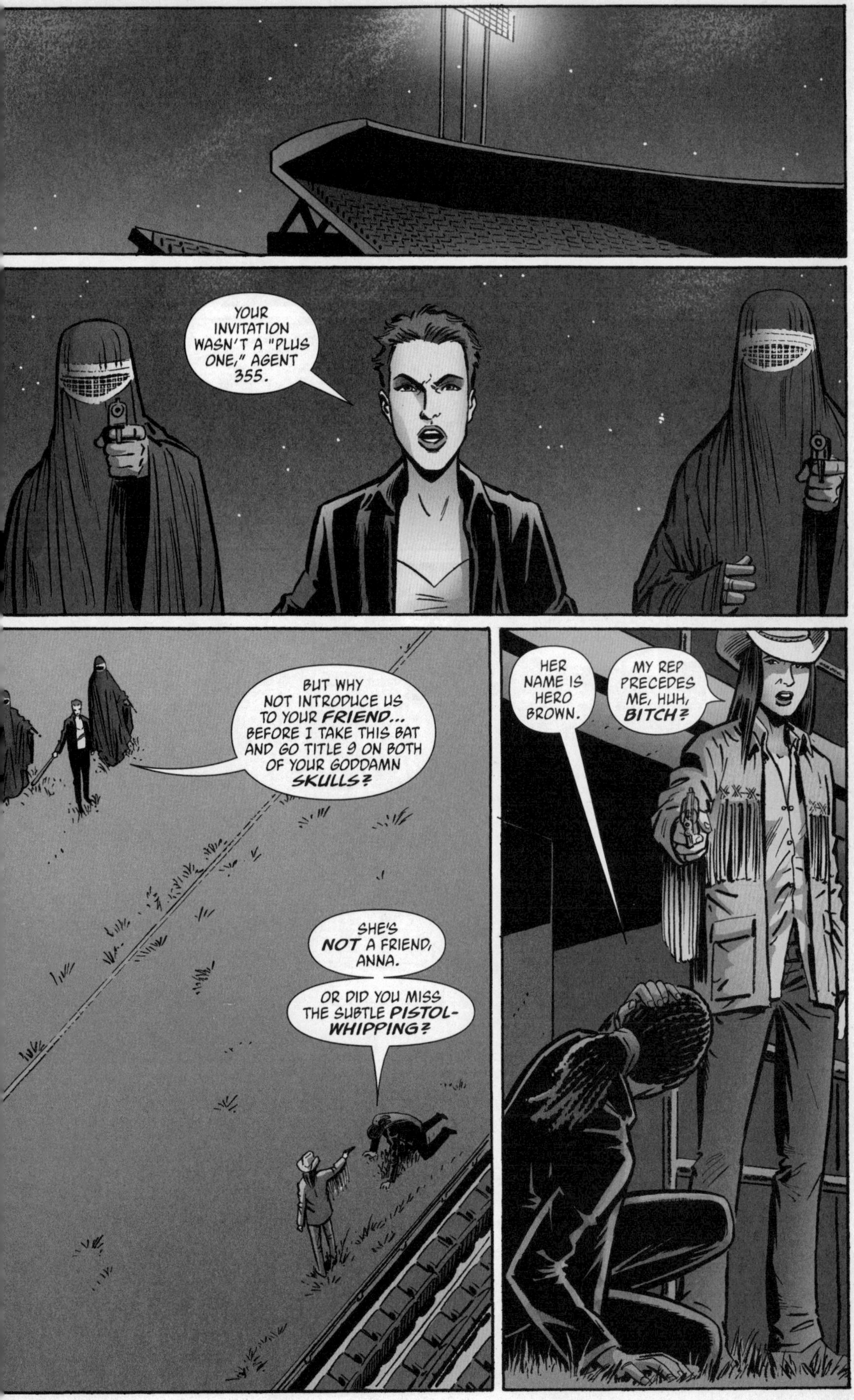
YOUR INVITATION WASN'T A "PLUS ONE," AGENT 355.
BUT WHY NOT INTRODUCE US TO YOUR FRIEND... BEFORE I TAKE THIS BAT AND GO TITLE 9 ON BOTH OF YOUR GODDAMN SKULLS?
HER NAME IS HERO BROWN.
MY REP PRECEDES ME, HUH, BITCH?
SHE'S NOT A FRIEND, ANNA.
OR DID YOU MISS THE SUBTLE PISTOL-WHIPPING?

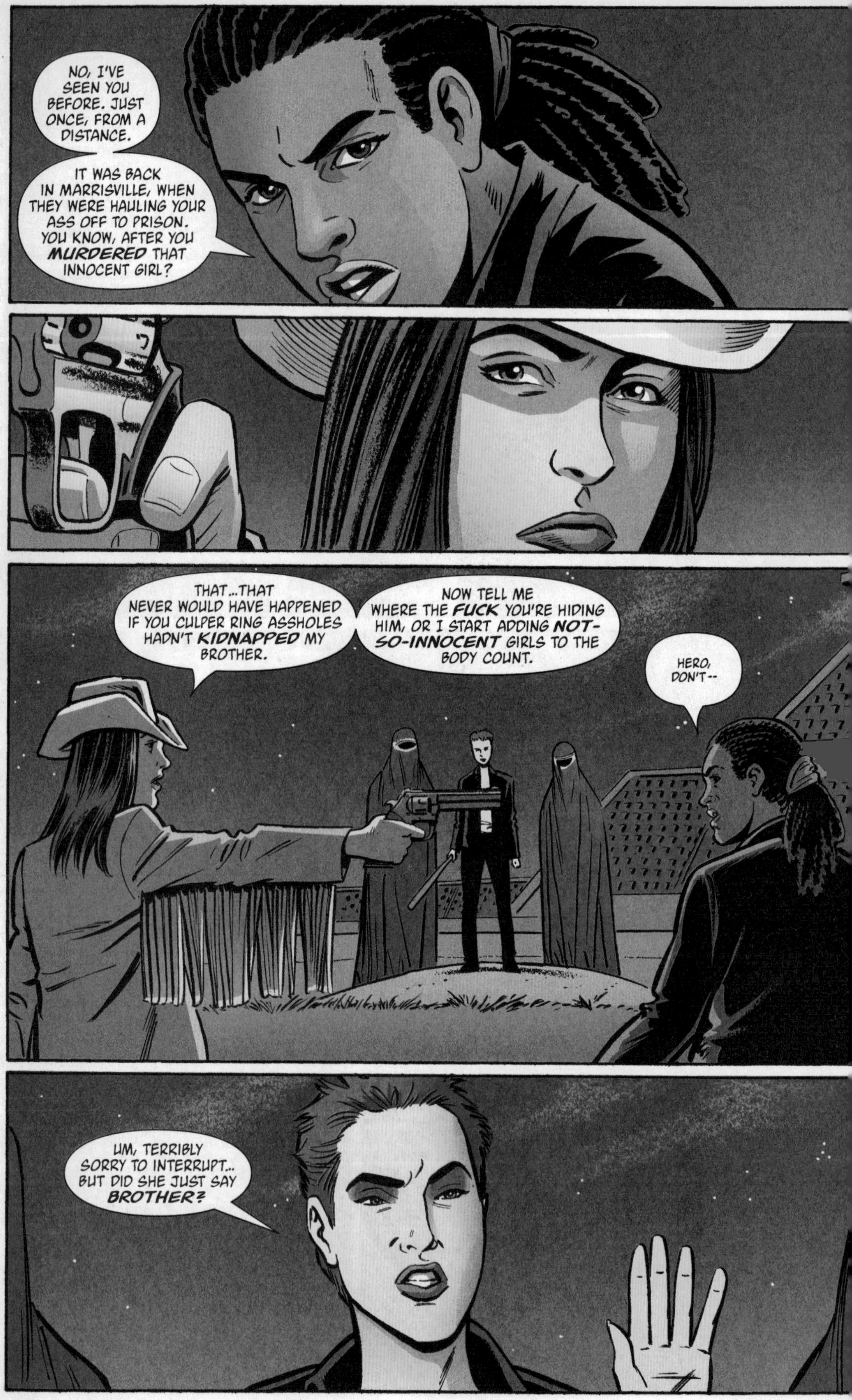
NO, I'VE SEEN YOU BEFORE. JUST ONCE, FROM A DISTANCE.
IT WAS BACK IN MARRISVILLE, WHEN THEY WERE HAULING YOUR ASS OFF TO PRISON. YOU KNOW, AFTER YOU MURDERED THAT INNOCENT GIRL?
THAT...THAT NEVER WOULD HAVE HAPPENED IF YOU CULPER RING ASSHOLES HADN'T KIDNAPPED MY BROTHER.
NOW TELL ME WHERE THE FUCK YOU'RE HIDING HIM, OR I START ADDING NOT-SO-INNOCENT GIRLS TO THE BODY COUNT.
HERO, DON'T--
UM, TERRIBLY SORRY TO INTERRUPT... BUT DID SHE JUST SAY BROTHER?

WHH...?

I'M DISAPPOINTED, YORICK.

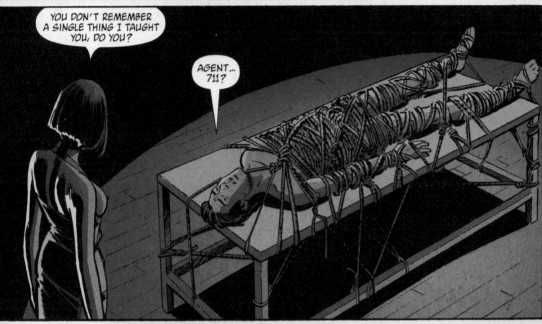

YOU DON'T REMEMBER A SINGLE THING I TAUGHT YOU, DO YOU?

AGENT... 711?

I THOUGHT YOU PROMISED TO *QUIT* YOUR FAGGY LITTLE SUICIDE ATTEMPTS?

SUICIDE? I DON'T *WANT* TO DIE, 711. I'M... I'M SICK. THE PLAGUE FINALLY CAUGHT UP WITH ME. THERE'S NOTHING I CAN DO ABOUT IT.

BULLSHIT. YOU CAN ESCAPE THIS, AS LONG AS YOU DON'T *PUSS OUT,* HARDLY HOUDINI.

I MEAN, WHAT HAPPENED TO WHATEVER THE FUCK YOU SAW WHEN YOU HAD YOUR *"EPIPHANY"*? THE THING THAT MADE YOU WANT TO *FIGHT* FOR LIFE?

WHAT WAS IT AGAIN...?

127

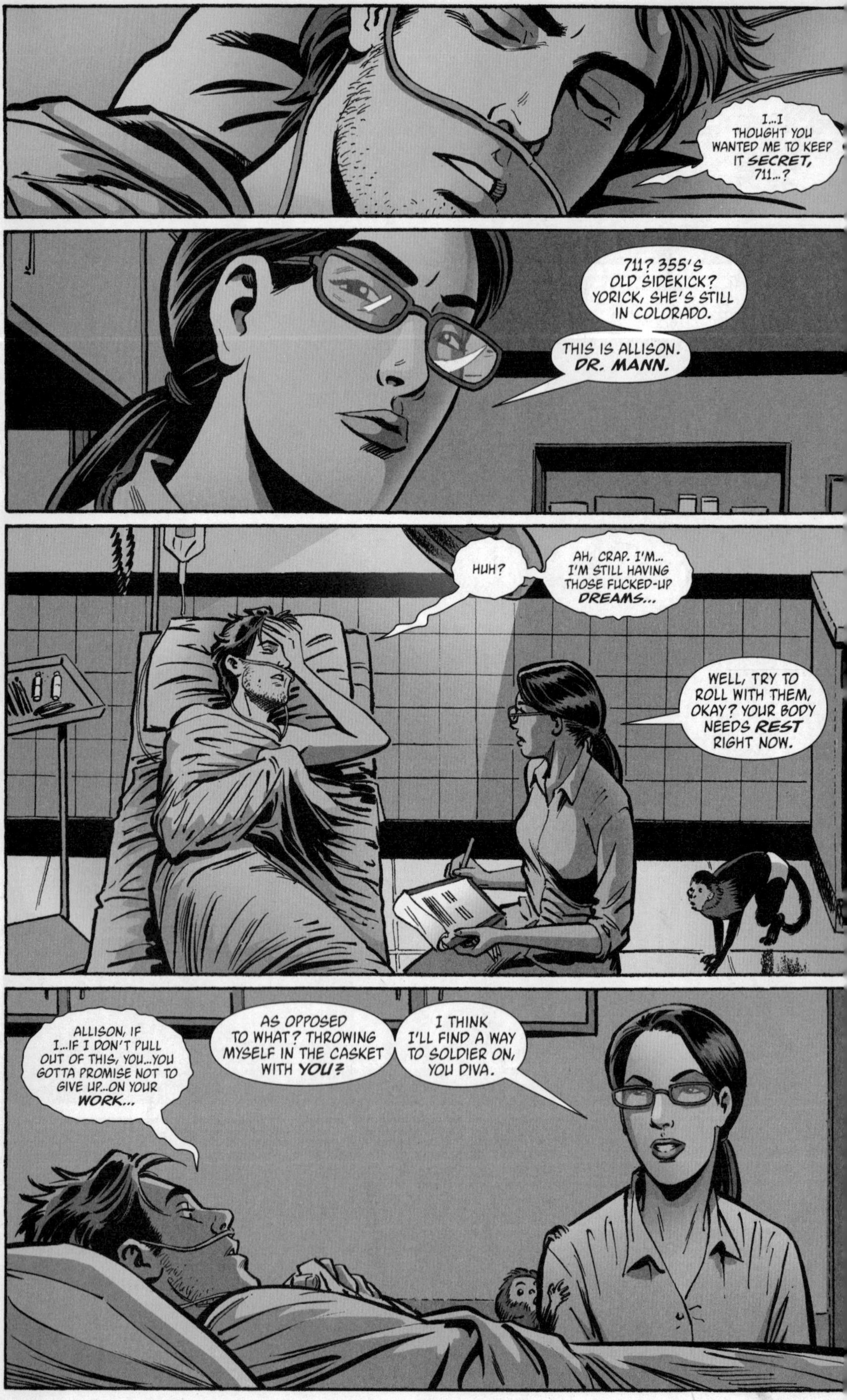
I...I THOUGHT YOU WANTED ME TO KEEP IT SECRET, 711...?
711? 355'S OLD SIDEKICK? YORICK, SHE'S STILL IN COLORADO.
THIS IS ALLISON. DR. MANN.
HUH?
AH, CRAP. I'M... I'M STILL HAVING THOSE FUCKED-UP DREAMS...
WELL, TRY TO ROLL WITH THEM, OKAY? YOUR BODY NEEDS REST RIGHT NOW.
ALLISON, IF I...IF I DON'T PULL OUT OF THIS, YOU...YOU GOTTA PROMISE NOT TO GIVE UP...ON YOUR WORK...
AS OPPOSED TO WHAT? THROWING MYSELF IN THE CASKET WITH YOU?
I THINK I'LL FIND A WAY TO SOLDIER ON, YOU DIVA.

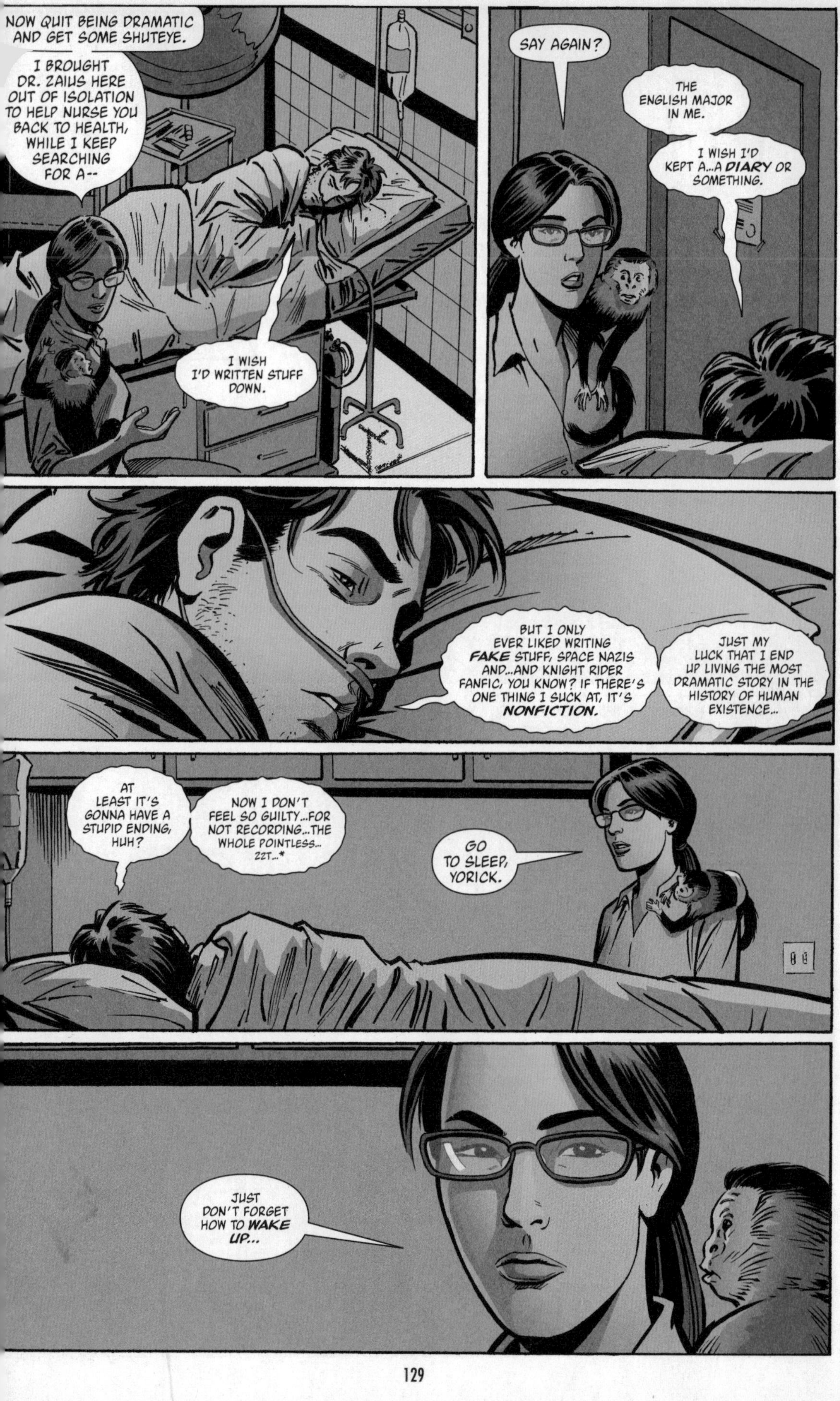
NOW QUIT BEING DRAMATIC AND GET SOME SHUTEYE.
I BROUGHT DR. ZAIUS HERE OUT OF ISOLATION TO HELP NURSE YOU BACK TO HEALTH, WHILE I KEEP SEARCHING FOR A--
I WISH I'D WRITTEN STUFF DOWN.
SAY AGAIN?
THE ENGLISH MAJOR IN ME.
I WISH I'D KEPT A...A DIARY OR SOMETHING.
BUT I ONLY EVER LIKED WRITING FAKE STUFF, SPACE NAZIS AND...AND KNIGHT RIDER FANFIC, YOU KNOW? IF THERE'S ONE THING I SUCK AT, IT'S NONFICTION.
JUST MY LUCK THAT I END UP LIVING THE MOST DRAMATIC STORY IN THE HISTORY OF HUMAN EXISTENCE...
AT LEAST IT'S GONNA HAVE A STUPID ENDING, HUH?
NOW I DON'T FEEL SO GUILTY...FOR NOT RECORDING...THE WHOLE POINTLESS... ZZT...*
GO TO SLEEP, YORICK.
JUST DON'T FORGET HOW TO WAKE UP...

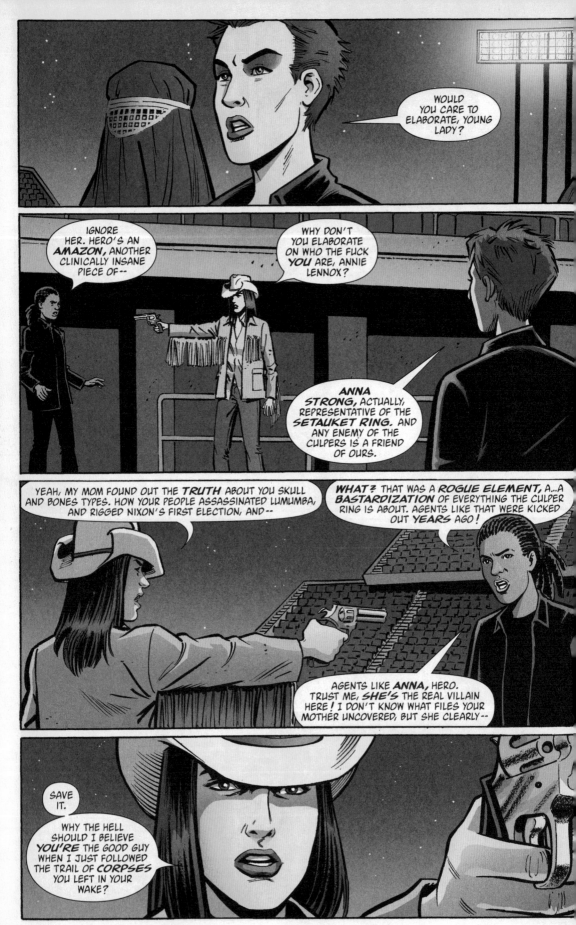

WOULD YOU CARE TO ELABORATE, YOUNG LADY?

IGNORE HER. HERO'S AN *AMAZON*, ANOTHER CLINICALLY INSANE PIECE OF --

WHY DON'T YOU ELABORATE ON WHO THE FUCK *YOU* ARE, ANNIE LENNOX?

ANNA STRONG, ACTUALLY, REPRESENTATIVE OF THE *SETAUKET RING*. AND ANY ENEMY OF THE CULPERS IS A FRIEND OF OURS.

YEAH, MY MOM FOUND OUT THE *TRUTH* ABOUT YOU SKULL AND BONES TYPES. HOW YOUR PEOPLE ASSASSINATED LUMUMBA, AND RIGGED NIXON'S FIRST ELECTION, AND --

WHAT? THAT WAS A *ROGUE ELEMENT*, A...A *BASTARDIZATION* OF EVERYTHING THE CULPER RING IS ABOUT. AGENTS LIKE THAT WERE KICKED OUT *YEARS* AGO!

AGENTS LIKE *ANNA*, HERO. TRUST ME, *SHE'S* THE REAL VILLAIN HERE! I DON'T KNOW WHAT FILES YOUR MOTHER UNCOVERED, BUT SHE CLEARLY --

SAVE IT.

WHY THE HELL SHOULD I BELIEVE *YOU'RE* THE GOOD GUY WHEN I JUST FOLLOWED THE TRAIL OF *CORPSES* YOU LEFT IN YOUR WAKE?

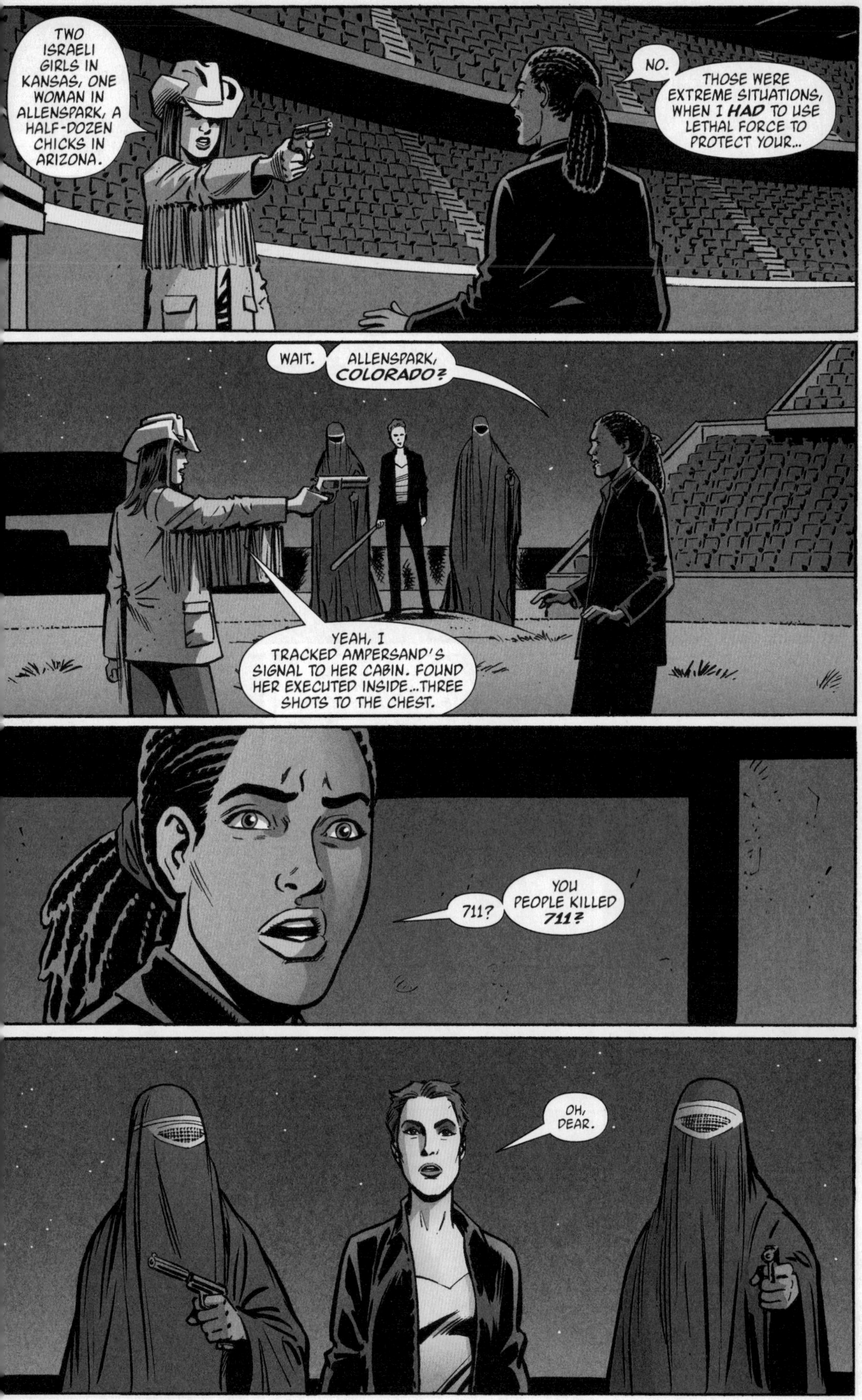
TWO ISRAELI GIRLS IN KANSAS, ONE WOMAN IN ALLENSPARK, A HALF-DOZEN CHICKS IN ARIZONA.
NO.
THOSE WERE EXTREME SITUATIONS, WHEN I HAD TO USE LETHAL FORCE TO PROTECT YOUR...
WAIT.
ALLENSPARK, COLORADO?
YEAH, I TRACKED AMPERSAND'S SIGNAL TO HER CABIN. FOUND HER EXECUTED INSIDE...THREE SHOTS TO THE CHEST.
711?
YOU PEOPLE KILLED 711?
OH, DEAR.

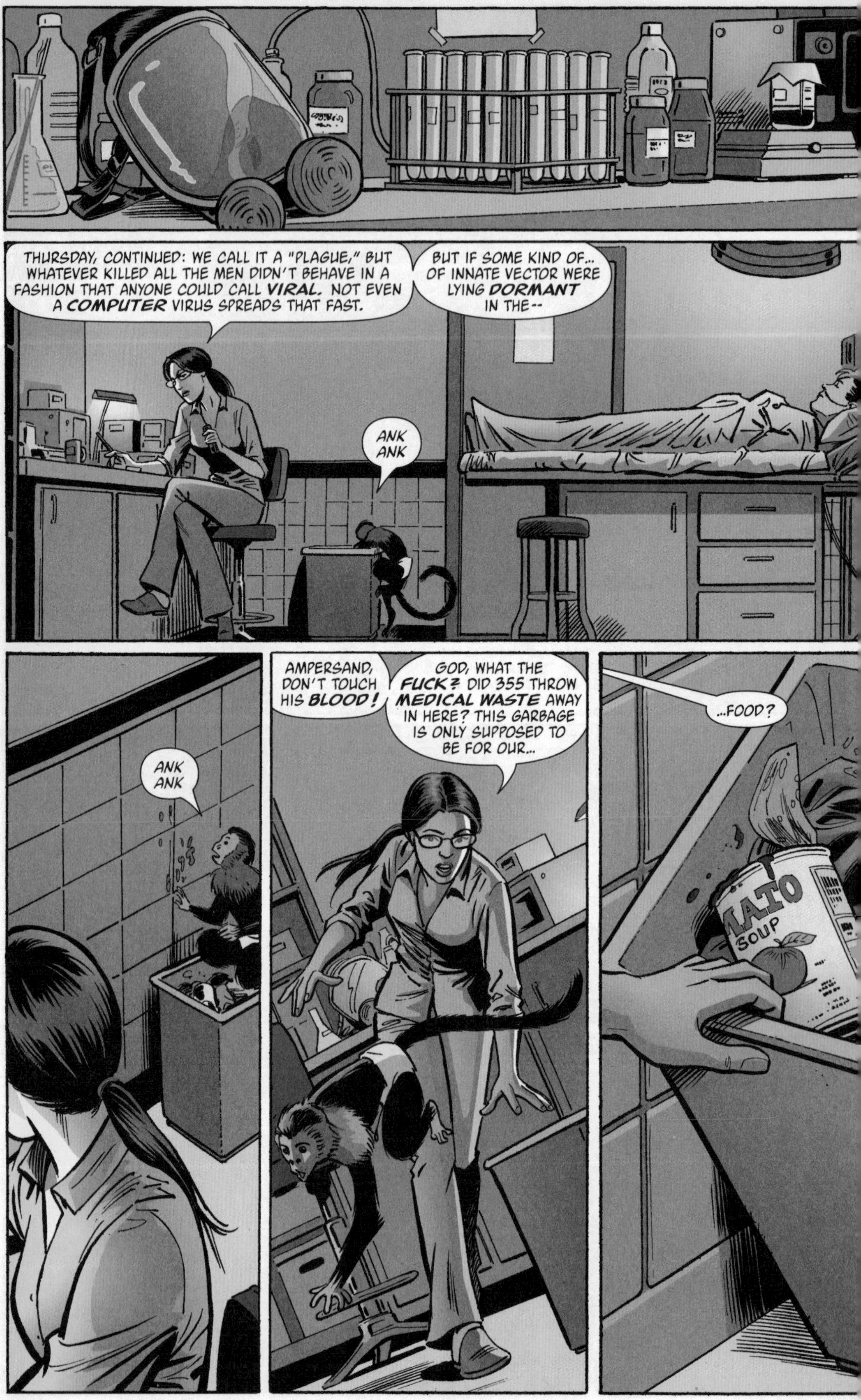

THURSDAY, CONTINUED: WE CALL IT A "PLAGUE," BUT WHATEVER KILLED ALL THE MEN DIDN'T BEHAVE IN A FASHION THAT ANYONE COULD CALL VIRAL. NOT EVEN A COMPUTER VIRUS SPREADS THAT FAST.
BUT IF SOME KIND OF... OF INNATE VECTOR WERE LYING DORMANT IN THE--
ANK ANK
ANK ANK
AMPERSAND, DON'T TOUCH HIS BLOOD!
GOD, WHAT THE FUCK? DID 355 THROW MEDICAL WASTE AWAY IN HERE? THIS GARBAGE IS ONLY SUPPOSED TO BE FOR OUR...
...FOOD?
MATO SOUP

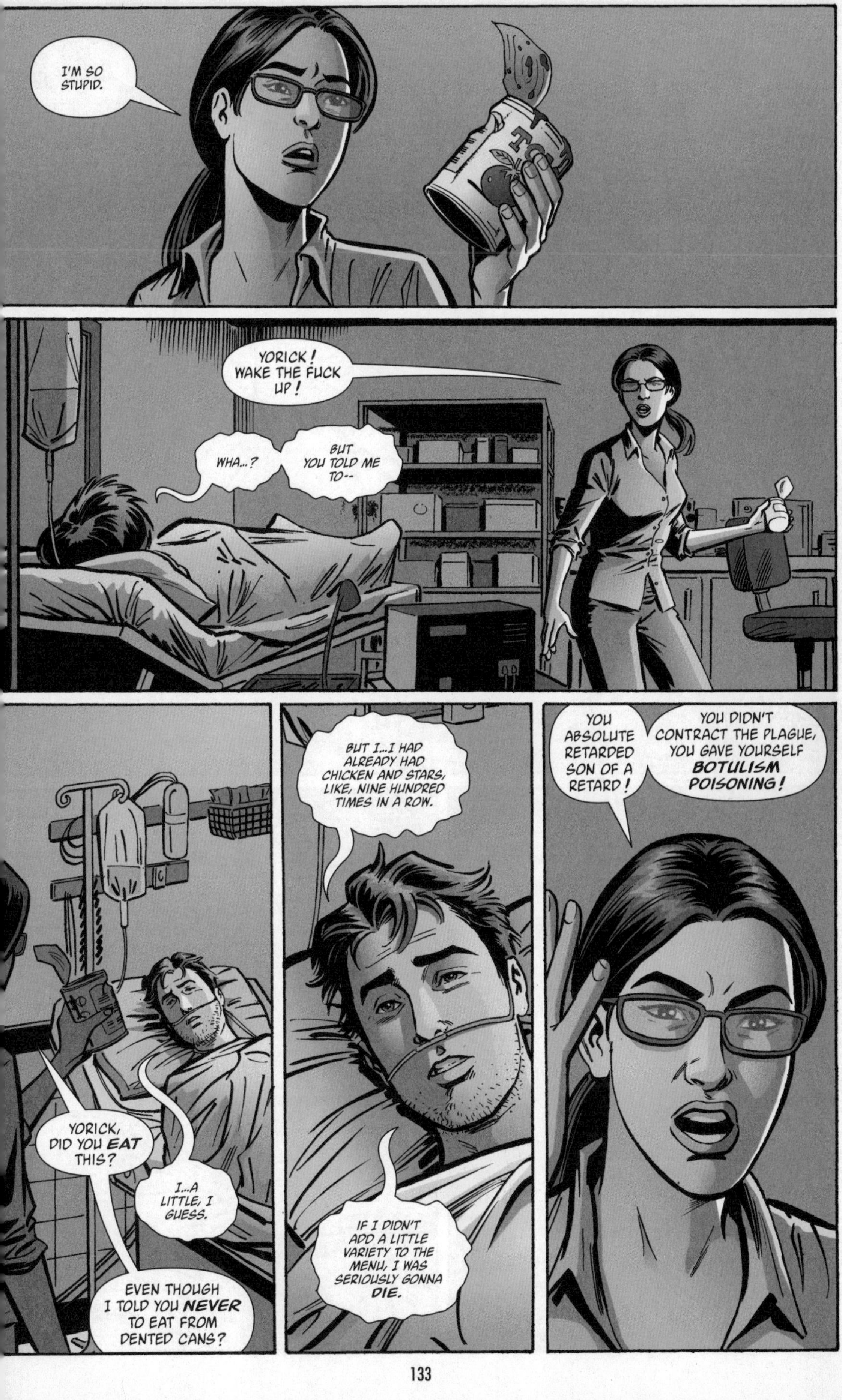
I'M SO STUPID.
YORICK! WAKE THE FUCK UP!
WHA...?
BUT YOU TOLD ME TO--
YORICK, DID YOU EAT THIS?
I...A LITTLE, I GUESS.
EVEN THOUGH I TOLD YOU NEVER TO EAT FROM DENTED CANS?
BUT I...I HAD ALREADY HAD CHICKEN AND STARS, LIKE, NINE HUNDRED TIMES IN A ROW.
IF I DIDN'T ADD A LITTLE VARIETY TO THE MENU, I WAS SERIOUSLY GONNA DIE.
YOU ABSOLUTE RETARDED SON OF A RETARD!
YOU DIDN'T CONTRACT THE PLAGUE, YOU GAVE YOURSELF BOTULISM POISONING!

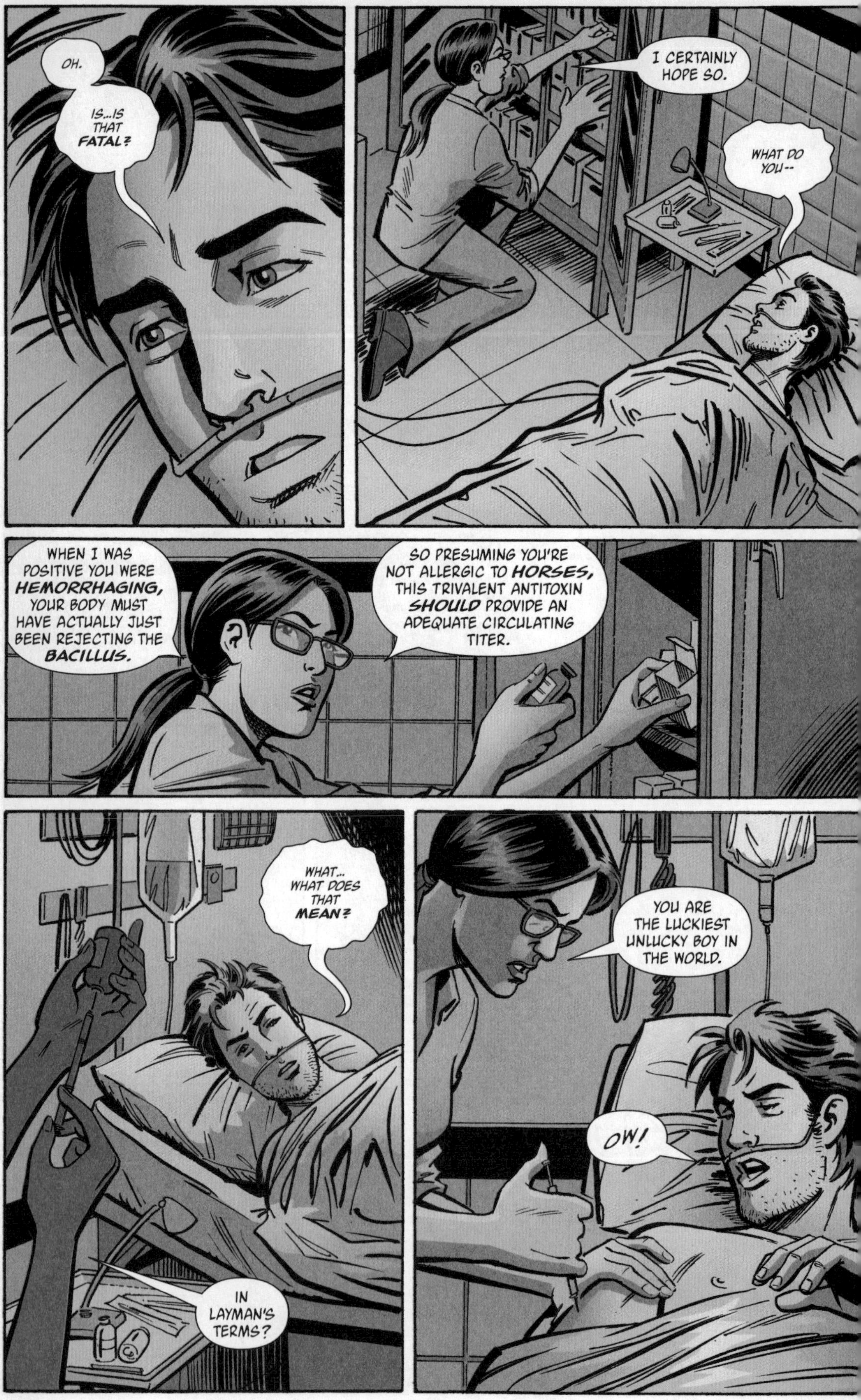
OH.
IS...IS THAT FATAL?
I CERTAINLY HOPE SO.
WHAT DO YOU--
WHEN I WAS POSITIVE YOU WERE HEMORRHAGING, YOUR BODY MUST HAVE ACTUALLY JUST BEEN REJECTING THE BACILLUS.
SO PRESUMING YOU'RE NOT ALLERGIC TO HORSES, THIS TRIVALENT ANTITOXIN SHOULD PROVIDE AN ADEQUATE CIRCULATING TITER.
WHAT... WHAT DOES THAT MEAN?
IN LAYMAN'S TERMS?
YOU ARE THE LUCKIEST UNLUCKY BOY IN THE WORLD.
OW!

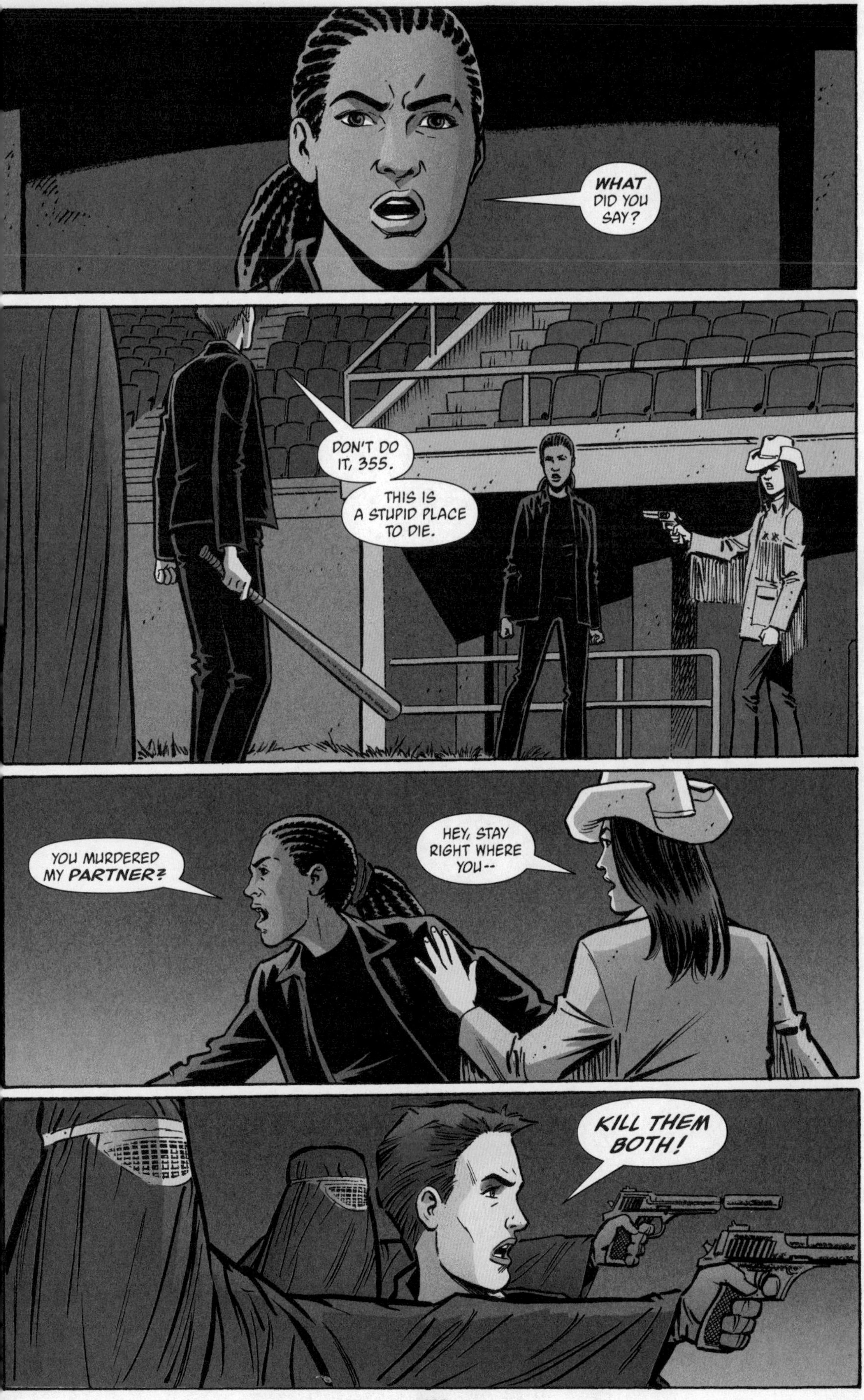
WHAT DID YOU SAY?
DON'T DO IT, 355.
THIS IS A STUPID PLACE TO DIE.
YOU MURDERED MY PARTNER?
HEY, STAY RIGHT WHERE YOU--
KILL THEM BOTH!

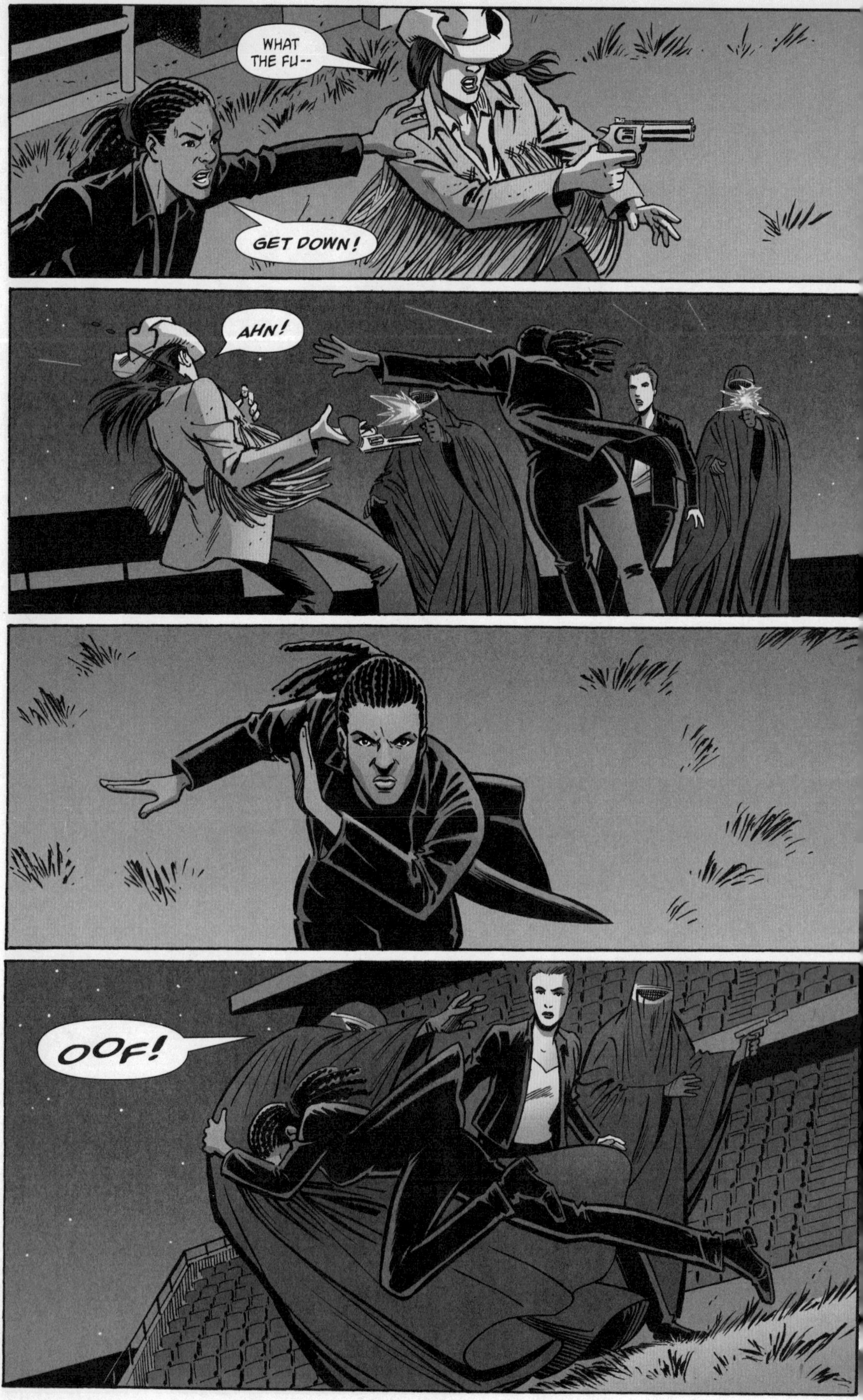
WHAT THE FU--
GET DOWN!
AHN!
OOF!

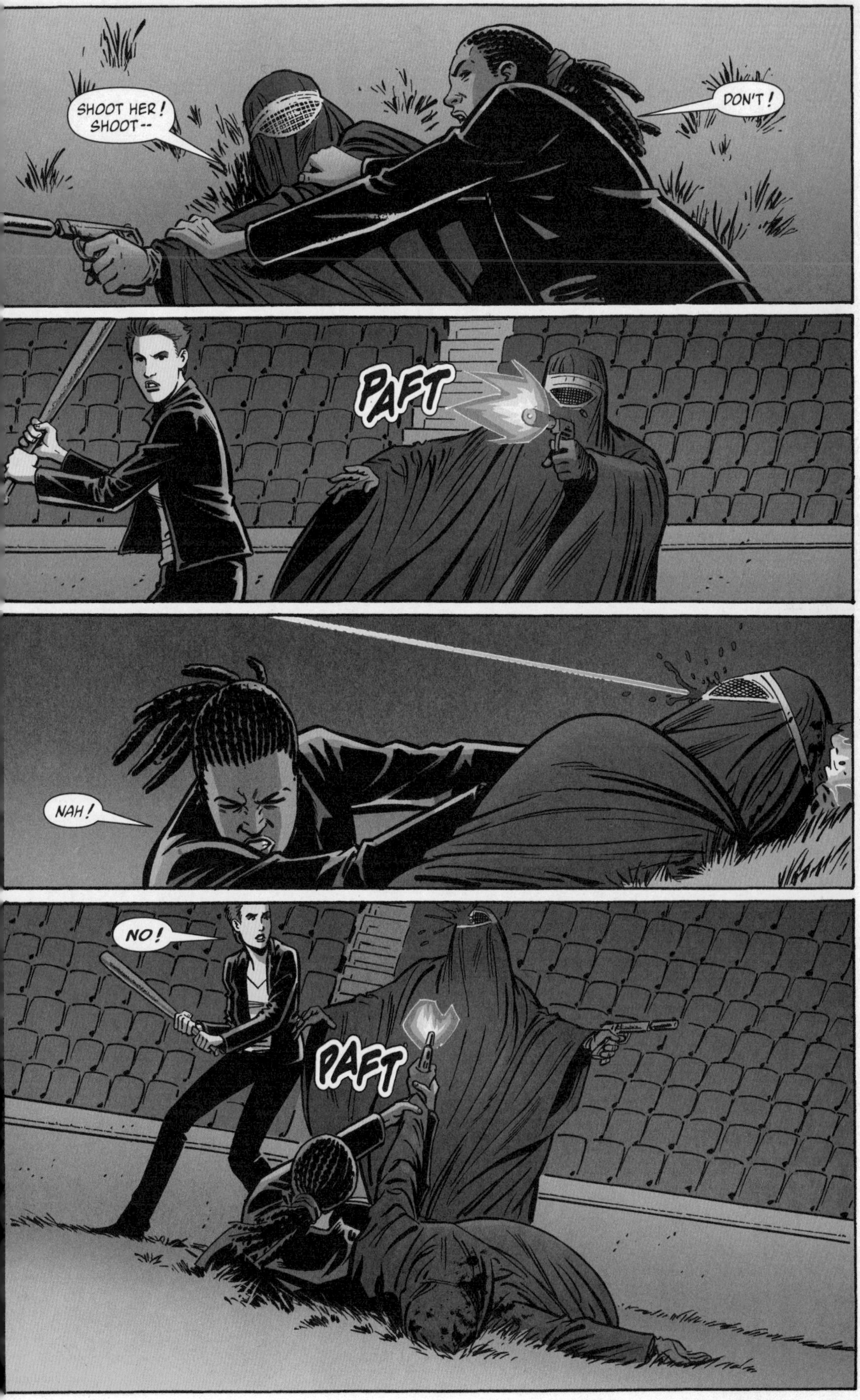
SHOOT HER! SHOOT--
DON'T!
PAFT
NAH!
NO!
PAFT

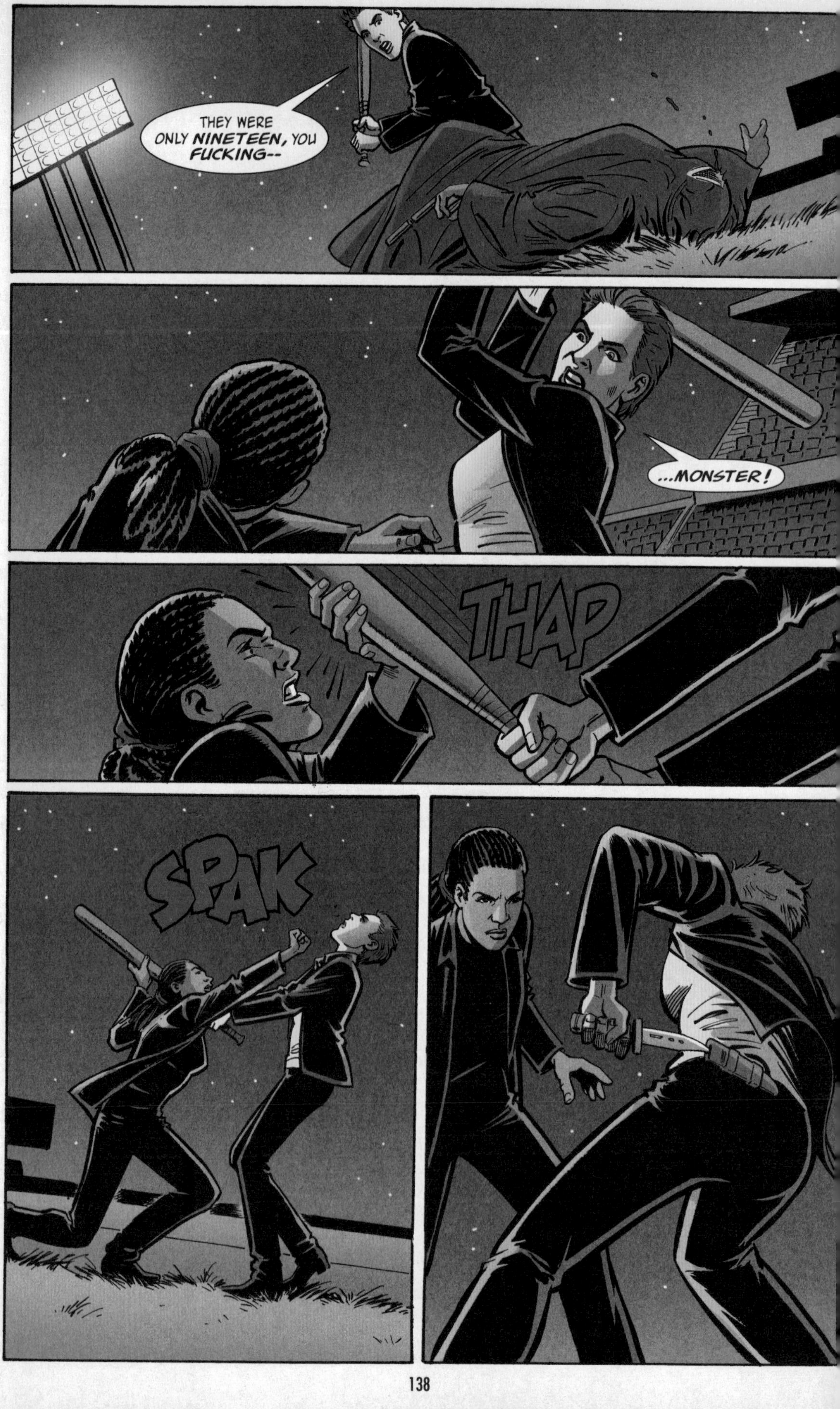
THEY WERE ONLY NINETEEN, YOU FUCKING--
...MONSTER!
THAP
SPAK

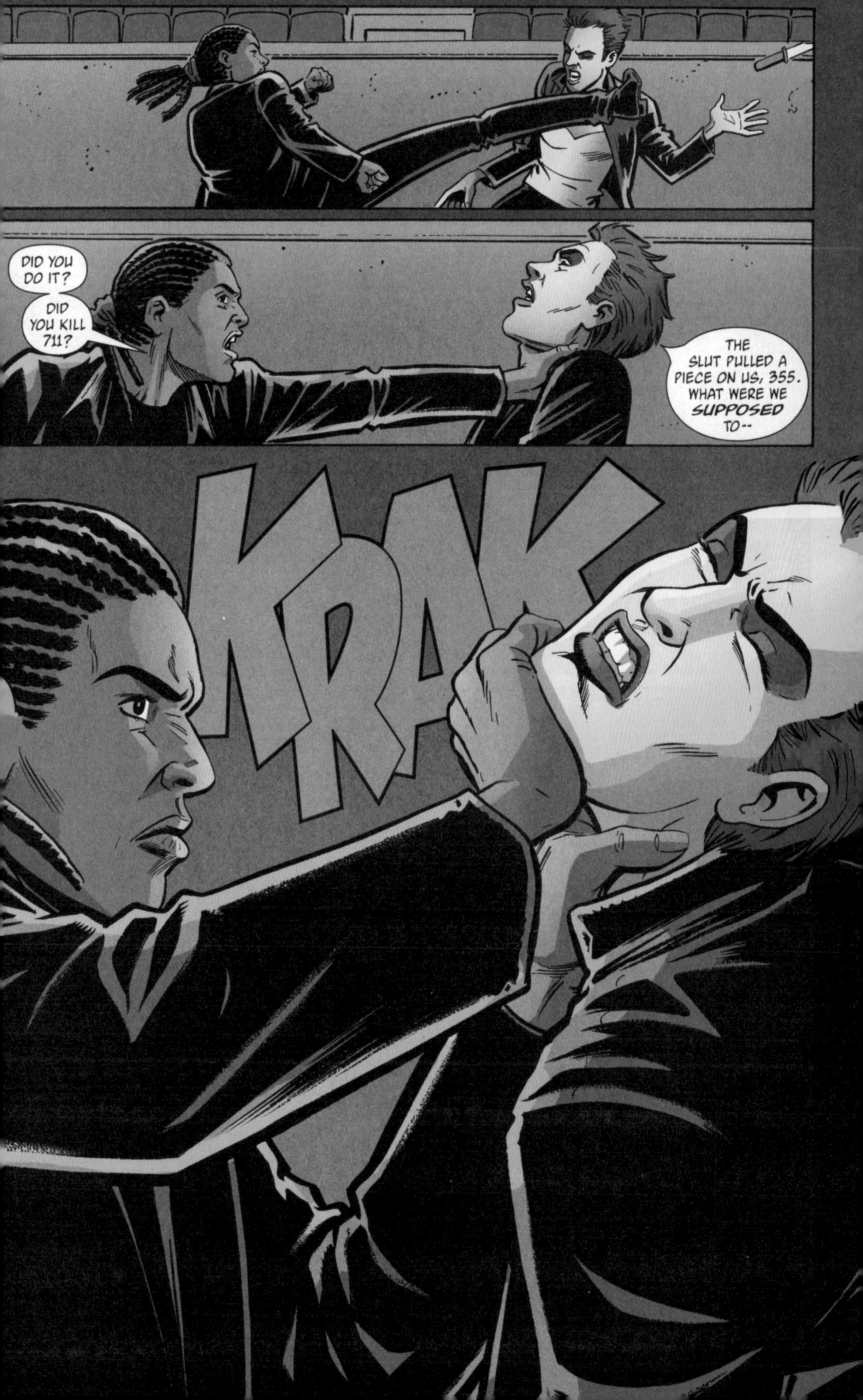
DID YOU DO IT?
DID YOU KILL 711?
THE SLUT PULLED A PIECE ON US, 355. WHAT WERE WE SUPPOSED TO--
KRAK

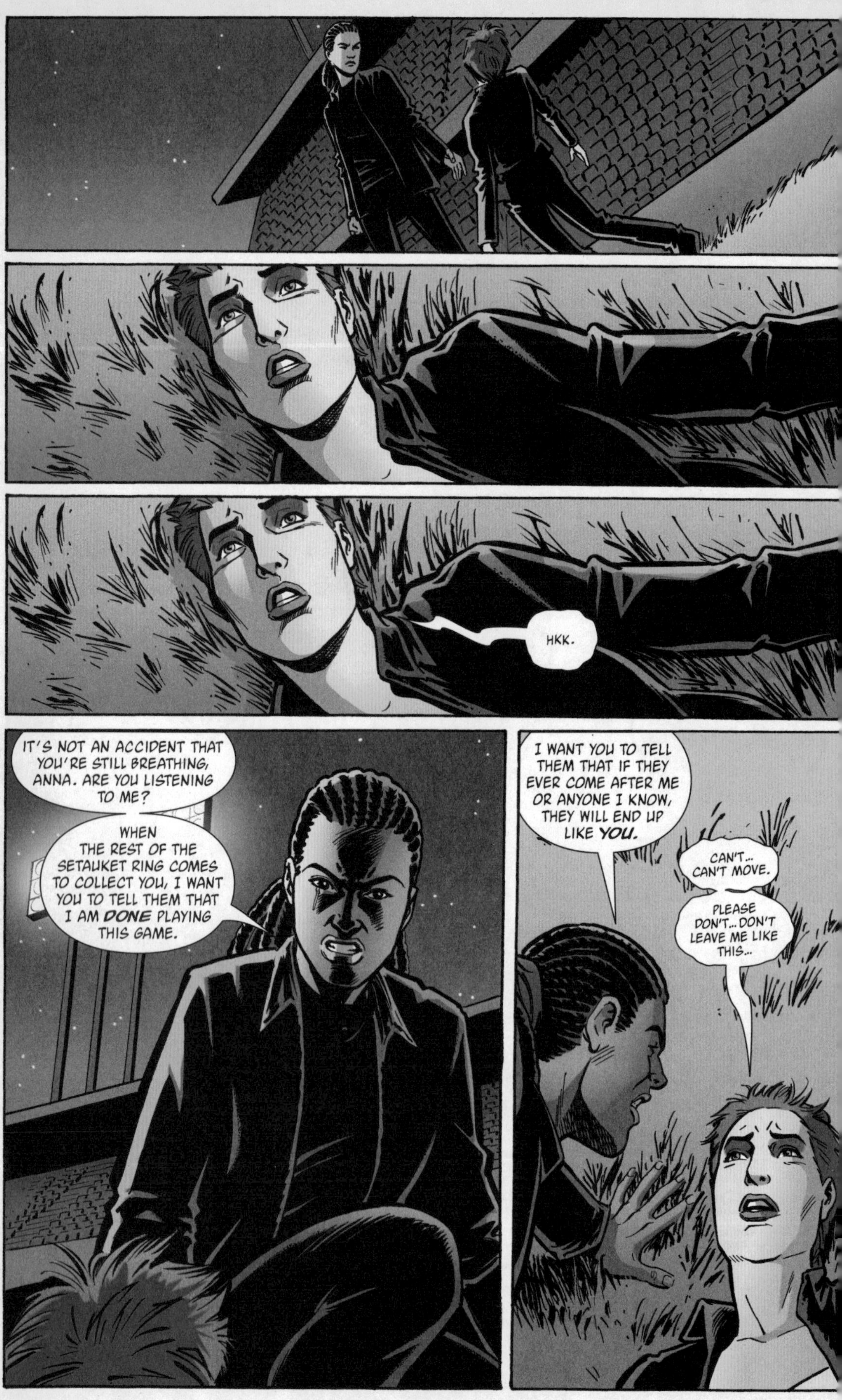
HKK.
IT'S NOT AN ACCIDENT THAT YOU'RE STILL BREATHING, ANNA. ARE YOU LISTENING TO ME?
WHEN THE REST OF THE SETAUKET RING COMES TO COLLECT YOU, I WANT YOU TO TELL THEM THAT I AM *DONE* PLAYING THIS GAME.
I WANT YOU TO TELL THEM THAT IF THEY EVER COME AFTER ME OR ANYONE I KNOW, THEY WILL END UP LIKE *YOU.*
CAN'T... CAN'T MOVE.
PLEASE DON'T... DON'T LEAVE ME LIKE THIS...

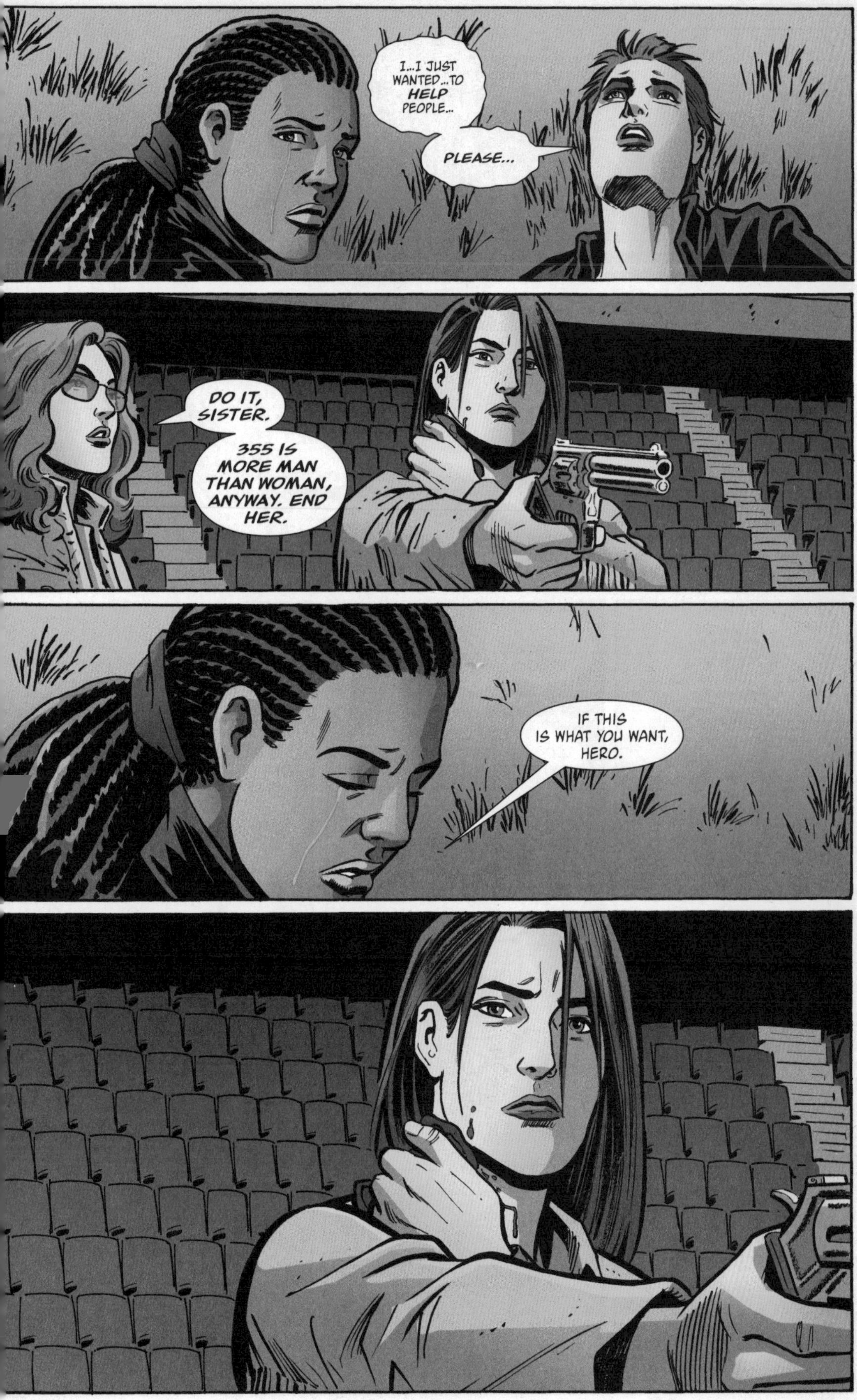
I...I JUST WANTED...TO HELP PEOPLE...
PLEASE...
DO IT, SISTER.
355 IS MORE MAN THAN WOMAN, ANYWAY. END HER.
IF THIS IS WHAT YOU WANT, HERO.

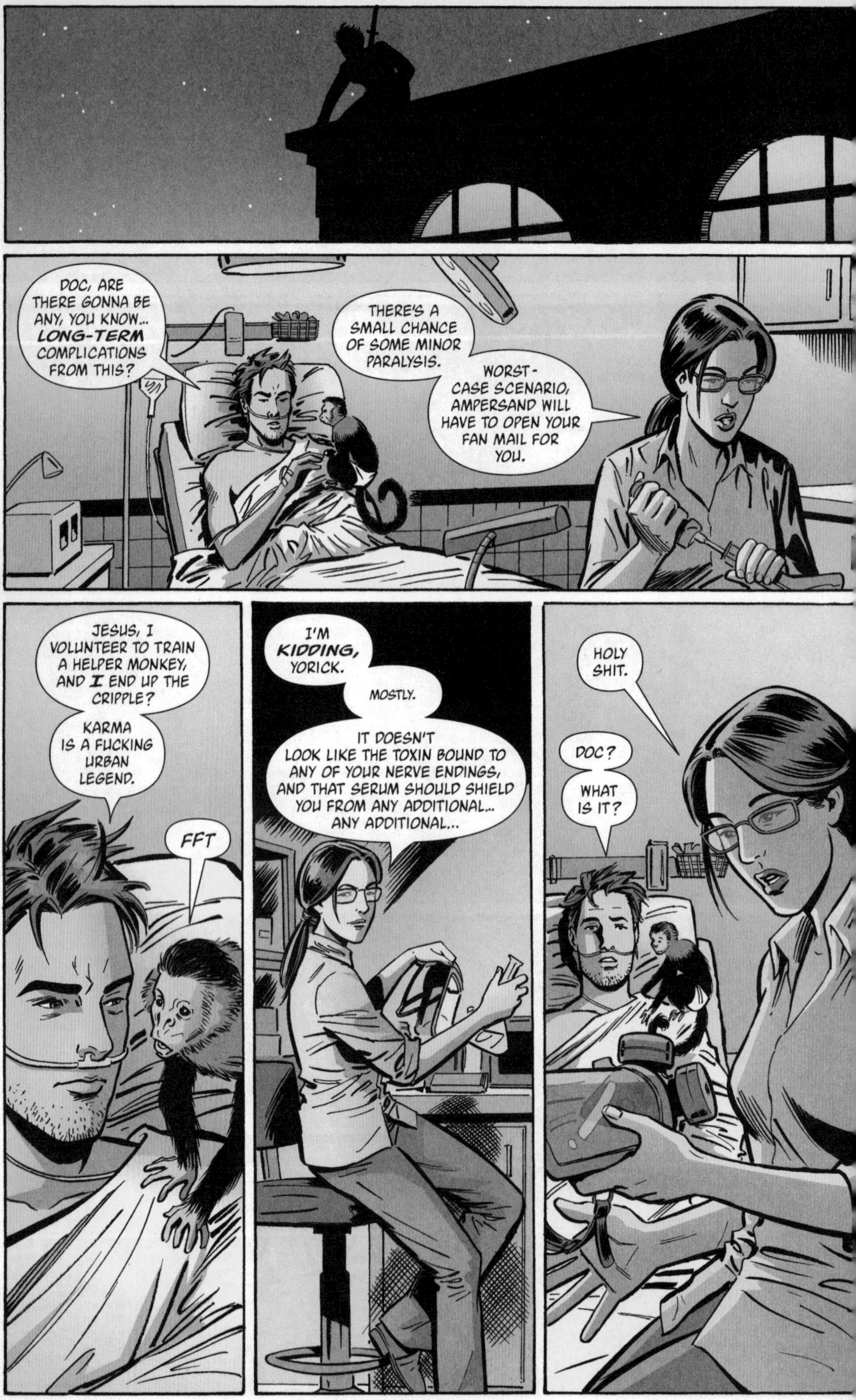

DOC, ARE THERE GONNA BE ANY, YOU KNOW... **LONG-TERM** COMPLICATIONS FROM THIS?
THERE'S A SMALL CHANCE OF SOME MINOR PARALYSIS.
WORST-CASE SCENARIO, AMPERSAND WILL HAVE TO OPEN YOUR FAN MAIL FOR YOU.
JESUS, I VOLUNTEER TO TRAIN A HELPER MONKEY, AND **I** END UP THE CRIPPLE?
KARMA IS A FUCKING URBAN LEGEND.
FFT
I'M **KIDDING,** YORICK.
MOSTLY.
IT DOESN'T LOOK LIKE THE TOXIN BOUND TO ANY OF YOUR NERVE ENDINGS, AND THAT SERUM SHOULD SHIELD YOU FROM ANY ADDITIONAL... ANY ADDITIONAL...
HOLY SHIT.
DOC?
WHAT IS IT?

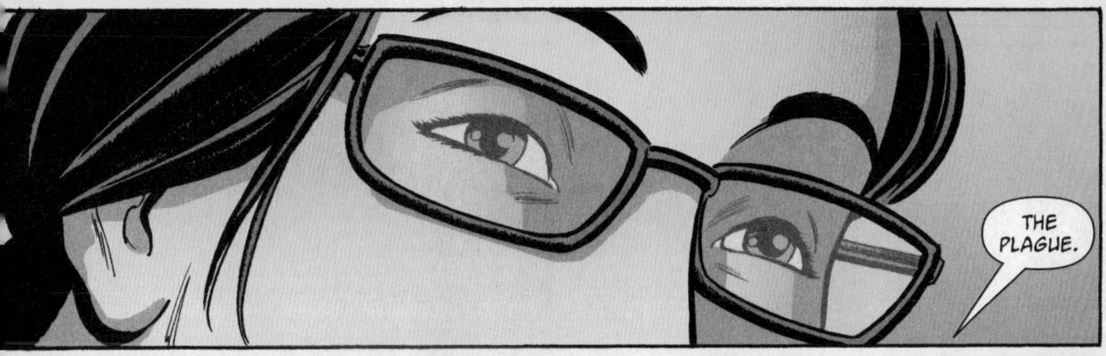
THE
PLAGUE.

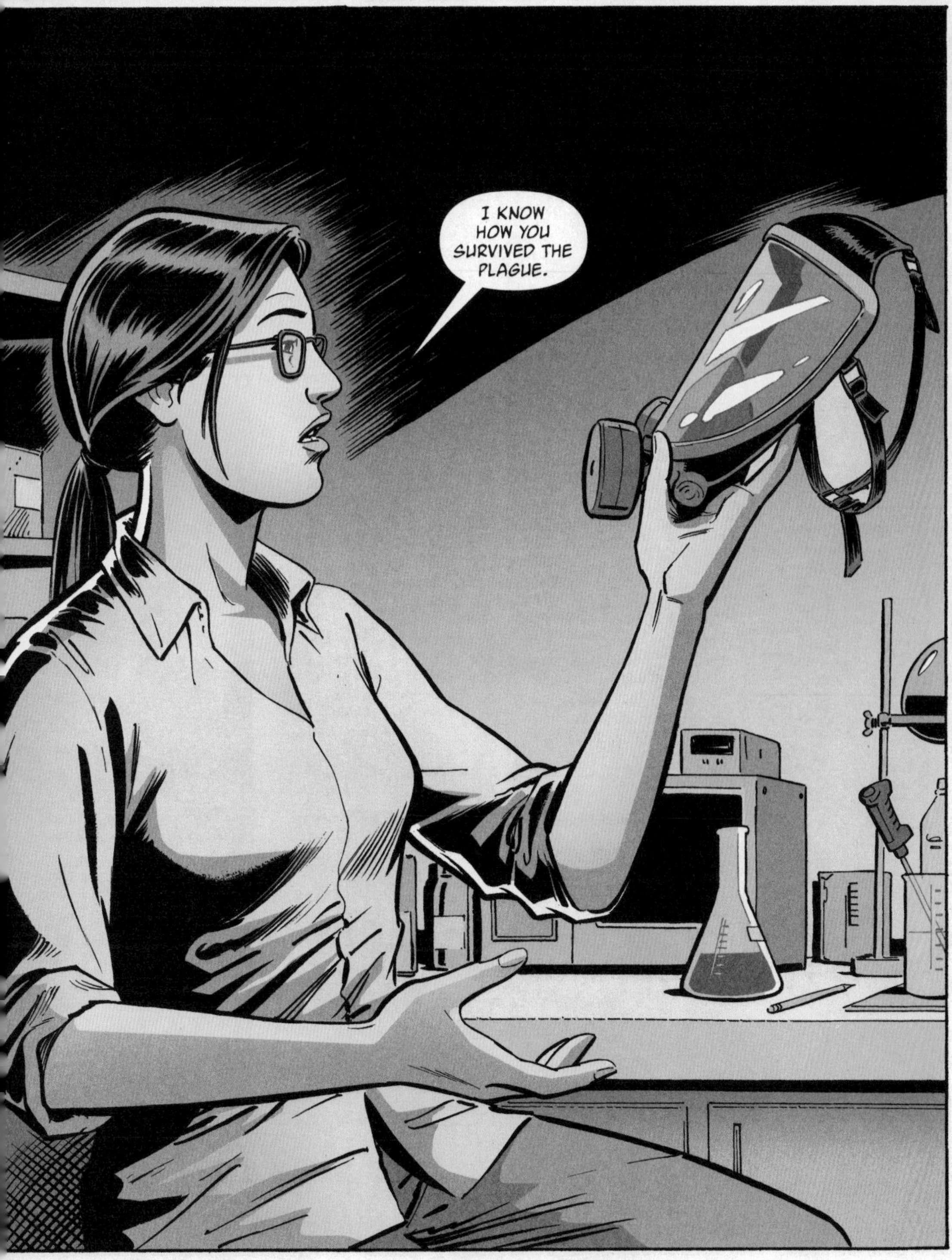
I KNOW
HOW YOU
SURVIVED THE
PLAGUE.

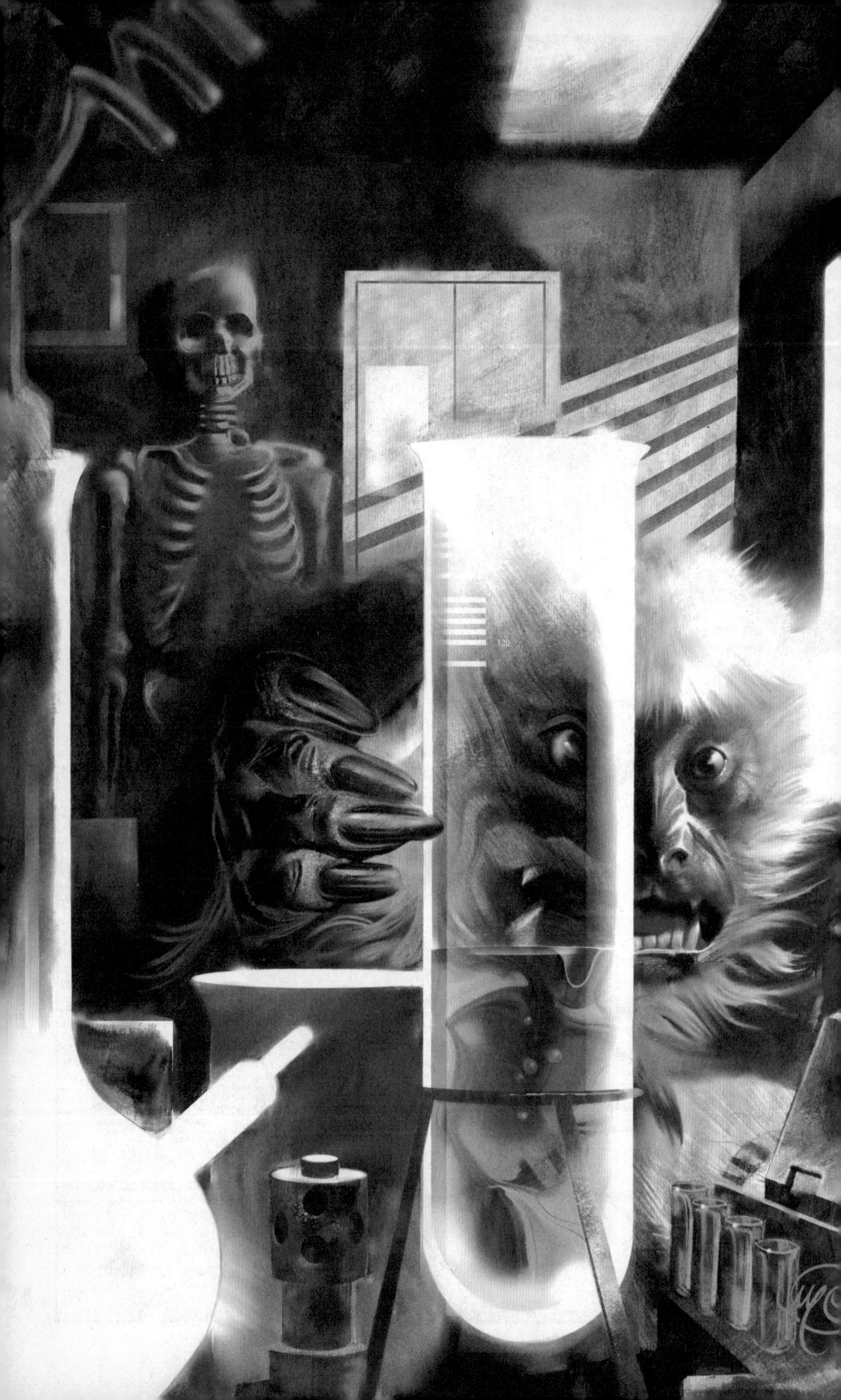

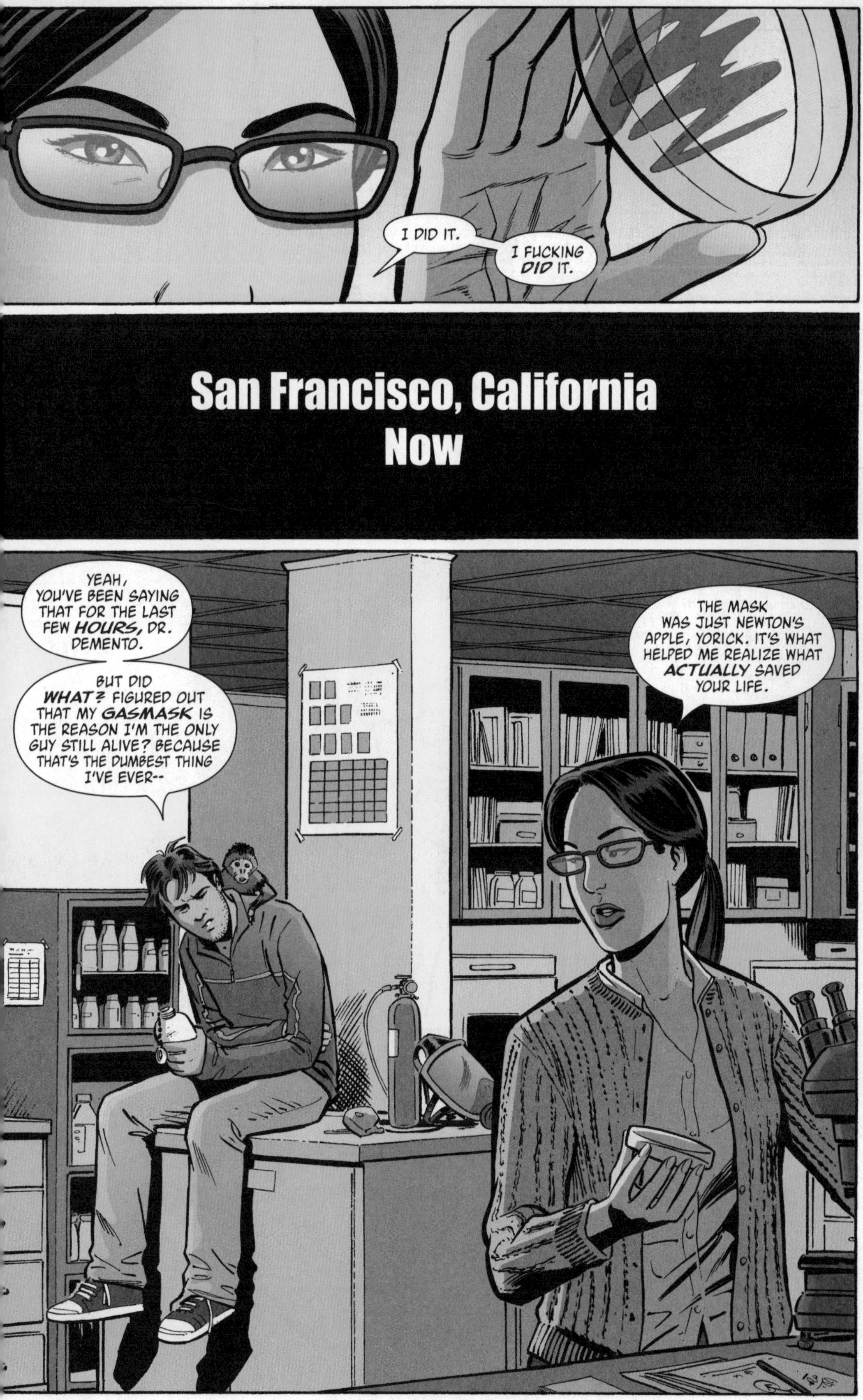
I DID IT.
I FUCKING DID IT.
San Francisco, California
Now
YEAH, YOU'VE BEEN SAYING THAT FOR THE LAST FEW HOURS, DR. DEMENTO.
BUT DID WHAT? FIGURED OUT THAT MY GASMASK IS THE REASON I'M THE ONLY GUY STILL ALIVE? BECAUSE THAT'S THE DUMBEST THING I'VE EVER--
THE MASK WAS JUST NEWTON'S APPLE, YORICK. IT'S WHAT HELPED ME REALIZE WHAT ACTUALLY SAVED YOUR LIFE.

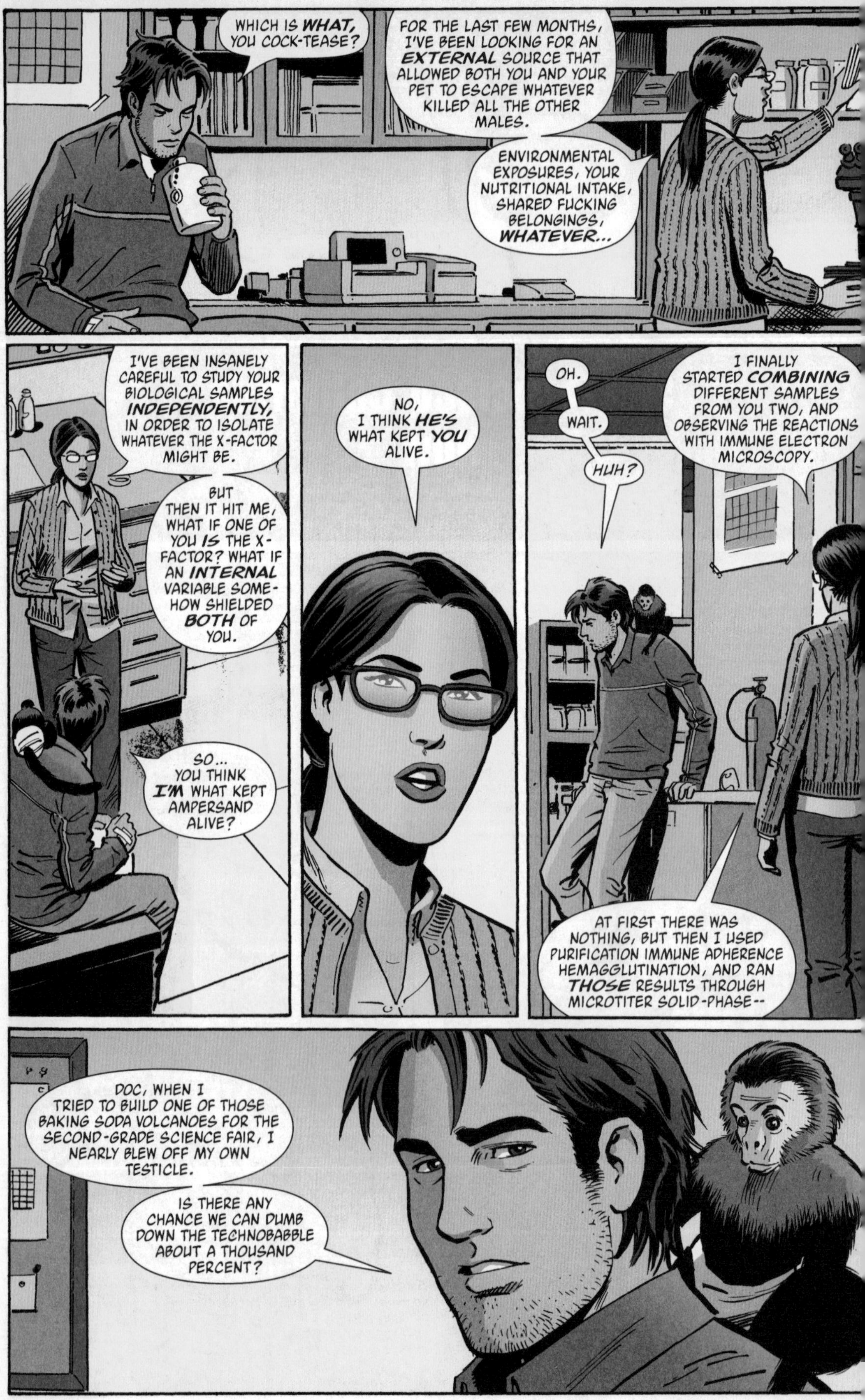
WHICH IS WHAT, YOU COCK-TEASE?
FOR THE LAST FEW MONTHS, I'VE BEEN LOOKING FOR AN EXTERNAL SOURCE THAT ALLOWED BOTH YOU AND YOUR PET TO ESCAPE WHATEVER KILLED ALL THE OTHER MALES.
ENVIRONMENTAL EXPOSURES, YOUR NUTRITIONAL INTAKE, SHARED FUCKING BELONGINGS, WHATEVER...
I'VE BEEN INSANELY CAREFUL TO STUDY YOUR BIOLOGICAL SAMPLES INDEPENDENTLY, IN ORDER TO ISOLATE WHATEVER THE X-FACTOR MIGHT BE.
BUT THEN IT HIT ME, WHAT IF ONE OF YOU IS THE X-FACTOR? WHAT IF AN INTERNAL VARIABLE SOMEHOW SHIELDED BOTH OF YOU.
SO... YOU THINK I'M WHAT KEPT AMPERSAND ALIVE?
NO, I THINK HE'S WHAT KEPT YOU ALIVE.
OH.
WAIT.
HUH?
I FINALLY STARTED COMBINING DIFFERENT SAMPLES FROM YOU TWO, AND OBSERVING THE REACTIONS WITH IMMUNE ELECTRON MICROSCOPY.
AT FIRST THERE WAS NOTHING, BUT THEN I USED PURIFICATION IMMUNE ADHERENCE HEMAGGLUTINATION, AND RAN THOSE RESULTS THROUGH MICROTITER SOLID-PHASE--
DOC, WHEN I TRIED TO BUILD ONE OF THOSE BAKING SODA VOLCANOES FOR THE SECOND-GRADE SCIENCE FAIR, I NEARLY BLEW OFF MY OWN TESTICLE.
IS THERE ANY CHANCE WE CAN DUMB DOWN THE TECHNOBABBLE ABOUT A THOUSAND PERCENT?

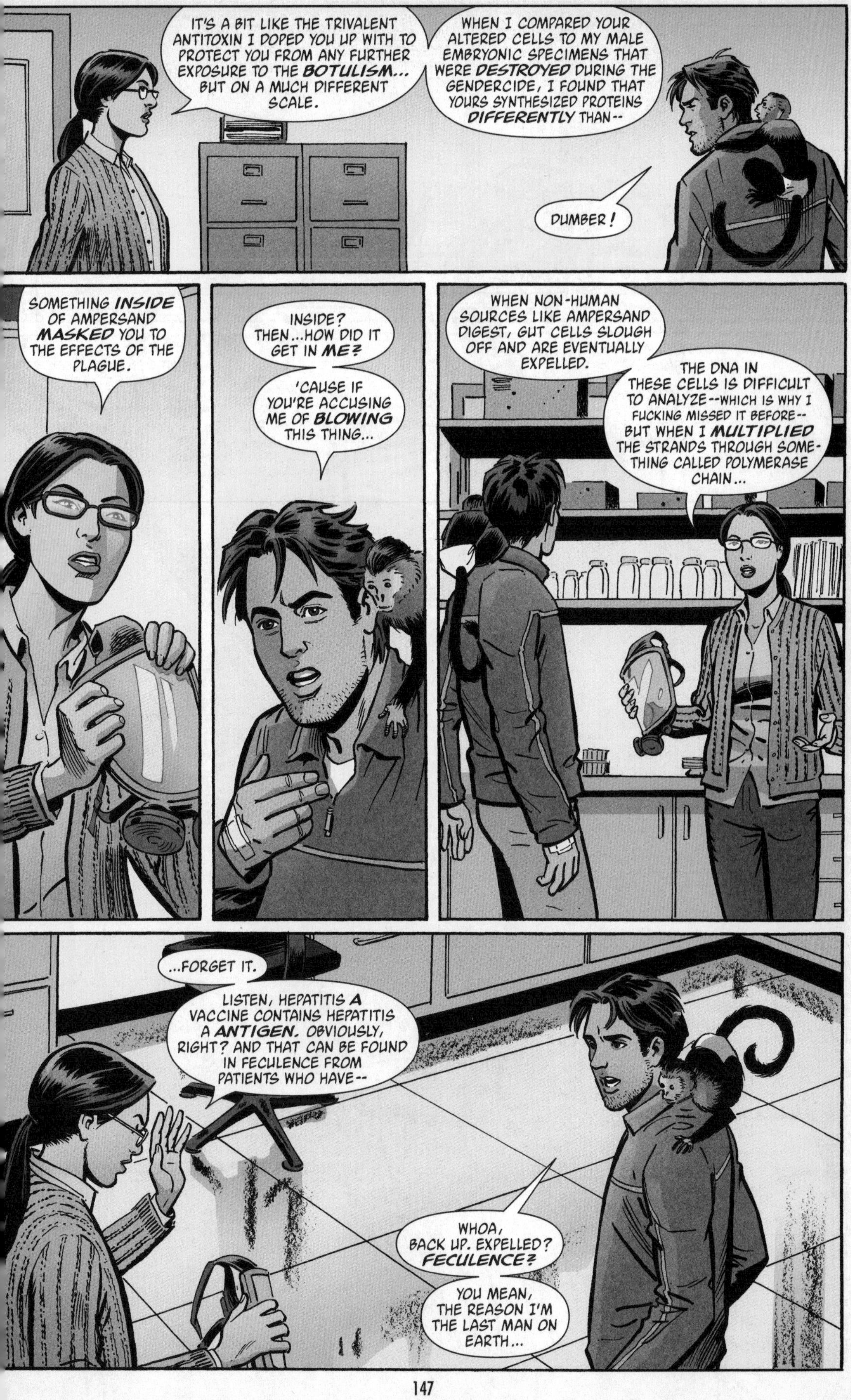
IT'S A BIT LIKE THE TRIVALENT ANTITOXIN I DOPED YOU UP WITH TO PROTECT YOU FROM ANY FURTHER EXPOSURE TO THE BOTULISM... BUT ON A MUCH DIFFERENT SCALE.
WHEN I COMPARED YOUR ALTERED CELLS TO MY MALE EMBRYONIC SPECIMENS THAT WERE DESTROYED DURING THE GENDERCIDE, I FOUND THAT YOURS SYNTHESIZED PROTEINS DIFFERENTLY THAN--
DUMBER!
SOMETHING INSIDE OF AMPERSAND MASKED YOU TO THE EFFECTS OF THE PLAGUE.
INSIDE? THEN...HOW DID IT GET IN ME?
'CAUSE IF YOU'RE ACCUSING ME OF BLOWING THIS THING...
WHEN NON-HUMAN SOURCES LIKE AMPERSAND DIGEST, GUT CELLS SLOUGH OFF AND ARE EVENTUALLY EXPELLED.
THE DNA IN THESE CELLS IS DIFFICULT TO ANALYZE--WHICH IS WHY I FUCKING MISSED IT BEFORE--BUT WHEN I MULTIPLIED THE STRANDS THROUGH SOMETHING CALLED POLYMERASE CHAIN...
...FORGET IT.
LISTEN, HEPATITIS A VACCINE CONTAINS HEPATITIS A ANTIGEN. OBVIOUSLY, RIGHT? AND THAT CAN BE FOUND IN FECULENCE FROM PATIENTS WHO HAVE--
WHOA, BACK UP. EXPELLED? FECULENCE?
YOU MEAN, THE REASON I'M THE LAST MAN ON EARTH...

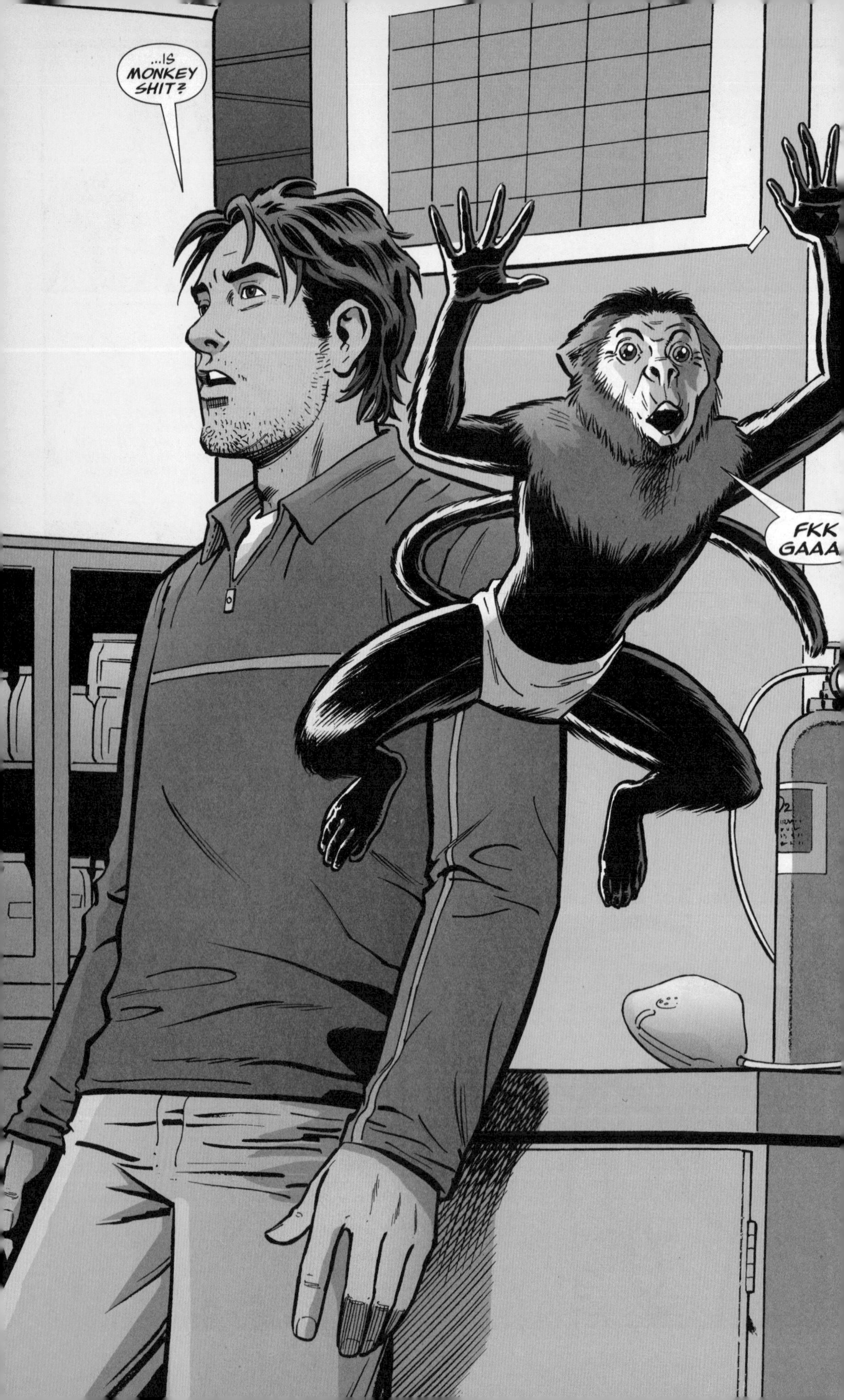
...IS MONKEY SHIT?
FKK GAAA

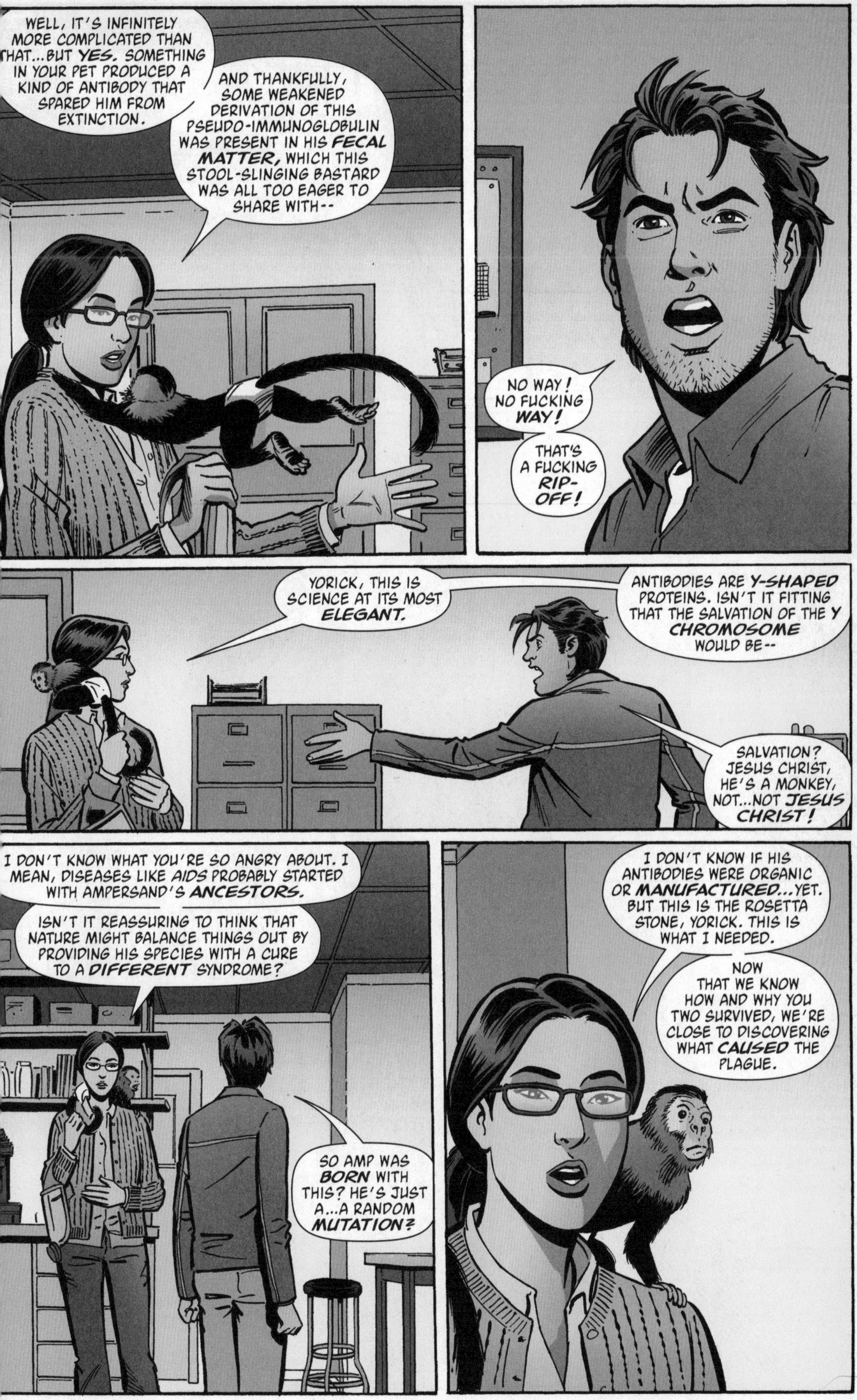
WELL, IT'S INFINITELY MORE COMPLICATED THAN THAT...BUT YES. SOMETHING IN YOUR PET PRODUCED A KIND OF ANTIBODY THAT SPARED HIM FROM EXTINCTION.
AND THANKFULLY, SOME WEAKENED DERIVATION OF THIS PSEUDO-IMMUNOGLOBULIN WAS PRESENT IN HIS FECAL MATTER, WHICH THIS STOOL-SLINGING BASTARD WAS ALL TOO EAGER TO SHARE WITH--
NO WAY! NO FUCKING WAY!
THAT'S A FUCKING RIP-OFF!
YORICK, THIS IS SCIENCE AT ITS MOST ELEGANT.
ANTIBODIES ARE Y-SHAPED PROTEINS. ISN'T IT FITTING THAT THE SALVATION OF THE Y CHROMOSOME WOULD BE--
SALVATION? JESUS CHRIST, HE'S A MONKEY, NOT...NOT JESUS CHRIST!
I DON'T KNOW WHAT YOU'RE SO ANGRY ABOUT. I MEAN, DISEASES LIKE AIDS PROBABLY STARTED WITH AMPERSAND'S ANCESTORS.
ISN'T IT REASSURING TO THINK THAT NATURE MIGHT BALANCE THINGS OUT BY PROVIDING HIS SPECIES WITH A CURE TO A DIFFERENT SYNDROME?
SO AMP WAS BORN WITH THIS? HE'S JUST A...A RANDOM MUTATION?
I DON'T KNOW IF HIS ANTIBODIES WERE ORGANIC OR MANUFACTURED...YET. BUT THIS IS THE ROSETTA STONE, YORICK. THIS IS WHAT I NEEDED.
NOW THAT WE KNOW HOW AND WHY YOU TWO SURVIVED, WE'RE CLOSE TO DISCOVERING WHAT CAUSED THE PLAGUE.

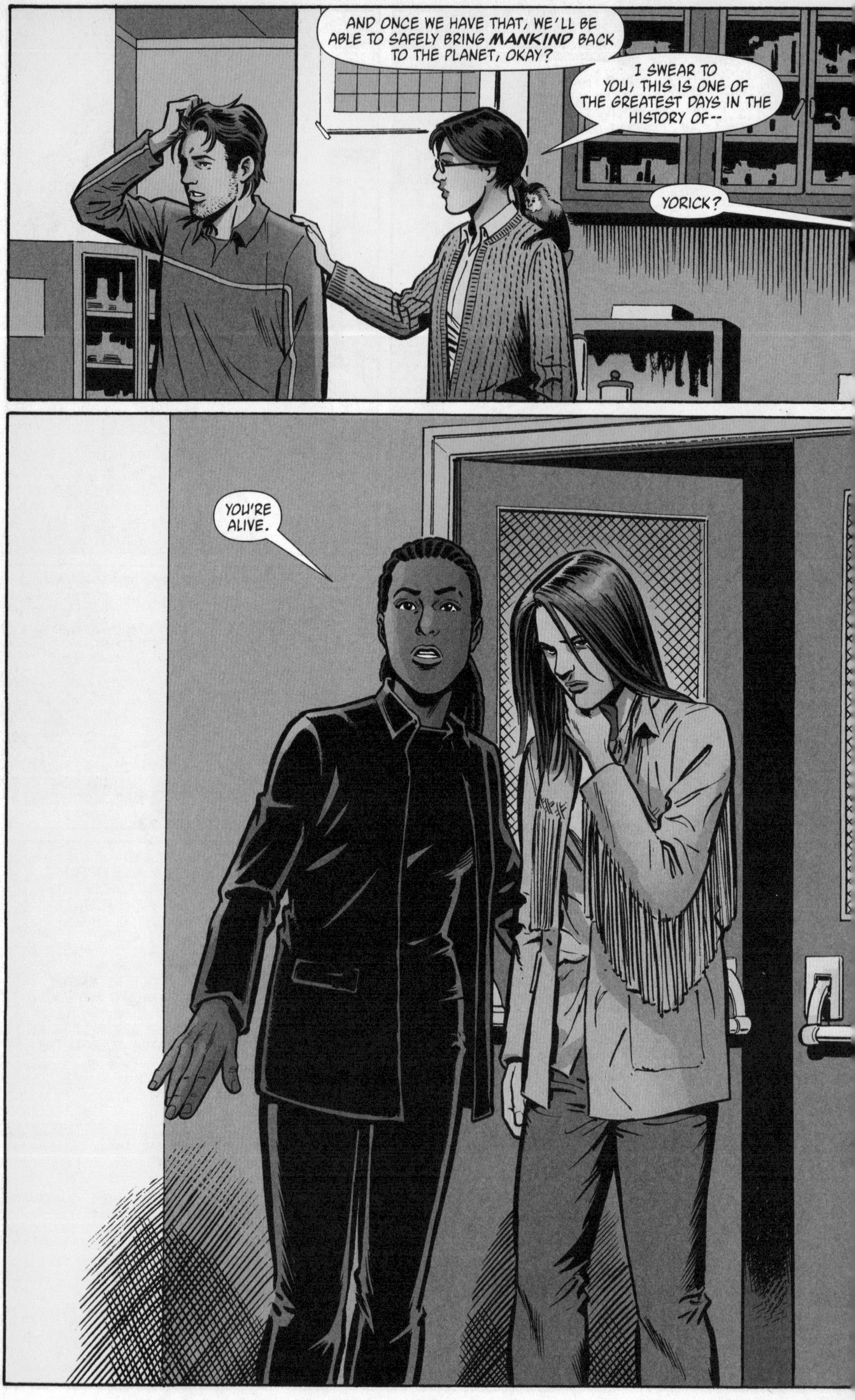
AND ONCE WE HAVE THAT, WE'LL BE ABLE TO SAFELY BRING **MANKIND** BACK TO THE PLANET, OKAY?
I SWEAR TO YOU, THIS IS ONE OF THE GREATEST DAYS IN THE HISTORY OF--
YORICK?
YOU'RE ALIVE.

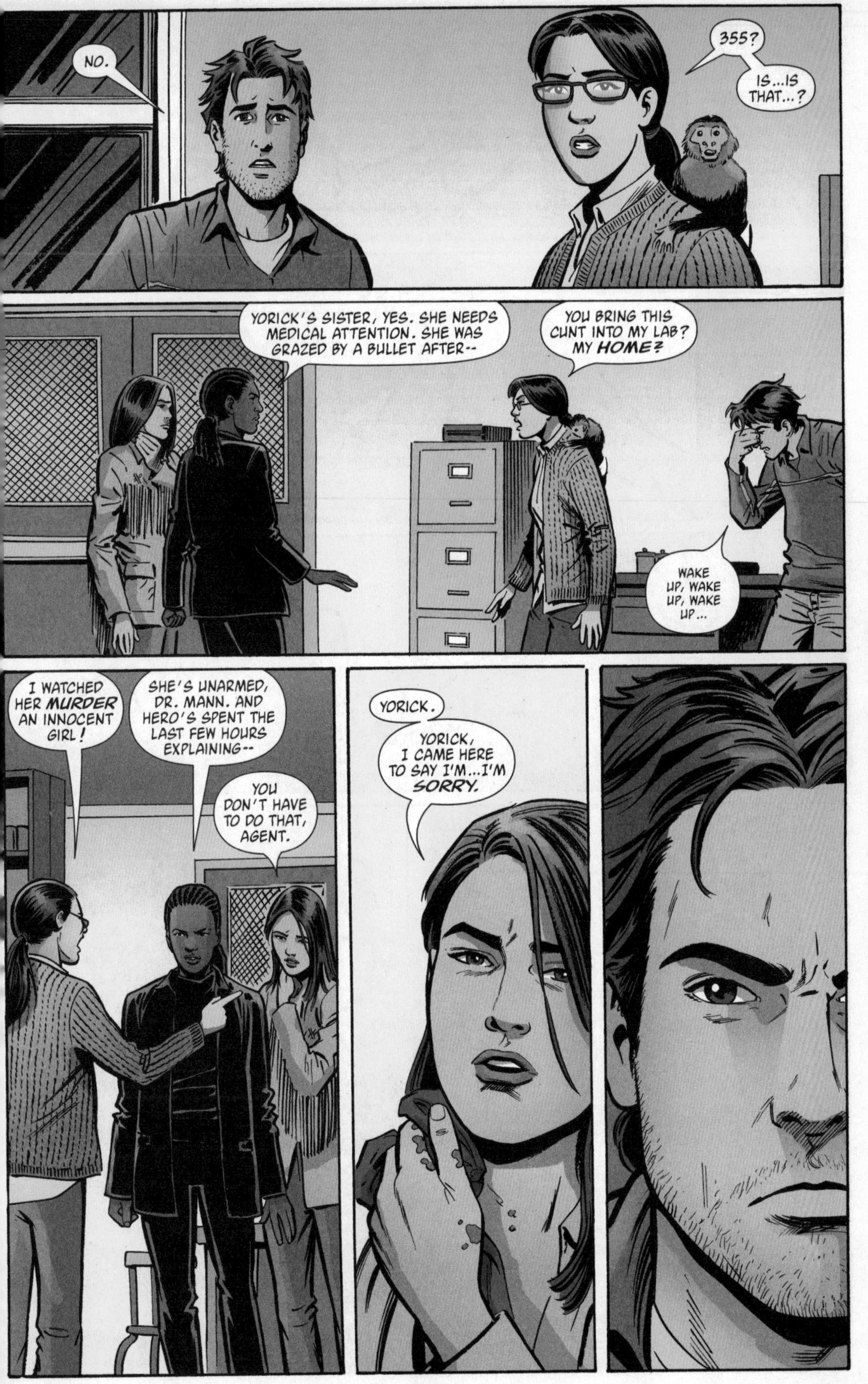
NO.
355?
IS...IS THAT...?
YORICK'S SISTER, YES. SHE NEEDS MEDICAL ATTENTION. SHE WAS GRAZED BY A BULLET AFTER--
YOU BRING THIS CUNT INTO MY LAB? MY HOME?
WAKE UP, WAKE UP, WAKE UP...
I WATCHED HER MURDER AN INNOCENT GIRL!
SHE'S UNARMED, DR. MANN. AND HERO'S SPENT THE LAST FEW HOURS EXPLAINING--
YOU DON'T HAVE TO DO THAT, AGENT.
YORICK.
YORICK, I CAME HERE TO SAY I'M...I'M SORRY.

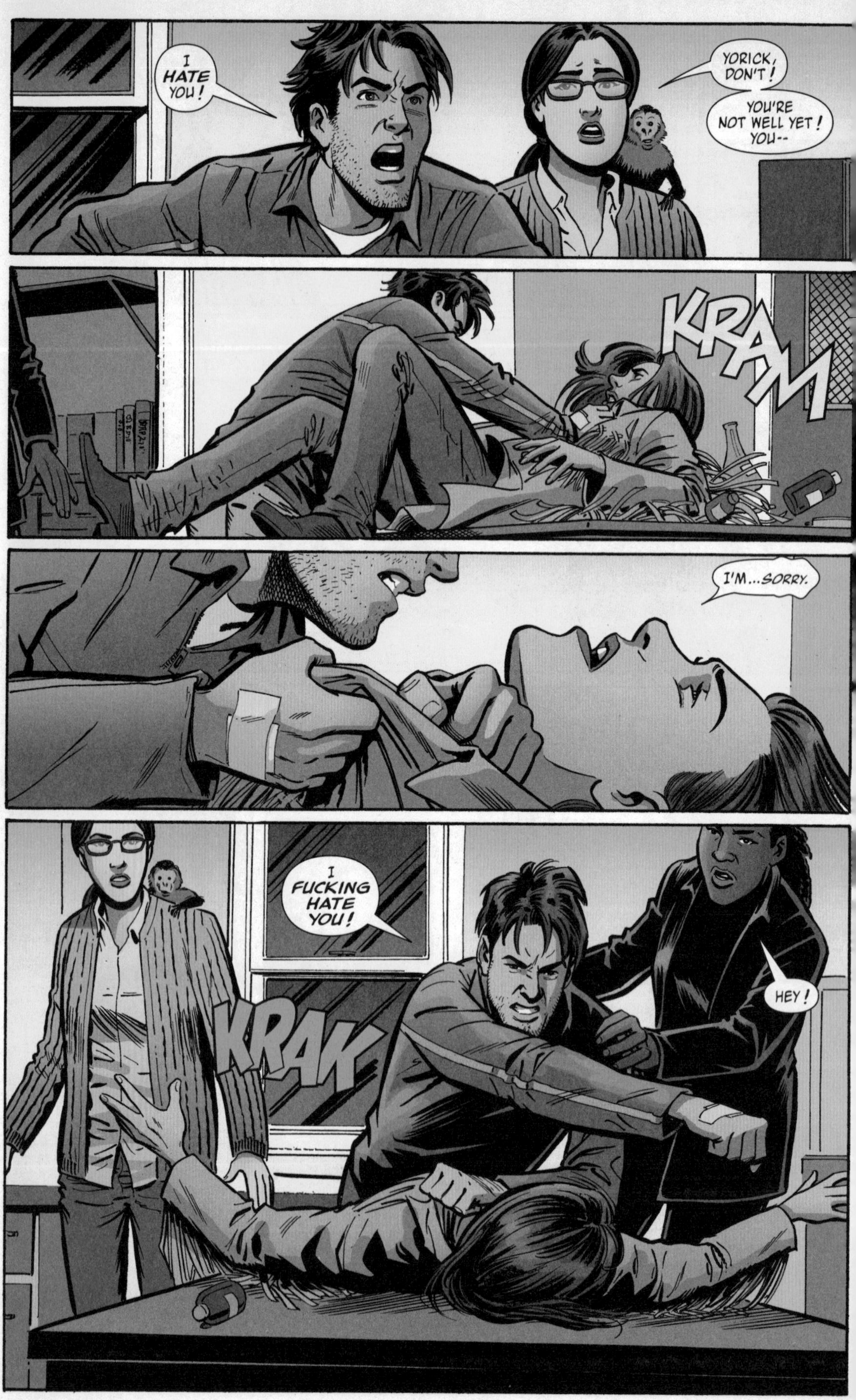
I HATE YOU!
YORICK, DON'T!
YOU'RE NOT WELL YET! YOU--
KRAM
I'M...SORRY.
I FUCKING HATE YOU!
HEY!
KRAK

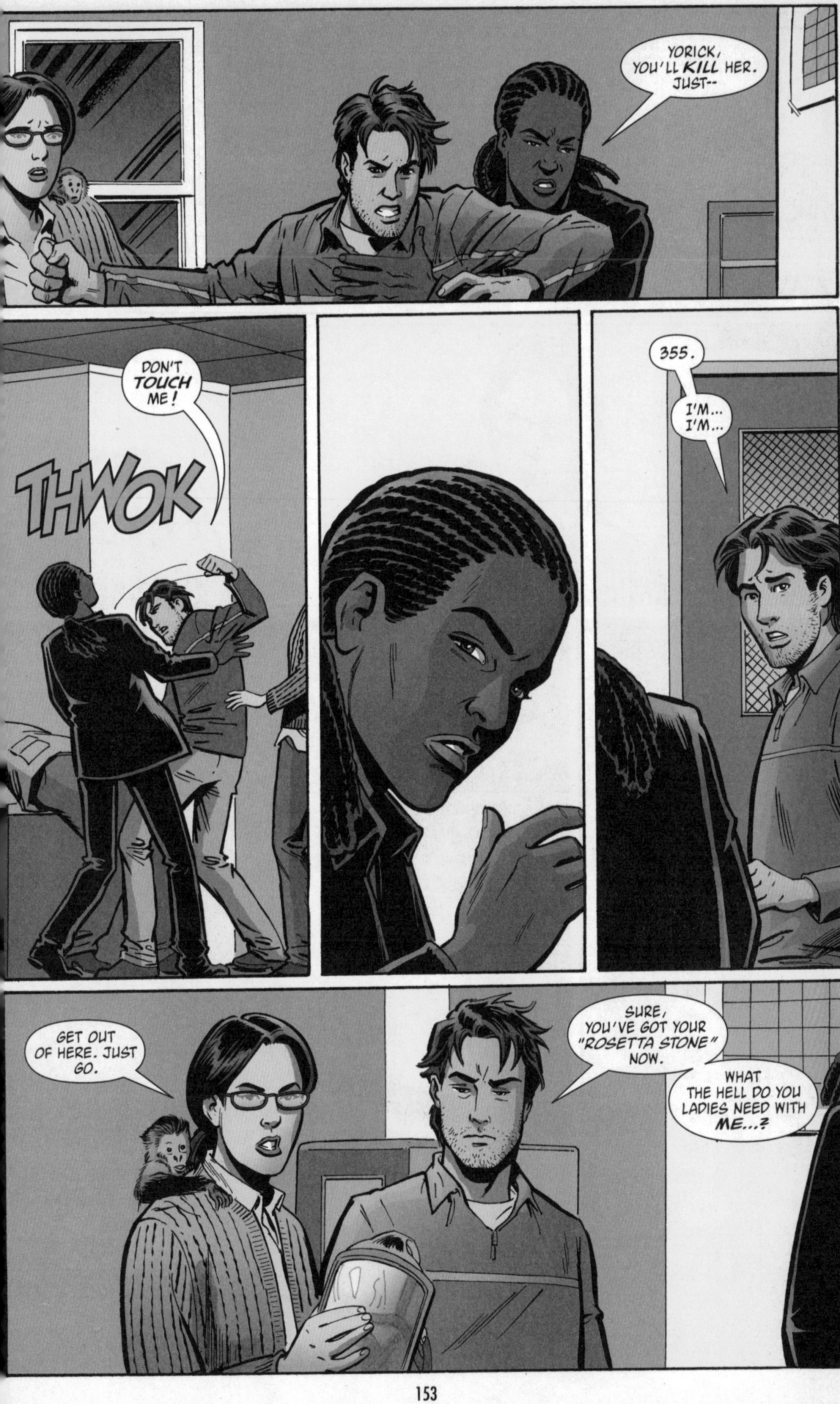
YORICK, YOU'LL KILL HER. JUST--
DON'T TOUCH ME!
THWOK
355.
I'M... I'M...
GET OUT OF HERE. JUST GO.
SURE, YOU'VE GOT YOUR "ROSETTA STONE" NOW.
WHAT THE HELL DO YOU LADIES NEED WITH ME...?

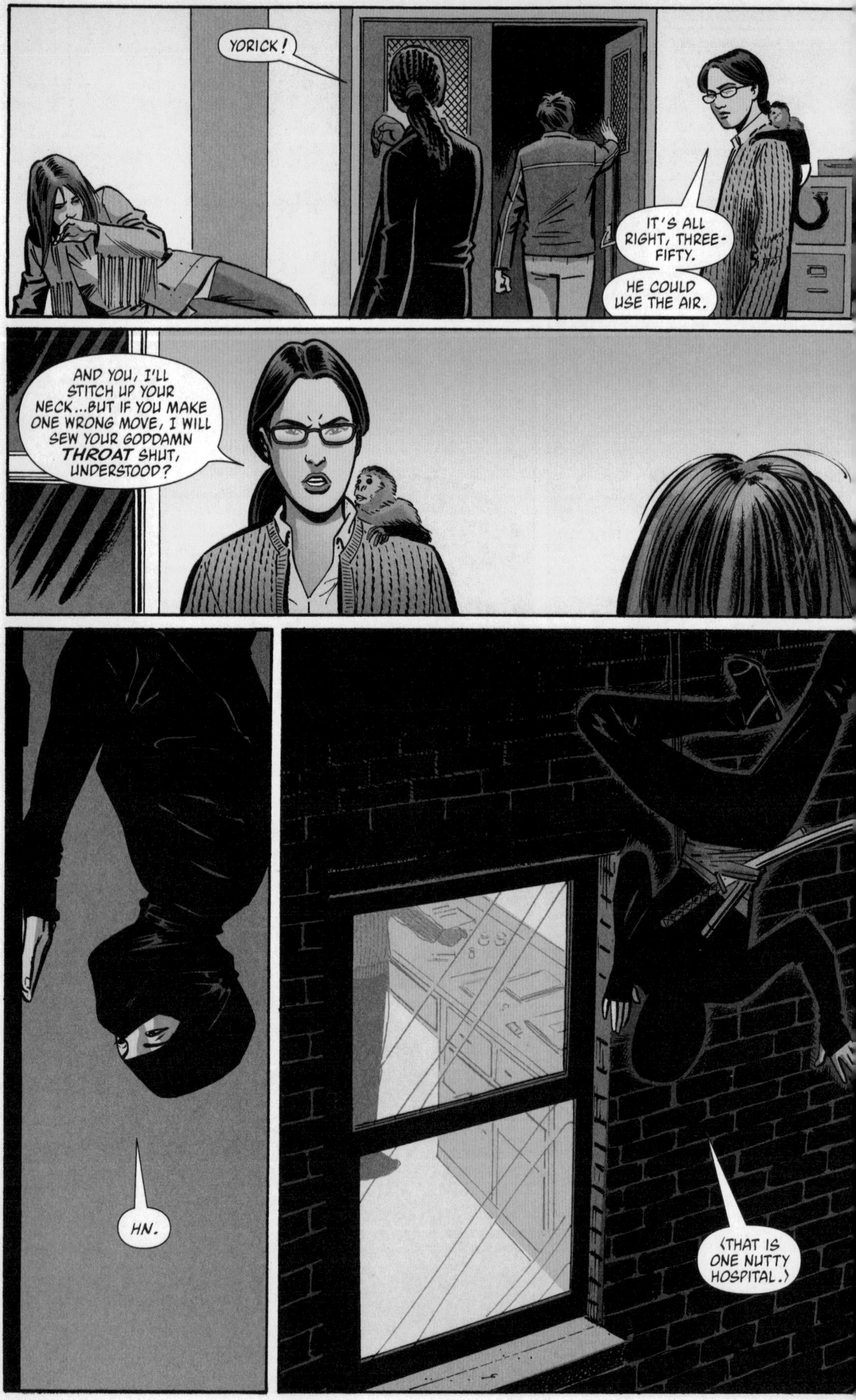

YORICK!
IT'S ALL RIGHT, THREE-FIFTY.
HE COULD USE THE AIR.
AND YOU, I'LL STITCH UP YOUR NECK...BUT IF YOU MAKE ONE WRONG MOVE, I WILL SEW YOUR GODDAMN **THROAT** SHUT, UNDERSTOOD?
HN.
⟨THAT IS ONE NUTTY HOSPITAL.⟩

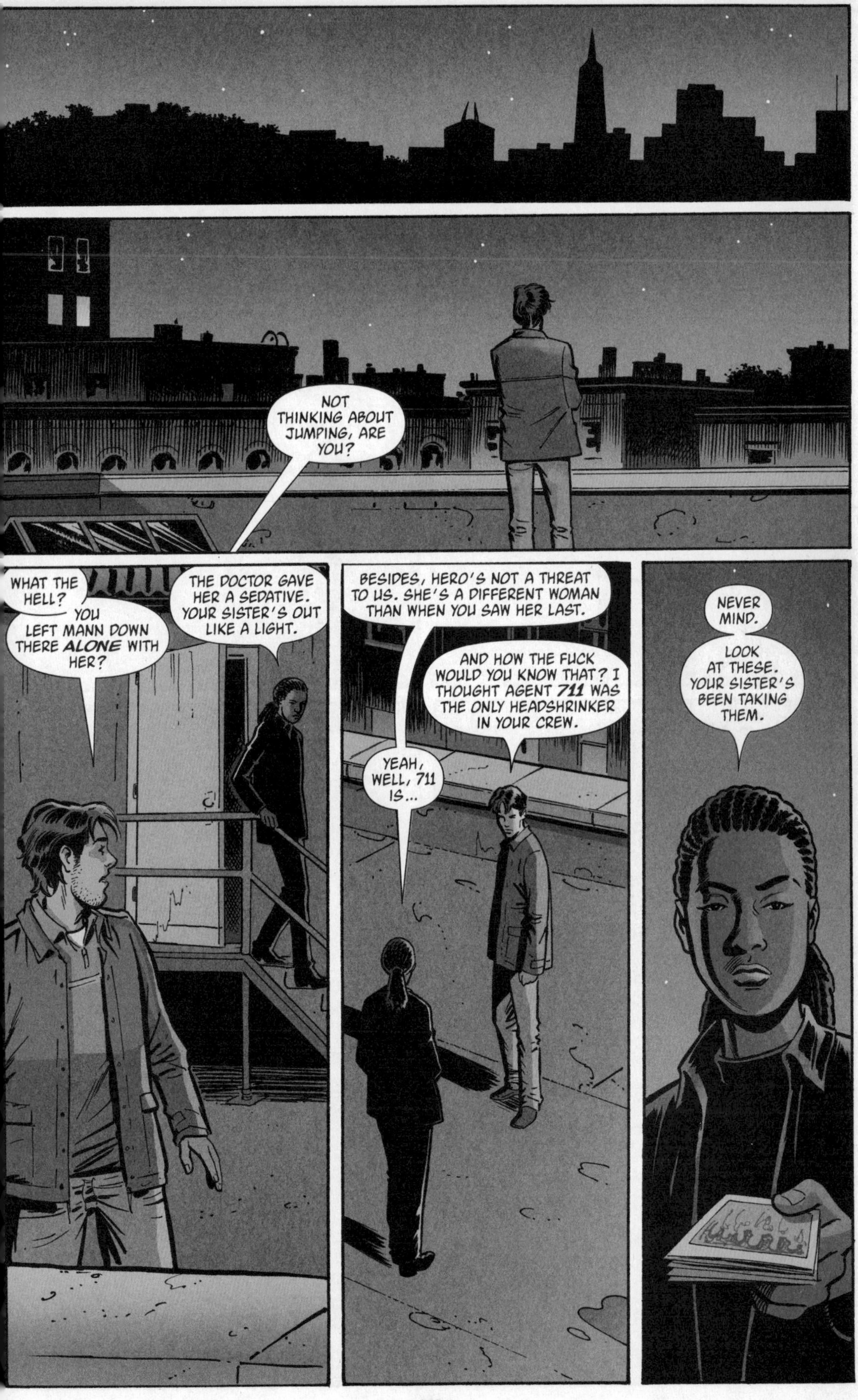
NOT THINKING ABOUT JUMPING, ARE YOU?
WHAT THE HELL?
YOU LEFT MANN DOWN THERE ALONE WITH HER?
THE DOCTOR GAVE HER A SEDATIVE. YOUR SISTER'S OUT LIKE A LIGHT.
BESIDES, HERO'S NOT A THREAT TO US. SHE'S A DIFFERENT WOMAN THAN WHEN YOU SAW HER LAST.
AND HOW THE FUCK WOULD YOU KNOW THAT? I THOUGHT AGENT 711 WAS THE ONLY HEADSHRINKER IN YOUR CREW.
YEAH, WELL, 711 IS...
NEVER MIND.
LOOK AT THESE. YOUR SISTER'S BEEN TAKING THEM.

last day in Marrsville
Lylia says she doesn't know
whether to hug me or
shiv me. Know the feeling.

Mom is doing better, but
still doesn't trust me. Won't
tell me how she was tracking
until she knows I'm "squared."
DON'T BLAME H

Vladimir and me, courtesy
Natalya. For the worlds
greatest sharp shooter, she
sure is a shitty photograph

IS THIS...?

THE ASTRONAUT'S CHILD.

HER SON.

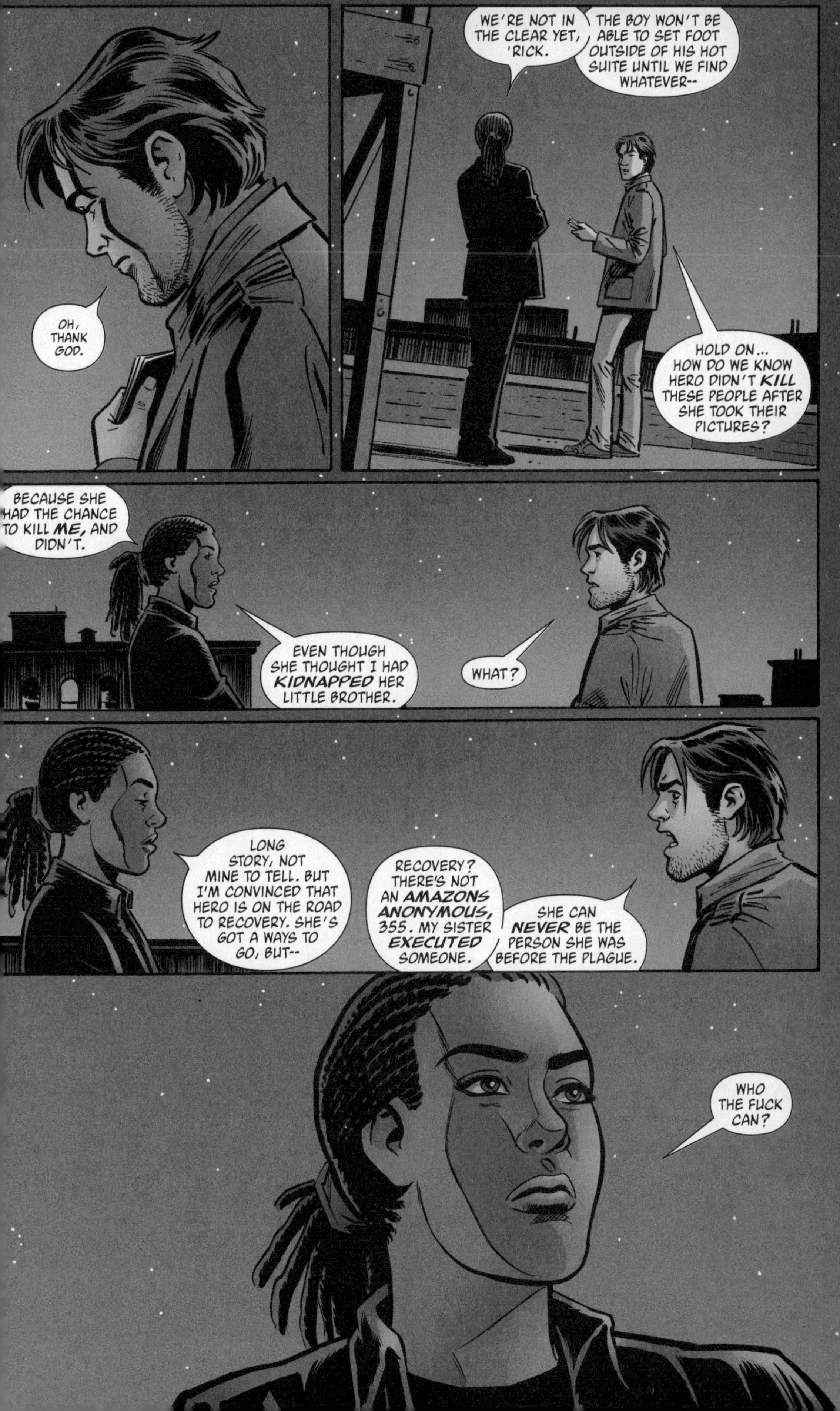
OH, THANK GOD.
WE'RE NOT IN THE CLEAR YET, 'RICK.
THE BOY WON'T BE ABLE TO SET FOOT OUTSIDE OF HIS HOT SUITE UNTIL WE FIND WHATEVER--
HOLD ON... HOW DO WE KNOW HERO DIDN'T KILL THESE PEOPLE AFTER SHE TOOK THEIR PICTURES?
BECAUSE SHE HAD THE CHANCE TO KILL ME, AND DIDN'T.
EVEN THOUGH SHE THOUGHT I HAD KIDNAPPED HER LITTLE BROTHER.
WHAT?
LONG STORY, NOT MINE TO TELL. BUT I'M CONVINCED THAT HERO IS ON THE ROAD TO RECOVERY. SHE'S GOT A WAYS TO GO, BUT--
RECOVERY? THERE'S NOT AN AMAZONS ANONYMOUS, 355. MY SISTER EXECUTED SOMEONE.
SHE CAN NEVER BE THE PERSON SHE WAS BEFORE THE PLAGUE.
WHO THE FUCK CAN?

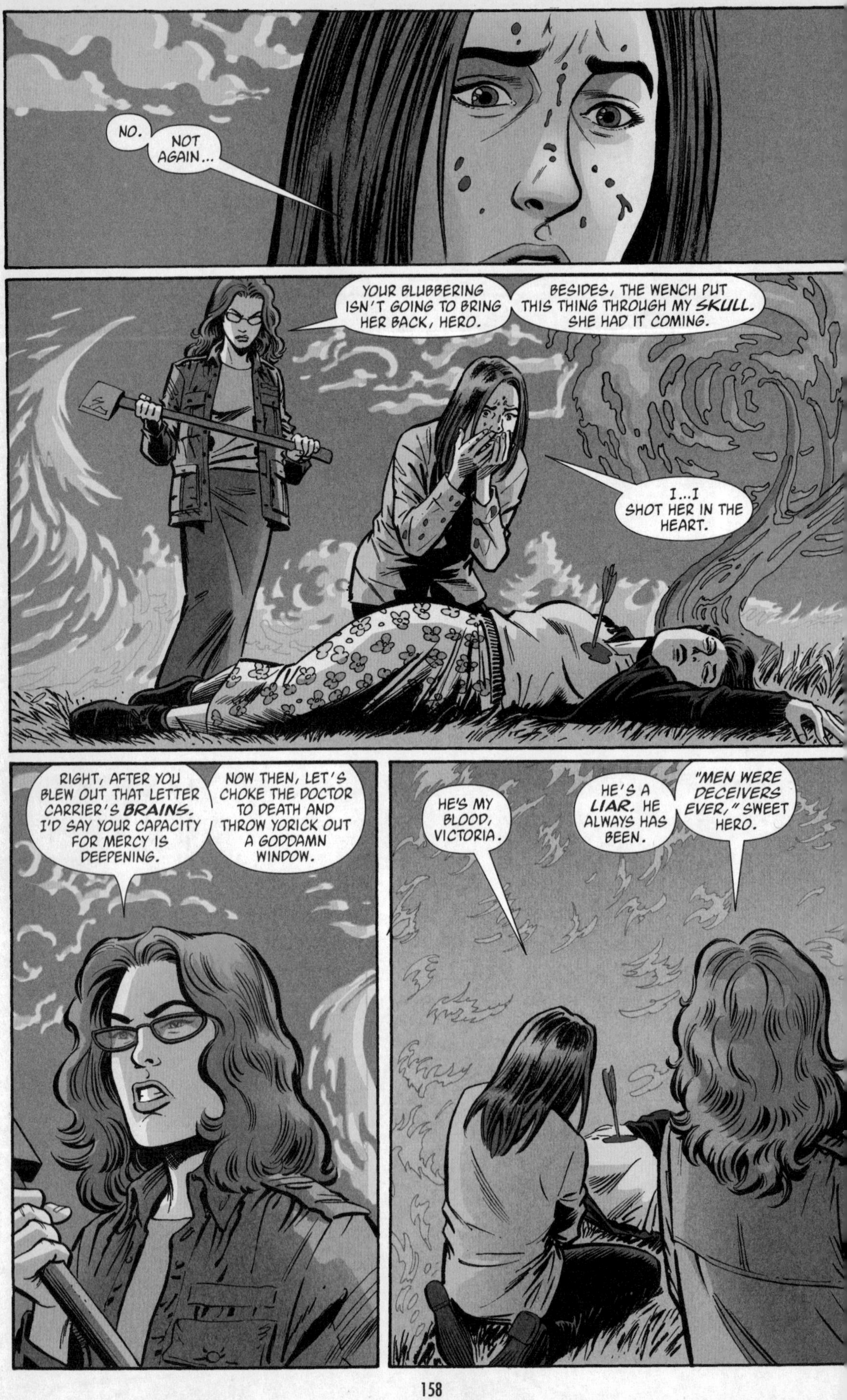
NO.
NOT AGAIN...
YOUR BLUBBERING ISN'T GOING TO BRING HER BACK, HERO.
BESIDES, THE WENCH PUT THIS THING THROUGH MY SKULL. SHE HAD IT COMING.
I...I SHOT HER IN THE HEART.
RIGHT, AFTER YOU BLEW OUT THAT LETTER CARRIER'S BRAINS. I'D SAY YOUR CAPACITY FOR MERCY IS DEEPENING.
NOW THEN, LET'S CHOKE THE DOCTOR TO DEATH AND THROW YORICK OUT A GODDAMN WINDOW.
HE'S MY BLOOD, VICTORIA.
HE'S A LIAR. HE ALWAYS HAS BEEN.
"MEN WERE DECEIVERS EVER," SWEET HERO.

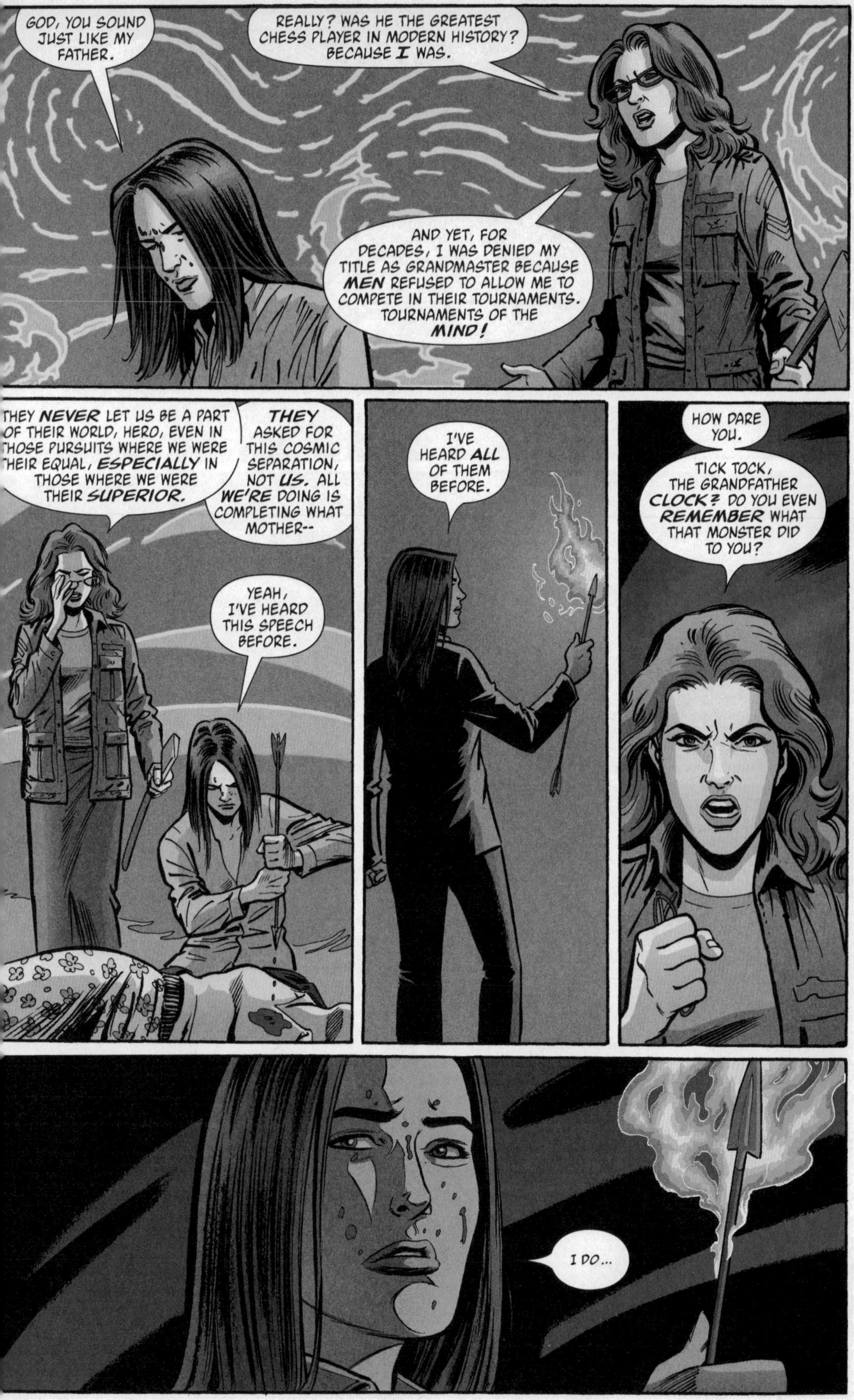

GOD, YOU SOUND JUST LIKE MY FATHER.
REALLY? WAS HE THE GREATEST CHESS PLAYER IN MODERN HISTORY? BECAUSE I WAS.
AND YET, FOR DECADES, I WAS DENIED MY TITLE AS GRANDMASTER BECAUSE MEN REFUSED TO ALLOW ME TO COMPETE IN THEIR TOURNAMENTS. TOURNAMENTS OF THE MIND!
THEY NEVER LET US BE A PART OF THEIR WORLD, HERO, EVEN IN THOSE PURSUITS WHERE WE WERE THEIR EQUAL, ESPECIALLY IN THOSE WHERE WE WERE THEIR SUPERIOR.
THEY ASKED FOR THIS COSMIC SEPARATION, NOT US. ALL WE'RE DOING IS COMPLETING WHAT MOTHER--
YEAH, I'VE HEARD THIS SPEECH BEFORE.
I'VE HEARD ALL OF THEM BEFORE.
HOW DARE YOU.
TICK TOCK, THE GRANDFATHER CLOCK? DO YOU EVEN REMEMBER WHAT THAT MONSTER DID TO YOU?
I DO...

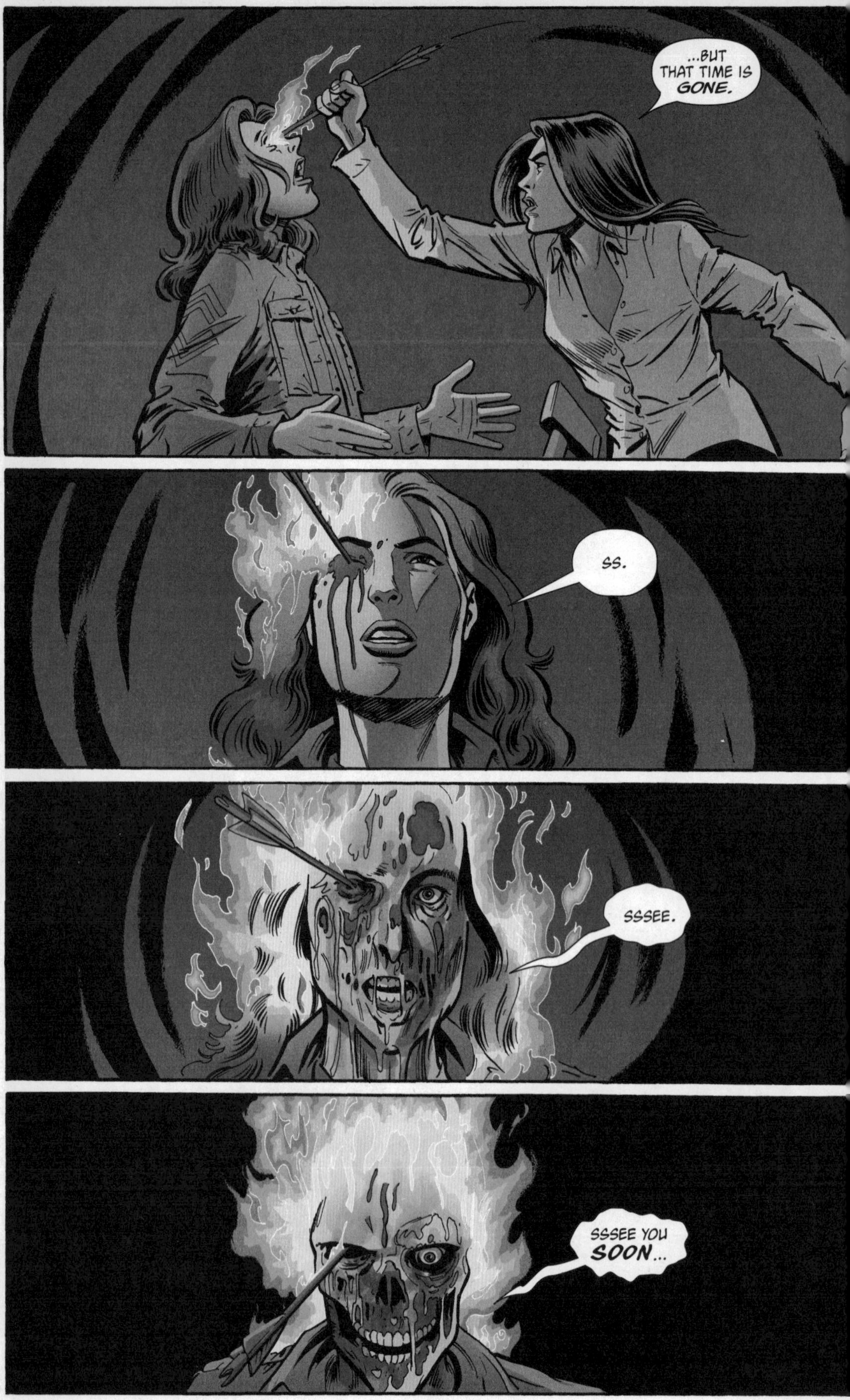

...BUT THAT TIME IS GONE.
SS.
SSSEE.
SSSEE YOU SOON...

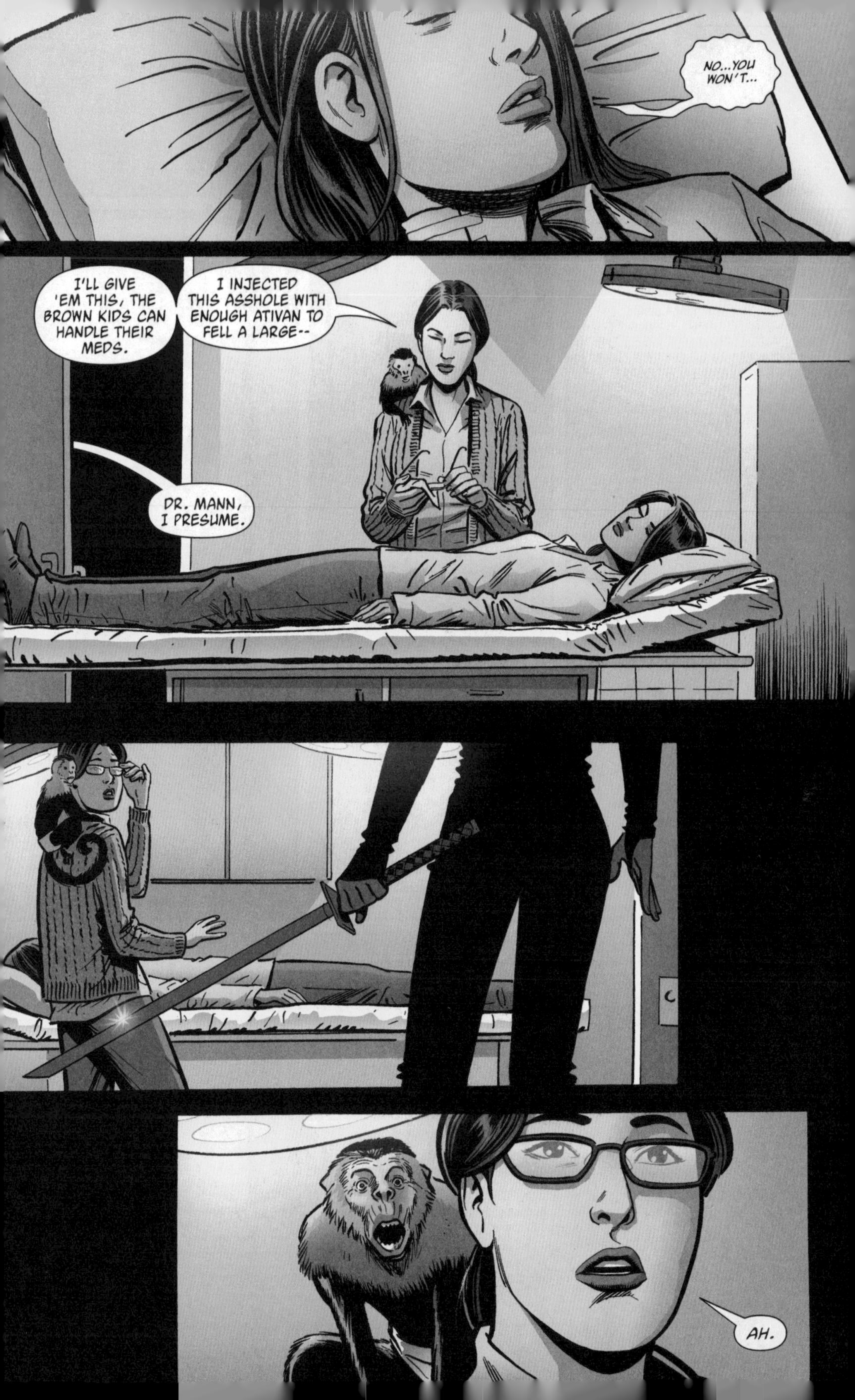
NO...YOU WON'T...
I'LL GIVE 'EM THIS, THE BROWN KIDS CAN HANDLE THEIR MEDS.
I INJECTED THIS ASSHOLE WITH ENOUGH ATIVAN TO FELL A LARGE--
DR. MANN, I PRESUME.
AH.

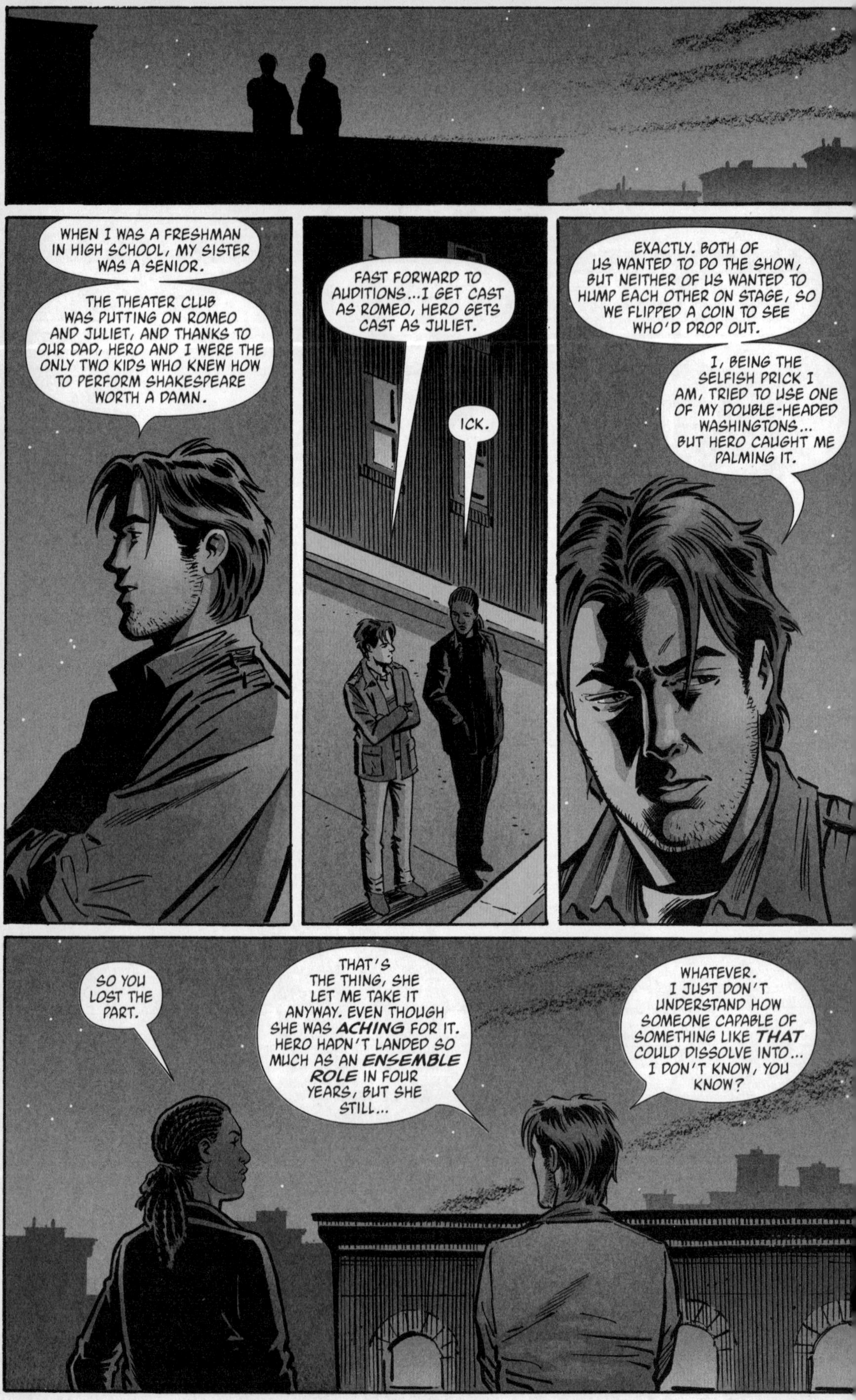
WHEN I WAS A FRESHMAN IN HIGH SCHOOL, MY SISTER WAS A SENIOR.
THE THEATER CLUB WAS PUTTING ON ROMEO AND JULIET, AND THANKS TO OUR DAD, HERO AND I WERE THE ONLY TWO KIDS WHO KNEW HOW TO PERFORM SHAKESPEARE WORTH A DAMN.
FAST FORWARD TO AUDITIONS...I GET CAST AS ROMEO, HERO GETS CAST AS JULIET.
ICK.
EXACTLY. BOTH OF US WANTED TO DO THE SHOW, BUT NEITHER OF US WANTED TO HUMP EACH OTHER ON STAGE, SO WE FLIPPED A COIN TO SEE WHO'D DROP OUT.
I, BEING THE SELFISH PRICK I AM, TRIED TO USE ONE OF MY DOUBLE-HEADED WASHINGTONS... BUT HERO CAUGHT ME PALMING IT.
SO YOU LOST THE PART.
THAT'S THE THING, SHE LET ME TAKE IT ANYWAY. EVEN THOUGH SHE WAS ACHING FOR IT. HERO HADN'T LANDED SO MUCH AS AN ENSEMBLE ROLE IN FOUR YEARS, BUT SHE STILL...
WHATEVER. I JUST DON'T UNDERSTAND HOW SOMEONE CAPABLE OF SOMETHING LIKE THAT COULD DISSOLVE INTO... I DON'T KNOW, YOU KNOW?

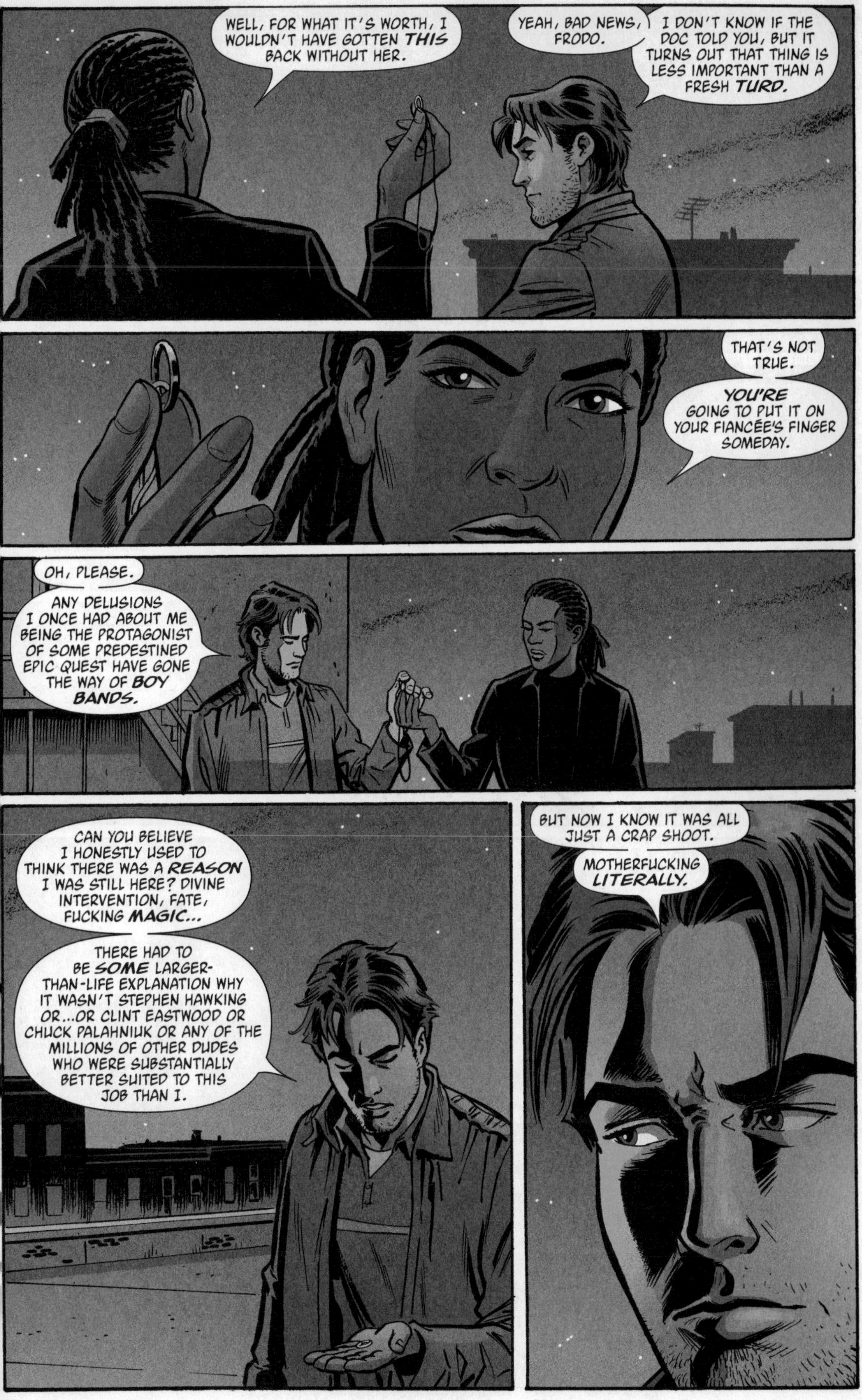
WELL, FOR WHAT IT'S WORTH, I WOULDN'T HAVE GOTTEN THIS BACK WITHOUT HER.
YEAH, BAD NEWS, FRODO.
I DON'T KNOW IF THE DOC TOLD YOU, BUT IT TURNS OUT THAT THING IS LESS IMPORTANT THAN A FRESH TURD.
THAT'S NOT TRUE.
YOU'RE GOING TO PUT IT ON YOUR FIANCÉE'S FINGER SOMEDAY.
OH, PLEASE.
ANY DELUSIONS I ONCE HAD ABOUT ME BEING THE PROTAGONIST OF SOME PREDESTINED EPIC QUEST HAVE GONE THE WAY OF BOY BANDS.
CAN YOU BELIEVE I HONESTLY USED TO THINK THERE WAS A REASON I WAS STILL HERE? DIVINE INTERVENTION, FATE, FUCKING MAGIC...
THERE HAD TO BE SOME LARGER-THAN-LIFE EXPLANATION WHY IT WASN'T STEPHEN HAWKING OR...OR CLINT EASTWOOD OR CHUCK PALAHNIUK OR ANY OF THE MILLIONS OF OTHER DUDES WHO WERE SUBSTANTIALLY BETTER SUITED TO THIS JOB THAN I.
BUT NOW I KNOW IT WAS ALL JUST A CRAP SHOOT.
MOTHERFUCKING LITERALLY.

GODDAMMIT!

ALLISON!

I *TOLD* YOU HERO HADN'T CHANGED! SHE--

NO...YOUR SISTER'S STILL ASLEEP.

THIS WAS SOMEONE ELSE. A...A WOMAN, DRESSED ALL IN BLACK. SHE HAD SOME KIND OF *SWORD*...

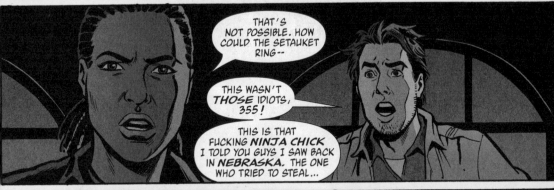

THAT'S NOT POSSIBLE. HOW COULD THE SETAUKET RING--

THIS WASN'T *THOSE* IDIOTS, 355!

THIS IS THAT FUCKING *NINJA CHICK* I TOLD YOU GUYS I SAW BACK IN *NEBRASKA*. THE ONE WHO TRIED TO STEAL...

...AMPERSAND?

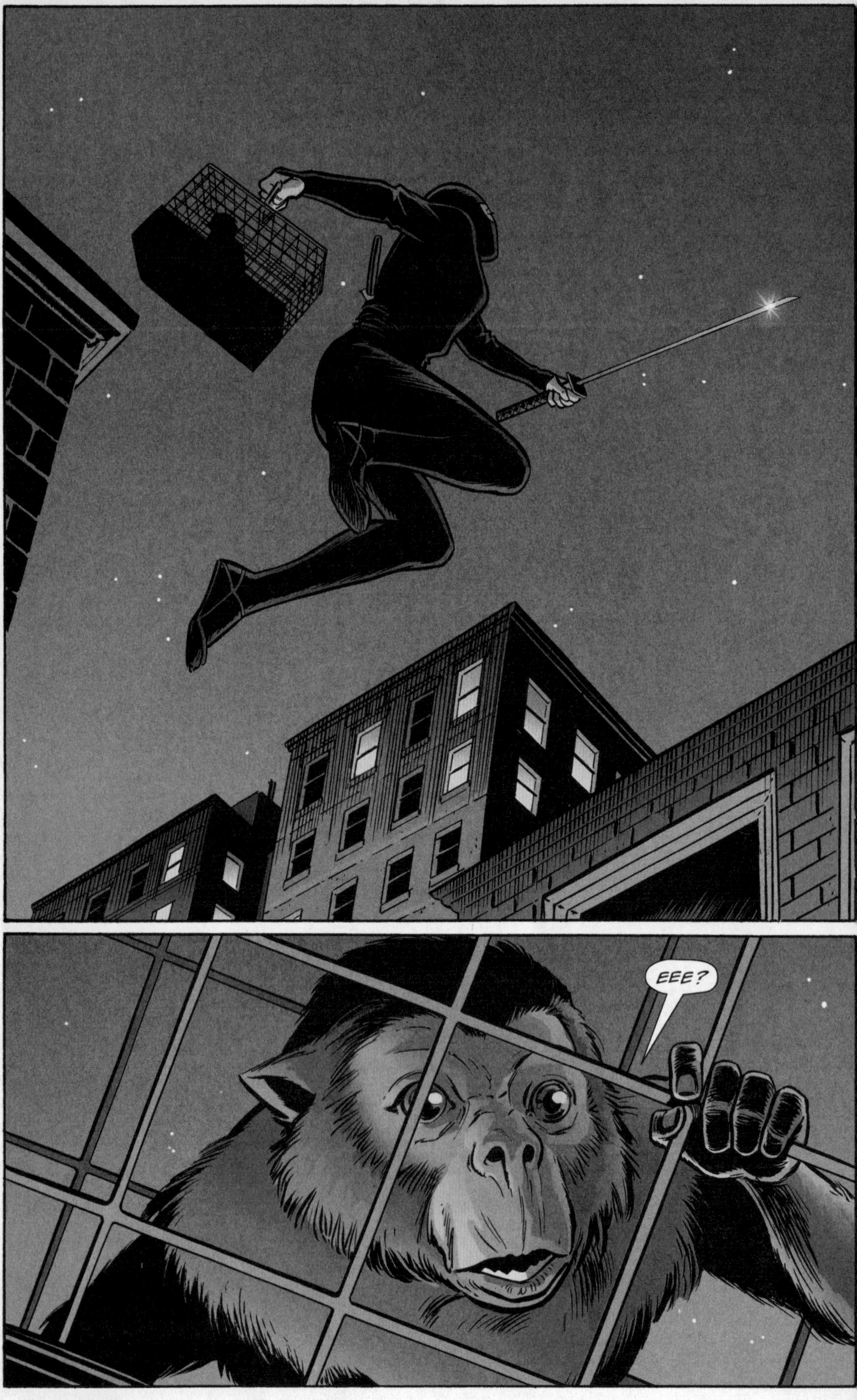
EEE?

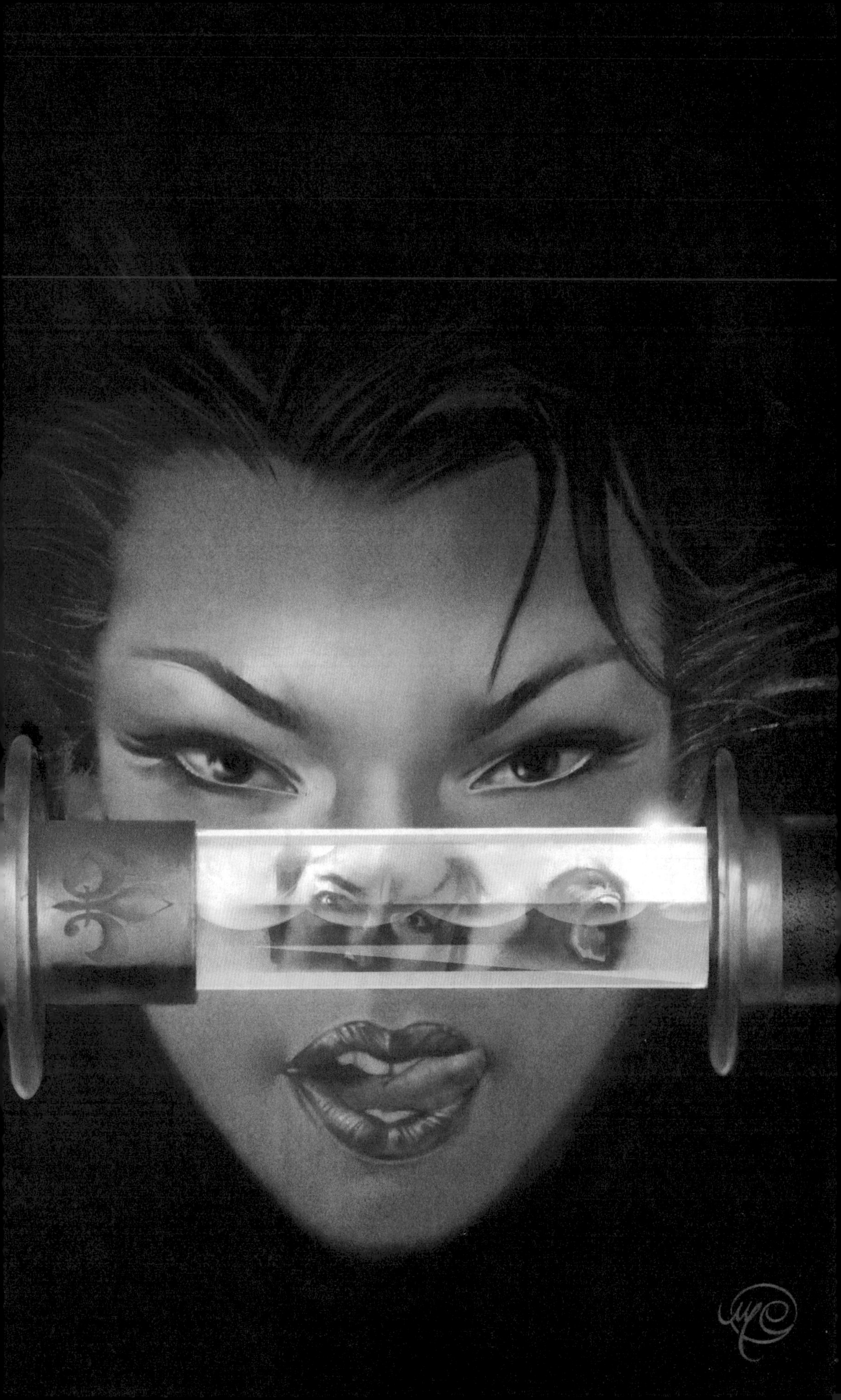

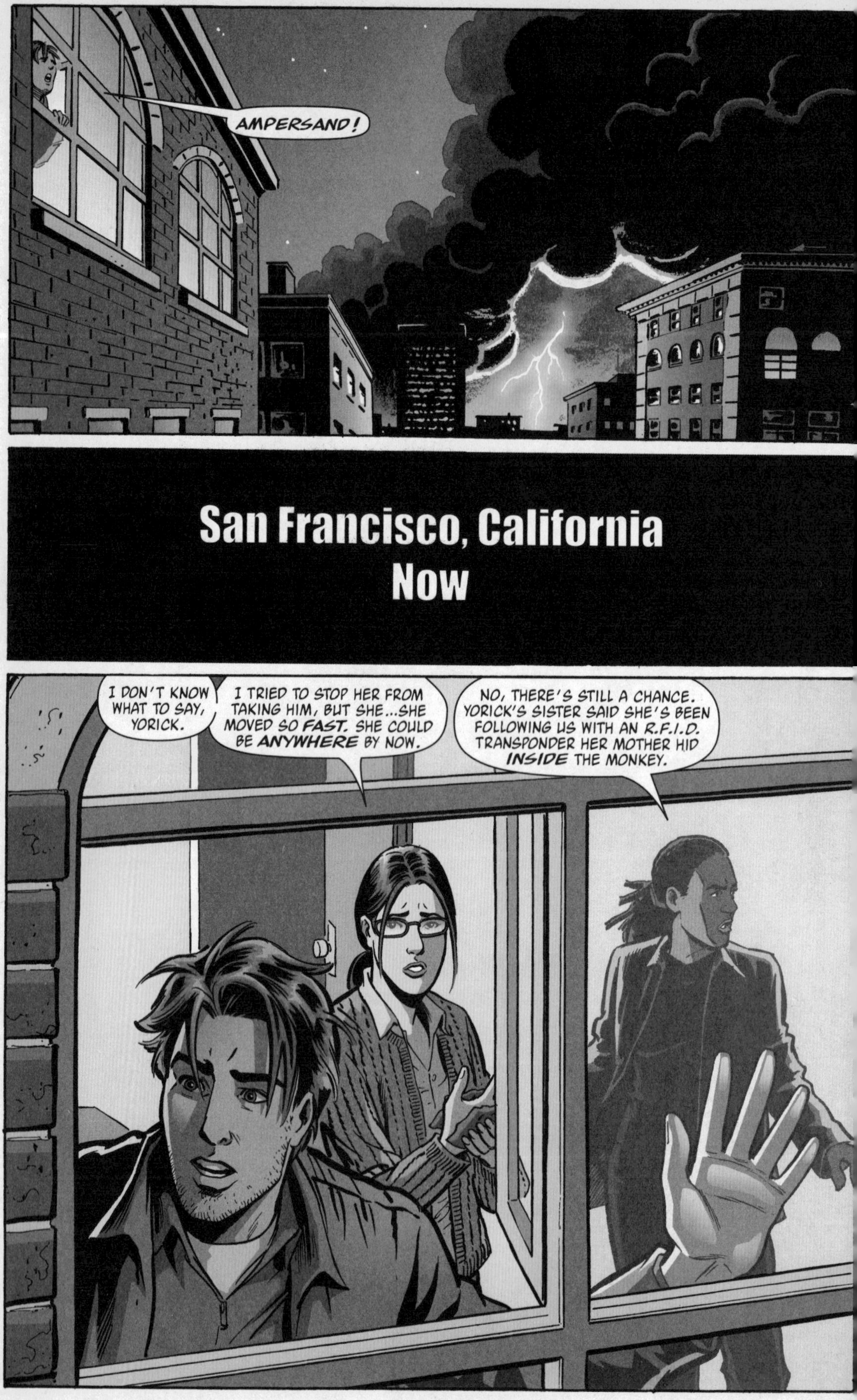
AMPERSAND!
San Francisco, California
Now
I DON'T KNOW WHAT TO SAY, YORICK.
I TRIED TO STOP HER FROM TAKING HIM, BUT SHE...SHE MOVED SO FAST. SHE COULD BE ANYWHERE BY NOW.
NO, THERE'S STILL A CHANCE. YORICK'S SISTER SAID SHE'S BEEN FOLLOWING US WITH AN R.F.I.D. TRANSPONDER HER MOTHER HID INSIDE THE MONKEY.

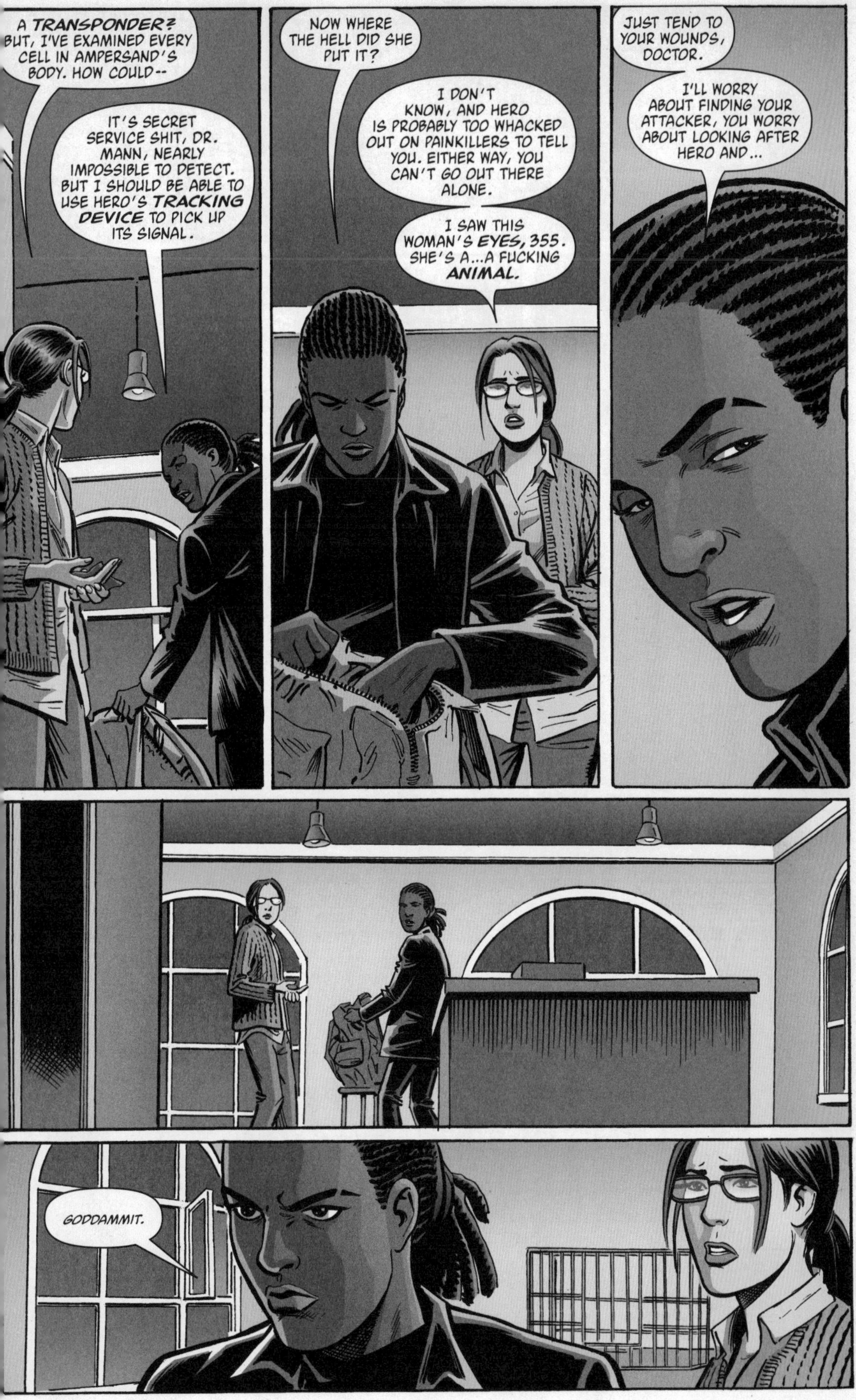
A TRANSPONDER? BUT, I'VE EXAMINED EVERY CELL IN AMPERSAND'S BODY. HOW COULD--
IT'S SECRET SERVICE SHIT, DR. MANN, NEARLY IMPOSSIBLE TO DETECT. BUT I SHOULD BE ABLE TO USE HERO'S TRACKING DEVICE TO PICK UP ITS SIGNAL.
NOW WHERE THE HELL DID SHE PUT IT?
I DON'T KNOW, AND HERO IS PROBABLY TOO WHACKED OUT ON PAINKILLERS TO TELL YOU. EITHER WAY, YOU CAN'T GO OUT THERE ALONE.
I SAW THIS WOMAN'S EYES, 355. SHE'S A...A FUCKING ANIMAL.
JUST TEND TO YOUR WOUNDS, DOCTOR.
I'LL WORRY ABOUT FINDING YOUR ATTACKER, YOU WORRY ABOUT LOOKING AFTER HERO AND...
GODDAMMIT.

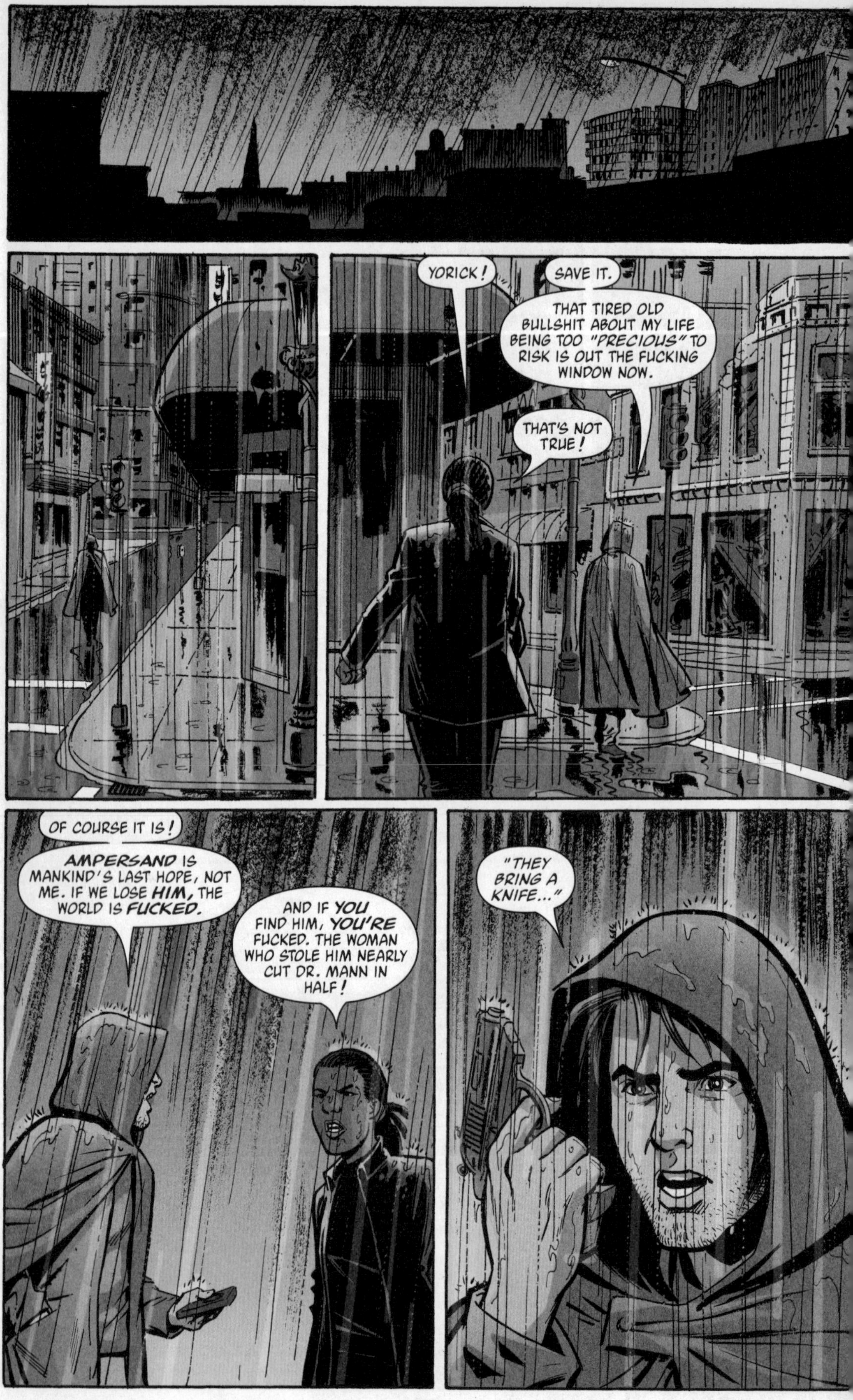
YORICK!
SAVE IT.
THAT TIRED OLD BULLSHIT ABOUT MY LIFE BEING TOO "PRECIOUS" TO RISK IS OUT THE FUCKING WINDOW NOW.
THAT'S NOT TRUE!
OF COURSE IT IS!
AMPERSAND IS MANKIND'S LAST HOPE, NOT ME. IF WE LOSE HIM, THE WORLD IS FUCKED.
AND IF YOU FIND HIM, YOU'RE FUCKED. THE WOMAN WHO STOLE HIM NEARLY CUT DR. MANN IN HALF!
"THEY BRING A KNIFE..."

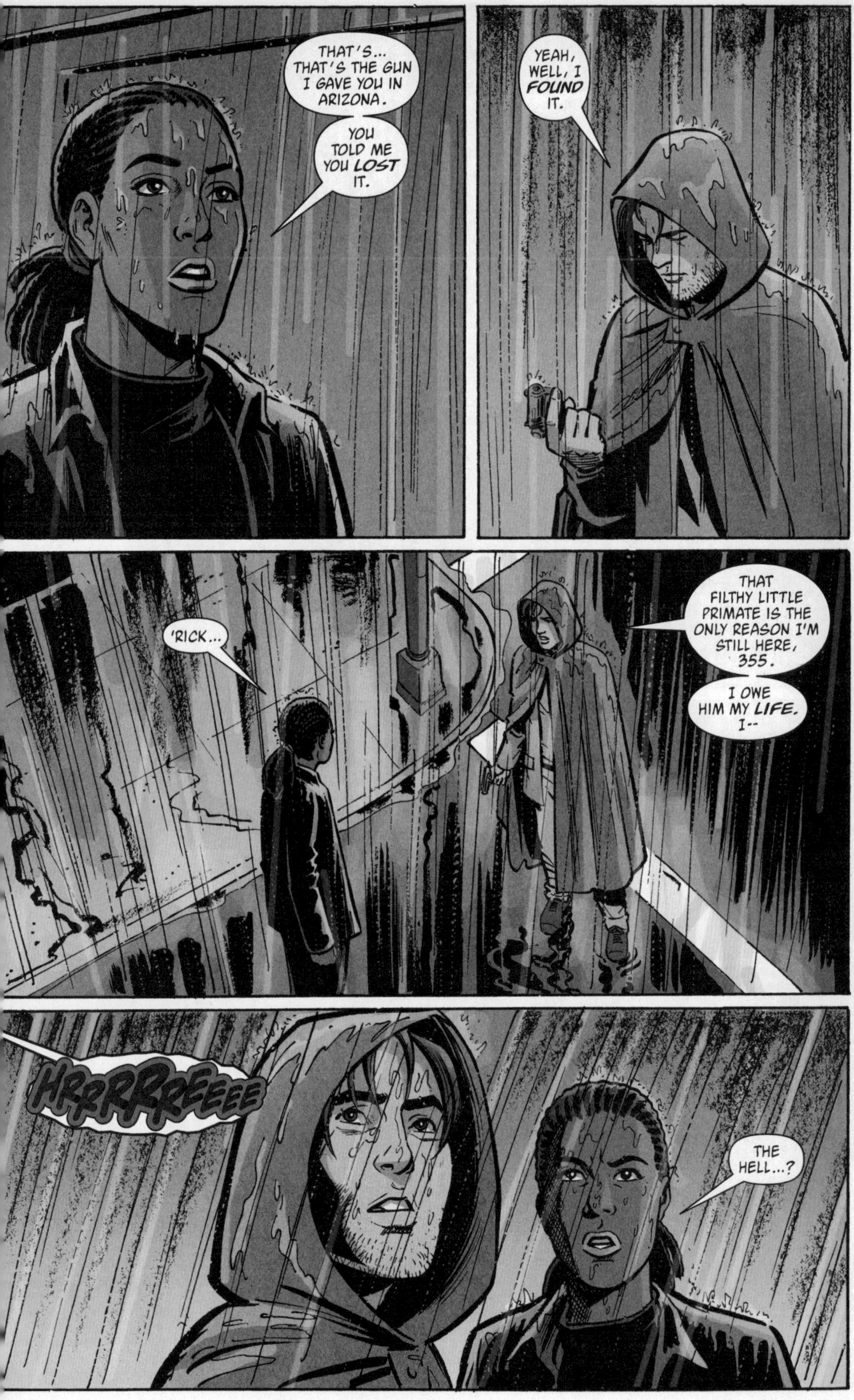
THAT'S... THAT'S THE GUN I GAVE YOU IN ARIZONA.
YOU TOLD ME YOU LOST IT.
YEAH, WELL, I FOUND IT.
'RICK...
THAT FILTHY LITTLE PRIMATE IS THE ONLY REASON I'M STILL HERE, 355.
I OWE HIM MY LIFE. I--
HRRRRREEEE
THE HELL...?

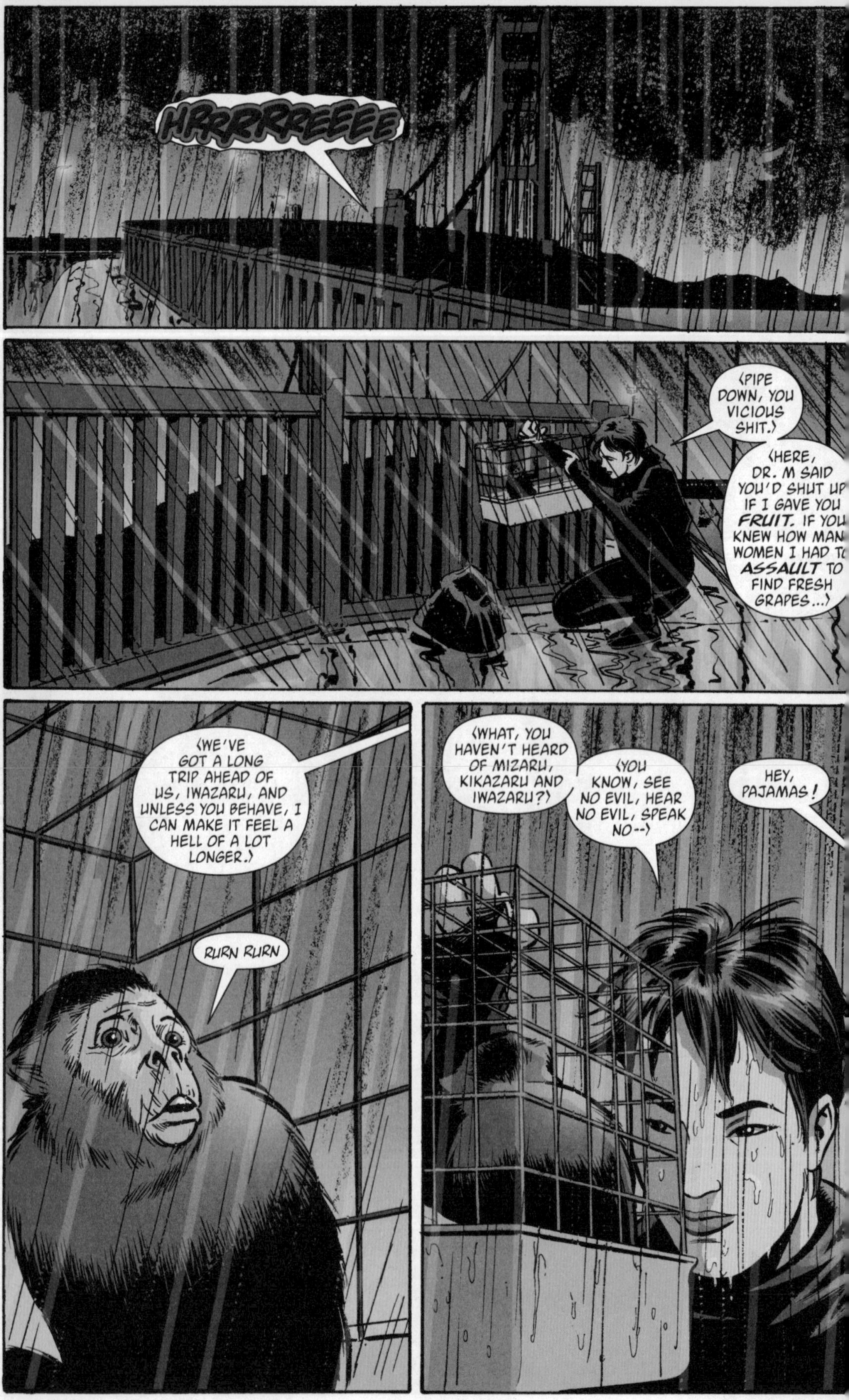
HRRRRREEEEE
‹PIPE DOWN, YOU VICIOUS SHIT.›
‹HERE, DR. M SAID YOU'D SHUT UP IF I GAVE YOU FRUIT. IF YOU KNEW HOW MANY WOMEN I HAD TO ASSAULT TO FIND FRESH GRAPES...›
‹WE'VE GOT A LONG TRIP AHEAD OF US, IWAZARU, AND UNLESS YOU BEHAVE, I CAN MAKE IT FEEL A HELL OF A LOT LONGER.›
RURN RURN
‹WHAT, YOU HAVEN'T HEARD OF MIZARU, KIKAZARU AND IWAZARU?›
‹YOU KNOW, SEE NO EVIL, HEAR NO EVIL, SPEAK NO--›
HEY, PAJAMAS!

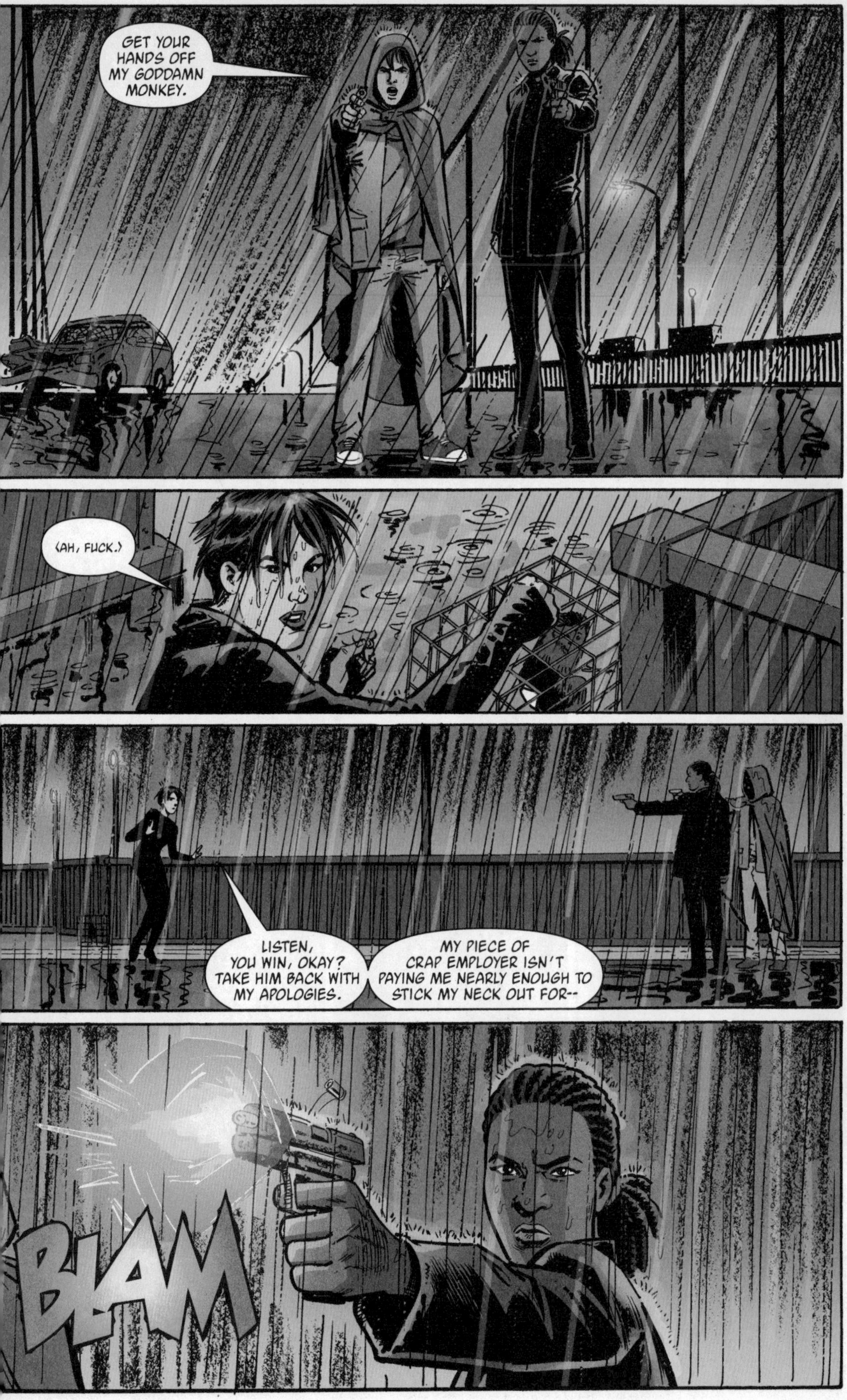
GET YOUR HANDS OFF MY GODDAMN MONKEY.
‹AH, FUCK.›
LISTEN, YOU WIN, OKAY? TAKE HIM BACK WITH MY APOLOGIES.
MY PIECE OF CRAP EMPLOYER ISN'T PAYING ME NEARLY ENOUGH TO STICK MY NECK OUT FOR--
BLAM

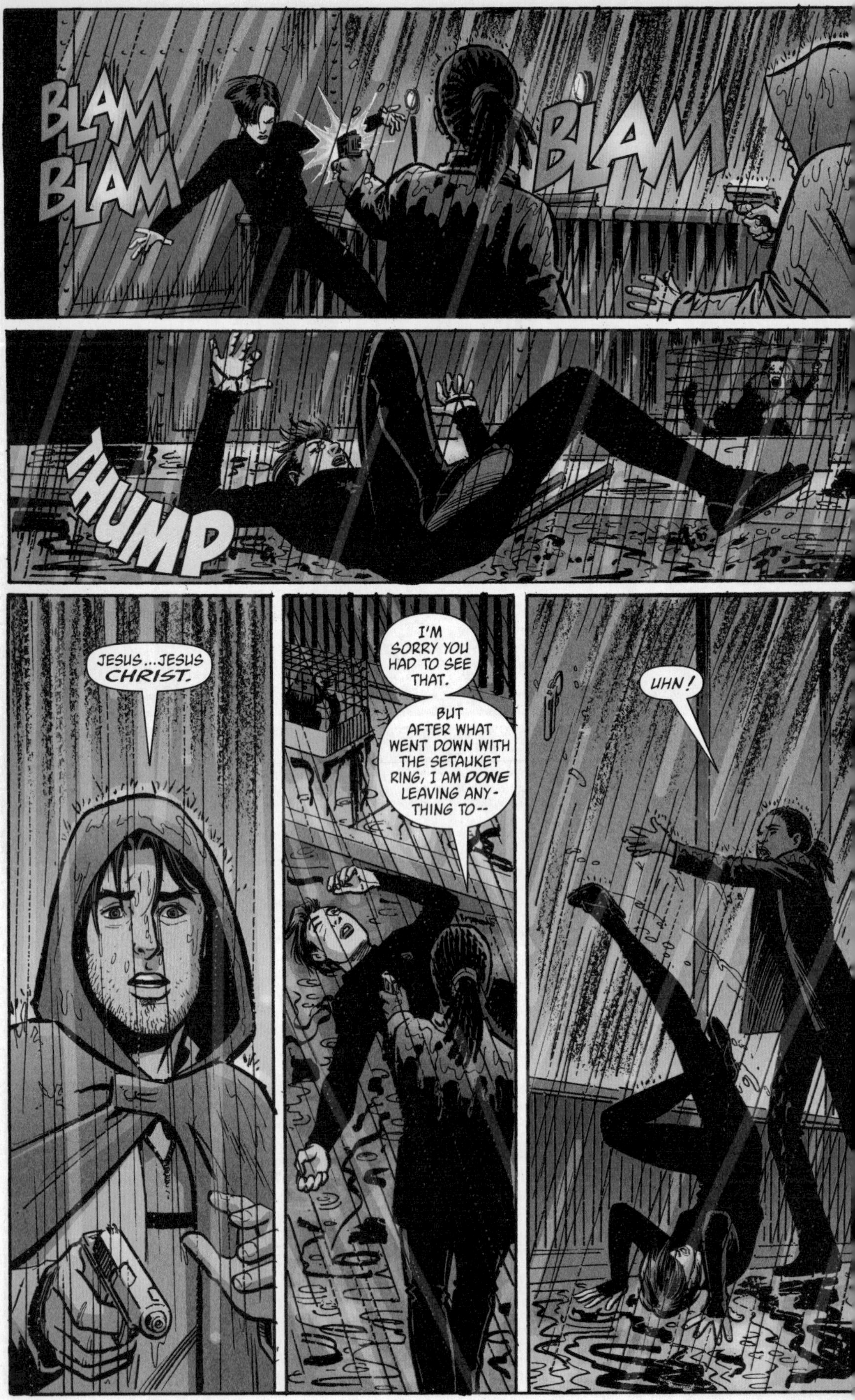
BLAM BLAM
BLAM
THUMP
JESUS...JESUS CHRIST.
I'M SORRY YOU HAD TO SEE THAT.
BUT AFTER WHAT WENT DOWN WITH THE SETAUKET RING, I AM DONE LEAVING ANY-THING TO--
UHN!

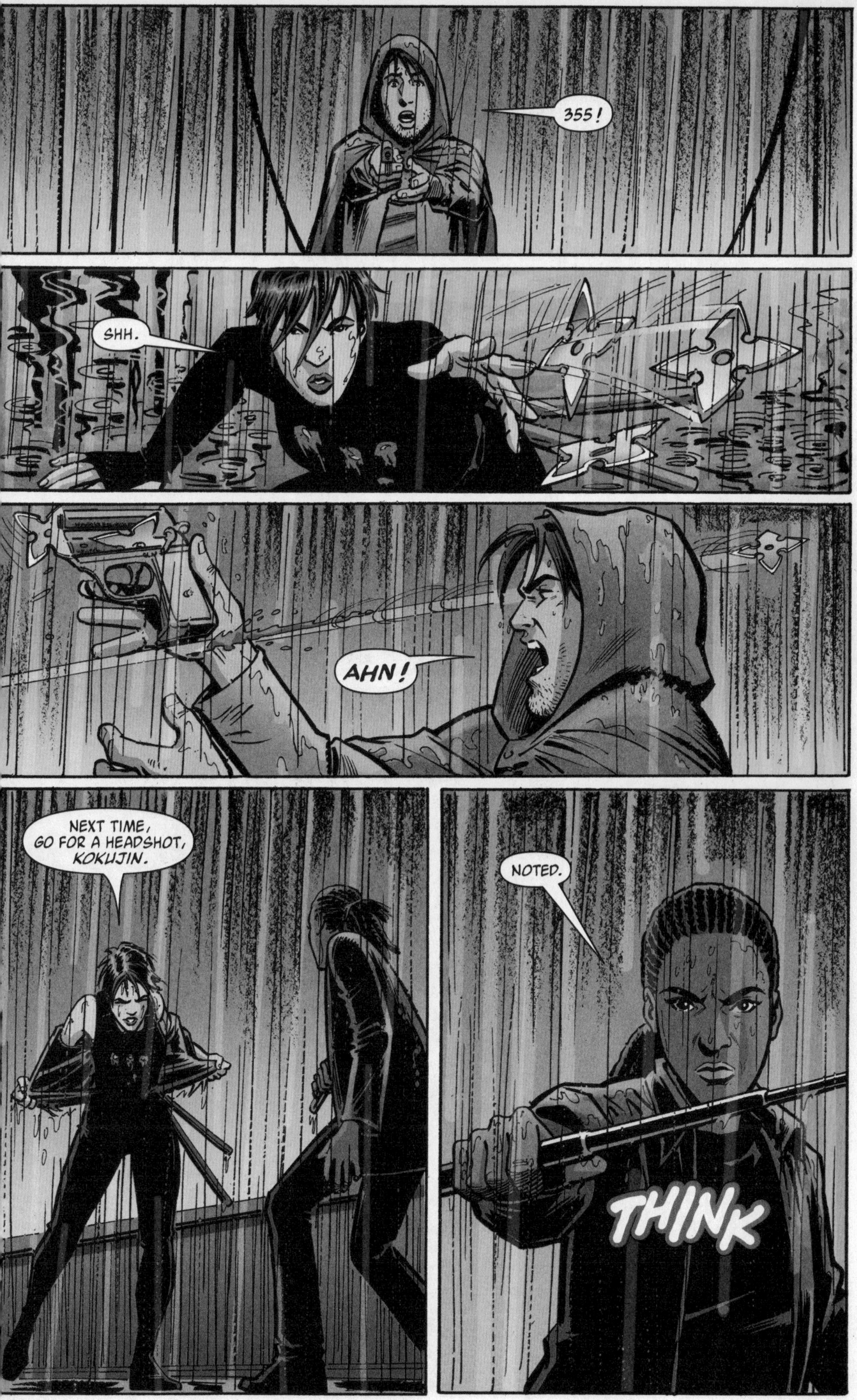
355!
SHH.
AHN!
NEXT TIME, GO FOR A HEADSHOT, KOKUJIN.
NOTED.
THINK

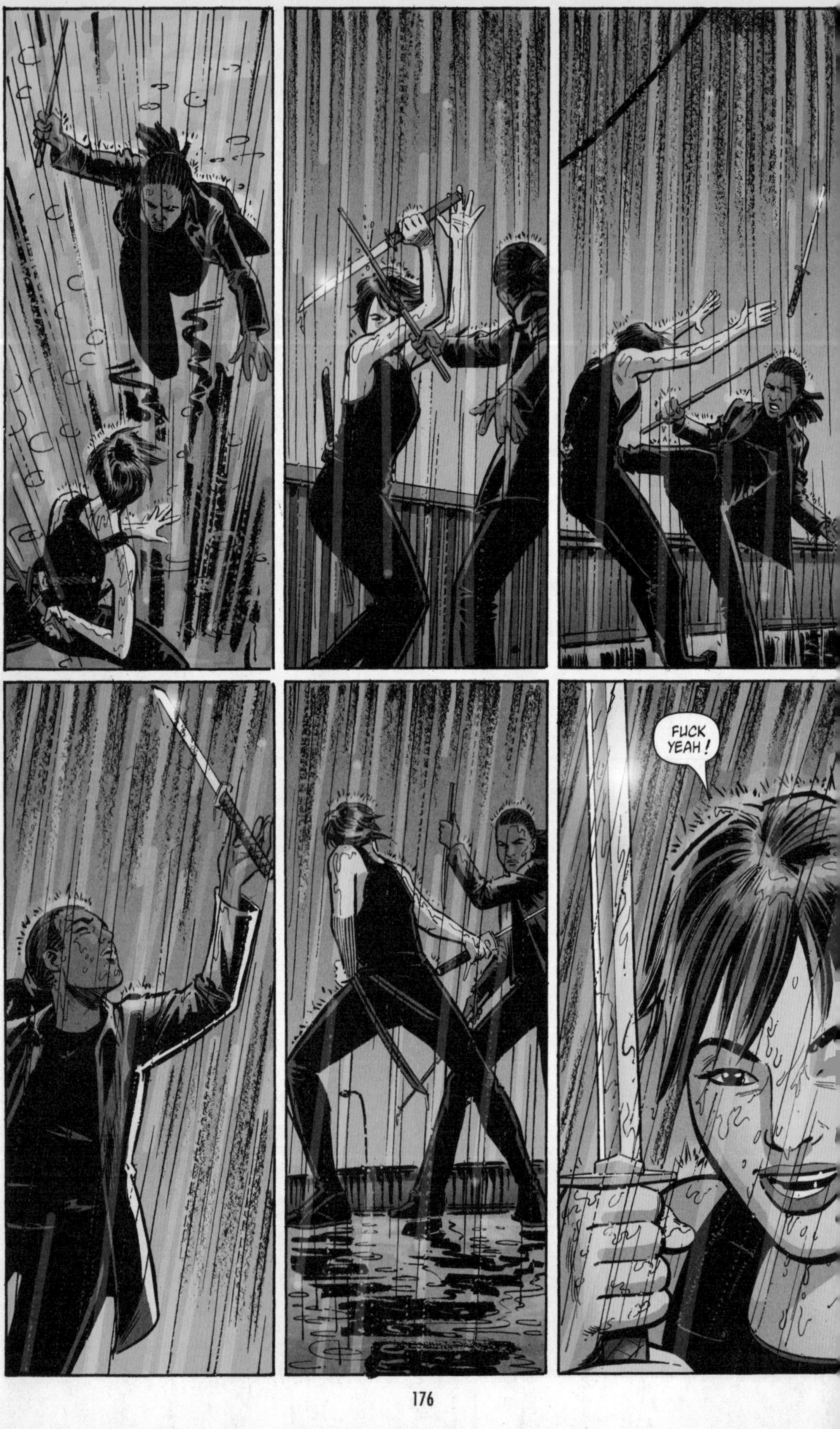
FUCK
YEAH!

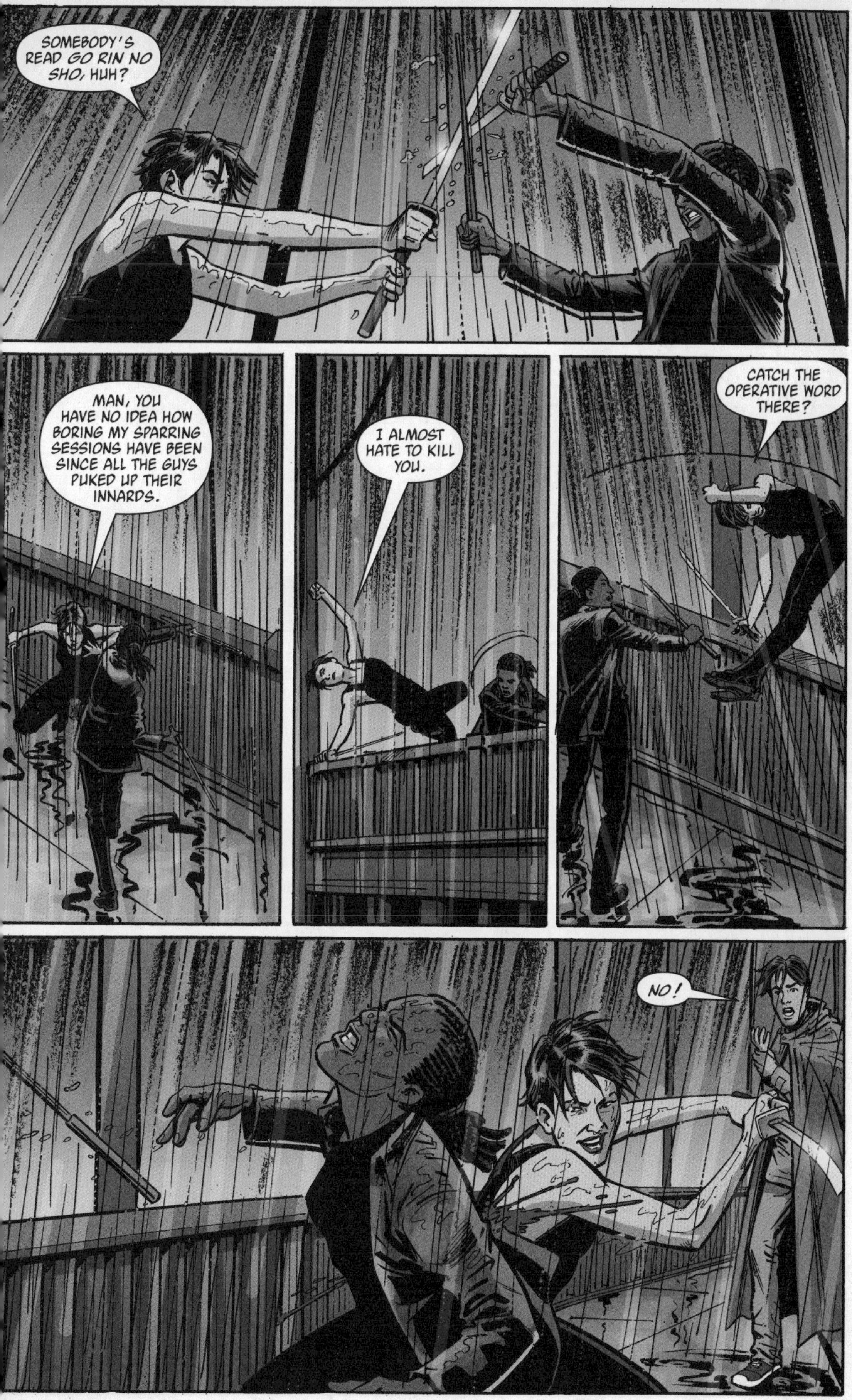
SOMEBODY'S READ GO RIN NO SHO, HUH?
MAN, YOU HAVE NO IDEA HOW BORING MY SPARRING SESSIONS HAVE BEEN SINCE ALL THE GUYS PUKED UP THEIR INNARDS.
I ALMOST HATE TO KILL YOU.
CATCH THE OPERATIVE WORD THERE?
NO!

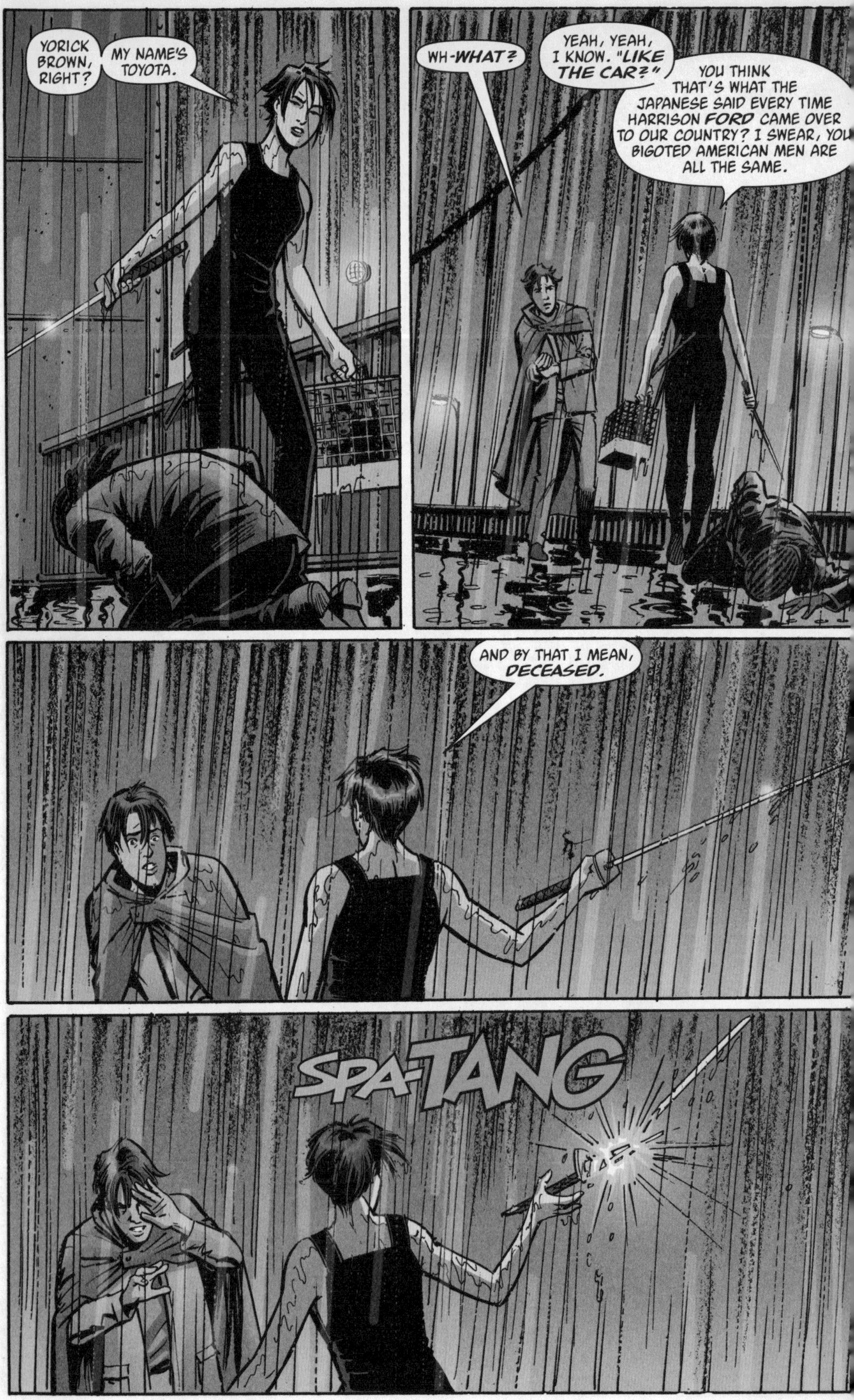
YORICK BROWN, RIGHT?
MY NAME'S TOYOTA.
WH-WHAT?
YEAH, YEAH, I KNOW. "LIKE THE CAR?"
YOU THINK THAT'S WHAT THE JAPANESE SAID EVERY TIME HARRISON FORD CAME OVER TO OUR COUNTRY? I SWEAR, YOU BIGOTED AMERICAN MEN ARE ALL THE SAME.
AND BY THAT I MEAN, DECEASED.
SPA-TANG

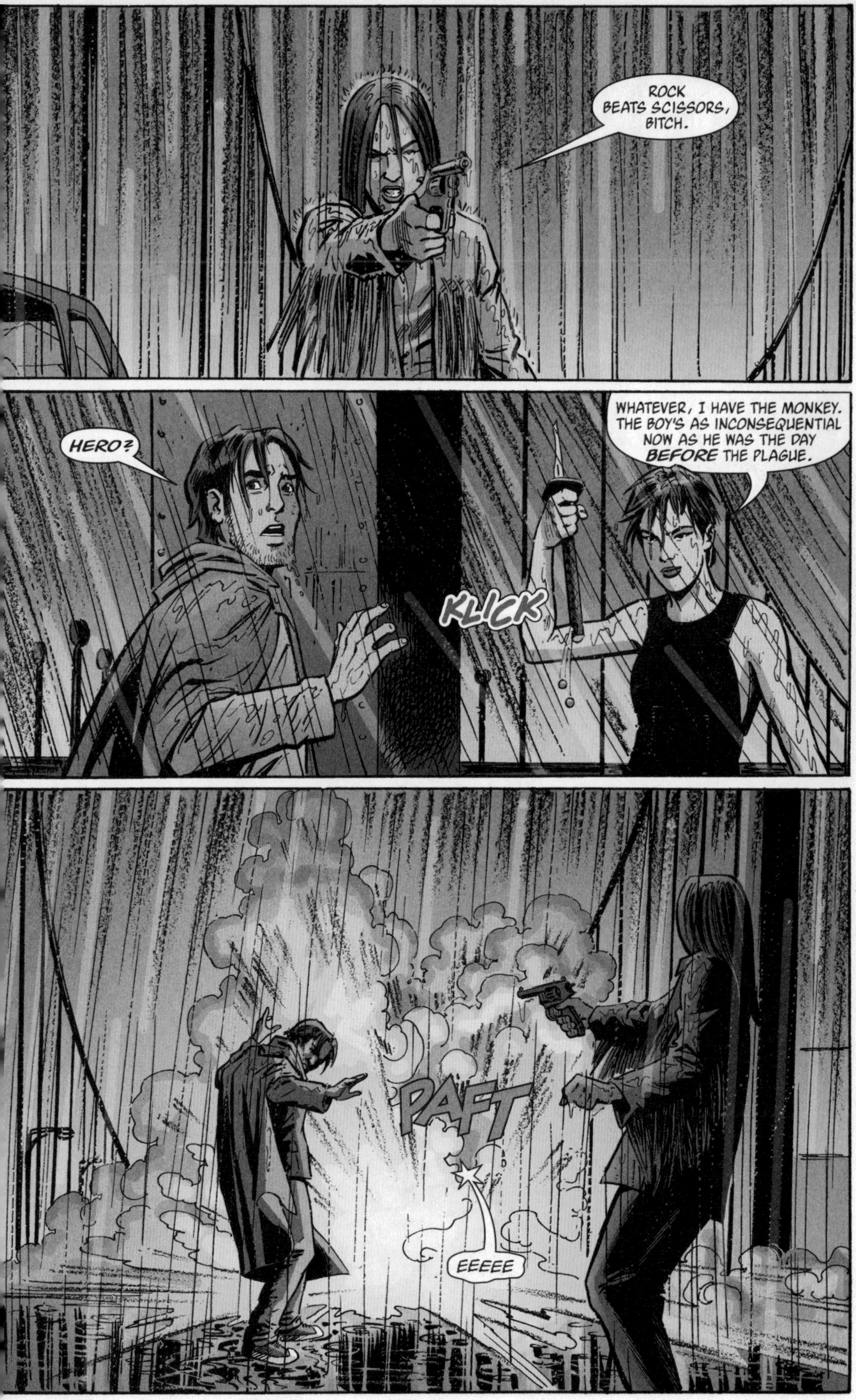
ROCK BEATS SCISSORS, BITCH.
HERO?
WHATEVER, I HAVE THE MONKEY. THE BOY'S AS INCONSEQUENTIAL NOW AS HE WAS THE DAY BEFORE THE PLAGUE.
KLICK
PAFT
EEEEE

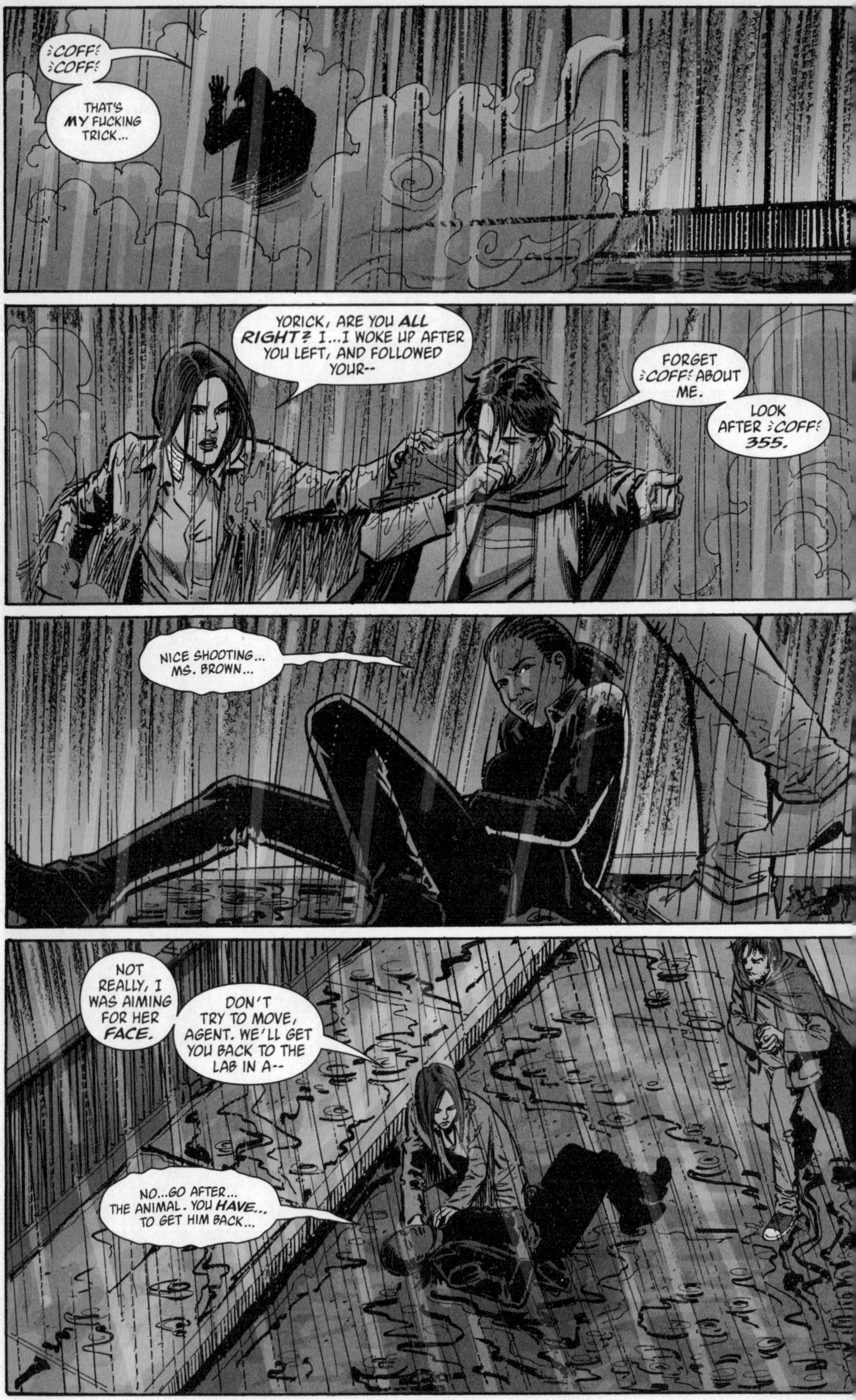

COFF COFF
THAT'S MY FUCKING TRICK...
YORICK, ARE YOU ALL RIGHT? I...I WOKE UP AFTER YOU LEFT, AND FOLLOWED YOUR--
FORGET COFF ABOUT ME.
LOOK AFTER COFF 355.
NICE SHOOTING... MS. BROWN...
NOT REALLY, I WAS AIMING FOR HER FACE.
DON'T TRY TO MOVE, AGENT. WE'LL GET YOU BACK TO THE LAB IN A--
NO...GO AFTER... THE ANIMAL. YOU HAVE... TO GET HIM BACK...

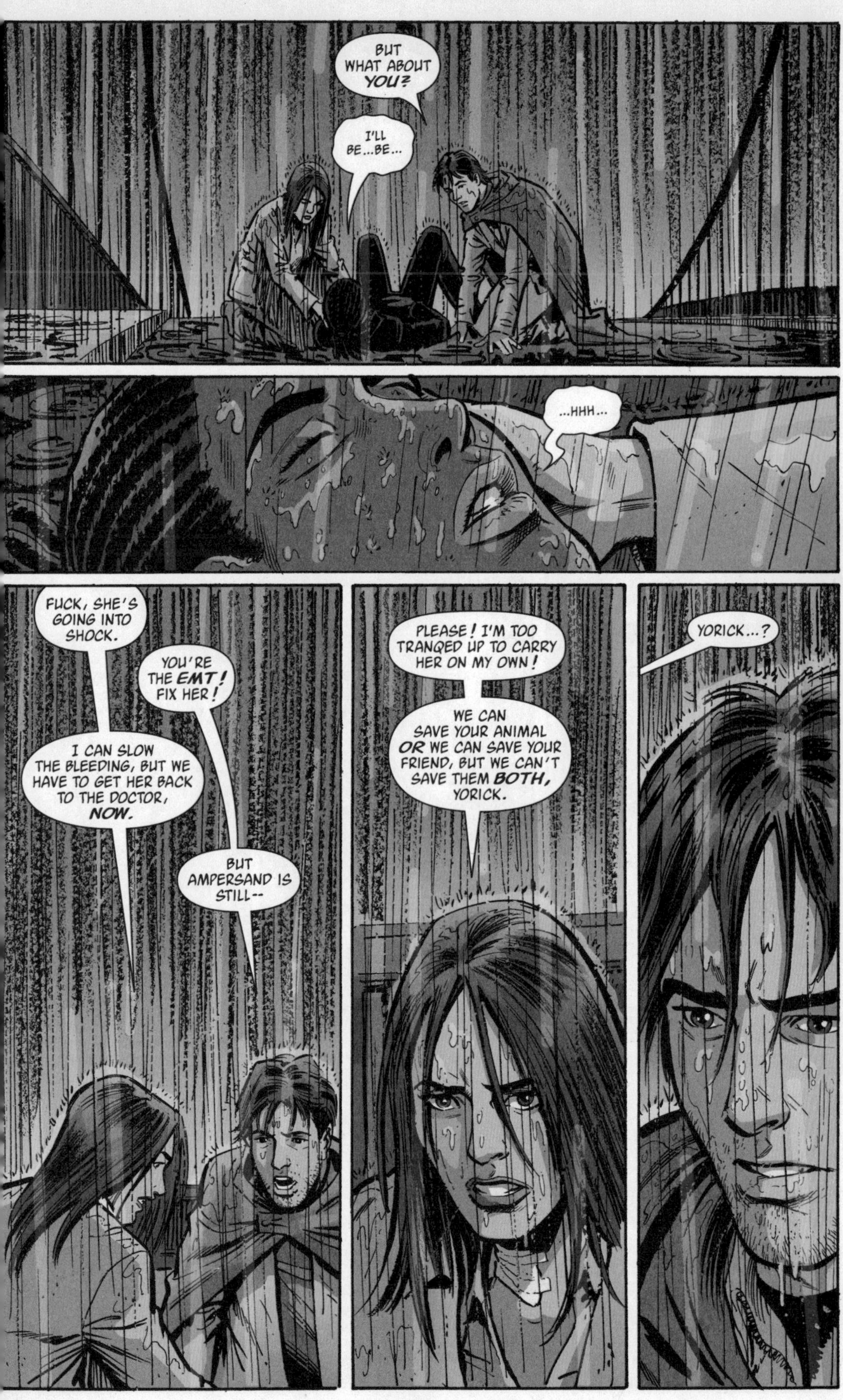
BUT WHAT ABOUT YOU?
I'LL BE...BE...
...HHH...
FUCK, SHE'S GOING INTO SHOCK.
YOU'RE THE EMT! FIX HER!
I CAN SLOW THE BLEEDING, BUT WE HAVE TO GET HER BACK TO THE DOCTOR, NOW.
BUT AMPERSAND IS STILL--
PLEASE! I'M TOO TRANQED UP TO CARRY HER ON MY OWN!
WE CAN SAVE YOUR ANIMAL OR WE CAN SAVE YOUR FRIEND, BUT WE CAN'T SAVE THEM BOTH, YORICK.
YORICK...?

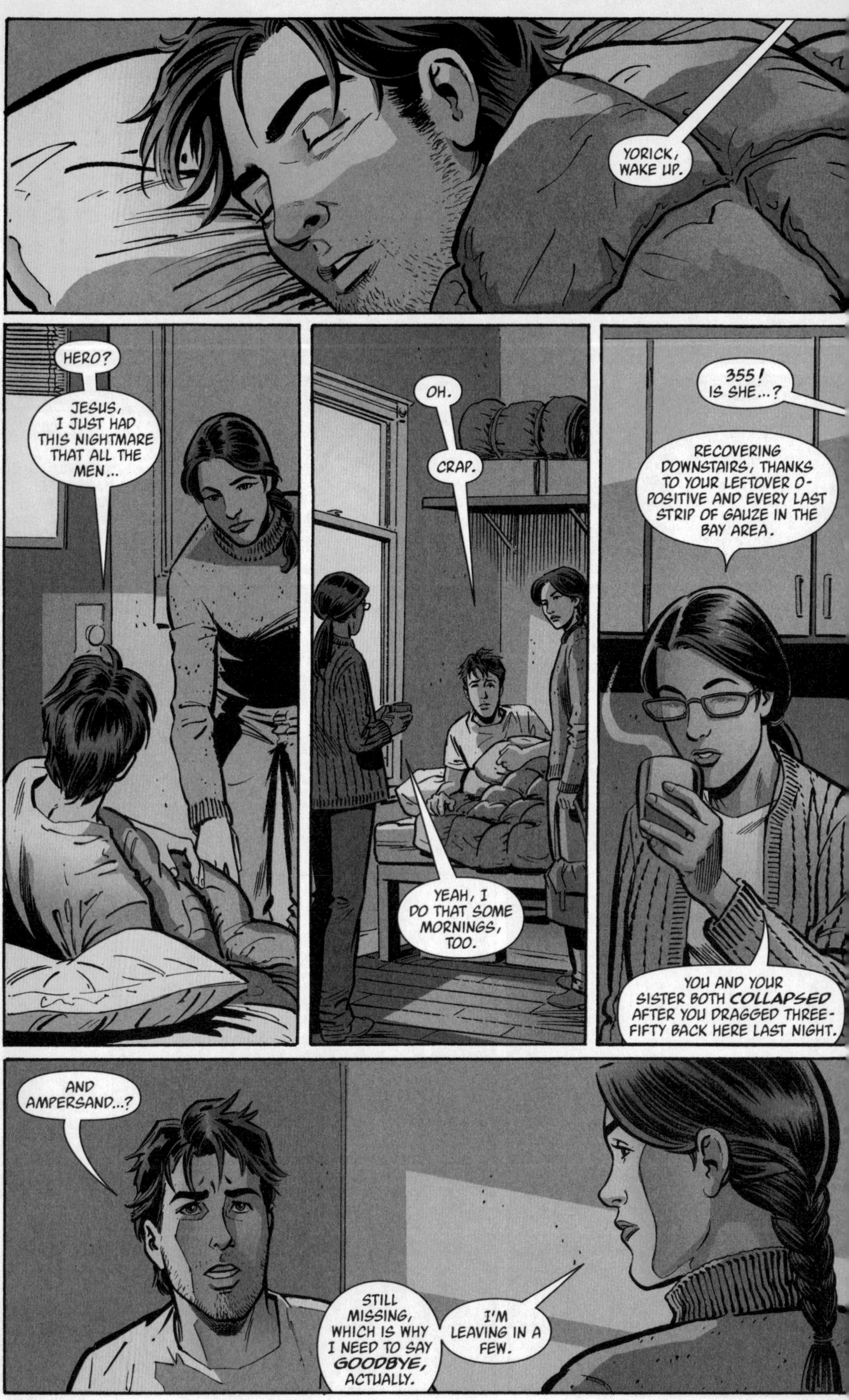
YORICK, WAKE UP.
HERO?
JESUS, I JUST HAD THIS NIGHTMARE THAT ALL THE MEN...
OH.
CRAP.
YEAH, I DO THAT SOME MORNINGS, TOO.
355! IS SHE...?
RECOVERING DOWNSTAIRS, THANKS TO YOUR LEFTOVER O-POSITIVE AND EVERY LAST STRIP OF GAUZE IN THE BAY AREA.
YOU AND YOUR SISTER BOTH COLLAPSED AFTER YOU DRAGGED THREE-FIFTY BACK HERE LAST NIGHT.
AND AMPERSAND...?
STILL MISSING, WHICH IS WHY I NEED TO SAY GOODBYE, ACTUALLY.
I'M LEAVING IN A FEW.

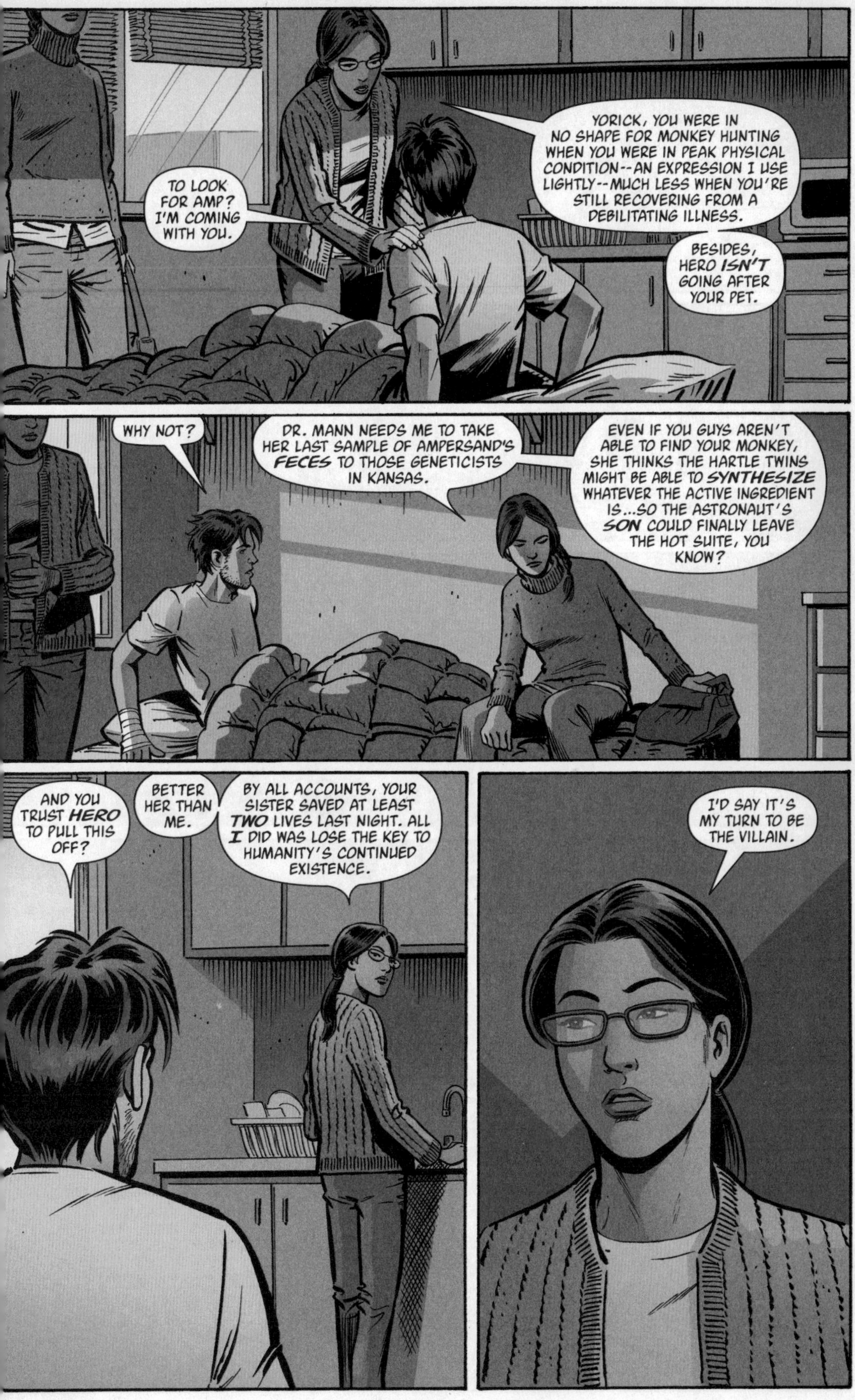
YORICK, YOU WERE IN NO SHAPE FOR MONKEY HUNTING WHEN YOU WERE IN PEAK PHYSICAL CONDITION--AN EXPRESSION I USE LIGHTLY--MUCH LESS WHEN YOU'RE STILL RECOVERING FROM A DEBILITATING ILLNESS.
TO LOOK FOR AMP? I'M COMING WITH YOU.
BESIDES, HERO ISN'T GOING AFTER YOUR PET.
WHY NOT?
DR. MANN NEEDS ME TO TAKE HER LAST SAMPLE OF AMPERSAND'S FECES TO THOSE GENETICISTS IN KANSAS.
EVEN IF YOU GUYS AREN'T ABLE TO FIND YOUR MONKEY, SHE THINKS THE HARTLE TWINS MIGHT BE ABLE TO SYNTHESIZE WHATEVER THE ACTIVE INGREDIENT IS...SO THE ASTRONAUT'S SON COULD FINALLY LEAVE THE HOT SUITE, YOU KNOW?
AND YOU TRUST HERO TO PULL THIS OFF?
BETTER HER THAN ME.
BY ALL ACCOUNTS, YOUR SISTER SAVED AT LEAST TWO LIVES LAST NIGHT. ALL I DID WAS LOSE THE KEY TO HUMANITY'S CONTINUED EXISTENCE.
I'D SAY IT'S MY TURN TO BE THE VILLAIN.

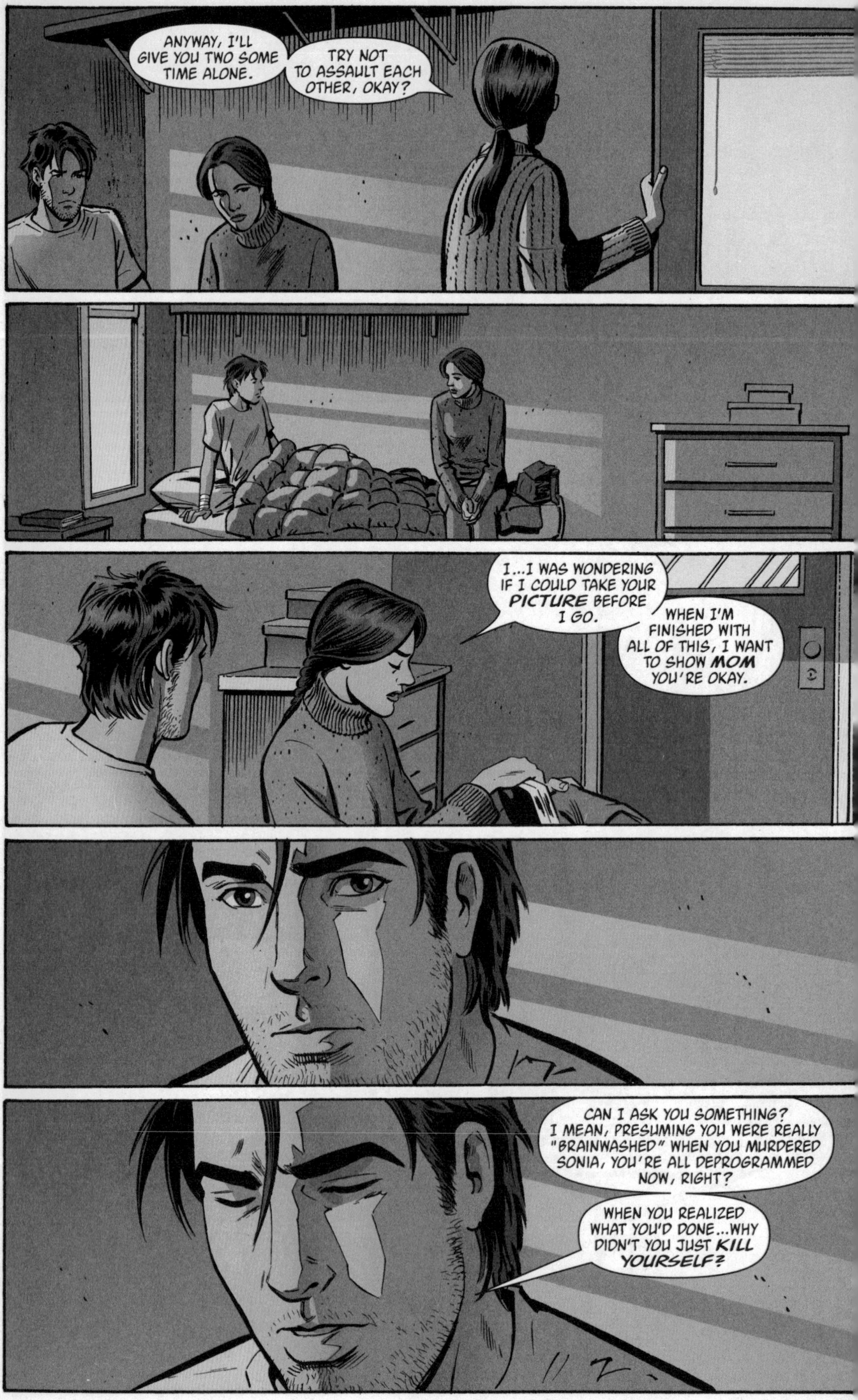
ANYWAY, I'LL GIVE YOU TWO SOME TIME ALONE.
TRY NOT TO ASSAULT EACH OTHER, OKAY?
I...I WAS WONDERING IF I COULD TAKE YOUR PICTURE BEFORE I GO.
WHEN I'M FINISHED WITH ALL OF THIS, I WANT TO SHOW MOM YOU'RE OKAY.
CAN I ASK YOU SOMETHING? I MEAN, PRESUMING YOU WERE REALLY "BRAINWASHED" WHEN YOU MURDERED SONIA, YOU'RE ALL DEPROGRAMMED NOW, RIGHT?
WHEN YOU REALIZED WHAT YOU'D DONE...WHY DIDN'T YOU JUST KILL YOURSELF?

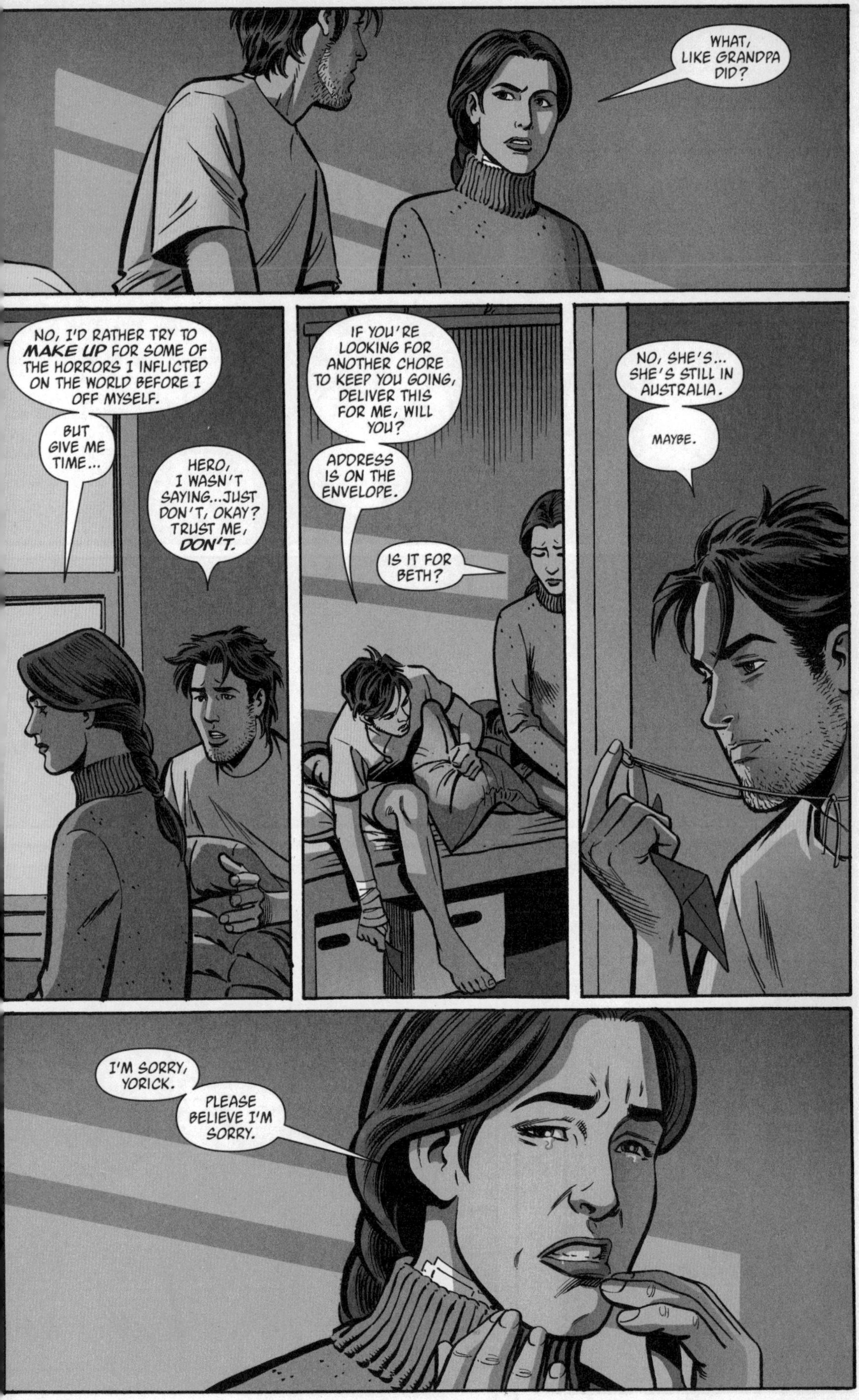
WHAT, LIKE GRANDPA DID?
NO, I'D RATHER TRY TO MAKE UP FOR SOME OF THE HORRORS I INFLICTED ON THE WORLD BEFORE I OFF MYSELF.
BUT GIVE ME TIME...
HERO, I WASN'T SAYING...JUST DON'T, OKAY? TRUST ME, DON'T.
IF YOU'RE LOOKING FOR ANOTHER CHORE TO KEEP YOU GOING, DELIVER THIS FOR ME, WILL YOU?
ADDRESS IS ON THE ENVELOPE.
IS IT FOR BETH?
NO, SHE'S... SHE'S STILL IN AUSTRALIA.
MAYBE.
I'M SORRY, YORICK.
PLEASE BELIEVE I'M SORRY.

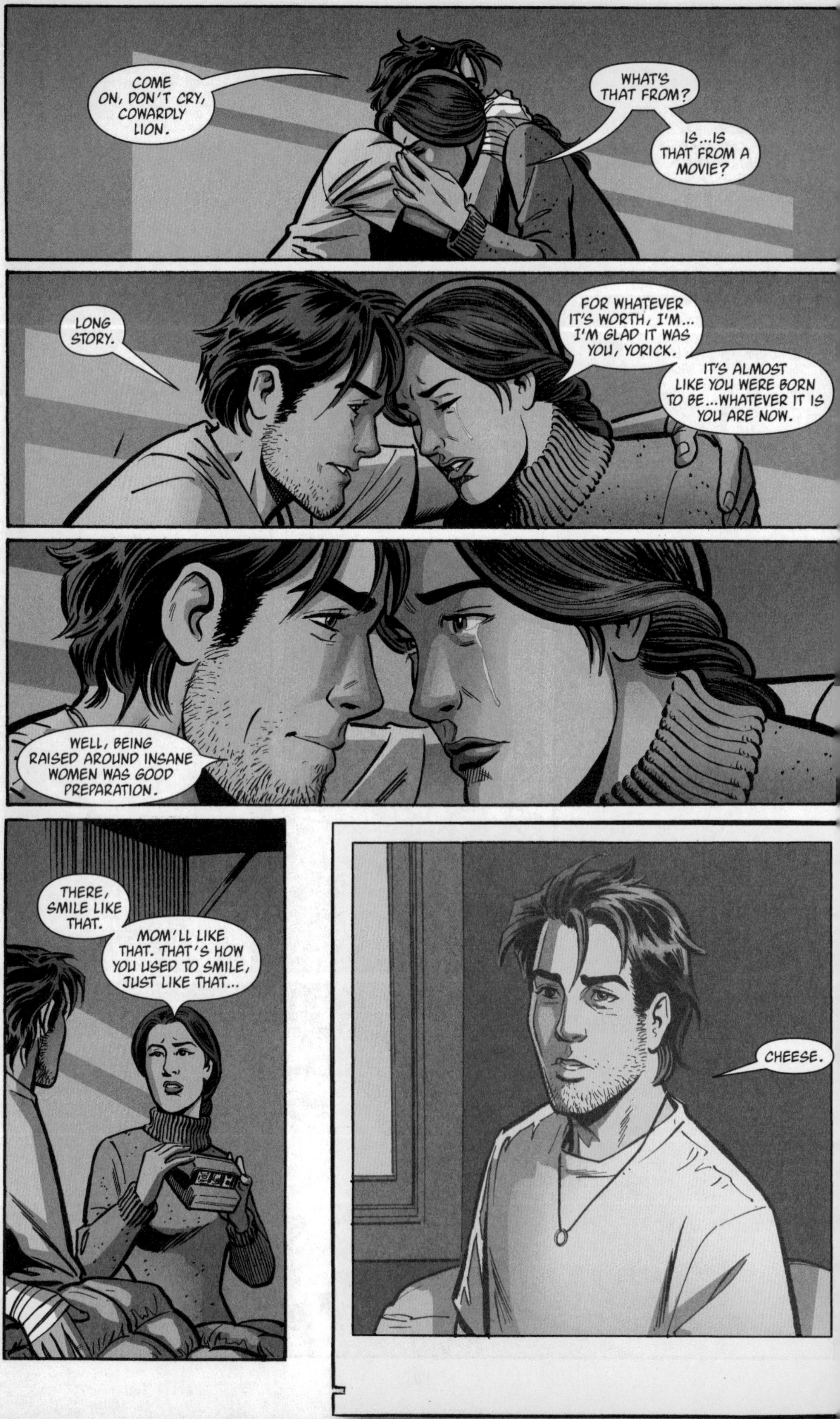

COME ON, DON'T CRY, COWARDLY LION.
WHAT'S THAT FROM?
IS...IS THAT FROM A MOVIE?
LONG STORY.
FOR WHATEVER IT'S WORTH, I'M... I'M GLAD IT WAS YOU, YORICK.
IT'S ALMOST LIKE YOU WERE BORN TO BE...WHATEVER IT IS YOU ARE NOW.
WELL, BEING RAISED AROUND INSANE WOMEN WAS GOOD PREPARATION.
THERE, SMILE LIKE THAT.
MOM'LL LIKE THAT. THAT'S HOW YOU USED TO SMILE, JUST LIKE THAT...
CHEESE.

San Diego, California
One Week Later

188

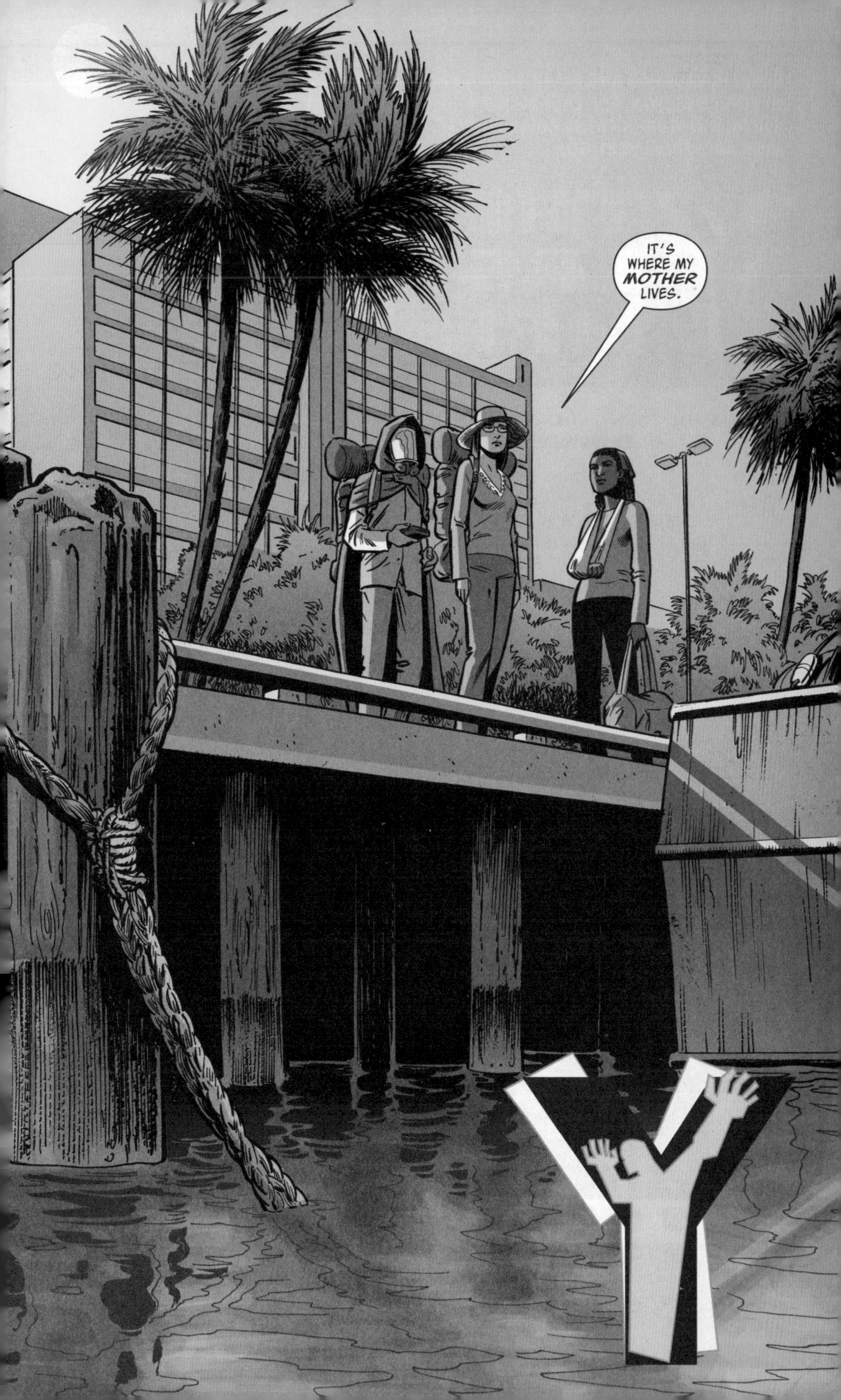
IT'S WHERE MY MOTHER LIVES.

ALSO FROM WRITER

BRIAN K. VAUGHAN

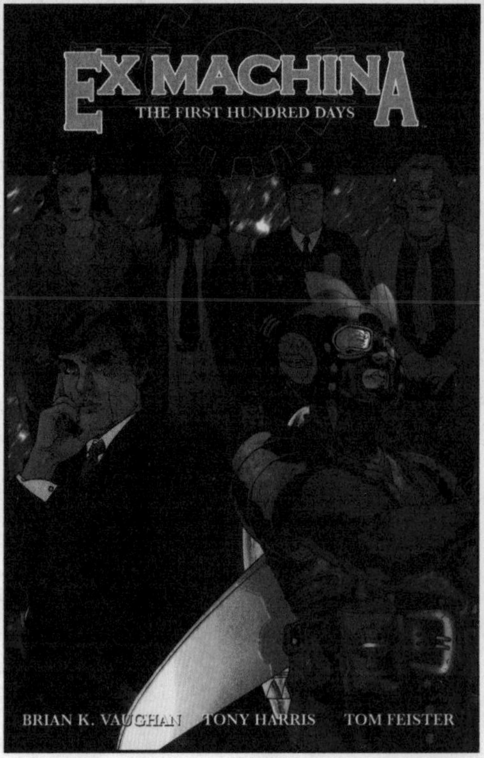
EX MACHINA
THE FIRST HUNDRED DAYS
BRIAN K. VAUGHAN TONY HARRIS TOM FEISTER

EX MACHINA: VOLUME 1: THE FIRST HUNDRED DAYS

WITH TONY HARRIS AND TOM FEISTER

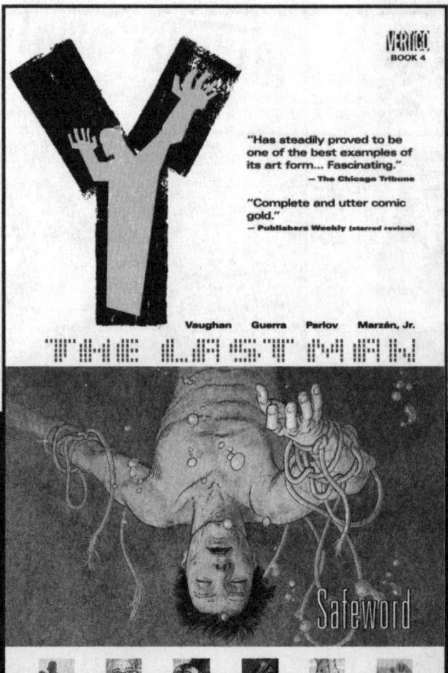
VERTIGO
BOOK 4
"Has steadily proved to be one of the best examples of its art form... Fascinating."
— The Chicago Tribune
"Complete and utter comic gold."
— Publishers Weekly (starred review)
Vaughan Guerra Parlov Marzán, Jr.
THE LAST MAN
Safeword

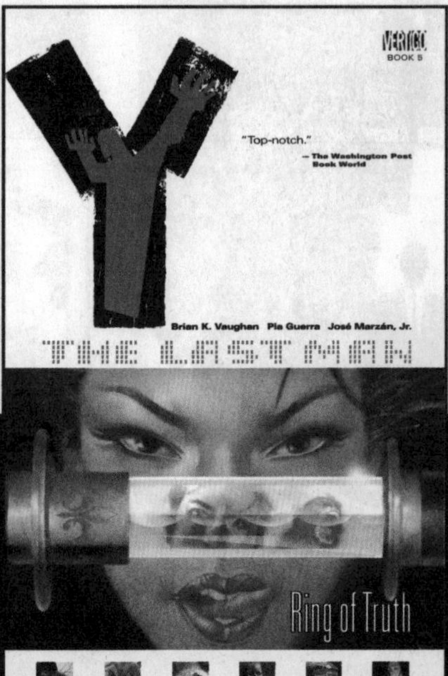
VERTIGO
BOOK 5
"Top-notch."
— The Washington Post Book World
Brian K. Vaughan Pia Guerra José Marzán, Jr.
THE LAST MAN
Ring of Truth

VOLUME 4:

VOLUME 5:

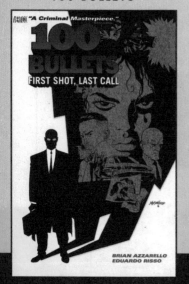